The Holy Madmen of Tibet

THE HOLY
MADMEN
OF TIBET

DAVID M. DiVALERIO

OXFORD
UNIVERSITY PRESS

OXFORD
UNIVERSITY PRESS

Oxford University Press is a department of the University of
Oxford. It furthers the University's objective of excellence in research,
scholarship, and education by publishing worldwide.

Oxford   New York
Auckland   Cape Town   Dar es Salaam   Hong Kong   Karachi
Kuala Lumpur   Madrid   Melbourne   Mexico City   Nairobi
New Delhi   Shanghai   Taipei   Toronto

With offices in
Argentina   Austria   Brazil   Chile   Czech Republic   France   Greece
Guatemala   Hungary   Italy   Japan   Poland   Portugal   Singapore
South Korea   Switzerland   Thailand   Turkey   Ukraine   Vietnam

Oxford is a registered trademark of Oxford University Press
in the UK and certain other countries.

Published in the United States of America by
Oxford University Press
198 Madison Avenue, New York, NY 10016

© Oxford University Press 2015

Cataloging-in-Publication data is on file at the Library of Congress
ISBN 978-0-19-939120-2 (hbk.); 978-0-19-939121-9 (pbk.)

9 8 7 6 5 4 3 2 1
Printed in the United States of America
on acid-free paper

Dedicated to the memory of Julian Paul Green

Contents

List of Illustrations

Acknowledgments

MANY PEOPLE HAVE played important roles in my development as a scholar and in the research that has resulted in this book. In the fall of 2001, Ben Bogin, Kabir Heimsath, and Hubert Decleer introduced me to Tibetan religion and culture through the School for International Training's Tibetan Studies program. Much of my research addresses questions raised during that extremely formative time.

While she was teaching at Wesleyan University, Kim Gutschow gave me guidance in how to pursue a graduate education in this field. I am grateful for her sincere encouragement at that crucial moment.

I thank the Department of Religious Studies at the University of Virginia for taking a chance on me. Thanks especially to Jeffrey Hopkins, Clarke Hudson, and Bob Hueckstedt. Karen Lang and John Nemec have supported me from the very start. Years after the fact, I have come to realize the important role Paul Groner played in shaping my thinking about Buddhism (at the time, I thought he was only being contrarian for the fun of it). David Germano has had an especially large impact on my development: since the first day we met I have been trying to live up to his uncompromising standards. Much of what I have accomplished is thanks to him. Most of all, I thank my dissertation advisor, Kurtis Schaeffer, whom I have always been able to count on for guidance and encouragement.

I am fortunate to have been able to draw on the work of other scholars working on these Tibetan "madmen" in recent years. Franz-Karl Ehrhard and Stefan Larsson have been gracious colleagues, always willing to share information and publications with me. I am deeply indebted to Andrew Quintman, who has encouraged me in my pursuit of this topic since the beginning. He and Roger Jackson offered helpful evaluations of my manuscript as part of Oxford University Press's review process. Bryan Cuevas, Marcus Filippello, Matt McMullen, and David Tomlinson read and provided useful feedback on late drafts of the book. Peter Dreyer and Michael

Durnin greatly improved this work through their skilled copyediting. I thank Cynthia Read at Oxford for believing in the project.

To the Tibetan language instructors I have had over the years: your dedication to teaching has given me the tools most vital to my research. I thank Rinchen (Dharamsala), Steve Weinberger, Tsering Wangchuk, Sönam Yankyi, Slava Komarovski, and the staff of the Foreign Students' Department at Tibet University, especially our departed friend Dawa.

I express heartfelt thanks to the learned Tibetans who have kindly volunteered their time to work with me on an individual basis, both before and during this project. These are Khensur Wangdak Rinpoché of Middletown, Connecticut, who patiently read Tibetan texts with me before I knew much of anything; Lama Ngawang Rinchen and the other members of Bengen Monastery in Kham; Khenpo Ngawang Dorjé of Charlottesville; and Sangyé Tendar Naga of the Library of Tibetan Works and Archives, with whom I spent many hours discussing the *Life of the Madman of Ü*. I especially enjoyed my conversations with Tashi Tsering of the Amnye Machen Institute in Dharamsala, who gave me many significant research leads.

I am grateful to the many Tibetan lamas, *khenpos*, and *rinpochés* I interviewed about the "holy madmen" during my fieldwork in India. In every instance I arrived at their monasteries without any announcement or introduction; without exception, I was met with remarkable candor and generosity. I express my very warmest thanks to Khenpo Tsülnam Rinpoché of Sherap Ling monastery in Bir. Rinpoché met with me daily during what were a very busy few months for him. I benefitted greatly from his knowledge.

Thanks to the late E. Gene Smith, Jeff Wallman, and the rest of the staff at the Tibetan Buddhist Resource Center (TBRC), who have greatly facilitated my research from start to finish. The staff of the Library of Tibetan Works and Archives in Dharamsala was most helpful during my time there. Nawang Thokmey, Tibetan language materials librarian at the University of Virginia, offered much assistance while I was writing my dissertation. Lastly, the kind help of Namraj Gurung and the staff of the Nepal Research Center and the Nepal–German Manuscript Preservation Project enabled me to get a remarkable amount done during my time in Nepal.

I thank Tom Pritzker, the TBRC, and the National Archives of Nepal for allowing me to use their images in this book. Tsering Wangyal Shawa made the two excellent maps.

Thanks to my colleagues at the University of Wisconsin–Milwaukee, who all contribute to making it a very nice place to work.

I would like to express my appreciation for the many friends I have made since this project began, in Charlottesville and Milwaukee, Tibet and India, and many places in between. In particular, I would like to acknowledge the formative (often spirited) conversations I have had with Jeremy Saucier, Gabe Popkin, Jongbok Yi, Zach Rowinski, Chris Hatchell, Dan Kent, Erin Burke, Ben Deitle, Brenton Sullivan, Chris Bell, Alison Melnick, Geoff Barstow, Nic Bommarito, Élise Turcotte, Nicolas Schlitz, David Slatkin, Alison Broach, Paul Hackett, Michael Sheehy, Alyson Prude, Tülku Ngawang Sönam (of Ganden Monastery in Mundgod), and Tsangsar Künga Rinpoché (formerly of Nangchen, now living in Taiwan). I especially appreciate my relationship with Jann Ronis, a friend and colleague without equal.

Lastly, I thank my mother, Jane, for all that she has done for me over the years. Without her many sacrifices, I never could have achieved anything. Although she expressed due motherly concern, she never discouraged me from any of my undertakings. The untimely passing of my uncle, Will Miller, created some opportunities that otherwise would not have been available to me. We remember him with affection.

In graduate school I received fellowships from the University of Virginia, as well as Foreign Language and Area Studies grants from the federal government. Fieldwork for this project was made possible by grants from the American Institute for Indian Studies and the University of Wisconsin–Milwaukee. My education and scholarly career have been supported by many tuition and tax dollars, paid mainly by people with little or no interest in what I do. Some of them I imagine would rather have their money back. I hope this book may mitigate the debts I owe in some small way.

Technical Note

TIBETAN TERMS AND proper nouns appearing in the body of the text are in most cases rendered according to the phonetic transcription scheme developed by the Tibetan and Himalayan Library. Spellings of Tibetan terms are given in parentheses using the orthographic transliteration system first developed by Turrell V. Wylie and revised somewhat in recent years. Transliterated spellings of proper nouns are given in a key at the end of the book. Wylie transliterations are used in the endnotes. Some of the Tibetan texts drawn from in this study use shorthand at times. For the sake of consistency, these abbreviations will be transliterated in their fully expanded forms, so that *rn+yor* is rendered as *rnal 'byor*, *srgyas* as *sangs rgyas*, *bzhuD* as *bzhugs*, with numerals spelled out, and so on. Because of the frequency of misspellings encountered in the texts drawn from in this study, they will only occasionally be pointed out using [*sic*].

The Tibetan phoneme rendered in this book as ü, as in the Madman of Ü, should be pronounced like a German umlauted u, such as in the word *für*. Its pronunciation is similar to the vowel sound in the French *rue*. An umlauted o, as in Götsang, should be pronounced like a German umlauted o, as in the first vowel sound in the name of the poet Goethe, which is similar to the vowel sound in the French *peu*. É should be pronounced like the "ay" in the English "day," so that Gyantsé is pronounced "Gyan-tsay."

The Sanskrit letter rendered as Ś should be pronounced "sh," as in the god Śiva. Ṭ, ḍ, and ṇ are pronounced as retroflexes, with the tip of the tongue folded back, touching the top of the mouth. Ṣ is a retroflex "sh." In Sanskrit words, *th* should not be pronounced as it would in the English word "the," but as a hard "ta." Thus the name of the buddha of our world age, Siddhartha, is pronounced "Siddharta," with the final *ta* heavily aspirated, rather than "Siddhar-tha." *Ca* should be read as "cha," with

Cakrasaṃvara pronounced "Chakrasamvara," *caryā* pronounced "charya," and so on. A line over a vowel indicates a slight lengthening of its sound.

The traditional Tibetan manner of counting a person's age differs from that which predominates in the European world. Rather than recognizing individual birthdays, everyone would be counted as a year older at the beginning of each new year. What's more, from the time a baby is born, she is considered "one" year old, because of the time spent in the womb. Thus a baby born late in the year could turn "two" after just a few months. For these reasons, Westerners would in most cases subtract one or two years from the age listed for a Tibetan person. As I draw from a wide range of sources, some using the Tibetan system of calculating ages, some using the European, discrepancies are bound to arise. All ages mentioned in this book are therefore approximate.

All translations are my own unless otherwise noted. The European-language sources drawn from in this study use varying conventions in their transcription of Tibetan words and names, the use of diacritical marks, the capitalization of terms like dharma and buddha, and so on. Except where specified in the endnotes, quoted passages have been left unaltered.

The Holy Madmen of Tibet

Introduction

His naked body was rubbed with ashes from a human corpse, daubed with blood, and smeared with fat. He wore the intestines of someone who had died as a necklace and ornamenting his wrists and ankles. His hair was bound up with a garland he had made from the corpse's fingers and toes, which he had cut off and strung together. He wore an incomplete set of bone ornaments that someone had offered to him. Sometimes he laughed, sometimes he cried. He did all manner of nonsensical things in the marketplace. Although the people of Tsari were very coarse in their ways, he overwhelmed them with his abilities and tamed them with his compassion. And so they became faithful, and since they unanimously praised him as "the Madman of Tsang," in every direction that name became as renowned as the sun and the moon.

GÖTSANG REPA, *The Life of the Madman of Tsang*[1]

SANGYÉ GYELTSEN, COMMONLY known as Tsangnyön Heruka—"the Madman from Tsang, the Heruka"—first became famous for making grotesque displays among crowds of people while wearing an outfit fashioned from human remains. Künga Zangpo, "the Madman from Ü," miraculously survived the many savage beatings he received for making daring affronts to powerful lords. Drukpa Künlé, "the Madman of the Drukpa [Kagyü sect]," is credited with composing verses that overturn all sense of propriety, paying homage, not to the Buddha, but to an old man's impotent member.

The central questions this book seeks to answer are: Why did these men (and a few women) behave in unexpected ways that would get them labeled "mad," with that term carrying generally positive connotations? In what sense were they "mad"? The aim of this book is to convey a well-rounded understanding of the human beings behind these colorful personas, by looking at the details of their lives and literary works in their due historical contexts. Previous studies have addressed aspects of the lives and legacies of a few of these "madmen," in particular Drukpa Künlé and the Madman of Tsang. This book seeks to offer a more comprehensive account of the "madman" phenomenon, offering new understandings of the more famous "madmen" and bringing many lesser-known ones into the conversation.

Traditional Tibetan worldviews hold that there are a number of factors that could cause mental derangement in an individual. In some cases, madness was thought to result from problems occurring inside an individual's body, as understood by Tibetan medicine. Traditionally madness was most commonly ascribed to a disorder of the psychophysical winds (*rlung* in Tibetan, *prāṇa* in Sanskrit) that carry thoughts and animate the body. Also believed capable of causing insanity were external harms (*gdon*), such as the influence of witches, demons, celestial bodies, and contact with poisonous or polluted substances. If correctly propitiated, a deity might even drive an enemy mad at one's behest.[2]

Distinct from all these possibilities, there have traditionally been individuals in Tibet called "mad," whose apparent mental unwellness was not seen as resulting from any unfortunate circumstance, but, in the view of some, as symptomatic of high achievement in religious practice. Although they are called "mad," through a series of inversions, the term comes to bear positive connotations. It is these individuals who are the subject of this book.

Tibetans most often simply call such a person a *nyönpa* (*smyon pa*), "madman," it being clear from context that they do not mean "mad" in the ordinary, negative sense. In these cases, *nyönpa* can often be taken as abbreviating one of three related terms: *druptop nyönpa*, "mad *siddha*"; *neljor nyönpa*, "mad yogin"; or *lama nyönpa*, "mad lama."[3] *Siddha* and "yogin" are Sanskrit terms; "lama" is the Tibetan translation of the Sanskrit "guru." A yogin is one deeply involved with the practice of meditation (*yoga* in Sanskrit). A *siddha* is an individual who has achieved *siddhis* (special qualities and supernatural powers) and perhaps enlightenment through advanced tantric practice. Yogin is a general term referring to a meditator, who may or may not have achieved some of the remarkable abilities of a *siddha*. As the Madman of Tsang himself wrote, "If one is a *siddha*, one is certainly a yogin. If one is a yogin, one is not necessarily a *siddha*."[4] In common usage, the term yogin carries some of the same positive connotations as *siddha*. "Lama" refers to a teacher who instructs one in meditation. Given the great respect that a student is expected to have for his guru, it is usually assumed or implied that one's lama has achieved an advanced spiritual state. Tibetans use the full terms that translate as "mad *siddha*," "mad yogin" and "mad lama" infrequently, although some examples of their doing so will be shown in the chapters that follow. Tibetans usually assume the more famous and exalted figures referred to as *nyönpa*, like Drukpa Künlé and the Madman of Tsang, to be "mad *siddhas*." Lesser-known figures referred to as *nyönpa* would likely be considered "mad yogins" or "mad lamas." In the vast majority of instances, they are simply called "madmen," leaving their perceived degree of spiritual attainment unstated.

Those writing in English about these figures have referred to them as crazy *siddhas*, divine madmen, saintly madmen, Mad Yogins, "Crazy Yogins," and so on. Each of these renderings has advantages and disadvantages. In this book I mainly use the term "holy madman" (sometimes in quotation marks, sometimes not), since this seems the most neutral phrasing. Although the term "mad *siddha*" may be more accurate in some respects, it is overly delimiting, putting these characters into the predetermined category of *siddha*. The term "holy madman," although less literal, will allow us to come to our own conclusions in our thinking about these figures. In referring to them as "holy madmen," I do not mean to imply that from my perspective these are in fact holy beings, but rather that they tend to be regarded as such by other Tibetans—although they often had critics who were skeptical of their spiritual worth. This book is an exploration of the nature of their holiness.

This book does not discuss individuals perceived as "mad" in the unfortunate sense, and as such is not a Foucault-style study of the shifting conceptions of madness in Tibetan culture historically. The saintly figures that are the subjects of this book did not constitute significant points of interface between Buddhist and medicalized discourses about madness (perhaps because a highly structured medical discourse was a later development in Tibet). However, the argument developed in this book is influenced by Michel Foucault's thought in other ways, as discussed below.

Nor does this book address the "mad saint" traditions of other religions and cultures. There are comparable traditions of "crazy" Buddhist saints in South Asia, China, and Japan. There are respected "mad" or "intoxicated" figures in branches of Hinduism and Islam as well. There is a long tradition of saintly "fools for Christ," and the figure of the "holy fool," or *yurodivy*, is a mainstay of Russian literature. Each of these traditions is deserving of its own close historical study. Once this has been accomplished, I hope more meaningful comparisons—rather than flights of fancy inspired by the evocative notion of holy madness—can someday be made.

This book only touches upon the ways the idea of Buddhist "holy madness" has become manifest in the imaginations of Western observers. For example, in *The Dharma Bums*, Ray Smith, the voice of Jack Kerouac, narrates: "I wrote a pretty poem addressed to all the people coming to the party: 'Are in your eyelids wars, and silk . . . but the saints are gone, all gone, safe to that other.' I really thought myself a kind of crazy saint."[5] Smith often refers to his circle as the "Zen Lunatics," expressing how they thought of themselves as emulating the ways of past Buddhist sages through their free-spiritedness. For Smith—and Kerouac—holy madness is a natural part of Buddhism. But the goal of the present book is to explore the idea and the workings of "holy madness" in Tibet. The way Buddhist holy madness has been imagined by modern-day Europeans and Americans will be addressed only briefly in chapter 7.[6]

From among the Nyingma, Sakya, Jonang, Geluk, and Kagyü sects of Tibetan Buddhism, it is with the last that most of the individuals discussed in this book are associated. The Kagyü presents itself as continuing a tradition initiated by famous practitioners of tantric yoga in India, with whom they remain connected through an unbroken lineage of guru–disciple relationships. The lineage begins with the Indian master Tilopa, who received instructions directly from the primordial buddha Vajradhara. Tilopa's foremost disciple was Nāropa, at one time a famous scholar at Nālandā monastery, who abandoned his monkhood to pursue a more tantric lifestyle. The Tibetan Marpa Chökyi Lodrö (1012–1097) traveled to India to train under Nāropa, then brought the teachings back to his homeland, where he imparted them to Milarepa. The poet-saint Milarepa (1028/40/52–1111/23) is discussed throughout this study, as his history is interwoven with that of the "holy madmen" in myriad ways.[7] Milarepa's life is one of the best-known stories in the Tibetan world. After having his inheritance stolen by his aunt and uncle, Milarepa's mother sent him off to learn black magic, in hope of someday exacting revenge. He performed dark rituals that caused the deaths of thirty-five people. After realizing the grave error of his deeds, Milarepa dedicated his life to the practice of Buddhism. He sought out Marpa, who submitted him to a series of grueling trials before accepting him as a disciple and initiating him into tantric practice. Then Milarepa meditated and endured an almost unimaginable asceticism in caves along what is today the Tibet–Nepal border, subsisting for years on nothing more than nettles.

In time Milarepa achieved highest enlightenment. He would instruct Gampopa (1079–1153), Rechungpa (1083/84–1161), and his many other disciples through songs expressing his spiritual insights. The individual responsible for composing and mass-disseminating the version of Milarepa's biography that would become most central to the mythology of the Kagyü sect was none other than the Madman of Tsang.

In the generations after Milarepa, a variety of subsects were established within the broader Kagyü. There were the Drukpa, Pakmodrupa, Drikung, Shangpa, Taklung, Karma, and other subsects, each with its own monastic institutions, favored texts, and eminent hierarchs—sometimes in the form of reincarnation lineages, as with the successive Karmapas of the Karma Kagyü, or the Drukchens (also known as the Gyelwang Drukpa) of the Drukpa Kagyü.

This book deals largely with the form of Buddhism referred to as Secret Mantra, Vajrayāna, tantra, or sometimes "esoteric" Buddhism.[8] First arising as a new movement in the latter half of the first millennium CE, tantra has continued as a subcurrent within certain Buddhist traditions, where it remains contrasted with exoteric or sūtric Buddhism. Tantra has proven notoriously difficult to define. It presents itself as the most potentially powerful form of Buddhism, since it offers the possibility of achieving enlightenment in a single lifetime. (Those who misuse tantra, however, will find themselves in Vajra Hell.) Tantra involves a wide variety of means to the desired transformation. Many of these are ritual actions intended to tap into various sources of power that exist in the universe, most important among them being enlightened deities with whom the meditator enters into a relationship and strives to achieve full self-identification. A practitioner must undergo a formal initiation ritual before beginning these practices, and they must be taught to him by a guru who has already undergone the training himself. A good deal of advanced tantric practice concerns itself with the movements of the psychophysical winds and "drops" (*bindu* in Sanskrit, *thig le* in Tibetan) that circulate within the yogic, "subtle" body, a system of channels running throughout the physical frame. Sexual intercourse is one means by which some practitioners have invigorated the flow of these energies. Intercourse was also the means to produce the sexual fluids that, for some tantric communities, were of central importance in rituals of initiation. The various forms of mental and physical alchemy that constitute the techniques of tantra involve directed visualization, the repetition of mantras, tactile rituals, the cultivation of specific experiences, and much more.

TIBETANS TODAY TEND to think of the "holy madmen" with great fondness. Many of the Tibetans I spoke with during my research for this book would immediately laugh when asked what they thought about the holy madmen (using the phrase *druptop nyönpa* or *neljor nyönpa*, "mad *siddha*" or "mad yogin"). This was because my question brought to mind tales of Drukpa Künlé or some other eccentric master of whom they had heard. Drukpa Künlé is by far the best known of all Tibetan "holy madmen." The Madman of Tsang and the Madman of Ü are second and a distant third best known, respectively. A few of the Tibetan lamas, *khenpos*, and *rinpochés* I spoke with mentioned these three figures together under the grouping "the Three Madmen" (*smyon pa gsum*).[9] Some mentioned the famous Tangtong Gyelpo, Milarepa, or an eccentric lama of more recent times.

Tibetans often point out that the term *druptop nyönpa*, "mad *siddha*," is an oxymoron. *Siddha* means one who is "accomplished [in tantric meditation]," and has thereby achieved supernormal abilities and intelligence. An insane person cannot be a *siddha*, and a *siddha*, by definition, cannot be insane—at least, not in the medical understanding of madness. This mutual exclusivity is part of the conceptual framework for the most predominant way in which Tibetans interpret the odd behavior of holy madmen: the holy madmen are highly realized—enlightened—beings who see everything as it truly is, and act accordingly. Their way of seeing the world is radically different from our deluded, unenlightened one. This puts them at odds with conventional expectations. In this understanding, their being labeled and labeling themselves "mad" is ironic, pointing out the radical disparity between enlightenment and nonenlightenment. This "madness" is at once a marker of the saint's state of awakening and a reminder of our own lack of it.

Based on this view, Tibetans often say that we ordinary beings cannot comprehend the actions, words, or thoughts of an enlightened "madman" like Drukpa Künlé, for they are "inconceivable" (*bsam gyis mi khyab pa*). Many of the lamas I interviewed would offer an interpretation of the "holy madmen" only after making clear their feeling that anything we might say on the topic is somewhat speculative, since we can never fully comprehend the minds of the enlightened.

Tibetan religious specialists employ a variety of related terms to describe the high level of spiritual realization that the eccentricity of the "holy madman" is so often taken as indicating. This "madness" is often said to result from the fact that these individuals have abandoned all *namtok* (*rnam rtog*; in Sanskrit, *vikalpa*), meaning conceptual formations or false ideations. *Namtok* are preconceptions, which are, from the Buddhist perspective, *mis*conceptions. These conceptual thoughts act like lenses, distorting our vision of the world around us. Only those who are free of such thoughts can experience reality directly. Thus, while unenlightened beings like us try to understand the world through such relative distinctions as big and small, hot and cold, dirty and clean, pleasant and unpleasant, comfort and pain, right and wrong, and so on, a highly realized Buddhist master lives without such discursive categories mediating and distorting his experience of reality. When viewed from this perspective, the Madman of Tsang's adorning himself in human remains indicates that he has transcended the unenlightened distinction between repulsive and nonrepulsive. In light of the emptiness of all phenomena and worldly distinctions, in truth there is no such thing as virtue or sin, which is why Drukpa Künlé can sleep with other men's wives with impunity. This state is sometimes explained as the yogin's having transcended "worldly concerns" (*'jig rten gyi chos*). Sometimes it is said that because the holy madmen have abandoned all *namtok*, they have only "pure vision" (*dag snang*), or see everything as a buddha realm (*zhing khams*). This idea can be formulated in a more general way by stating that the holy madmen behave in their eccentric ways because they have an abundance of "realization" (*rtogs pa*).

Some learned Tibetans with whom I spoke mentioned Saraha, Virūpa, Nāropa, or other Indian *siddha*s in the process of explaining the nature of holy madness. Often these *siddha*s were cited as individuals who appeared strange to the world but secretly harbored great wisdom. On other occasions they were referred to because of their ability to perform miracles, which is taken as an indication of their having achieved *siddhi*s or of their realization of the emptiness of all phenomena.

Those adhering to this most widely held understanding of holy madness—that it is a symptom of the individual's being enlightened and having transcended ordinary worldly delusions—tend to see the irreverent behavior of the "holy madman" as occurring naturally (*rang bzhin gyis*), rather than having some sort of purpose or intention behind it. Alternatively, Tibetans sometimes see the eccentric behavior of these yogins as something engaged in with a specific purpose in mind: either to help unenlightened beings realize the emptiness of phenomena, or as part of the yogin's own training toward that realization.

The idea that the behavior of the holy madman is by nature pedagogical tends to be articulated in a few different ways. The most common is to say that the madman does and says wild, unexpected things in order to dispel the conceptual thoughts or misconceptions (*rnam rtog*) of those who behold him. Drukpa Künlé is often cited as one who exemplified this. A person taking this view would interpret the Madman of Tsang's dressing in human remains as intended to be a lesson to us unenlightened beings about the falsity of worldly distinctions. The yogin's purposeful crossing of boundaries and calling into question the observer's preconceptions is sometimes said to constitute the "introduction [to the nature of reality]" (*ngo sprod*) that is essential for a trainee's progress toward realization. When viewing the phenomenon from this perspective, it is sometimes said that the "mad" yogin is "simulating the behavior of a madman" (*smyon pa'i spyod pa 'khrab*). Some may see this behavior as exemplifying the Buddhist concept of "skillful means" (*thabs* in Tibetan, *upāya* in Sanskrit).

A yogin can also teach others by performing a miracle. Many Tibetan yogins like our holy madmen are said to have had the ability to leave impressions on boulders with their hands and feet, to tie metal swords into knots with their bare hands, and so on. These supernatural feats are sometimes interpreted as a lesson to the unenlightened, teaching us that because everything is ultimately empty, nothing is impossible. Even that which seems most solid is in truth completely malleable.

The third way in which Tibetan religious specialists tend to explain the behavior of the "holy madman" also involves an element of intentionality, but the yogin's concern is directed inwardly rather than outwardly. This view maintains that the yogin's shocking behavior is meant to foster his own spiritual development, as part of a deliberate process through which he trains himself to overcome conceptual distinctions and realize emptiness. By embracing the impure and the disgusting, by doing the utterly unimaginable—like stripping naked in the middle of a bustling marketplace—one can have the invigorating experience of crossing the invisible boundaries we draw around ourselves and which define the way we live. By purposefully transgressing conventions, one can begin to do away with them, and progress into a more immediate way of experiencing the world—a way that is based on the truth of emptiness, rather than our imperfect habits of mind. When viewed in this way, the yogin's odd behavior can be said to be for the sake of changing his "experiential understanding" (*nyams myong*) or overcoming conceptual formations (*rnam rtog*). It can also be said to advance his training toward "experiencing [all phenomena] to be of a single taste" (*ro snyoms*): in other words, to experience everything as empty.

All commentators recognize that the "holy madmen" appear to live free from the concerns that define life for ordinary individuals fully participating in society. The question is whether this deviance is a natural by-product of the yogin's state of realization, or part of his mode of teaching, or something purposefully pursued for the sake of his own edificatory experience. The first possibility is cited most often, and is nearly ubiquitous; the third is least commonly appealed to. The idea that a "holy madman's" eccentric behavior may be for the sake of his own training is almost never applied to famous saints like the Madman of Tsang or Drukpa Künlé, whom people assume were fully enlightened. The idea is occasionally used to explain the behavior of lesser-known "holy madmen," who do not have such well-established reputations as highly realized beings.

Many of the lamas I interviewed expressed doubts about whether we can ever be sure which of these interpretations is most accurate in a given situation. As His Holiness the Seventeenth Karmapa explained, any of these three motivations might lie behind the eccentric behavior of a "mad" yogin at a particular moment, and it is difficult for us to be sure which applies. Is the yogin in question fully enlightened or still working toward that goal? Is his activity for his own training or for the purpose of instructing others? With figures like Drukpa Künlé and the Madman of Tsang, it is generally agreed that they have long since completed their spiritual training. But for yogins of lesser renown and stature, who can say for certain what they have achieved?

When asked pointedly whether or not there are any mad *siddhas* (*grub thob smyon pa*) living in the world today, Tibetan religious specialists offer a wide range of responses. One lama stated that "holy madmen" are difficult to find, but as long as there is good meditative practice in the world, they will exist somewhere. One lama said that they surely do exist, but that they are very rare; they were easier to find in old Tibet. Another lama said that these days holy madmen are more likely to exist in Tibet than in other places, because of the political situation there, but would not elaborate on why. Differences of opinion and interpretation abound.

There is also ambivalence with respect to the question of "real" and "fake" crazy yogins. Some lamas say it would be impossible to tell whether or not an eccentric individual was a holy madman, for there are no limitations on how a holy madman might act or disguise himself. The behavior of a real holy madman may appear the same as that of a pretender; the only thing differentiating them would be their respective states of mind. Other Tibetan religious specialists see a more appreciable distinction, maintaining that if you were to put a "real" holy madman alongside a "fake" one, it would become obvious which was which. This can also be framed as a question of faith. As one lama told me, those who are open to being taught will learn a valuable lesson from the holy madman, while those who are not will walk away from the encounter unchanged. It is not the motivations of the yogin that matter so much as the attitude with which one beholds him. The most famous holy madmen, with the weight of tradition behind them, tend to be accepted as "real" holy madmen. There is less certainty regarding lesser-known and more recent figures sometimes said to be holy madmen, although an attitude of respect toward them generally prevails.

These few pages have summarized some of the main modes of thinking about "holy madmen" that tend to be expressed by Tibetan religious specialists and laymen today. Some of the other ways Tibetans have thought about the "holy madmen" will be examined in the course of this book. At any given moment, past or present, one can find evidence of a wide range of attitudes and opinions about Tibet's "holy madmen," moved at times by great faith or skepticism, and based upon differing understandings of individuals, of history, and of the nature of religion. There is no single traditional Tibetan view. What's more, many of the lines of thinking I apply toward understanding "holy madmen" in the course of this book have long been exercised by Tibetans, in various times and places—including by some of the "holy madmen" themselves. Any perceived chasm between "my" and "their" ways of thinking about the "holy madmen" is an illusion.

THIS BOOK IS in large part a study of how certain people came to be perceived as holy. It takes it for granted that, for the sake of academic research, we should view all things and people as existing on the same ontological plane, which is material in nature. However, in the course of human history certain entities have been conceptually set aside, and have thereby become imbued with a sense of holiness—at least in the eyes of some observers.

I do not contend that ghosts, demons, and gods truly exist, or that the miracles described in these saints' biographies—flying, disappearing, walking through solid walls—actually occurred. And although history has witnessed a broad spectrum of human capabilities and intelligence, I take there to be no specific moment in a person's development when he or she gains supernatural abilities or omniscience. In the world described in the pages that follow, there is no point at which an individual truly achieves a different ontological state as a *siddha* or a buddha. For the purposes of scholarly research, I assume that all of these designations are tropes and categories produced out of human discourse. It is not the case that holiness or enlightenment or gods or demons or miracles exist, independently and objectively, and that there is a Tibetan discourse describing them. Rather, beliefs in things such as these have been generated out human discourse.

Take, for example, the very notion of enlightenment. At any given moment in Buddhist history there have existed competing understandings of what constitutes liberating knowledge. This undermines the idea that enlightenment might exist as objectively real, independent of the discourses that describe it. Therefore, it must be said that those discourses do not *describe* enlightenment, but that they have in fact created the very idea of it.

Rather than accepting the view that through extraordinary religious achievement an individual can attain a different ontological state or the ability to perform miracles, we should examine the histories, needs, and intentions of the people who have made such claims, which brings us back into the domain of language and culture, of "truth" and power. The argument about Tibet's "holy madmen" that unfolds in the course of this book is in large part about competing models of truth, and the relations of power with which they are associated, and is thus inspired by Foucault's work in a general way.

Instead of trying to somehow plumb the inner, experiential dimension of being a "holy madman," this book explores its external dimensions—the effects or side effects of taking on the persona of a "holy madman," for historically and socially embedded individuals. Here sainthood is viewed as something that arises out of the dynamic between a saintly figure and his public, both during his lifetime and after. This allows us to explore the texture and workings of the social medium in which holiness exists. This book thus takes as a starting point arguments advanced by Aviad Kleinberg in *Prophets in Their Own Country* and by Robert Campany in *Making Transcendents*.[10] In the chapters that follow, I draw from both of these works in ways too innumerable to point out. Like Kleinberg and Campany, my aim is to understand these "holy madmen" as real people, as ordinary humans. As commonsensical as this approach may seem to some readers, it has not always been employed by scholars of religion. Viewing the "holy madmen" as creative, self-aware, meaning-producing *people* enables us to better appreciate their unique and brilliant contributions to the world. A view that sees the holy madmen as enlightened *siddhas*—and their odd behavior as a natural by-product of that state—actually divests them of genuine agency.

Readers should take my use of the term "saint" with a grain of salt, understanding this to mean "saintly figure," rather than something more reified or traditionally defined. There are differences in the mythologies, ideologies, and relationships that surround saintly figures of the world's various religions (and at different historical moments within any particular religion). Nevertheless, across cultures and time there are meaningful similarities to be identified in the processes through which individuals come to be perceived by others as having achieved an exalted religious state, and subsequently become the subject of devotion or worship. For this reason, a general phenomenon of "sainthood," unmoored from the specificities of any particular religion, is a worthy term and object of study.

One observation that catalyzes the research presented in this book is that Tibetan "holy madmen," like the vast majority of Buddhist renunciants, still live within the matrix of worldly activity. In the course of Buddhist history, there have undoubtedly been rare individuals who have pursued the hermetic ideal to its fullest, truly turning their backs on the world, undoing all social ties, and living entirely off the grid. But we know nothing of such figures, since they by definition would not have been involved with the production of literature or have associated with communities or institutions that would have transmitted their legacies to us. By contrast, we know of the holy madmen who are the subjects of this book only because they were social and cultural actors, with audiences who knew of them and saw preserving their stories as worthwhile.

There is also the inescapable fact of embodiment. The basic biological need to eat keeps the hermit in a relationship of exchange with the mundane world. Moreover, by separating himself from human society (spatially, symbolically, rhetorically) an ascetic can achieve a degree of sanctity. Paradoxically, this sanctity often serves to draw interested parties—faithful laypeople, potential patrons, disciples—to the ascetic, inasmuch as they hope to receive his blessings or his favor. Announcing one's rejection of society is an act that can carry profound consequences in the social sphere.

As a traditional Tibetan adage observes, "When practitioners meditate in mountains, food will roll uphill."[11] Those whose livelihoods come from religious practice—monks, ascetics, ritualists, and so on—are as aware as anyone of the ever-unresolved tension between renunciation and engagement with the world. As we shall see throughout this book, one of the most common criticisms a religious individual or group might level against a competitor is to say that they are worldly-minded, only masquerading as being devoted to higher renunciatory ideals. This exposes a concern that lurks perennially beneath the surface of the discourse. Many of these "holy madmen" were particularly attuned to the dynamics of exchange that inevitably surrounded them. Taking on a new identity as a "holy madman" in many cases had clear social, institutional, political, and economic ramifications. As skilled cultural and social actors, these individuals were aware—consciously or unconsciously—of what kinds of ramifications their decisions were likely to have. This is not to say that such decisions are always fully calculated or strategic, but it is having this basic awareness of how others within their society are likely to respond to their words and actions that defines them as participants in their culture (as it does us in our own).

The ascetics discussed in this book (as with the vast majority of all Buddhist ascetics, despite what rhetoric they may espouse) had various social ties and were engaged in worldly activities throughout their lives. The Madman of Tsang, for example, performed his antinomian behavior for all to see and hear of. He also mass-produced Tibetan-language literature using the most advanced printing technology available during his time. And although he underwent periods of meditative retreat, during which he greatly reduced his engagement with the affairs of the outside world, those connections were never severed absolutely, and these periods of withdrawal were temporary, having the effect of profoundly altering his standing in society once he emerged from them. This was not a man striving for hermetic anonymity. This study focusing on individual yogins is necessarily a study of yogic communities, and the ways individuals relate to them.

Finally, this book is in large part about narratives, both oral and textual. It considers how narratives are formulated in discrete acts of meaning making, and the way ideals are commodified through those narratives. This study also considers how those narratives circulate, affect people, and change over time, which enables new perspectives on historical questions.

The first five chapters are dedicated to developing a comprehensive understanding of two figures: the Madman from Tsang (1452–1507) and the Madman from Ü (1458–1532). Chapter 1 offers a brief discussion of the nature of the religious biographies that are the main sources used in this study, followed by abridgments of the biographies of these two "holy madmen." This serves to establish the basic trajectories of their lives and to introduce readers to the religious culture in which they operated.

Chapter 2 examines the shocking, antinomian lifestyles assumed by the Madmen of Ü and Tsang as being a form of religious practice. Despite the apparent strangeness of their behavior, it in fact resulted from their enacting a very literal reading of certain passages of tantric Buddhist texts that tended to be taken figuratively in Tibet.

Chapter 3 considers the Madmen of Ü and Tsang as public figures. The fact that they had both supporters and impassioned critics suggests that any degree of saintliness they achieved existed in the eyes of their beholders. The two acted in ways that led others to compare them to the enlightened *siddha*s of India, which was cause for controversy. By describing broader patterns in their interpersonal encounters, this chapter argues that the lifestyles assumed by the Madmen of Ü and Tsang were meant to position them as diametrically opposed to representatives of scholastic, monastic Buddhism, which is significant to the question of what may have motivated them to take on their distinctive personas.

A brief intermezzo explores the relationship that seems to have played out between the Madmen of Ü and Tsang, and how that relationship is portrayed in their respective biographies.

Chapter 4 considers how the "madness" of the Madmen of Ü and Tsang may have been related to the broader religious and sociopolitical events of fifteenth- and sixteenth-century Tibet, which was a period of civil war and tense sectarian rivalry. This chapter suggests that the Madmen of Ü and Tsang's decisions to enact such a literal reading of the tantras was part of an attempt to reimagine and redefine the Kagyü sect in response to its waning fortunes and influence. This decline was caused mainly by the dramatic rise of the Geluk sect and the reformed style of Buddhism it espoused. The specifics of the unique political and religious situation of the moment are what enabled the Madmen of Ü and Tsang to achieve such significance and influence during their lifetimes.

Chapter 5 describes the various cultural projects taken up by the Madmen of Ü and Tsang later in their lives, which were important means through which they worked to redefine and invigorate the Kagyü. These projects include the Madman of Ü's monastery-founding activities, and the Madman of Tsang's writing and printing the *Life* and *Songs* of Milarepa, his setting to paper the teachings of the Aural Transmission, and his renovating Nepal's Swayambhūnāth stūpa in 1504. This chapter considers the ways these projects served to continue the agendas the madmen earlier pursued through personal identity formation.

The final two chapters consider the lives and legacies of other "holy madmen" in Tibet. Chapter 6 attempts to separate the historical Drukpa

Künlé, Madman of the Drukpa (born in 1455), from more recent and popular representations of him. A close reading of Drukpa Künlé's four-volume *Miscellaneous Writings* suggests an individual very different from the one that lives on in popular memory. Attendant to the transformation from the historical Drukpa Künlé to the one so well known today was a dramatic change in the nature of his "madness." This chapter also explores the relationships Drukpa Künlé had with the Madmen of Ü and Tsang, and his views on the politics of his day.

Chapter 7 offers a brief survey of the "holy madman" phenomenon throughout Tibetan history, as well as the broader rhetoric of religious madness to which it is related. We will see that individual holy madmen were influenced by what they knew of other holy madmen who preceded them, and also that representations of holy madmen were often recycled. This shows that the holy madmen existed within a literate and self-aware tradition. The final section considers how some of the ideas about holy madness that currently predominate among European and American commentators were produced, and how those ideas have shaped understandings of the history of the phenomenon.

Much of this book focuses on Tibet in the fifteenth and sixteenth centuries, which was a society at once as admirable and as problematic as any that has ever existed. Religion dominated, as almost every aspect of Tibet's culture—conceptions of the self and the world expressed through literature and art, the basic categories through which people thought and communicated—was filtered through Buddhist discourse. Despite its pervasiveness, the influence of Buddhism was by no means totalizing, for people experienced other ways of viewing the world, held competing values, and at times behaved in ways that opposed Buddhist ideals. This Tibet was a place of faith and good works, but also of self-interest and treachery. Civil war carved a path of destruction across the regions of Ü and Tsang (figure 0.1, figure 0.2). Sectarian conflict was commonplace. Wrongdoing like murder was rarely punished, with clerics on occasion both the targets and perpetrators of this kind of violence. There was no separation of church and state, and the shifting relationships between religious hierarchs and members of the nobility drove the politics of the day. Meanwhile, the majority of the population worked in subsistence agriculture, subject to the nobles or monasteries whose land they farmed, in some cases as serfs. For those who had the freedom to do so, entering the monk- or nunhood was one of the few alternatives to this lot. Anyone invoking the traditional Buddhist historiographic trope of our living in a degenerate age (*snyigs dus*; similar to the Indian notion of a Kali Yuga), when Buddhism and the human condition have devolved grossly, would have had much to point to in support of that view.

In the individuals described in this book we witness the full range of human emotions, motivations and foibles: faith and doubt, affection and disdain, selfishness and selflessness, pride, compassion, jealousy, allegiance, and opportunism—anything that one can imagine. We see examples of remarkable creativity coming up against deeply entrenched structures of thought, as well as personal striving that is at times in the service of, at times in tension with, the concerns of various collectives. These people are as complicated as we would ever imagine our own selves to be.

The years I have spent studying Tibet's "holy madmen" have been filled with many kinds of conversation. I have spoken with lamas and *khenpo*s of the various sects, and given lectures on my findings to Tibetan scholars. I have had countless conversations with Tibetan laypeople, mostly in India, in which they asked me, "What is it that you're doing here?" Some thought holy madmen an odd subject to spend one's time studying, there being a strong sentiment among Tibetans that there is little sense to be made of the holy madmen: they are enlightened masters, so what hope do we have of understanding their behavior? Conversations about my research with other American and European scholars have often given way to debates about our most basic understandings of what religions are. It is my hope that the publication of this book will lead to further meaningful conversations—about these "holy madmen" and the history of Tibet, but also about the nature of religion and the methodologies and assumptions we employ when studying it.

In framing my arguments in ways that challenge some readers' preconceptions, I hope to do justice to the legacy of the holy madmen, for as a friendly Tibetan layman said to me one morning as we switch-backed down the steep hill to the Library of Tibetan Works and Archives in Dharamsala, the holy madmen have always been important, because "if there were no madmen, there would be no new [ways of thinking]" (*smyon pa med na gsar pa yod ma red*). I hope in the pages that follow to portray these "holy madmen" as forward-thinking individuals, who had a clear understanding of the workings of the world around them, and who, through their words and actions, challenged others' assumptions about how things ought to be.

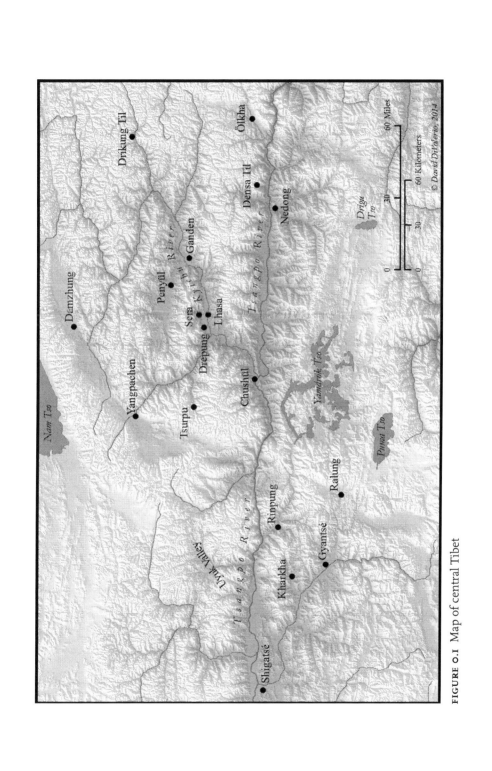

FIGURE 0.1 Map of central Tibet

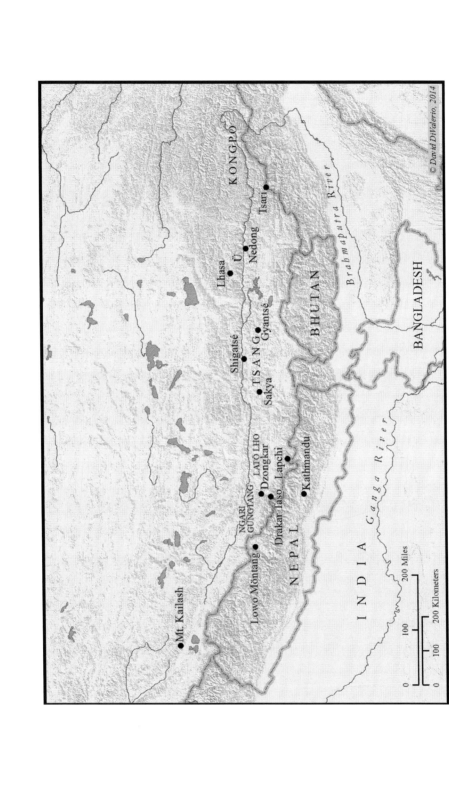

FIGURE 0.2 Map of Tibet and the greater Himalayas

1

The Lives and *Lives* of the Madmen of Ü and Tsang

The master [the future Madman of Ü] entered his mother's womb in the fire-female-ox year [1457]. At that time there were a variety of wondrous good omens, such as his mother's and father's dreaming that the sun, moon and stars were all shining together; that they built and paid reverence to representations of enlightened body, speech and mind; that conch shells, drums and other instruments were blown and played and flew into the air; about a canopy of rainbow light, and other things—so it is renowned.

Then when he was born in the year called "abundant grain" in the Indian system, or the earth-male-tiger year in the Chinese [1458], the infant was beautiful and pleasing to behold. His head was broad like a parasol, his brow was wide, and all of his limbs were fully articulated and lovely: one endowed with all the marks of a great being had been born.

NYUKLA PENCHEN, *The Life of the Madman of Ü*[1]

Hagiography and History

This chapter describes the basic trajectories of the lives of the Madmen of Ü and Tsang—birth, childhood, entering the religious life, abandoning monkhood to take on an alternative ascetic lifestyle, rising to prominence, passing away—while conveying some of the flavor of the biographies that relate the stories of their lives to us. These summaries are based on religious biographies, or hagiographies, of the Madmen of Ü and Tsang, which were composed by their respective disciples. These texts function as the official records of these yogins' lives within the Tibetan tradition and are our main sources of information about them.

There are certain problems inherent in using religious biographies as sources for historical information, since they offer mundane details of their subjects' lives alongside descriptions of miraculous feats. Many of these problems stem from the fact that while the authors of these biographies were striving to make accounts that were accurate and convincing, they also sought to make accounts that would inspire readers or listeners to gain faith in the spiritual accomplishments of their respective subjects. The intention of generating "goosebumps of faith" is announced in the very titles of biographies of both madmen.[2] These authors were not objective, journalistic observers, but were personally invested in their masters' reputations.

The dual nature of these biographies is best described using Dominick LaCapra's observation that texts can be both *documentary*, in their capacity to convey information about empirical reality, and *work-like*, in the way they actively shape understandings of that reality.[3] These texts tell us about what happened in the past while also manipulating our understanding of that history. The author of any narrative plays an important role in shaping the truth, whether he acknowledges it or not. But the places where these hagiographies exaggerate or diverge from the truth are no less meaningful and useful to the historian, because by determining which aspects of the story were altered, and when and how those changes took place, we can come to important conclusions about the means through which and the ends to which these texts were produced. This exposes the texts' work-like nature and tells us meaningful things about the historical past.

To put this another way, parts of these hagiographies can be taken as accurate descriptions of events that really did take place. Other parts may not relate events exactly as they occurred, but describe something similar to what took place—perhaps an inaccurate accounting of the gifts that were exchanged during a meeting, or an indirect quotation capturing the gist of what someone said, but not his exact words. Other parts of these hagiographies may relate exaggerated versions of the truth. For example, we have no reason to doubt that the Madman of Ü was at times physically assaulted by people who objected to his provocative behavior. But when his biography says that he was attacked by an entire army of angry Nepalese, with the air becoming "so full with weapons and a rain of stones that there was not space for even a little bird to fly," it is reasonable to view this as an exaggeration introduced by the author or by other faithful contemporaries of the yogin.[4] The logic behind this exaggeration is that the more harrowing a trial the yogin was capable of enduring, the more impressive his level of spiritual accomplishment must therefore have been. Meanwhile other parts of these hagiographies may be more thoroughly fictional. I take the many miracles described in these texts—the yogins' walking on water, flying through the air, passing through solid walls—as falling into this category. I understand these miracles as pious fictions imagined by the hagiographers—or imagined by other contemporaries and repeated by the hagiographers—for the purpose of bolstering their masters' reputations as *siddhas* who have achieved enlightenment and miraculous powers through meditation, and who are therefore worthy of our awe and respect. These miracles reflect the need to externalize and quantify the internal states these yogins are maintained to have achieved. There is no skirting the fact that, in order to make a meaningful argument about these matters, the scholar will at times have to decide which of these four categories any part of the hagiography may or may not fall into. Historical studies that attempt to remain agnostic on this question tend not to amount to much.

Volumes could be written about the nature of hagiographies and how they can and cannot be used for historical study. This book will not offer a comprehensive discussion of these issues, but will show a number of examples of how one might use this kind of text as a historical document. One technique that will be employed throughout this study to shed light on authors' decisions is to compare how different texts—an alternative biography of the individual, a biography of someone else, or some other textual source—portray a single statement, person, or event. As will be seen, these biographies can be "saved" as historical sources, in a limited way, through close attention to the authors' various agendas and the ways they pursue them.[5]

This brief discussion of the nature of these biographical texts highlights the fact that the process through which men like the Madmen of Ü and Tsang came to be seen as enlightened, saintly beings, was a collaborative one, involving many agents aside from the yogins themselves. Ultimately this book is a study of the efforts of various agents of meaning-making: from the "holy madmen" to those who beheld them, wrote descriptions of their lives, or perpetuated and modified stories about them generations after their deaths. I am another of these agents, because by saying what I say about them in this book, I play a role in shaping who and what the "holy madmen" were—exercising a work-like function, in addition to the documentary.

The famous holy madmen are, in a way, prisoners of the dynamics of representation—what tends to go on in the space between who a real human being was and what is thought about him by others. This is to some extent the inevitable fate of anyone who becomes the subject of historical study. But the famous holy madmen are susceptible to the dynamics of representation in a particularly thorough manner. This is because of how skillfully they negotiated those dynamics during their lifetimes. As I hope to show in the course of this book, these "holy madmen" are best seen as true masters of the alchemy of identity formation.

The Life of the Madman of Ü (1458–1532)

The following account is based on the only substantial biography of the Madman of Ü. The text was written in two parts by two of his disciples. The first part was written by the monk Nyukla Penchen Ngawang Drakpa (1458–1515, figure 1.1) in 1494, when the Madman of Ü was about thirty-six years old. Nyukla Penchen may have been a cousin of the warlord Dönyö Dorjé (1463–1512), who was a member of the Rinpung family and an important character in the story that will unfold in the course of this book. The second part was written in 1537, five years after the yogin's death, by Lhatong Lotsāwa Shényen Namgyel (born in 1512). The latter part was

FIGURE I.I "Homage to the great *paṇḍita*, Ngawang Drakpa"

composed based on records maintained by the Madman of Ü's nephew and successor, Künzang Nyida Pembar. The first part bears the title *The Life Story of the Noble Künga Zangpo, Glorious Holy Lama, the Preeminent Siddha Whose Practice Is Totally Victorious in All Respects, Called "That Which without Restriction Gives Goosebumps of Faith."* A consistent chapter structure runs throughout the two parts of the *Life*, which together form a single, continuous narrative. Readers interested in the text should consult my complete translation.[6]

The future Madman of Ü was born in a village called Ölkha, in the central Tibetan region of Ü, in 1458. He was the youngest of five sons born into a farming family of the Nyang clan. They called him Kyepo Dar. When he was five or six years old (the hagiography itself expresses this uncertainty) his mother would carry him on her back to a nearby monastery, where he listened to stories about the lives of past masters of the Kagyü sect. When he was eight or nine, he began to learn reading and writing at that same monastery.[7]

Following the death of his mother, while struggling under the weight of corvée labor (compulsory work imposed on the family as a tax) and other hardships, Kyepo Dar decided to dedicate his life to the practice of Buddhism, rather than participate in the self-perpetuating cycle of suffering that was village life. Despite his earnest wish to leave home and become a monk, his father and brothers prevented him from doing so for two years.

When he was fifteen or sixteen, Kyepo Dar fled to Tsari, a holy mountain and a locus of tantric activity. There he met Chuworipa Künga Namgyel, whom he took as his master. Kyepo Dar took his novice monastic vows and was given the name Künga Zangpo. He would spend the next three years with Chuworipa, who transmitted many tantric teachings and ritual empowerments to him. We are told that because of the teenager's ardent meditation, warmth blazed in his belly, giving him a feeling of bliss. He understood the emptiness of all phenomena and experienced waking life as if it was a dream.

In 1475, at around seventeen, Künga Zangpo took full monastic ordination at the Forest of Glorious Samantabhadra, a site for meditative retreat near Densa Til monastery, not far from his home village. After this, he traveled to various monasteries around Ü to receive transmissions from other masters, including Drakchokpa Rinchen Zangpo, who would replace Chuworipa as his main guru from then on.

Künga Zangpo traveled to southwestern Tibet, where he spent eight years in meditative retreat at Lapchi, Chubar, and other sites. He undertook great austerities during this period, fearlessly exposing himself to extreme weather while eating and wearing very little.

Künga Zangpo then underwent a transformation that would profoundly change the course of his life. One day he went before a statue of the Buddha and removed his maroon monks' robes. Then he smeared himself with the ashes and blood of a corpse, and put on bangles and a necklace made from human bone. He dressed in a cloak of human skin and a skirt made from a tiger pelt. He took up a trumpet made from a thighbone, a cup made from a human skull, and a *khaṭvāṅga*, an ornate ritual staff incorporating skulls and other tantric symbols. In this way he took on the guise of the wrathful deity Heruka.

Shortly after making this dramatic change in his appearance, Künga Zangpo began to engage in the provocative behavior that would make him famous. He went to Dzongkar, capital of the western Tibetan kingdom of Ngari Gungtang, where he stole into the presence of the king. Then the palace guards threw him out into the courtyard and savagely beat him. He danced like a wrathful deity, pronouncing the divine syllables *hūṃ* and *phaṭ*. Upon seeing this, the king and his ministers and subjects became convinced that Künga Zangpo was a *siddha*. From this time on, he was renowned as "the Madman from Ü" (figure 1.2).

After this, the yogin went for the first time to what is today Kathmandu, Nepal. He meditated in the inauspicious places where corpses were burned. According to his biography, he also desecrated many statues of Hindu deities by urinating on them and dancing on their heads. The outraged locals beat and stoned the yogin in a manner sufficient to kill any ordinary man. When he survived, they started to honor and praise him, and were even swayed to revere images of Buddhist deities and to stop performing animal sacrifices.

Künga Zangpo returned to central Tibet, traveling from one monastery to the next, receiving teachings and transmissions he had not gotten previously. After visiting his home village, he spent a year meditating and performing rituals at many holy places around Tsari. By this time the yogin had attracted a circle of disciples. He instructed them in the Six Dharmas of Nāropa, the Mahāmudrā, and other practices of defining importance to the Kagyü. In Kongpo, he continued to win people over through his miraculous yogic feats. He visited the provincial governor (*khri dpon*, "lord

FIGURE I.2 "Homage to the Madman of Ü, Künga Zangpo"

of ten thousand" or "myriarch"), Tashi Dargyé of Ja (died in 1499), who became his first major patron.

The Madman of Ü traveled to Tsang, visiting many monasteries and retreat sites along the way. During the autumn harvest in Gyantsé, he danced all over some grain that had been laid out to dry. The people beat him mercilessly, but he survived. He made his second and final trip to Kathmandu, during which, we are told, he punched and urinated on a local king, frightening the people so much that they began to revere him.

He then established a meditation center called the Fortress of the Expanse of Being in Tsang, which was made possible by financial support from a powerful lord. This served as the yogin's base for the next few years, as he occasionally returned there to meditate and teach between his travels.

In 1488, when the yogin was about thirty years old, he attended an enormous gathering of religious practitioners at Zambulung in the Shang valley, marking the anniversary of the birth of the tantric saint Padmasambhava. It is said that wearing his Heruka costume, he stood out from everyone else in attendance. Around this time, he visited the respected scholar-monk of the Sakya sect Śākya Chokden (1428–1507), at Serdokchen monastery.

One time the Madman of Ü dug up the corpse of a monk who had died of smallpox. He cracked open the skull and ate some of the brains. Everyone who witnessed this was left nauseated.

Much of Künga Zangpo's life during his thirties revolved around his relationship with the Rinpung family, who by this time had taken control of most of the Tsang region through timely power grabs, alliance-making, and military engagements. Künga Zangpo had first met Dorjé Tseten, one of the heads of the family, when he rudely burst into the presence of the great lord seated at court in Shigatsé. As the Rinpung faction extended their domain into Ü, drawing ever closer to Lhasa, the yogin moved along with them. He spent a significant amount of time with Dönyö Dorjé— younger brother of Dorjé Tseten and the most powerful layman in all of Tibet—at Chushül Lhünpo fortress, strategically located at the confluence of the Tsangpo and Kyichu rivers, west of Lhasa. The yogin stayed in a cave at the foot of the fortress and met daily with the great lord.

Around this time, the Madman of Ü endured a particularly vicious beating at the hands of the people of Nyukla, who were skeptical of the man who had arrived dressed like a wrathful deity. After he miraculously survived, he was hosted at Nyukla fortress. There the yogin gave teachings to Ngawang Drakpa, "the Great Paṇḍita of Nyukla," who shortly thereafter wrote this first part of the biography.

After visiting his father in Ölkha, the yogin circled through Kongpo, then stayed for some time at the Yöl Rinchen Ling retreat site. An official from Kharak gave him the gift of an estate called Liberation Park, where he established a second meditation center.

Künga Zangpo traveled through Tsang, stopping at Serdokchen monastery, where he saw Śākya Chokden a second time. He began to use the wealth at his disposal to sponsor festivities at various monasteries, including a religious service at the Forest of Glorious Samantabhadra before the enshrined skull of Drakchokpa, who must have died in the years since the yogin had last seen him.

PART TWO OF the biography begins by relating the events of 1495, when the Madman of Ü was around thirty-seven years old. He returned to Ölkha to be present at the death of his father, then took his final trip through Kongpo and Tsari.

After this the yogin's lifestyle became much less itinerant, with his activities limited to the Penyül area, northeast of Lhasa. In winter of 1499, he went into meditation at Kya-lhuk cave, where he gave advanced instructions to some of his closer disciples. They held a special event in which those advanced practitioners used yogic heat to dry wet sheets they had wrapped around themselves.

The Madman of Ü then set his sights on acquiring a monastery situated on an auspicious site in Penyül. It was called Tsimar Pel. The yogin tasked one of his disciples with getting them ownership of the complex, which may have been sitting vacant. On the fifteenth day of the eleventh month of 1502, the Madman of Ü took residence at the monastery, where he would remain until his death thirty years later.

The yogin spent the next ten years in strict meditative retreat, focusing on his own practice rather than teaching. For some or perhaps all of this decade he stayed in a sealed retreat, confined to a single room and interacting with the world through a small window. It is said that during some of this time he consumed nothing but flowers and berries.

In 1511, one of Künga Zangpo's disciples returned after having spent a long period in eastern Tibet. The Madman of Ü granted him leave to visit his mother in Tsang. While stopping over briefly in Lhasa, he performed some version of the provocative behavior for which his master was famous. Because of his doing so, he was attacked and killed.

In 1512, at the age of about fifty-four, the Madman of Ü finished his ten-year retreat. When word spread that he would begin giving teachings again, five hundred practitioners arrived from all over Tibet. To a small circle of disciples, he gave more advanced instructions, like the Aural Transmission (*snyan rgyud* or *snyan brgyud*), a rare and secret body of higher teachings relating to the *Cakrasaṃvara Tantra*. When the teaching session was over, he instructed some of his close disciples to make offerings, raise statues, and meditate at holy sites he himself had visited earlier in his career, including Mount Kailash, Lapchi, Chubar, the Swayambhūnāth stūpa, and the Six Fortresses of Milarepa.

During the last twenty years of the Madman of Ü's life, many local officials would arrive to give offerings in exchange for blessings and teachings. The great yogin also corresponded with powerful figures from afar. He received letters and gifts from heads of minor kingdoms throughout the Himalayas, like the king of Lowo Möntang (also known as Mustang, inside present-day Nepal), who sent carpets, five hundred pearls, and other gifts. He also received a flattering letter from the Eighth Karmapa,

Mikyö Dorjé (1507–1554), a leading hierarch of the Kagyü sect, who sought his counsel on some difficult points in the practice of tantra.

During these twenty years, the Madman of Ü was also visited by many religious figures. Another "madman," Drukpa Künlé, came bearing gifts and a praise of the Aural Transmission he had written at the yogin's request. He was also visited by two Indian ascetics known as Tilmarwa of Bodhgaya and Jaharbhi, who declared that even in India there was no guru greater than the Madman of Ü.

In 1514, the Madman of Ü's nephew, who was thirteen years old, came to Tsimar Pel from Ölkha to become a monk and train as the master's spiritual heir. The yogin dubbed him Künzang Nyida Pembar.

Shortly after the autumn harvest of 1516, when most of the master's disciples were away collecting offerings, a troop of monks and laymen surrounded the Madman of Ü's residence and began bombarding it with stones and arrows. (It is unclear which faction these attackers represented; they may have been based in Lhasa or near Ganden monastery, and were likely on their way to some more significant military engagement, since this was a time of open conflict between Ü and Tsang.) A few soldiers who broke into the residence and found the yogin wearing his wrathful deity costume immediately prostrated themselves at his feet. But overcome with craving, they took all of his belongings and left. That night the guilty parties saw bad signs portending punishment for what they had done. They returned the great yogin's possessions the next morning.

In 1518, when the Madman of Ü was about sixty, he announced that it was time to appoint replacements for his lineage-holders who had died. In recent years he had lost the disciple who was killed in Lhasa; Nyukla Penchen, who died in 1515; and Chokro Penchen Rinchen Samtenpa. Many aspiring meditators surrounded the yogin. He imparted his highest transmissions to a hundred advanced ascetics.

Throughout the 1520s the Madman of Ü taught regularly, holding instructional assemblies in winter, spring, and summer. At the end of these sessions, he would send his disciples (who in many cases had disciples of their own) to meditate and spread their brand of Buddhism in different regions, in southwestern Tibet, eastern Tibet, and even China.

To prolong the life of his uncle, Künzang Nyida Pembar made offerings and sponsored the performance of rituals at Drikung Til monastery, Tsari, Mount Kailash, the Six Fortresses of Milarepa, Ramoché temple, the Jokhang temple, the Drak Yerpa caves, and before the skull of Drakchokpa.

According to his biography, in 1531 the Madman of Ü made the following announcement: "If you want to meet with papa, come this year! I do not know if we'll be able to keep meeting again and again."[8] People flocked to Tsimar Pel as never before. That summer, the yogin announced that he had decided to cease teaching the dharma. Then he told many stories about the deaths of famous lamas of the past, which was taken as a sign that his own time would soon come. He told his disciples that for their salvation, remaining diligent in meditation was the most important thing—even more important than relying on their lama. He then entered a very strict retreat, meeting with no one.

In 1532, on the holiday marking the anniversary of the Buddha's descent from Trāyastriṃśa heaven, the Madman of Ü died at dusk, sitting in the meditation posture. He was seventy-five years old in the Tibetan reckoning.

The great yogin's casket was adorned with his set of bone ornaments. His nephew was installed as the head of the Tsimar Pel spiritual community. People gathered at the monastery, making offerings and reciting prayers. After the corpse was cremated, the Madman of Ü's skull and some pearl-like relics were left behind. A stūpa containing his relics, hair, fingernails, teeth, and other blessed objects was erected at Tsimar Pel. This holy stūpa would remain there as a "material support enabling sentient beings of this degenerate age to accumulate merit," thus allowing the master to continue his compassionate activity even after death.[9]

The Life of the Madman of Tsang (1452–1507)

Of the three biographies of the Madman of Tsang composed after his death by his disciples, the following account is based on *The Life Story of the Madman of Tsang, the Heruka, Who Is Victorious in All Respects, Called "The Heart of the Sun, Clarifying the Vajrayāna,"* by Götsang Repa Natsok Rangdröl (1482–1559, figure 1.3). The text was most likely completed in 1512. Götsang Repa's *Life* draws extensively from a shorter one penned by Ngödrup Pembar (1456–1527) in 1508, as well as from the *Collected Songs* of the Madman of Tsang, which were compiled and printed at that same time. A third biography of the great yogin, by Lhatsün Rinchen Namgyel (1473–1557), also draws extensively on Ngödrup Pembar's biography and the *Collected Songs*. I have chosen to base the following account on the biography composed by Götsang Repa because it is the most detailed of the three (figure 1.4). In the chapters that follow, I make reference to all three

FIGURE I.3 "Homage to Götsang, the great *repa*"

versions of the biography, which agree with and diverge from one another in significant ways. I have written about the contents of and the relationships between these biographies in an article published elsewhere.[10]

The future Madman of Tsang was born in 1452, in a village called Kharkha, in Upper Nyang (*myang stod*), in the Tsang region. Like the Madman of Ü, he was of the Nyang clan. He was the second of three brothers, all of whom would have careers as noncelibate tantric practitioners, as the men in the family had done for generations. After his birth he was given the name Chögyel Lhünpo. When playing with friends, he would pretend to be a tantric master teaching the dharma. At the age of seven he took the novice monastic vows and was given the name Sangyé Gyeltsen. It is said that at the age of thirteen, he tied a small bundle of poison around his neck, proclaiming that he would kill himself if he ever broke his vows. He tried to run away to the famous meditation site of Lapchi, but was caught by his mother and brought back home to continue his studies.

In his late teens, Sangyé Gyeltsen went to Tsari, where he met Shara Rapjampa Sangyé Sengé (1427–1470, figure 1.5), whom he took as his guru. Sangyé Gyeltsen served as Shara Rapjampa's attendant for a year, during which time he received the Six Dharmas of Nāropa, the Mahāmudrā,

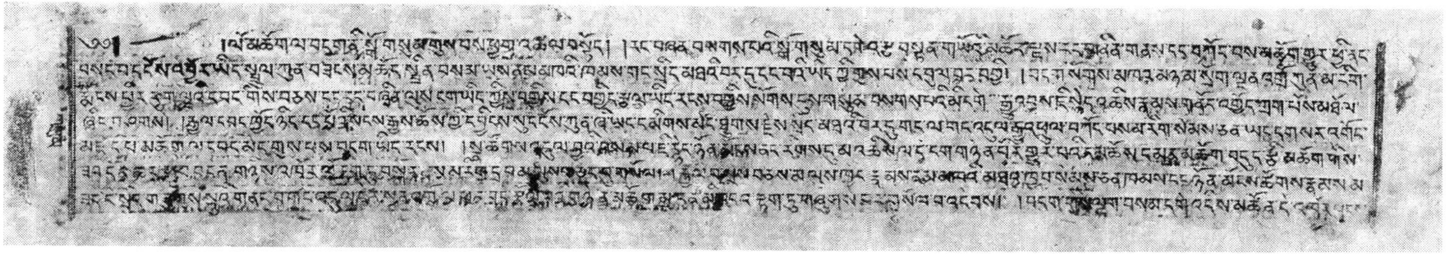

FIGURE 1.4 A page from Götsang Repa's version of the *Life of the Madman of Tsang*

Saraha's *Dohā Trilogy*, the Aural Transmission, and other teachings. He showed signs of success in meditation, such as a yogic warmth that enabled him to go about wearing nothing but a thin cotton cloth. Before their tearful final parting, Shara Rapjampa told Sangyé Gyeltsen to seek out tantric transmissions from other masters, to dedicate himself to the study of the *Hevajra Tantra*, and to wear tattered clothes and practice austerities.

Sangyé Gyeltsen returned to Tsang and enrolled in the Gurpa college of the renowned Pelkhor Chödé monastic complex in Gyantsé. For three or four years he studied and received empowerments for a number of tantric systems, including the *Hevajra Tantra* and the Path and Fruit (*lam 'bras*). He became a master of ritual, the proper construction of religious images, and ceremonial singing and dance. He is said to have shown great aptitude in everything he studied, knowing the words of the teachings but also their deeper meanings.

It is said that while living in the monastery, Sangyé Gyeltsen entered into a state of "divine pride," in which he saw himself as having the same nature as his chosen tantric deity.[11] At the same time, he experienced all phenomena as empty of their own inherent existence. Accordingly, he would no longer bow or use respectful language to kings or ministers, or to the monks who outranked him. He began acting out in strange ways.

One day a formal assembly was being held, and the ruler of Gyantsé came to the monastery with his ministers. When all the monks were seated in rows, Sangyé Gyeltsen arrived carrying a thighbone trumpet and a skull cup, from which he ate and drank. When scolded by the monastery's disciplinarian for acting in such a disruptive manner, Sangyé Gyeltsen responded by asking, "Where in the *sūtras* and tantras does it say one cannot bring a skull cup and thighbone trumpet into the line of monks?"[12] The disciplinarian was unable to say. After this, Sangyé Gyeltsen began to think seriously about leaving the monastery. He reasoned that he should be meditating diligently, rather than only studying the teachings, and that living as a monk was antithetical to the genuine practice of tantra. So he renounced his novice monk's vows (he does not seem to have taken full ordination) and ritually returned his maroon robes to the monastic assembly.[13] After spending a night on the roof of his dormitory reciting the *Hevajra Tantra*, he departed from the monastery. He was about twenty-one years old. For some years, Sangyé Gyeltsen would wear ornaments made from human bones and carry a skull cup and a *khaṭvāṅga* staff.

On his way to Tsari, traveling with his younger brother Könchok Gyeltsen, Sangyé Gyeltsen stopped in a Lhasa marketplace, where he tore apart a thread cross and ate a ritual cake (*gtor ma*, pronounced *torma*). Some people attacked him for acting so strangely, but miraculously he was not hurt. In Tsari, where he would stay for the next three years, he behaved in even more shocking ways. He told a female religious dignitary being hosted by Tashi Dargyé of Ja that he wanted to copulate with her. When the yogin successfully justified his impertinent behavior by saying that it was as instructed by the *Hevajra Tantra*, the powerful lord was won over and promised to provide for Sangyé Gyeltsen's upkeep as long as he stayed in Tsari.

Another local lord asked Sangyé Gyeltsen to ritually prepare the ground at a site where he intended to build a temple. The yogin smeared his body with blood, adorned himself with intestines from a human corpse, and danced about. On a different occasion Sangyé Gyeltsen went amid a large gathering of people while holding a chunk of brown sugar in his right hand and human feces in his left, taking bites from both. The people were shocked by this unfathomable behavior. Some believed that he had achieved a higher spiritual state and started to call him "the 'Hero' of Tsari" (*dpa' bo*, the Tibetan equivalent of the Sanskrit *vīra*, the male counterpart to the *ḍākinī*; these are low-level tantric gods and goddesses).

We are told that one night Sangyé Gyeltsen had a vision of the wrathful deity Hevajra, who gave him four tantric initiations and the title of "King of the Blood Drinkers." The next morning, he ate the brains of someone who had died of smallpox. It is said that from this time on, Sangyé Gyeltsen was completely free from all misunderstanding and dualistic grasping. *Saṃsāra* and *nirvāṇa* became one and the same to him. After some further gruesome and shocking behavior, people began to revere him as "the Madman from Tsang" (figure 1.6).

During an assembly at a lord's manor near Lhasa, the yogin got into an argument with some scholar-monks (*dge bshes*, pronounced *geshé*) from Sera and Drepung monasteries concerning the validity of his odd ways of acting and dressing. He argued that they were based on the tantric scriptures and the example of the great *siddhas* of the past. From Lhasa, the Madman of Tsang traveled to his home village in Tsang, where his mother implored him to give up his eccentricities and resume his education at Pelkhor Chödé. She reasoned that unless he at least changed his clothes, people might see him as a demon and try to kill him.

FIGURE 1.6 "Homage to the lord of victors, the Madman of Tsang, the Heruka"

The next period of the Madman of Tsang's life would be spent in south-western Tibet, meditating at sites made holy by their associations with Milarepa, like Lapchi, Chubar, and Kangtsuk cave. During his stay in the area, he had occasional contact with the rulers of Ngari Gungtang and Tsamda. It was around this time that he made his first of three visits to Kathmandu.

While on his way to Dzongkar in Ngari Gungtang, the Madman of Tsang met a meditator known as "the Lama from [Densa] Til" (*bla ma thel pa*). After arriving at the palace, the Madman of Tsang stole into the king's chambers and woke him from his slumber. The king, queen, and princess were all terrified, but soon saw the yogin's spiritual worth. The Madman of Tsang stayed there for some time as a guest of the king. When the Lama from Densa Til arrived at the palace gate, the king refused to let him in and even had him beaten. The Madman of Tsang protested that it was wrong to treat a renunciant in such a way. The king was persuaded to receive the Lama from Densa Til, who from then on was renowned as "the Madman from Ü." The Madmen of Ü and Tsang would have a tenu-ous relationship for some years after this meeting, until their relationship dissolved completely in the wake of some unpleasantness between their disciples, to be described shortly.

After spending these years in southwestern Tibet, the yogin decided to return to Tsari, stopping along the way at Kharkha (the third of at least six such visits to his mother), Lhasa, and Nedong. Tashi Dargyé again offered to provide for the yogin's upkeep, this time having to take into account his disciples as well. Corvée laborers were conscripted to transport these goods. Some refused to carry the Madman of Tsang's things, which led to a heated exchange. They threw rocks at the yogin, but he was unharmed.

After meditating and teaching in Tsari for some time, he journeyed back to southwestern Tibet, visiting various patrons and monasteries along the way. When he stopped at a monastery called Samten Ling in southern Latö (Latö Lho), the elderly abbot invited Sangyé Gyeltsen to take over the monastery, as he felt the yogin to be the greatest living vessel for the Kagyü teachings. Sangyé Gyeltsen declined, saying that he intended to continue living as a wandering ascetic, as he had been instructed by his guru. He remained a homeless itinerant all his life.

While staying in caves near Lapchi one winter, the yogin got the idea of composing and printing versions of the *Life* and *Collected Songs* of the famous poet-saint Milarepa. The Madman of Tsang began by sending his disciples to various places to gather existing songs by and narratives about Milarepa. After he finished composing his versions of the *Life* and *Collected Songs*, woodblocks bearing the imprint of each page of text were carved. Copies were made and sent all over Tibet. The printing project was completed in 1488, when the yogin was about thirty-six years old.

One night Sangyé Gyeltsen had a dream in which a woman wearing bone ornaments offered him some jewels. The next day, Küntu Zangmo, the daughter of a minor lord, who had run off to become a nun after the death of her husband, came to him. The Madman of Tsang readily accepted her as a disciple. She would remain his consort and patron throughout the rest of his life, and would sponsor the printing of his biographies and his *Collected Songs* after his death.

The great yogin was invited to Rinpung by Dönyö Dorjé, who was impressed by the versions of the *Life* and *Songs* of Milarepa he had produced. They entered into a patron–priest relationship that would continue for the rest of the yogin's life.

The Madman of Tsang went to Lapchi in southwestern Tibet, where he spent three years in meditative retreat. During this time he wrote a number of texts related to the Aural Transmission.

After another visit to Ü and his second journey to the Kathmandu valley, Sangyé Gyeltsen embarked on a pilgrimage to Mount Kailash, in the far west of Tibet. He was welcomed with a grand reception arranged by some of his students who were living by the holy mountain. While visiting the blessed caves in the area, he showed off his clairvoyance, knowing other people's thoughts before they even voiced them. He was visited by faithful nomads, who gave him yaks, goats, and sheep. He doled out payments to support his disciples staying in meditative retreat.

At this time the Madman of Tsang's patron in Lowo Möntang was at war with the minor kingdom of Gugé Purang over some territory. Much blood had been shed. Both factions requested that the Madman of Tsang mediate in the conflict, which the yogin compassionately agreed to do. Despite his best efforts, he was unable to broker a lasting peace. Eventually, Lowo Möntang prevailed and order was restored.

Around this time, the Madman of Tsang composed a letter of safe passage, ensuring that while they traveled, his disciples would be sheltered by the various lords with whom he had connections. This letter, and how it was received by other contemporaries, are discussed in chapter 6.

The Madman of Tsang made a vow to stay for three years in meditation at Chubar, where he continued to write texts that would go into a grand collection of Aural Transmission teachings. Two years into his retreat, he received word that his mother had died. He vowed to do an additional three years of practice on her behalf.

One winter the Madman of Tsang sent some of his disciples on pilgrimage to the Swayambhūnāth stūpa in Nepal. When they returned, he learned that they had had a conflict with some of the Madman of Ü's disciples. Harsh words were exchanged. With tempers fueled by alcohol, a fight broke out, and disciples on both sides were killed. This was followed by more retaliatory killings. The great yogin was saddened by this turn of events.

Around this time the Madman of Tsang decided to take on the task of overseeing the renovation of the exterior of the Swayambhūnāth stūpa. He had been receiving requests to do so for some time. He sent his disciples to various patrons with letters asking for support. When enough funding and materials had been gathered, the great yogin departed for Nepal, where he oversaw the work of artisans and conscripted laborers. The renovations were completed in two and a half months in 1504. The Madman of Tsang then returned to Tibet, more famous than ever.

For the next three years, the yogin spent his summers in Onjung and his winters in Chubar. He used some of his resources to put finishing touches on the Swayambhūnāth stūpa and to make woodblocks for a new version of the *Life* of Marpa, Milarepa's guru.

After this, the Madman of Tsang returned to central Tibet, spending a great deal of time with his longtime patron Dönyö Dorjé, visiting him in Rinpung, Shigatsé, Chushül, and Lhasa, which the Rinpungpas now controlled. Along the way he visited his natal village, where he saw his mother's remains.

With the great yogin's health in obvious decline, he stayed at Zelmo cave, where five hundred practitioners came to receive teachings from him. Some of Sangyé Gyeltsen's followers suggested he go into meditative retreat in order to prolong his life, but he was resigned to the inevitability of death and chose to continue teaching. Day and night the master's disciples and patrons circumambulated and prostrated to the place where he stayed, praying to find themselves in his presence again in some future lifetime.

The yogin relocated to Rechung cave, where he entered a strict retreat, not meeting anyone for ten days. After calling his students before him, the Madman of Tsang encouraged them to practice deep asceticism. He passed away on the fifteenth day of the fifth month of 1507. In the Tibetan manner of counting, he was fifty-six years old.

According to Götsang Repa's version of the biography, the faithful offered so many butter lamps that it looked as if the stars had fallen to earth in the area around Rechung cave. The cremation rites were carried out by forty of the yogin's disciples. When the cremation chamber was opened a week later, two thousand five hundred were in attendance. Bits of the master's bone, hair, ash, and pearl-like relics, along with his various possessions, were distributed to his disciples.

Tea ceremonies and virtuous offerings were sponsored at many centers of religious activity. Feasts for 824 and 1,500 religious practitioners were held at Rechung cave and Tsari. Offerings poured in from the madman's many patrons. Statues of the master were made. At a mountain retreat near Chubar, where Milarepa had passed away in the twelfth century, a memorial prayer service lasting three months was held. It is said to have been attended by Dönyö Dorjé, other government ministers, and commoners. Some of the master's disciples made vows to go into retreat for one, three, or six years, perhaps the most fitting way to honor the memory of the great enlightened one.

2

Of Scripture and Bone

THE TANTRIC DISCIPLINE OF THE
MADMEN OF Ü AND TSANG

At that time, when the great one [Künga Zangpo] had become a great preeminent *siddha*, never to revert from that state, in succession he received prophetic assurances from his lama and the *ḍākinīs*, leading him to think, "My continuum is ripened and liberated, so whatever I do is just as well. However, in accordance with the prophetic commands given by my lama and the *ḍākinīs*, I should give up the indicators and attire of monkhood and take on the accoutrements of the Heruka. Having combined practice with an 'intimate one' [i.e., a consort] with the yogas of the Generation and Perfection Stages, which are derived from the short path of the Vajrayāna, the swift path of the definitive secret of the *ḍākinīs*, I will enhance the aspects of my method visible to others, and show the manner of traversing the stages of the Stages and Paths as easily as if they were mere illusions. In one life and one body I will make manifest the body of a sovereign *vajradhara*."

In order to overwhelm all of phenomenal existence with his greatness through the Practice [*spyod pa*; in Sanskrit, *caryā*]; in order to subdue all the nonhuman spirits that are enemies of and obstacles to the Teachings; in order to take care of every last worthy being and set them on the Stage of Accomplishment; in order to proclaim the greatness of the Vajrayāna and highlight the profundity of its essential meaning; in order to fulfill the intentions of the heroes and *ḍākinīs* of the three realms; in order to project heaps of offerings like Samantabhadra for the Victor and his Sons; in order to spread and increase the teachings of the Victor in general, and especially to initiate a tradition dedicated to the definitive meaning of the precious Kagyü, the master laid down the indicators and attire of monkhood before an image of the Lord of Sages and took on the accoutrements of glorious blood-drinking Heruka.

Upon his naked body he was adorned with a crown of long hair, as well as a circlet, earrings, a necklace and bangles made of bone, a sash, and a Sacred Thread—the Six Bone Ornaments—as well as clumps of ash, drops of blood, and smears of grease from human tissue. For a shawl he wore a human skin, with hair and nails still attached. He wore a tiger's hide as a skirt. He wore a *brahmin*'s cord made from human hair. He took up a *ḍamaru* made of *catechu* wood, a smaller hand drum made from the tops of skulls, a trumpet made from human bone, and an authentic *kapāla* [skull cup] that was fissured and yellowed. He had a *vajra*, a bell, and a "sky-staff" or *khaṭvāṅga*, which was decorated with bells, strips of silk, and so on. All of these were associated with *samaya* vows.

Thus he was adorned with the Six Accoutrements of the Heruka, or the Eight Accoutrements of the Great Glorious One. For his *samaya*s he drew from such volumes as the root text of the *Two-Parted* [the *Hevajra Tantra*], the *Laghusaṃvara* [*Cakrasaṃvara*] *Tantra*, and the *Dohā Trilogy*. For his appearance he drew from the forms of Hevajra, Cakrasaṃvara, the glorious four-faced vitality-sapping Mahākāla, and so on. He would consume *samaya* substances. . . . He also took up a sword symbolizing Wisdom, an arrow and a bow symbolizing Means and Discernment, and so on.

NYUKLA PENCHEN, *The Life of the Madman of Ü*[1]

THIS CHAPTER EXPLORES some aspects of Künga Zangpo and Sangyé Gyeltsen's distinctive religious practice, showing that despite the apparent strangeness of their behavior, it in fact resulted from their enacting a specific tantric discipline. The final section begins the task of considering how performing this tantric discipline positioned the Madmen of Ü and Tsang within the religious culture of their day.

The Practice of the Observance

In order to identify what was unique about the Madmen of Ü and Tsang, we must first note that much of their religious activity was entirely customary for elite practitioners of the Kagyü in fifteenth- and sixteenth-century Tibet. They received instructions and initiations for a range of tantric systems, which they would practice throughout the rest of their lives. They traveled to holy sites across the Himalayas, seeking to tap into sources of great power. Through meditation and ritual, they communed with various deities and protector spirits. They devoted great effort to inner fire meditation and the rest of the Six Dharmas of Nāropa. The superlative meditative goal they sought to achieve was described through the rhetoric of the Mahāmudrā, or "Great Seal," a radically nondual understanding of existence. In all of this, Künga Zangpo and Sangyé Gyeltsen were operating within the bounds of the ordinary for highly dedicated Kagyüpas during their day.

But in addition to their more conventional religious activities, Künga Zangpo and Sangyé Gyeltsen behaved in ways that set them apart from their contemporaries and led to their being labeled "mad." They are many times said to have accosted powerful lords, to have done obscene things among crowds of people, and to have spent parts of their lives smeared with ashes and blood, wearing ornaments made of bone. According to their biographies, their respective appearances were so gruesome and out of the ordinary that people sometimes thought they were demons.[2]

Despite the immediate strangeness of this behavior, it was neither random nor meaningless, but represents Künga Zangpo's and Sangyé Gyeltsen's performing a certain advanced practice that is prescribed in the tantric scriptures. In the madmen's biographies, this distinctive practice is referred to as *tülzhuk*, *chöpa*, or *tülzhuk chöpa* (*brtul zhugs*, *spyod pa*, *brtul zhugs spyod pa*), terms that are used nearly interchangeably. *Tülzhuk* is a translation of the Sanskrit term *vrata*, meaning a religious vow or observance. *Chöpa* is a translation of *caryā*, meaning practice, performance, or activity. *Tülzhuk chöpa* translates *vratacaryā*, meaning "the practice of the observance," or *caryāvrata*, "the observance of the practice." The terms *vrata* and *carya* were widely used in both the Buddhist and non-Buddhist traditions of India to refer to various aspects of religious practice, which is true of *tülzhuk* and *chöpa* in Tibetan as well. But in the context of late Buddhist tantra, these terms sometimes designated a specific practice, leading Christian Wedemeyer to describe them as "terms of art" in this usage. When describing the distinctive activity of the Madmen of Ü and Tsang, it is in this sense, as terms of art, that these words are used.[3]

Tibetan exegetes gloss the term *tülzhuk* in various ways. Broken into its parts, it means "taming" (*brtul*) and "entering" (*zhugs*). The fourth in the Red Hat incarnation lineage, Chödrak Yeshé (1453–1524), an elite hierarch of the Kagyü sect, takes the term as meaning that one intends to "*tame* the afflictive emotions and conceptual formations that are to be abandoned, and *enter* into the potent wisdom that is their antidote." The term can also be interpreted as meaning "taming inappropriate activity and entering into perfected activity."[4] *Tülzhuk* and *tülzhuk chöpa* have been translated into English as "deliberate behavior," "practice of spiritual discipline," "observance practice," and "disciplined conduct."[5] In this book I render *chöpa/caryā* as the Practice, *tülzhuk/vrata* as the Observance, and *tülzhuk chöpa/vratacaryā* as the Practice of the Observance, with all three referring, in this context at least, to the same basic practice.

Various tantric texts composed in the second half of the first millennium in India describe the Practice of the Observance as a time-delimited period of wandering homelessness during which an advanced meditator takes on new dress, practices, and attitudes toward the world. The tantras often dedicate a chapter to describing this practice, which is the case in the *Hevajra*, *Laghusaṃvara* (which I refer to as the *Cakrasaṃvara Tantra* throughout this book), *Guhyasamāja*, *Buddhakapāla*, and others.[6] Wedemeyer has shown that among the Indian Buddhist tantric texts that describe the Practice, no two are in full agreement about how it ought to be performed. If taken in aggregate, however, the texts do align with one another in significant ways.

In terms of *when* in the practitioner's development it should be undertaken, it is agreed that the Practice is not for beginners, but for those already well accomplished in tantra. The degree of success in meditation one should have achieved before beginning the Practice is often referred to as having "achieved heat" (*ūṣman* in Sanskrit, *drod thob* in Tibetan), which refers to having an advanced realization of emptiness. The prerequisite is also described in terms of having achieved certain supernatural powers, or high accomplishment in meditation quantified in some other way.[7]

In terms of *where* the Practice should be performed, the texts usually offer a list of isolated, impure, and liminal spaces, suggesting that the yogin reside on a mountain, under a solitary tree, in the home of a low-caste person, in a charnel ground, and so on. The tantras are particularly divergent on the question of *how long* the Practice should be performed, prescribing a period of a fortnight, six months, a year, twelve years, or the rest of one's life. As for what should be *worn* while doing the Practice, the texts most often mention wearing a set of bone ornaments, a tiger skin, ashes, and carrying a *khaṭvāṅga*, a *ḍamaru* drum, and a skull cup. Some scriptures suggest that the practitioner go naked.

As for what *practices* the yogin should perform during this time, the texts prescribe wandering, consuming impure substances, drinking alcohol, eating whatever one finds, singing and dancing, behaving fearlessly, like a lion, or without concern for what others might think, like a child. As will be expanded upon in the next section, some texts say the practitioner should behave "like a madman," insofar as he lives without reliance on ordinary conceptual distinctions. It is repeatedly stated that the practitioner should act without taking into account the relative purity or pollution of things, thereby dramatically disregarding one of the most fundamental orienting concerns of life in India during this time. Almost all of the texts suggest that sex should be a part of the yogin's practice during this period. The texts are also careful to mention certain practices the yogin should be certain *not* to perform while pursuing the Observance: he should not read texts, recite prayers, or offer worship in the usual ways. The yogin should not engage in value judgments or conceptuality.

As for what the yogin is meant to gain from the Practice of the Observance, there are a number of related possibilities. After having deeply contemplated the nature of things while seated in meditation and training in the conventional way, the practitioner enters into the Practice, during which he seeks out experiences that will challenge his habitual modes of thinking, which could lead to his having deeper and more transformative realizations. Forcing oneself to eat filth could play a significant role in the process of *training* oneself to view the world in a way that transcends all dualities. At the same time, submitting oneself to these powerful experiences could serve to *test* whether or not the practitioner has achieved such a state of transcendence. Meanwhile, doing these things can also serve to *attest* to the practitioner's having completed such a transformation, putting his realization on display for others to see. Given the semiotic structures surrounding this practice, Wedemeyer has described it as "a way of viscerally instantiating and ritually attesting to the attainment of the aim of Buddhist Tantric yogins: a nondual gnosis that sees through (and acts without regard for) the delusive sense that the constructed categories of conceptual thought are real and objective."[8] The practice is thus a means to the most profound of Buddhist transformations and the expression of its achievement collapsed into one.

But what did the Practice of the Observance entail for the Madmen of Ü and Tsang specifically? As seen at the opening of this chapter, taking on the dress of a wrathful tantric deity was an essential part of the Practice for Künga Zangpo, as well as for Sangyé Gyeltsen, which will be detailed in the third section of this chapter. The Practice also entailed having sex. The Madman of Tsang had a long relationship with a woman named Küntu Zangmo (figure 2.1), who was his sexual consort, disciple, and patron (her arrival presaged by a dream about a goddess giving him jewels). It is likely that Künga Zangpo also took a consort, as the passage translated at the beginning of the chapter would seem to suggest. Both madmen probably had a series of consorts with whom they practiced sexual yoga once they renounced their monks' vows, although their biographies provide little detail on this. In the tantric circles in which they operated, sexual practice would have been common enough not to warrant special mention.[9]

As to what else the Practice of the Observance entailed for the two yogins, one passage in the *Life of the Madman of Tsang* states: "In charnel grounds, under solitary trees, and on the banks of rivers; on open plains,

FIGURE 2.1 "Homage to the great mother, Küntu Zangmo"

in abandoned homes and temples; in alleyways and marketplaces; and in frightening haunted places that make one's skin crawl, he roamed, doing the Practice of the Observance."[10] This passage echoes the lists of sites appropriate for the Practice offered by the tantric scriptures. All of the places listed here are distinguished either by the absence of human inhabitants or their presence. It is common for Tibetan yogins to meditate in caves or other isolated places in order to avoid the distractions inherent in being around other people. Tantric practitioners also sometimes seek isolation in charnel grounds or other liminal spaces believed to be inhabited by malicious spirits, where the yogin can confront and hopefully overpower those beings. Uniquely distinguishing Künga Zangpo and Sangyé Gyeltsen was the fact that they would do shocking things among crowds of people or in marketplaces—the marketplace being the most public space in fifteenth-century Tibet, filled with people from near and far, exchanging goods, news, and everything else. One instance of the Madman of Tsang's exhibitionistic Practice of the Observance is described as follows:

> The next morning he rubbed his body with ashes from a corpse that had been burned and thrown to the birds. He made a neck-lace, bracelets, and anklets out of the intestines. He went among a crowd of people making a full moon offering, where he ate the ritual cakes. He jumped among the people. He would dance and sing, then he would cry and beat his chest. Letting his *vajra* hang out, he chased and climbed on all the women, kissing and hugging them and grunting. Then he would tuck his *vajra* inside, so there was only a hole with hair around it, and chase all the men, saying "Screw me!" while grabbing and hugging them. He would throw feces and urine at the people, and consume it himself. No matter what kind of Practice of the Observance he performed, out of fear and shock, no one could contest him.[11]

There are few things that could more palpably signify a person's existing in a profoundly abnormal state than their not being repulsed by human waste. In adorning himself with human remains and eating filth, the yogin may have been furthering, testing, or attesting to his realization of the ultimate falsity of the distinction between pure and impure. In sexu-ally accosting men and women, he may have been furthering, testing, or attesting to his realization of the conventionality of society's behavioral norms. By eating the ritual cakes and thus interfering with the relationship between people and the gods, which was seen as a dangerous undertaking, he may have been showing his transcendence of such fears. The passage translated as the epigraph to the introduction gives another example of the Madman of Tsang's overturning norms in the course of the Practice. The Madman of Ü is also said to have done the Practice amid crowds of people, although not recounted in the same vivid detail. As mentioned in chapter 1, when one of the Madman of Ü's disciples performed the Practice of the Observance in Lhasa, it provoked such a violent reaction from people that he was killed. Performing this kind of antisocial behavior must have been a dangerous enterprise.[12]

In many instances in the biographies of the Madmen of Ü and Tsang, the terminology of the Practice of the Observance is used to refer to a moment of violent confrontation, with the ascetic disrespecting or assault-ing a powerful lord or doing something to provoke the ire of a gathering of people. The purpose of this kind of confrontation may have been to over-come, or test if one had overcome, or make a display of having overcome fear—behaving "like a lion," as the texts often say. Another aspect of this confrontational behavior may have been the yogins' imitating the behavior of the fierce deity they impersonated, as described later in this chapter. In the *Life of the Madman of Ü*, the Practice of the Observance most often comes as part of the phrase "the Practice of the Fierce Observance" (*drag po brtul zhugs kyi spyod pa*), which he used to cast Hindus out of some Buddhist holy sites near Kathmandu that they had taken over, and to bring to heel a curmudgeonly Tibetan lord. When he performed the Practice of the Fierce Observance at one monastery, it is said to have caused the monks to attack him with stones, swords, arrows, spears, and other weapons.[13]

Similarly, on one occasion the Madman of Tsang's Practice of the Observance entailed rudely snatching a cup of *chang* (a light alcoholic drink made from barley, the Tibetan equivalent of beer) from a lord's hand. When the guards made ready to attack the yogin with their swords and spears, he threatened them with his *khaṭvāṅga*. It seems that by the middle of his career, Sangyé Gyeltsen had gained a reputation for violence. Götsang Repa's version of the *Life* describes how Chöwang Lhündrup (1440–1503), the first in the Pawo incarnation lineage, sent his younger brother to train under the Madman of Tsang, who, the Pawo is quoted as saying, "maintained the teachings of Secret Mantra through his mastery of fierce activity and the Practice of the Observance." The younger brother would soon return to the Pawo, saying that he "didn't get" the Madman of Tsang's ways of dressing and practicing tantra.[14]

The Madmen of Ü and Tsang were sometimes understood as progress-ing through specific phases in their practice of this distinctive asceticism. Sangyé Darpo, a grand-disciple of the Madman of Tsang, wrote in his *History of the Kagyü: The Combined Luster of a Heap of Jewels* that during his career the Madman of Tsang performed "the Secret Practice, the Public Practice, the Awareness Observance, and the Practice that Is Victorious in All Respects."[15]

To spell out what kinds of practices these distinctions may have been meant to indicate, in his commentary on the *Hevajra Tantra*, Dakpo Peṇchen Tashi Namgyel (1512/13–1587) explains that in the *Cakrasaṃvara* system, there are understood to be four different stages through which a practitioner progresses. First, there is the All-Good Practice, which refers to living a virtuous lifestyle in accordance with the conventional vows and commitments, while living at one's home monastery. This is followed by the Secret or Covert Practice, which refers to a period during which the practitioner engages in "mantric" or "tantric conduct" (*sngags kyi kun spyod*) without letting on to others that this is religious practice; he should pair with a consort and consume *samaya* substances in secret (*samaya* or "pledge" substances, *dam rdzas*, would here refer to alcohol and various foods usually considered disgusting or impure, perhaps including the "five meats," discussed in the final section of this chapter).[16] Then comes the Practice of the Awareness Observance, which denotes a phase in which the practitioner "puts on the accoutrements of a yogin" (*rnal 'byor pa'i chas su zhugs*), and should, along with his consort, perform mantric activity at gatherings (*tshogs su*). Lastly, there is the Practice that Is Victorious in All Respects, which means that the practitioner has subdued all adverse circumstances and can overpower existence with his brilliance.

Here Dakpo Peṇchen uses the term "Practice of the Awareness Observance" to refer to a period during which one performs tantric practices among other people. In other accounts, practicing for others to see is referred to as the "Public Practice" (*tshogs spyod*) (as in Sangyé Darpo's presentation).[17] Karma Trinlepa (1456–1539), a well-respected Kagyüpa scholar, treats the "Practice of the Awareness Observance" as synonymous with the "Practice of the Observance," as an umbrella term, stating that it can include within it the Public Practice, the Secret Practice, the All-Good Practice, and so on, depending on the practitioner's mental capacities. Other commenters see the "Practice of the Awareness Observance" as involving sexual yoga specifically. Some regard "Secret Practice" as synonymous with "Practice of the Observance," while others see it as a specific practice within it, or even a prerequisite for it.[18]

This consideration of a few different presentations of these practices gives a sense of the lack of agreement among fifteenth- and sixteenth-century Kagyü commentators regarding significant facets of the Practice— questions of how many stages of practice there are, what exactly those entail, what terminology denotes those practices, and so on. When taking into account other descriptions, the divergences increase exponentially.[19] It seems that the various commentators were unsure about what exactly these terms referred to, or that there was simply no greater consensus about their meanings. This might suggest that the practices were not commonly performed in Tibet. In his reading of the late Indian sources available in Sanskrit, Wedemeyer was unable to find meaningful differences between many of these labels, determining that they were synonymous, nearly synonymous, or at least of the "same class of ritual behaviors." These terms may never have been differentiated without ambiguity.[20]

Putting these uncertainties aside, it seems that the Madmen of Ü and Tsang moved through a series of stages in the course of their distinctive asceticism. After a period of living in accordance with conventional discipline as a monk (All-Good Practice), each spent time practicing in out-of-the-way places (Secret Practice), which was followed by a period in which he did outrageous things among crowds of people (Public Practice), after which he enjoyed the fruits of his years of training (Practice that Is Victorious in All Respects). The madmen's biographers saw fit to resort to these categories when describing their lives. Similarly to how Sangyé Darpo described the activities of the Madman of Tsang, in describing what the Madman of Ü had done in his spiritual career up to his mid-thirties, Nyukla Penchen writes, "The master completed most of the Mother [Yoginī] tantra instructions on the Secret Practice, the Public Practice, the Practice that Is Victorious in All Respects, and the All-Good Practice—however it is that they are defined."[21] For Nyukla Penchen, it was important to make sense of the great yogin's life through reliance on these terms, despite his admitted uncertainty over what exactly they meant.

The Madman of Tsang is in one instance said to have used these categories to explain his vision of the religious path. The story maintains that someone questioned the Madman of Tsang in the following manner:

> Concerning the dress and implements of the Heruka—the matted hair and other things that pertain to the Secret Mantra Vajrayāna: although there are many yogins actually taking them up in India, before the arrival of the master [the Madman of Tsang] there were none in Tibet wearing the complete garb of the Heruka, just some individuals with dreadlocks or plaited hair. These days there are many who do not have good qualities or experiential realization but nevertheless take on an external manner of dress like this. If your disciples do not have your authorization, they are not allowed to wear the emblems of the Heruka. Regarding this, how much experiential realization and what good qualities must one have on the inside before one is allowed to adopt the emblems of the Heruka?

The Madman of Tsang is said to have replied,

> Once a person has developed nausea with *saṃsāra* and bad rebirths; once one has entered the door of the Teachings, and is unattached

to life or the eight worldly concerns; after one has faultlessly upheld the instructions for individual liberation [i.e., monkhood] and bodhisattvahood, just as he promised; after having gotten the ripening and liberating empowerments from an authentic lama of the Vajrayāna, along with the instructions, tantras, and practices; and having become learned in both their words and their meanings; and then thanks to practicing them, experiential realization is born in one's continuum—one such as this has arrived at the time for the Practice and takes on the emblems of the Heruka.

When is it time for the individual practices? At the time of the Path of Accumulations, one does the All-Good Practice. At the time of the Path of Connection, one does the Secret Practice. At the time of the Path of Seeing, when one has directed the winds and the mind into the central channel, and externally can use one's clairvoyance and supernatural abilities to convert the unfaithful and bear difficulties as part of the path, then one enters into the Awareness Observance and the Public Practice.[22] At that time one adorns oneself with the emblems of the Heruka.

But even if one does not have abilities like those, as long as one's Secret Mantra *samaya*s and vows are unbroken, and internally one has the antidote to the afflictive emotions, and externally one is benefitting the Teachings, then it is suitable [to put on the garb of the Heruka and enter into the Practice].

This passage is significant for a number of reasons. It gives a sense of the surprise some of the great yogin's contemporaries felt toward his manner of dress. This passage also shows the prerequisites the Madman of Tsang thought necessary (or not) before entering into the Practice, and how the practitioner transitions from one phase of the Practice to the next as he reaches certain conventionally defined milestones on the path to liberation.

In some lists, the All-Good Practice is given last, and thereby put in the position of honor in the graduated succession of practices that is implied. In other lists, the All-Good Practice is given first. The difference seems to stem from whether the person formulating the list holds pure monastic conduct (which the All-Good Practice is often understood to mean) to be the highest ideal for one living a Buddhist life, or only a stepping-stone to tantra.[23] In cases where the All-Good Practice is placed first, the last phase is usually referred to as the Practice that Is Victorious in All Respects, which expresses the total freedom and boundless capacities that a yogin successful in these practices is asserted to achieve. "The Practice that Is Victorious in All Respects" is used at times in the biographies of the Madmen of Ü and Tsang to refer to their distinctive behavior.[24] The phrase is also featured as part of the titles of their biographies, expressing the amazing states they achieved through their many years of religious practice. The yogins' entire biographies are meant to be understood as testaments to the efficacy of the Observance.

The odd-seeming behavior that distinguished Künga Zangpo and Sangyé Gyeltsen from other Tibetan yogins and paved the way for them to become "madmen" was not the unrestrained activity of wild men, but rather their enacting a practice with a long precedent in the tantric tradition. Each took up the Practice in his twenties after abandoning monkhood. The Madman of Tsang's lifestyle was marked by the Practice for about a decade, after which he began to focus on his writing. The Madman of Ü persisted in the Practice for about fifteen years before settling down to take on intensive retreat and instruct his many disciples. Although the active Practice of the Observance was a temporary pursuit for both "madmen," they would continue to be associated with it for the rest of their lives, as it had become a central feature of their public personas.

The Secret Practice, the Insane Observance

Based on his analysis of tantric Buddhist sources written in India, Wedemeyer has observed that the terms *caryā* and *vrata* "frequently occur in compound with qualifiers related to ideas of secrecy or madness," yielding terms like *guhyavrata*, "secret observance"; *guhyacaryā*, "secret practice"; *prachannavrata*, "concealed observance"; *unmattavrata*, "insane observance," and so on. In Wedemeyer's understanding of the literature, these terms are synonymous, or very nearly so.[25] Some of these terms, such as *guhyacaryā/sangchö* (*gsang spyod*) and *unmattavrata/nyönpé tülzhuk* (*smyon pa'i brtul zhugs*), appear in the literature surrounding the Madmen of Ü and Tsang.

The Madmen of Ü and Tsang each received and gave teachings on a practice or practices referred to as the Secret Practice of Nāropa, the Secret Practice of India, the Secret Practice, and so on, sometimes as part of a collection called "the Eight Great Instructions of the Drukpa."[26] It is unclear whether these titles refer to a single practice and text, or to different ones. Regardless, the Secret Practice played a central role in the Madmen of Ü and Tsang's spiritual programs. On one occasion the

Madman of Ü stated that the Secret Practice of India was one of the distinctive teachings of the Kagyü sect, along with the Mahāmudrā, the Six Dharmas of Nāropa, and the *Dohās*. He then instructed Nyukla Penchen to make a printing of a text referred to as the *Secret Practice of India*. More telling still, when the Madman of Ü was giving one of his last teachings, he said, "The essence of all the teachings [of the Buddha] and all the treatises is this . . .," then proceeded to give oral instructions on the Secret Practice of India.[27]

The best indication of what the Secret Practice probably entailed for the Madmen of Ü and Tsang is the *Instructions for the Secret Practice of Great Glorious Nāropa*, a seventeen-folio text authored by the Madman of Tsang.[28] This text is contained within the collection of Aural Transmission texts compiled by the Madman of Tsang (discussed in chapter 5). The Madman of Tsang wrote down this Secret Practice of Nāropa text after his disciples repeatedly asked him to do so, and says that the text reflects the practice exactly as it was taught to him by his own guru, Shara Rapjampa.[29] Echoing the Madman of Ü's comment about the significance of the practice, it is here said to express the "intended meaning" (*dgongs don*) of all of tantra.

The Secret Practice as described in this text was probably understood as part of the larger ascetic regimen of the Practice of the Observance. According to the Madman of Tsang, the meditation is to be performed while sitting under a tree, in a charnel ground, alongside a river or an ocean, in an empty house or a dilapidated temple, or in any frightening place where nonhuman spirits are believed to dwell. It should be performed at night, or whenever one is afflicted by the fault of grasping at the existence of the self. The stated purpose of the practice is to help one achieve "heat" or to increase the "heat" one already has. Ultimately it can lead to one's achieving the supreme *siddhi* of the Mahāmudrā.

The main part of the practice is as follows: the meditator visualizes his body being chopped into pieces by the goddess Vajrayoginī, which are then offered to the inhabitants of the six realms of existence, whom he has invited to gather by blowing a thighbone trumpet and playing a hand drum. After offering his body in this way, the practitioner is to compose himself in meditation and hopefully progress toward overcoming any notion of the self. By mentally giving up his body, he should experience a decrease in his attachment to it, which is the basis for all fears. This process is repeated, as the practitioner then offers his body in the same fashion to his lama, to the deities of the maṇḍala, and to the *ḍākinīs*. This is followed by an extended meditation in which the practitioner tries to resolve his understanding of himself with the true nature of existence.

The next part of the meditation is a test of the practitioner's level of accomplishment. He is to try to tame various spirit-beings present in the area where he is meditating—but according to the text, he is ultimately not taming entities external to himself, but his own delusions and failings, which are externalized and personified as independent entities. The "demons" referred to throughout the text are in fact conceptual formations (*rtog pa*, here synonymous with *rnam rtog*).

Next the Madman of Tsang describes the kind of lifestyle that one doing the Secret Practice should take on. As the values of the Mahāyāna still hold, the practitioner is to maintain a compassionate attitude and an awareness of emptiness at all times. He is to remain respectful to his lama and to the others who preceded him in his lineage. But he is not to make any show of respect to statues of deities, to other lamas, or to wielders of worldly power, who are likely to be filled with misguided self-regard. With the divine pride that one generates during the yogas of the Generation and Perfection Stages, one is to act like a mighty lion among deer.

While maintaining a divine pride that entails seeing all beings as divine and all food and drink as divine nectar, the practitioner should enjoy all potential consumables, as pigs and dogs do, without distinguishing between what is clean [like brown sugar] or dirty [like feces]. Remembering that all appearances are illusory, he should not give in to feelings of attachment or aversion. The practitioner should wander from place to place: when he wants to stay somewhere, he should leave; when he wants to leave a place, he should stay there. He should be like a leaf or a feather blown by the wind. He should live from day to day, without planning for the future in any way. He should have no worldly aspirations. He should think and act in any way that will counter his tendency to grasp at the notion of a self. He should not fall into dualistic differentiation of any sort. By practicing in this way, the true intention of the Buddha will arise from within, so there will be no need to look at scripture or modes of reasoning external to oneself.

The text then explains that during the practice one should "behave like a madman," without differentiating between what is pleasing and displeasing (*bde sdug gi yul la gza' gtad med par smyon pa ltar spyad*). He should behave like a child, without any concern for how others may perceive him. He should live as if already dead, without differentiating between *saṃsāra* and liberation.

While performing this kind of practice, the yogin should take up the Six Bone Ornaments, a tiger-skin skirt, a *khaṭvāṅga* staff, and a hand drum made from skulls. He should couple with a worthy consort.

Within the text the Madman of Tsang makes a point of defending the value of this practice. He says that even though this lifestyle may appear to be nonvirtuous in the eyes of ordinary people and those adhering to lower forms of Buddhism, it does have canonical backing. By the same token, the practitioner should abandon actions that are called virtuous but in fact promote grasping at the notion of the self or cause harm to other beings.

Sangyé Gyeltsen states that it is best if the practitioner can completely abandon his home, his monastery, all relatives and friends who are not dharma practitioners, as well as books, representations of deities, and whatever else he might be attached to, and do the Secret Practice continuously in rugged places in the mountains. If the practitioner cannot do that, he should at least abandon his home region and worldly relations, and, while living within a monastery, go out to a rugged place to do the Secret Practice two nights each month (presumably this means spending the entire night out of doors). If the yogin cannot do that, he should go out to do the practice once a month. The absolute minimum is to go out once a year.

Götsang Repa's version of the *Life of the Madman of Tsang* describes the yogin's training in the Secret Practice under Shara Rapjampa, decades before he wrote down this text. We are told that during the day, the young Sangyé Gyeltsen would receive the instructions for the Secret Practice of Glorious Nāropa. Then at night he would wander in haunted places and do the Secret Practice, which caused many nonhuman spirits to offer their lives to him before he bound them with oaths; he practiced Cutting (*gcod*) beneath a tree, and thereby made great progress.[30]

This passage and the practice described above raise the question of the relationship between the Secret Practice and Cutting. Some readers will have noticed that the practice described in the *Instructions for the Secret Practice of Great Glorious Nāropa* is similar in many ways to the meditative and ritual system known as Cutting, in which the practitioner imagines his or her body being cut up by Vajrayoginī; the pieces then feed and appease various types of spirit-beings, with the ultimate goal of leading the meditator to overcome false notions of self. Traditionally, Cutting also involved the practitioner's meditating in charnel grounds and haunted places, and even making use of a *ḍamaru* drum and a thighbone trumpet, and perhaps taking up an animal's hide, a trident, skull cup, and so on.[31]

The Madmen of Ü and Tsang received, performed, and taught meditation practices referred to as Cutting, showing that it was a distinct category in their conceptual world. But it also seems that Cutting and the Practice of the Observance bled into one another. Exemplifying this, the terms Practice and Cutting are often mistaken for one another or used interchangeably in the biographies. In Götsang Repa's version of the *Life of the Madman of Tsang*—which is replete with spelling mistakes and phonologically similar words mistaken for one another—it is mentioned that he once taught the practice of Secret Cutting (*gsang gcod*), with Cutting mistakenly inserted in the place of Practice (*spyod*).[32] In the passage described above, the mention of Sangyé Gyeltsen's doing Cutting under a tree may also be a mistake. We may wonder how many times the inverse mistake is made, with the author referring to the Practice when in fact he means Cutting. A major contributing factor to why the terms spelled *spyod* and *gcod* might be mistaken for one another is the fact that they are pronounced the exact same way in the central Tibetan dialect (*chö*). But we can probably also say that the practices referred to are so similar, and the two terms are used interchangeably so often, that the boundary between them was not entirely clear. Reflecting how other learned Tibetans thought about these practices at the time, in the *Blue Annals*, written in 1476, Gö Lotsāwa Zhönnu Pel (1392–1481) states that *spyod* and *gcod* are in fact synonymous, the former representing an older orthography.[33] The history of the relationship between Cutting and the Practice is a topic deserving of further investigation. Finally, as will be shown in chapter 7, the connection between Cutting and Tibet's "holy madmen" is a long-standing one, dating to well before the fifteenth century.

Beyond the Secret Practice, another means by which a rhetoric of secrecy or concealment comes into play in the lives of the holy madmen is in the idea of being a "secret" or "covert yogin." When the Madman of Ü was practicing and converting people to Buddhism in Nepal, it is said that he "assisted many sentient beings in the manner of a covert yogin" (*sbas pa'i rnal 'byor*). When the Madman of the Drukpa came to visit the Madman of Ü at his monastery, he was referred to as a "covert yogin."[34] This term, which has a long history of usage in Tibetan Buddhism, may imply that one has gone undercover, disguising the fact of being a religious practitioner. A passage from the *Life of the Madman of Tsang* suggests that doing so had been a part of his asceticism for some time. Between leaving the monastic life and beginning the outrageous behavior for which he became notorious, it is said that Sangyé Gyeltsen thought to himself, "Now that I have become fully accomplished for my own sake, it is time to work for the benefit of others." So he entered a deep meditation and in his wisdom saw that, in the degenerate time in which we live, sentient beings have short lives and teem with afflictive emotions and false views. Therefore, he concluded, he should engage in behavior directly beneficial to others: he would "wander in every direction doing the Practice of the Observance, and, keeping his excellent qualities thoroughly covert [*shin tu sbas pa*], align himself with the manner of ordinary people, establish pure connections with people of lesser faculties, and achieve great benefit for the Teachings and for sentient beings." Thinking thus, he smeared himself with ashes and blood, donned a necklace of intestines, and paid a disruptive visit to a religious gathering at Tsari. Further suggesting the importance of the notion of the "covert" meditator is the fact that a grouping called the "eighteen covert *mahāsiddhas*" are listed among the Madman of Tsang's disciples.[35]

In the Madman of Tsang's text describing the Secret Practice of Nāropa, it is said that the practitioner should strive to "behave like a madman," meaning to live without differentiating between what is pleasing or displeasing. Similarly, in his expansive commentary on the *Vajra Verses on the Aural Tantra* also included in his collection of Aural Transmission teachings, the great yogin again mentions "activity like that of a madman" (*smyon pa lta bu'i spyod pa*) as an aspect of the yogic practice of Illusory Body (*sgyu lus*), here referring to cultivating a mind-set in which the practitioner has overcome dualistic distinctions. The use of "mad" in this sense has a long precedent in the Tibetan commentarial tradition.[36] A similar rhetoric appears in Götsang Repa's *Life of the Madman of Tsang*: "Then, unafraid of anything, like a lion; without any doubts, like an elephant in pursuit of water; without clinging to anything, he roamed unpredictably in every direction, like a leaf blown by the wind. Without regard for anything, with nothing to eat or drink, he went about in the manner of a madman."[37] The yogin acts "in the manner of a madman" through his wandering, nondiscriminating lifestyle.

In the biography of Künga Zangpo there is only one place where "mad" is used to directly describe his behavior, here appearing as part of the phrase "the Practice of the Insane Observance" (*smyon pa brtul zhugs kyi spyod pa*, which in Sanskrit would be *unmattavratacaryā*). Nyukla Penchen uses this phrase while summarizing the yogin's practices and accomplishments up to the age of thirty-six:

He would go into the middle of a marketplace or a town and subject himself to minor difficulties, which he made part of the path. When he had no fear of such things and went out on the road, he did the Practice of the Insane Observance. Keeping secret his lineage, clan, family, and so on, he wandered in various unfamiliar places. He abided without any concern for conditions or appearances, distinctions like high or low, good or bad, praise or censure, pleasant or unpleasant to hear, pleasure or pain, expectations or apprehensions, things to be adopted or rejected, and so on—none of these; nor for hot or cold, hunger or thirst, weariness and fatigue, and so on—not one of these. Nor did he have any fear of avalanches or roofs collapsing on him, and so on; nor of fire, water, wind and the like. Without any fear or apprehension about any of those things, he overwhelmed all with his greatness by means of his assurance in his realization of the nature of reality and his *samādhi* of the Great Illusion.[38]

"The Practice of the Insane Observance" is used here to refer to living in a completely free manner, without making the sort of conceptual distinctions by which ordinary, sane people orient their lives. While commenting on the Practice, Karma Trinlepa describes this state as being "like a madman, without any fears, anxieties, or conceptuality."[39]

For these reasons, it should not be thought that pretending to be insane was central to Künga Zangpo's or Sangyé Gyeltsen's asceticism. Rather, the meaning of the term "mad" in reference to them was complex, carrying a variety of rich associations, including a nondistinguishing mental state. This rhetoric of madness was intertwined with the rhetoric of secrecy, and with the rhetoric of being a Heruka, which was of central importance to the distinctive lifestyles of the Madmen of Ü and Tsang.

"You, the Hero, Glorious Heruka Himself . . ."

A key aspect of Künga Zangpo and Sangyé Gyeltsen's Practice of the Observance was dressing in the garb of the Heruka. The connection between the Practice and dressing in the garb of the Heruka is maintained throughout the Tibetan commentarial tradition, where the two become nearly synonymous. In the commentary on the *Hevajra Tantra* attributed to Marpa and titled the *Sun of the Little Collection* (which the Madman of Ü knew and taught to his disciples), the author glosses the meaning of *tülzhuk chöpa* as follows: "As for the meanings of 'taming' and 'entering,' having tamed the activity of one's ordinary body, one enters into the way of dressing in the ornaments of the Heruka."[40]

In this context, Heruka refers to Cakrasaṃvara or Hevajra (most often Cakrasaṃvara), supreme wrathful deities that are prominent in the Unexcelled Yoga Tantras (*anuttarayogatantra, rnal 'byor bla na med pa'i rgyud*), including the *Cakrasaṃvara, Hevajra*, and other tantras. Tibetans most often leave the Sanskrit term *heruka* untranslated. When translated, it is rendered as *traktungwa*, "blood-drinker," connoting the absorbent ground in which bodies are buried, showing the deity's deep association with the macabre.[41]

As the Madman of Tsang glosses the term in one of his compositions on the Aural Transmission, in the name Śrī Heruka, the syllable *Śrī* expresses how appearances and emptiness are inseparable, like a wave and the water it is made of. *He* expresses how all appearances are produced by specific causes and conditions, but nevertheless do not diverge from the great universality of emptiness. *Ru* expresses how, given the emptiness of all phenomena, that which is perceived and that which perceives it cannot be established as independent entities. Lastly, *Ka* expresses how emptiness and the consciousness that perceives it are not in fact independent of one another; this same kind of mutual dependence characterizes the relationship between *saṃsāra* and *nirvāṇa*. The Madman of Tsang goes on to state that all of reality is represented by the maṇḍala and the deities that inhabit it, and that the maṇḍala and its deities are represented by the single deity Heruka. Therefore, Śrī Heruka represents all the phenomena of reality and the mode in which they exist.[42]

The distinctive dress adopted by the Madmen of Ü and Tsang is described throughout their biographies as "the emblems of the Heruka" (sometimes said to be eight-fold), "the mode of dress of the Heruka," "the emblems of the charnel ground," or "the bone ornaments" (often said to be six-fold).[43] Within the tradition there is less than total agreement over what precisely each of these designations refers to. For example, some commentators list the Six Bone Ornaments as consisting of a head ornament, earrings, necklace, Sacred Thread, bangles on the wrists, and bangles worn on the ankles, while others count the bangles as a single item and add ashes to the list.

The sixth chapter of the first book of the *Hevajra Tantra*, which outlines the Practice, states that the practitioner should wear earrings, a circlet (which may have served to bind up the hair), bangles on the wrists, bangles on the ankles, a sash, upper-armlets, a bone necklace, and the hide of a tiger. The chapter later adds that the practitioner should also wear ashes, a Sacred Thread strung together with hair, a headdress representing the five buddhas, and should carry a drum and *khaṭvāṅga*. This Sacred Thread (*mchod phyir thogs*), typically sported by wrathful deities, is a set of interconnected garlands of bone, worn over the torso and crossing over the chest and back. The twenty-seventh chapter of the *Cakrasaṃvara Tantra*, on the Practice, prescribes a similar list of adornments.[44]

Also pertinent is the question of how the deity Cakrasaṃvara/Heruka is typically described, visualized, and depicted. In one of his compositions the Madman of Tsang describes the deity as adorned with the Six Bone Ornaments; smeared with ashes, blood, and fat from a corpse; wearing a human skin, a tiger-pelt skirt, and an elephant-skin cloak; a crown containing five skulls, a garland of fifty dripping heads, and a snake. In his many hands he holds a *vajra*, bell, hand drum, *khaṭvāṅga*, hook, skull, arrow, spear, sword, and other items.[45]

The only instance in either madman's biography where his dress is described in detail is the passage from the *Life of the Madman of Ü* translated at outset of this chapter. Many of the elements of Künga Zangpo's garb match closely the prescriptive lists given in the *Cakrasaṃvara* and *Hevajra* tantras from which he drew. Other elements of his dress clearly go beyond this, and are taken from the iconography of Cakrasaṃvara—for example, his wearing a human skin in addition to the tiger pelt prescribed in the tantras, and his being smeared with fat and blood, beyond the more typical ashes. It thus seems that Künga Zangpo was attempting to dress as prescribed in the Practice chapters of the tantras, but going further, toward dressing as best he could like the deity himself. No full description of the Madman of Tsang's dress is ever given, but various elements of his attire are mentioned in passing. Woodcuts from early printings of the madmen's biographies show many elements of their dress mentioned here, with the Sacred Thread, armlets and so on clearly visible (figures 2.2, 2.3). A statue of the Madman of Tsang seated on a deerskin, made in the sixteenth century, shows his costume in vivid detail (figure 2.4).

One important element of the madmen's distinctive garb was the *khaṭvāṅga*. These staffs have long been used in South Asian religions in varying forms—sometimes as a trident, sometimes with a single point; with one skull or three; with actual skulls, or skulls shaped from metal or carved from wood. According to one of his biographies, the Madman of Tsang was once asked by a disciple to explain the significance of the many features of the *khaṭvāṅga*. The yogin explained that when carried by a female practitioner, the staff represents Means, or her male counterpart. When carried by a male practitioner, it represents the Wisdom

FIGURE 2.2 "Homage to the noble Heruka from Tsang" (from his *Collected Songs*)

of emptiness, or his female counterpart. The staff should be about the length of the person who is to carry it. It should be festooned with a pot (which represents the Jar Empowerment, the first in the standard series of tantric initiations), a "wet" head with flesh still attached (which represents the Secret Empowerment), a half-desiccated head (representing the Wisdom Empowerment), and a "dry" head without flesh (representing the Word Empowerment). The staff is topped with three trident points, which represent the three "bodies" (*kāya* in Sanskrit) or levels on which buddhahood can become manifest. The staff should be ornamented with a five-pronged *vajra*, a lotus, a crossed *vajra*, small bells, hair from different kinds of people (both living and dead), and so on. Each of these features has a symbolic meaning.[46]

Künga Zangpo carried a *khaṭvāṅga* from the time of his assuming the Heruka costume. Years later, a new *khaṭvāṅga* named "Blazing Auspicious

FIGURE 2.3 "Homage to the noble Heruka from Tsang" (from Ngödrup Pembar's version of his *Life*)

Light" was made for him by some supporters. Over the years, these staffs would be stolen from and returned to him a number of times. If we are to believe his biography, the yogin was not above occasionally using his ritual staff to hit people or ward off angry dogs. At the time of his death, he passed it on to his nephew, along with other objects of symbolic importance.[47] It is not clear whether the Madmen of Ü and Tsang's *khaṭvāṅga*s were made with real skulls or artificial ones, but it is certain that they were supersaturated with tantric signification.

The biographies of Künga Zangpo and Sangyé Gyeltsen mention their wearing of human skins. They may well have done so, since crossing the boundary into the grotesque was their forte. It is stated specifically in the *Life of the Madman of Tsang* that at a certain point he handed over to his mother a skin (*g.yang bzhi* [*sic*]), probably from a human corpse, that he had with him at the time, suggesting that he had been wearing it before then.[48] The passage that serves as the epigraph to chapter 3 would also

FIGURE 2.4 The Madman of Tsang

suggest that the Madman of Tsang really did wear a human skin—or at least was renowned to have done so.

Another question we remain uncertain about is whether the Madmen of Ü and Tsang wore these rather uncomfortable costumes at all times after initially putting them on, or only intermittently. Suggesting that Künga Zangpo and Sangyé Gyeltsen each wore the accoutrements of the Heruka for some years is the fact that their biographies mention people trying to steal or destroy these items. We are told that on one occasion some people beat the Madman of Ü, trying to break his bracelets, earrings, and Sacred Thread, hitting him so savagely that the ornaments even sank into the wood of the weapons they struck him with. Similar stories are told of the Madman of Tsang. These instances suggest that the Madmen of Ü and Tsang continued to wear the garb of the Heruka for some years after initially putting it on, if not at every moment, and may perhaps have donned the garb for special occasions later in life.[49] After the Madman of Ü's death, his casket was decorated with the six bone ornaments he had worn, showing their central symbolic importance to his identity. The holy madmen themselves were not the only ones to take on this mode of dress, as among the Madman of Tsang's disciples was a grouping called "the twenty-eight realized heartsons who wore the garb of the Heruka."[50] It seems the great yogin had to give approval before one of his students was allowed to adopt this attire.

Beyond being a prescribed element of the Practice of the Observance, Künga Zangpo's, Sangyé Gyeltsen's, and their students' dressing in the garb of the Heruka must be understood in light of tantric meditative and ritual practice in general. A defining feature of tantric Buddhism is that the practitioner must train to self-identify with a deity. The deity is a representation of enlightenment and likewise the practitioner's own true nature. The practitioner is to learn to identify with the deity, come into his own enlightened nature, and thereby achieve liberation.[51] Many individual elements of tantric practice serve as means toward this end. Mantras effect the immediate presencing of the deity in sonic form and can represent the deity's divine speech, spoken by the practitioner. Maṇḍalas, used in initiatory rituals and subsequent visualizations, help foster the practitioner's understanding of himself as the deity by positioning him at the center of the deity's idealized realm. Most important of all is deity yoga meditation, in which the practitioner visualizes himself as the deity, bearing the deity's outward physical form and all of his or her sublime qualities. The late tantras often articulate the individual's goal as being to become the deity, to achieve "union" with it.[52]

The bulk of the Madmen of Ü and Tsang's meditative practice would have involved deity yoga and other means of effecting their personal transformation into the deity. But in the course of their Practice of the Observance, Künga Zangpo and Sangyé Gyeltsen enacted the ideal of self-identification with the deity more literally, by dressing like him and taking on his persona in waking life. Beyond dressing like the deity,

Künga Zangpo and Sangyé Gyeltsen fostered their self-association with him through other sorts of behavior, such as their singing and dancing. It is said numerous times in the biography of the Madman of Ü that he performed the "nine demeanors expressed through dance" (*gar gyi nyams dgu*). These are the modes through which wrathful deities express themselves and are especially associated with the Heruka. When the Madman of Ü did the Practice of the Fierce Observance in Shang, a lord and his servants assembled to beat him up. Throughout the beating he intoned *hūṃ* and *phaṭ*—the divine speech of the god—and assumed the poses representing the nine demeanors—imitating the god's bodily movements. The Madman of Tsang also at times pronounced the syllables *hūṃ* and *phaṭ* and danced about in imitation of the deity.[53] Künga Zangpo and Sangyé Gyeltsen's performance of sexual yoga would have been another way of enacting their identity with the deity, as Cakrasaṃvara remains in perpetual union with his consort, Vajravārāhī.

Another means through which Künga Zangpo and Sangyé Gyeltsen enacted this sort of lived deity yoga was their "fierce" confrontational behavior. Herukas are wrathful deities, and the madmen's engaging in "the Fierce Practice" or "the Fierce Observance" (*drag po'i spyod pa, drag po'i brtul zhugs*) may have been attendant to their larger purpose of emulating the deity. Exemplifying the overlap between the Practice of the Observance, emulating the deity, and enacting wrathfulness, at the end of the chapter in which the Madman of Ü exchanged his monks' robes for the garb of the Heruka, his biographer summarizes that he had thus "taken on the Observance of fierce Heruka." The many instances of the Madmen of Ü and Tsang's engaging in "the Practice of the Fierce Observance" can be taken as to some extent meaning "the Practice of the Observance in the manner of the fierce one [Heruka]."[54]

Thus in addition to training to self-identify with the deity through meditation and ritual practice, Künga Zangpo and Sangyé Gyeltsen lived as the deity in the present: dressing like him, speaking like him, acting like him. In a sense, they turned long periods of their lives into a very literal form of deity yoga. Rather than leaving the achievement of self-identity with the deity as an abstract or internal affair, Künga Zangpo and Sangyé Gyeltsen chose to enact their union with him bodily and publicly. Further indicative of the way they actively collapsed their identities with that of the deity is the fact that Künga Zangpo and Sangyé Gyeltsen referred to themselves as Herukas. In one of his texts on the Aural Transmission, the Madman of Tsang refers to himself in the midst of his lineage as "the Heruka." He signed the *Life of Marpa* as "the yogin who wanders in charnel grounds, the king of the blood-drinkers." (In the colophon to the *Life of Milarepa* he styles himself "the yogin who wanders in charnel grounds, wearer of the bone ornaments.") It seems that Künga Zangpo and Sangyé Gyeltsen were successful in fostering this association, as people sometimes referred to them (and occasionally the Madman of the Drukpa) by titles that include "Heruka." To this day Tibetans most often refer to Sangyé Gyeltsen as Tsangnyön Heruka—"the Madman of Tsang, the Heruka."[55]

The deity Heruka, the Practice of the Observance, and a rhetoric of madness were key aspects of the public personas adopted by Künga Zangpo and Sangyé Gyeltsen, and became central to their contemporaries' perceptions of them. Exemplifying this, Karma Trinlepa wrote a versified praise of the Madman of Ü that begins:

> You who are identical with glorious Cakrasaṃvara,
> whose name is everywhere renowned as "the Madman of Ü,"
> lord of *siddhas*, emanation of father Tilopa,
> master of the Observance, please lend an ear!

It is nothing out of the ordinary for a Tibetan Buddhist author to compare a great master with a tantric deity like Cakrasaṃvara. But to refer to the Madman of Ü as *pel demchok korlö ngowo nyi* (*dpal bde mchog 'khor lo'i ngo bo nyid*)—"identical with," "the quintessence of," "the very being of" Cakrasaṃvara—takes on added significance here. A separate praise to the Madman of Ü by Karma Trinlepa may be read as saying something like,

> You, the hero, glorious Heruka,
> have taken the form of a madman from Ü in the here and now
> in order to perform the Awareness Observance;
> so you can do the Public Practice for the sake of others
> after having "achieved heat."[56]

Here Karma Trinlepa states explicitly that the Madman of Ü *is* the deity Heruka, manifested in our world. The yogin's Practice of the Awareness Observance is put forth as a divine mission.

In the opening verse of his biography, Götsang Repa describes the Madman of Tsang as "the supreme glorious protector, the Heruka fully perfected in the Observance." In another verse Götsang Repa praises Sangyé Gyeltsen as:

> Great Vajrasattva, in the form of a man,
> with the strength to perform the Practice of the Observance,
> the master from Tsang, unequalled in the three realms—
> to that glorious Heruka I prostrate![57]

Further indicating the sort of reputation they had during their time, in a verse composition included within his *Miscellaneous Writings*, Drukpa Künlé observes:

> There is no rivaling Sakya Paṇḍita in intellect.
> . . .
> There is no rivaling Atīśa and his sons in terms of *bodhicitta*.
> There is no rivaling the Dakpo Kagyü in terms of realization.
> There is no rivaling the Madman of Tsang or the Madman of Ü in
>   the Observance.[58]

Just as Tibetans forever associate the great scholar Sakya Paṇḍita with wisdom and know that one of Atīśa's main contributions to the Buddhist heritage of Tibet was to emphasize generating the altruistic aspiration to achieve enlightenment, during their lifetimes Künga Zangpo and Sangyé Gyeltsen were indelibly associated with the Observance.

Tantric Literalism

Readers more familiar with the religious culture of South Asia might not sense the full impact of Künga Zangpo and Sangyé Gyeltsen's distinctive mode of dress. In India and Nepal today there is a great diversity of ascetic traditions featuring remarkably different attires, many of which have been worn for centuries. In addition to Buddhist and Hindu monks, a *baba* or *sādhu* dressed in a loincloth is not an uncommon sight. He may be a devotee of Śiva or of Viṣṇu, display one of many possible forms of *tilak* on his forehead and face, have dreadlocks or a shaved head; he may be smeared with ashes, and carry ritual implements like a skull cup or a staff. Orange signifies asceticism in South Asia, with many renunciants, celibate or not, tending toward that color. Meanwhile the most dedicated practitioners of Jainism go completely naked, as they have for more than two thousand years.

Although career religious practitioners in Tibet have always displayed a variety of modes of dress, their appearances were never as diverse as among their South Asian counterparts. In Tibet, religious specialists may let their hair grow long and dress in variant ways, but the shaved head and maroon robes of monkhood have long been the most common form of dress for renunciants. Even nonmonastic practitioners tend to dress in maroon, and noncelibate yogins who dress in white often conform to the normative shawl-and-skirt model for their robes. In the late fifteenth century, the monastic norm was less potent than it is today, but it was well on its way to becoming the most pervasive model of clericalism in Tibet.

When a few dozen yogins traveled around central Tibet in the late fifteenth century smeared with ashes, dressed in loincloths and bone ornaments, and carrying cups made from skulls, it would have been a remarkable sight. One can imagine the effect that was produced when the Madman of Tsang and two dozen of his students dressed in the garb of the Heruka went traipsing through the Barkor in Lhasa, or when the Madman of Ü burst into the formal assembly of a powerful lord like Rinpungpa Dorjé Tseten and threatened him with his *khaṭvāṅga*. As we saw in the passage from his biography quoted above, some thought the Madman of Tsang's wearing the complete garb of the Heruka to be completely unprecedented on Tibetan soil; others charged that this mode of dressing and acting was not even Buddhist. The records from the time show that the appearance of the fifteenth-century holy madmen dressed in the garb of the Heruka was surprising to most, threatening to some, and deplorable in the opinion of others. The Madman of Tsang's mother feared that people might mistake him for a demon. This did happen, according to one version of his biography, providing us with an anecdote that exemplifies how the mad yogins' manners of dressing and behaving were received, and what they may have signified in late fifteenth-century Tibet.

According to his biography, on one occasion when Sangyé Gyeltsen arrived in Lhasa, the people said, "A demon has arrived!" and everyone fled. That night, whenever anyone approached him, the yogin played his hand drum and blew his thighbone trumpet, which frightened them off. The next day some people said that he was a ghoul, while others wondered if he was a *siddha*. Finally, some monks who had known Sangyé Gyeltsen from his days in the monastery in Gyantsé recognized him and invited him to Neudzong fortress (just south of Lhasa, on the other side of the Kyichu river), the seat of the local lord (*sde pa*), Penjor Gyelpo. There some scholar-monks from the nearby Geluk monasteries of Sera and Drepung began to argue with Sangyé Gyeltsen. The *geshés* said, "We have not heard of this way of dressing [*cha lugs*] and behaving [*spyod pa*] among the teachings of the Buddha. There is no precedent for it. From whose system [*su'i lugs*] is your manner of dressing and behaving derived?" The Madman of Tsang responded:

> The ant cannot see the whole mountain. The frog living in a well cannot fathom the size of the ocean. The child's hand cannot cover the whole sky. There are many teachings and phenomena that you have not heard of.
>
> If there is no precedent for this way of dress, then the tantric deities and the eighty *mahāsiddhas* of India never existed! Haven't you seen it drawn in pictures? My manner of dressing and behaving is explained in the Unexcelled Yoga Tantras of Vajradhara, particularly in the glorious *Two-Parted*, the condensed root tantra of glorious Hevajra.

The yogin continued, stating that the questions of who should do this kind of practice, where, when, with whom, for what purpose, and so on, are all clearly explained in the tantras. Therefore, what reason did these monks have for expressing such doubts?

The *geshés* countered by asserting, "This is not an age in which one is to enact Secret Mantra [i.e., tantra] in that way." This prompted the yogin to ask, "Is one to practice Secret Mantra when born into one of the Eight Restricted States?[59] Where does it say that this is not an age in which we are to practice Secret Mantra [in this way]? Tell me!" Unable to answer, the *geshés* got up and left the assembly, while the Madman of Tsang remained to be feted and honored by the now-faithful lord.

At the heart of the conflict between Sangyé Gyeltsen and these scholar-monks was a debate over how to interpret and practice the late tantric scriptures. Clearly, he and Künga Zangpo had chosen a way of following those texts that seemed extreme in the eyes of some of their contemporaries. And their way of enacting those scriptures was extremely literal. When Künga Zangpo renounced his monkhood in favor of his new lifestyle, his biographer portrays his new way of acting and dressing as adhering closely to the dictates of the *Hevajra* and *Cakrasaṃvara* tantras. The biographies even show the madmen themselves citing the tantras to justify their behavior. When the Madman of Tsang snatched and drank a nobleman's cup of *chang* during a banquet, the lord asked him if this did not constitute breaking his vow against stealing, which is one of the most basic of Buddhist vows, prescribed for monks and laymen alike. In response, Sangyé Gyeltsen quoted two lines from the *Hevajra Tantra*: "You should take things that haven't been given / You should take recourse to others' women" (the twenty-ninth verse of the third chapter of the tantra's second book). The lord had no response. Just as one would refer to scripture in supporting a written philosophical argument or during an oral debate, the Madman of Tsang quoted tantric scripture to justify his seemingly inappropriate behavior. It seems he had found a good use for his intensive study (and perhaps memorization) of the *Hevajra Tantra* years before.[60]

On another occasion Sangyé Gyeltsen behaved impertinently during a banquet, telling a female religious hierarch that he wanted to copulate with her. He was asked what value there was in behaving in such a manner. In the discussion that followed, the yogin made an impressive exposition on the *Hevajra Tantra*'s chapter on the Practice, making reference to other tantras as well. In the end, one of the interlocutors exclaimed that a yogin who enacts the Observance in this way, with such a thorough understanding of the tantras to back it up, is in our degenerate age "as rare as a star during daylight."[61]

To mention one last example, when the Madman of Tsang was asked to explain his religious training and his mode of behavior before a large monastic assembly, the presiding religious dignitary expressed his wonderment that the yogin's explanation of tantra and his mode of practicing it were all aligned. It would seem that people were surprised that the tantras could support what the Madmen of Ü and Tsang were doing, so much did their way of applying them differ from the norms of the day.[62]

The tantras that Künga Zangpo and Sangyé Gyeltsen cite as the inspiration for their lifestyle are of the Yoginī tantra class (often called the Mother Tantras, *ma rgyud*), which were a subset of the Unexcelled Yoga tantras. Written in India between the eighth and tenth centuries, the Yoginī tantras represent the latest stage of the development of Buddhist tantra in India.[63] It is in these texts that the themes of sex, violence, and things macabre—so central to many people's perceptions of tantra—become prominent. These texts prescribe ritualized sex, and the consumption of alcohol, meat, sexual fluids, and other transgressive substances, both as part of the Practice and outside of it. The deities on whom these tantras are centered are usually depicted as wrathful, trampling on corpses, adorned with skulls and weapons, drinking from cups of blood.

Shortly after these texts were penned, they became subject to many divergent interpretations and modes of enactment. Indian scholars and practitioners would write commentaries to these texts, each offering its own way of interpreting and practicing what is stated in the root scripture. The tantras would continue to be interpreted and enacted in a wide range of ways in Tibet. One of the most pressing issues in this ongoing conversation was the question of how to reconcile the transgressive aspects of the Unexcelled Yoga tantras with the demands of the monastic code. This issue became a perennial concern in Tibet, since the form of Buddhism that developed there was at once the most thoroughly monasticized and the most highly tantric in all of Asia. Could one maintain the monastic vows while engaging in these practices, or were being a monk and adhering to the transgressive elements of these tantras mutually exclusive endeavors?

Atīśa (982–1054), a Bengali monk who became hugely influential in Tibet after spending the last part of his life there, addresses this question in his *Lamp for the Path to Enlightenment*, where he argues that monks should practice tantra without taking the "higher" empowerments, which, if practiced literally, would cause them to break their vows of celibacy. Sakya Paṇḍita (1182 1251) writes about this issue in his *Clear Differentiation of the Three Codes*, where he argues that a monk should practice tantra in a careful manner, so as not to contravene his monastic vows. In Sakya Paṇḍita's presentation, adherence to the monk's and bodhisattva's vows is integrated into tantric practice, and tantra is practiced so as to not contradict the lower sets of vows. In contrast, Gampopa, a disciple of Milarepa and a famous systematizer of the Kagyü, maintained that tantra supersedes the "lower" forms of Buddhist practice, and thus any transgression of the monastic code that occurrs in the course of tantric practice is justified.[64] Of major influence would be the solution offered by Tsongkhapa Lozang Drakpa (1357–1419), founder of what would become the Geluk sect: that ordained monks should practice the transgressive aspects of these texts only through visualization, thus allowing them to keep their vows pure.

The many different approaches Indian and Tibetan Buddhists have taken to the question of how to interpret and enact the tantras is a topic worthy of more sustained discussion than can be given here. But one theme that must be highlighted is the way Indian and Tibetan commentators seeking to resolve the tension between the dictates of monasticism and the antinomian behaviors prescribed in the tantras would commonly suggest a mode of enacting the tantras in which the literal was made figurative, the embodied made imagined, and the external internalized.[65] For an example of how this typically worked, we will look at the sixth chapter of the first book of the *Hevajra Tantra*, describing the Practice, and how it was reinterpreted by an elite Kagyüpa, the Third Karmapa, Rangjung

Dorjé (1284–1339), in his commentary titled *The Stainless Light Explaining the Two-Parted.*

Near the beginning of this chapter, when stating where the Practice should be performed, the root text reads:

> Herein will be explained good meditation,
> which is practiced under a tree, in a charnel ground,
> in a house of female spirits, at night,
> in an empty place, or in solitude.[66]

In telling the reader what he regards as the "inner meaning" of the passage (*nang don*), Rangjung Dorjé offers an understanding very different from what the verse would at first glance seem to express. In its "inner meaning," the word "tree" refers to the central channel that runs through one's subtle, yogic body. "Charnel ground" means the doors to one's senses. "Night" refers to the thirty-two channels of the yogic body. The practitioner's aim is to make the yogic winds and *bodhicitta* (here referring to a psychophysical substance manipulated during subtle body meditation) enter the "empty place," which refers again to the central channel. Finally, we are told that "in solitude" refers to stopping the yogic winds from escaping through the doors to the senses. All of this is what is meant by "good meditation." In Rangjung Dorjé's presentation, the root text's directives that the yogin should meditate in these various places have been completely transformed, now taken as referring to a meditation process contained entirely within the yogin's own body. The yogin is no longer required to perform the practice anywhere in particular, as these external possibilities have all been made figurative and internalized. Rangjung Dorjé is careful to state that this interpretation is not idiomatic, but based on precedent established in commentaries on other tantras.

The Karmapa suggests this kind of internalization a number of times in the course of this short chapter. When the root text states that the yogin should take a beautiful woman as his consort, Rangjung Dorjé asserts that in the "definitive meaning" of the passage (*nges pa'i don*), "consort" actually refers to the letter *ah* one visualizes in one's belly during subtle body meditation.[67] In this way an overt statement about the necessity of sexual intercourse has been completely sanitized through reinterpretation, and the practice made suitable even for a celibate monk.

The Karmapa again prescribes a process of internalization when he says that the holy sites of the Indian subcontinent—the Twenty Four

Divine Abodes, the Eight Charnel Grounds, and so on—correspond to the thirty-two major channels of the subtle body, and are thereby mapped onto the yogin's own physical frame. Similarly, according to Rangjung Dorjé, the holy region of Jālandara corresponds to the top of the head, Oḍḍiyāṇa corresponds to the right ear, and so on.[68]

It would have been difficult for Tibetan meditators to visit these sacred sites, and yet they were listed in the tantras as essential locales for practice. By being mapped onto the practitioner's own body, the sacred sites were made completely portable. This remapping and internalization was key to the process of making the more extreme aspects of the tantras amenable to institutionalized monastic life, and to making them transportable to a distant locale like Tibet.

Describing the dress a meditator should wear in the course of the Practice, the *Hevajra Tantra* reads:

> Akṣobhya is symbolized by the form of the circlet,
> Amitābha by the earrings themselves,
> Ratneśa by the necklace,
> and Vairocana by the bangles on the wrists.
> Amogha[siddhi] is symbolized by the sash,
> Wisdom by the *khaṭvāṅga*,
> and Means by the drum.
> The Wrathful One himself is represented by the yogin.[69]

The most straightforward reading of this passage would suggest that in the process of becoming Hevajra/Heruka, the practitioner should take on these various accoutrements, and that each has symbolic value, invoking various deities or special qualities. In Rangjung Dorjé's presentation, the physical emblems become irrelevant. The line, "Akṣobhya [a buddha whose name means 'immovable'] is symbolized by the form of the circlet," is reinterpreted as meaning that the *bodhicitta* originating from the "*cakra* of great bliss," at the crown of one's head, is unwavering. "Amitābha ['boundless light'] by the earrings themselves" is reinterpreted as meaning that the white *bodhicitta* is restrained and the inner yogic fire burns. According to Rangjung Dorjé, "Ratneśa by the necklace" actually means that the *bodhicitta* is bound up at the subtle body's node at the throat. "Vairocana by the bangles on the wrists" means that the body's ancillary winds are bound up. "Amogha[siddhi] ['meaningful accomplishment'] is symbolized by the sash" actually means that the downward-voiding yogic wind is restrained, whereby one is "accomplished" in "meaning-fulness" (*don yod par 'grub pa*). Instead of indicating that the practitioner should actually carry a *khaṭvāṅga* staff and a drum, which would represent Wisdom and Means, the passage is said to indicate that the yogin himself should embody these special qualities, rendering the physical implements unnecessary.

Another passage from the *Hevajra Tantra*'s chapter on the Practice reads:

One certainly eats "medicine,"
one always drinks "water";
one is not afflicted by old age or death,
and will always be protected.[70]

The Karmapa's commentary indicates that on a surface level, "medicine" and "water" refer to feces and urine. This is a normative reading that was established shortly after the tantra was penned. Commentaries commonly expand on this reading, saying that "medicine" refers to the "five meats" and "water" to the "five nectars." The "five meats" are the meat of a bull, dog, elephant, horse, and human; the "five nectars" are feces, blood, semen, bone marrow, and urine—all highly polluting substances in the ancient Indian conceptual world.[71] But in his commentary, Rangjung Dorjé overturns the traditional reading of the passage, stating that its "definitive meaning" is that if one can stop the yogic winds from entering the left and right channels of the subtle body, one can prevent aging and death.

On two separate occasions, this chapter of the *Hevajra Tantra* instructs the practitioner to sing and dance, by means of which he communes with the deity. In the "definitive meanings" offered by Rangjung Dorjé, this "singing" and "dancing" refers to the movement of the elements of the subtle body, or to the pronunciation of mantras and meditation in general.[72]

The version of the Practice prescribed by Rangjung Dorjé hardly resembles what we know of it from the description given at the beginning of this chapter. Through a systematic and creative process involving a good deal of wordplay, and his assertion of "definitive" or "inner" meanings quite different from what a more straightforward and literal reading of the text would suggest, the Third Karmapa is able to offer a way of enacting the Practice that involves nothing at all transgressive and is suitable even for the fully ordained.

Having considered this example of a rather typical approach to the interpretation of the transgressive tantras, we can get a better sense of what was unique about Künga Zangpo and Sangyé Gyeltsen. What made Künga Zangpo and Sangyé Gyeltsen stand out from other religious practitioners of their day was the fact that their lifestyle and spiritual program were defined by a concerted attempt to enact a very literalist manner of following the Yoginī tantras, which necessarily meant rejecting other more popular modes.

In Tibet there had always been practitioners who performed the more antinomian aspects of the late Buddhist tantras, as a subset of lamas took tantric consorts, used sexual fluids in initiation rituals, and held gatherings in which transgressive substances were consumed. There were yogins who sported dreadlocks, and perhaps some aspects of the Heruka attire. The Secret Practice was passed down to Künga Zangpo and Sangyé Gyeltsen as a living tradition. The biography of the first Pawo, Chöwang Lhündrup—twelve years the Madman of Tsang's senior—tells of his performing some form of the Practice of the Observance. The yogin Lhatsün Künga Chökyi Gyatso (1432–1505) was praised as "supremely accomplished in the Observance," and some of his disciples took on aspects of this practice.[73] Nevertheless, the lifestyle adopted by Künga Zangpo and Sangyé Gyeltsen set them apart. (Even the Pawo's younger brother, we should remember, struggled to understand the Madman of Tsang's odd manner of dressing and practicing tantra.) Although others certainly performed some of these Unexcelled Yoga Tantra practices, none did so as comprehensively as the Madmen of Ü and Tsang. Künga Zangpo and Sangyé Gyeltsen made aspects of this transgressive, less-seen form of tantra utterly central to their practice, and to their public personas.

For these reasons, the distinctive behavior of the Madmen of Ü and Tsang can be thought of as exemplifying a *tantric fundamentalism*. I use the term "fundamentalism" to indicate a religious movement that promotes a specific lifestyle it claims is derived from a more literal reading of canonical texts. This is in line with the definition of fundamentalism articulated by Henry Munson, who states that religious movements can be considered fundamentalist "insofar as they insist on strict conformity to holy writ and to a moral code ostensibly based on it." (In the Madman of Tsang's reading, the moral code of the higher tantras sometimes meant doing things that seemed immoral.) Similarly, Martin E. Marty and R. Scott Appleby have somewhat provisionally defined fundamentalism as:

a tendency, a habit of mind, found within religious communities and paradigmatically embodied in certain representative individuals

and movements, which manifests itself as a strategy, or set of strate-
gies, by which beleaguered believers attempt to preserve their distinctive identity as a people or group. Feeling this identity to be at
risk in the contemporary era, they fortify it by a selective retrieval of
doctrines, beliefs, and practices from a sacred past. These retrieved
"fundamentals" are refined, modified, and sanctioned in a spirit
of shrewd pragmatism: they are to serve as a bulwark against the
encroachment of outsiders who threaten to draw the believers into
a syncretistic, areligious, or irreligious cultural milieu.[74]

I would add two qualifications to this understanding of the phenomenon.
First, that "fundamentalists" may not only be "preserv[ing]" their distinctive identity, but in fact formulating one that did not actually exist in the
past; and second, that the perceived threat in the face of which a fundamentalism arises does not need to be a secularizing force coming from
outside a religion, but could be a trend within it.

It was not the case that Künga Zangpo and Sangyé Gyeltsen had no
regard for tantric commentaries, liturgies, practice manuals, or other texts
that might offer a more mediated way of enacting the tantric scriptures,
since they studied and taught such texts, and in the Madman of Tsang's
case even composed them. The madmen still had regard for nontantric
practices, and even for the dictates of monasticism, as some of their disciples were monks. But on the wide spectrum of modes of interpreting
and enacting the late tantric scriptures that existed in fifteenth-century
Tibet, the Madmen of Ü and Tsang were positioned at the furthest possible extreme on the side of literalist applications. Rather than an absolute position, the tantric fundamentalism adopted by Künga Zangpo and
Sangyé Gyeltsen is better understood as a rhetorical stance. Symbolically
and rhetorically, vis-à-vis the religious movements of their day, they stood
out as fundamentalist literalists.

Künga Zangpo and Sangyé Gyeltsen were successful in positioning themselves as the upholders of tantra par excellence. When Künga
Zangpo gave up his monks' robes to take on the garb of the Heruka, his
biographer asserts that this was in part "in order to proclaim the greatness of the Vajrayāna." Decades later, he received a letter from the Eighth
Karmapa, Mikyö Dorjé, in which the great hierarch asked the yogin some
questions about tantra, praised him for his accomplishments in meditation, and exhorted him to continue "setting beings on the path of the
Vajrayāna during this degenerate age."[75] The subtitle to Götsang Repa's

version of the *Life of the Madman of Tsang* is *The Heart of the Sun, Clarifying the Vajrayāna*. It would seem that the madman's very life was to be taken as exemplifying the correct practice of tantra.

Conclusion

The seemingly eccentric—in some people's estimations, utterly inexplicable—behavior for which Künga Zangpo and Sangyé Gyeltsen became famous was neither spontaneous nor nonsensical. This was not the wild eccentricity of men who had transcended all worldly concerns. Quite to the contrary, these were the ways of individuals steadfastly upholding a well-defined set of spiritual commitments in a purposeful and ordered, if uncommon, manner.

In the course of their literalist application of the *Hevajra* and *Cakrasaṃvara* tantras, through which they presented themselves as the upholders of tantric Buddhist orthodoxy, Künga Zangpo and Sangyé Gyeltsen acted and dressed in ways that to some of their contemporaries seemed to be of a different time, a different place, and perhaps even a different religion. This is not an entirely inaccurate way to think of Künga Zangpo and Sangyé Gyeltsen, since their manner of enacting the Buddhist tantras would have been more commonplace five hundred years prior in India. What's more, the tantric practices enacted by Künga Zangpo and Sangyé Gyeltsen were directly or indirectly influenced by a great many South Asian religious movements, both Buddhist and non-Buddhist. The tantric Buddhist practice referred to as *vrata*, *caryā*, or *vratacaryā* must be seen as related to the practices of such non-Buddhist groups as the Pāśupatas, who would go into marketplaces and pretend to be crippled or insane, with the intention of provoking the scorn of passersby. There were the *kāpālika*-style practitioners, who smeared themselves with ashes and wore a set of six ornaments made from bone, whose mythology included a potent rhetoric of madness, and who worshipped Bhairava, "the Terrible," the form of Śiva that the deity Heruka was based on. There were the Kālāmukha, Lākula, Trika Tantra, and diverse other communities, many of which affected the lifestyles of degraded, outlaw, or outcaste groups, smearing themselves with ashes, engaging in sexual yoga, carrying *khaṭvāṅga*s and skull cups. There are the Hindu Avadhūtas, the Bauls, the Nāths, and the Aghoris. In many of these traditions, even going back to the *Upaniṣad*s and the *Veda*s, there was a consistent rhetoric of holy "madness" and/or intoxication.[76] The histories of these groups and the dynamics of sharing and exchange of ideas and ritual forms between them, over hundreds and thousands of years, are topics worthy of a whole series of books, falling well outside the scope of the present study.[77]

In their distinctive asceticism, Künga Zangpo and Sangyé Gyeltsen were showing mastery of and strict adherence to the canon of Buddhist scriptures, which incidently meant performing practices with centuries of precedent in the religious traditions of South Asia, including by groups against which Buddhists at times defined themselves. This is quite different from viewing Künga Zangpo and Sangyé Gyeltsen's behavior as an expression of enlightened spontaneity.

In the course of my many interviews with Tibetans, none alluded to the Practice of the Observance or any closely related terminology to explain the behavior of the holy madmen. When I suggested that the Madmen of Ü and Tsang's distinctive behavior ought to be understood as an example of these practices, and thus perhaps part of the yogin's spiritual training, some lamas accepted this as a possibility, while others did not. It seems that the idea that the eccentric behavior of the "holy madmen" was a by-product of their enlightenment (articulated in a variety of ways) has taken such firm root in some people that they struggle to conceive of them in any other way. The general explanation sometimes offered by Tibetans, that the holy madmen's eccentric behavior was a form of training for overcoming conceptual thinking (*rnam rtog*), does touch upon aspects of the Practice of the Observance. And the explanation that the madmen's behavior indicates their having transcended worldly distinctions is consistent with some meanings of their "madness," as described in this chapter. But the awareness that the Madmen of Ü and Tsang's eccentricity resulted from the specific tantric discipline described in this chapter has been completely lost. Indicative of this is the fact that although many recognize that the madmen were often referred to as Herukas, none of the lamas I interviewed seemed aware that the Madmen of Ü and Tsang had spent much of their lives wearing the fearsome garb of the deity; instead they seemed to take the designation Heruka as indicating a high degree of accomplishment in meditation. It is clearly the case that during the time in which Künga Zangpo and Sangyé Gyeltsen lived, many people were aware that their distinctive behavior resulted from their particular way of adhering to the tantras. But as decades and centuries passed, many significant details about the lives of the Madmen of Ü and Tsang were forgotten, and understandings of who these "madmen" were underwent a dramatic change in the minds of the Tibetan people in the process.

It is only in recent years that European and American scholars like Stefan Larsson, Geoffrey Samuel, and Cyrus Stearns have begun to recognize the importance of the Practice of the Observance for interpreting the odd-seeming behavior of some of Tibet's "holy madmen." A lack of appreciation for the importance of the Practice historically can be observed in our thinking, not only about the "holy madmen," but about tantric Buddhism in general, although there is some indication that this is being rectified. The Practice of the Observance is also little known among Tibetan lamas and *khenpos* today. Of the many I asked, only one claimed to have performed it, and in a much simplified and reduced form.[78]

3

Sainthood in the Making

THE MADMEN OF Ü AND TSANG IN PUBLIC

At that time, a tea merchant who had been to Lhasa
mentioned that there was a yogin called "the Madman of Tsang"
who dressed in a human skin. As soon as I heard this,
I got goosebumps and wept.

From the verse autobiography of GÖTSANG REPA, describing an event
that occurred when he was eight years old[1]

IN ADOPTING THE garb of the Heruka and performing the Practice of the Observance, Künga Zangpo and Sangyé Gyeltsen were also assuming new identities. This had significant social consequences. To conceptualize the relationship between the two yogins and their public, this chapter examines the reputations they acquired through their distinctive behavior, and how those reputations were generated and circulated.

The Drum Sound of Their Fame

Although Künga Zangpo and Sangyé Gyeltsen had many faithful supporters, they were also met with indifference, criticism, or worse by those who doubted their religious achievements or disapproved of their lifestyle. The Madman of Ü's biography states that the first time he arrived at Nyukla fortress dressed in the garb of the Heruka, "With no one having the slightest idea that the master was an excellent yogin or that he was a lord of *siddhas*, they thought that he was undoubtedly an unsurpassed fraud acting like a madman." He was beaten badly, even thrown from a cliff and pinned under a boulder, which he miraculously survived. This account was written by Nyukla Penchen, who was present when these events occurred and was won over by this display of the yogin's abilities. Various sources point to this event as contributing significantly to the spread of Künga Zangpo's fame.[2] If we accept the version of events presented in Götsang Repa's biography of the Madman of Tsang, it would seem that the king of Ngari Gungtang had such doubts about Künga Zangpo's level of spiritual accomplishment that he wanted to submit him to a series of tests, as will be described in the intermezzo.[3]

In the colophon to the part of the *Life of the Madman of Ü* that he authored, Nyukla Peṇchen addresses the issue of the Madman of Ü's numerous detractors. He states that at the time, some people were unable to believe some of the stories circulating about the Madman of Ü (probably referring to tales of his miracles), but these were "unfortunate people who have fallen under the powerful influence of false views, counterfeit logic, and sectarian hatred." Elsewhere Nyukla Peṇchen contends that there is ample scriptural backing for the various aspects of the Madman of Ü's seemingly eccentric activity. Those who maintain that the yogin's lifestyle harms the teachings of the Buddha are "fools who do not have the wealth of great learning; very unfortunate beings whose intellects are obscured by partisan jealousy, whose mouths have been poisoned by demons." The passage continues: "Although some people do not know what to make of this kind of yogin and say that his manner of enacting the Practice does harm to the Teachings," this is only the prattle of the uninformed and the sinful, so what would be the point of responding to their criticisms?[4] When this was written, the Madman of Ü was about thirty-six years old, indicating that in the middle of his career the great yogin faced formidable criticisms for the lifestyle he had assumed. The passage also indicates that at the time, some saw this criticism as motivated in part by sectarian competitiveness.

The Madman of Tsang was also attacked, physically and verbally, directly and indirectly, by those who regarded him with skepticism. His biography tells of how an artist at Dingri Langkhor monastery was moved by faith to begin making 108 statues of the great yogin. One day the abbot saw those statues and proclaimed that "making a statue of the Madman of Tsang is even more sinful than destroying a stūpa!" He took one of the statues and purposefully denigrated it by placing it a lowly position beneath his seat. Each day when the monks assembled for tea, the abbot would drag the statue across the floor by a string tied around its neck while hurling invective at it: "False one! Destroyer of the teachings of the Buddha! It is wrong that you should delude living beings!" The abbot charged the Madman of Tsang with teaching a false dharma, the most unpardonable of sins.

The biographer informs us that shortly after this, the abbot died a horrific death, to be understood by the reader as due punishment for his lack of faith. According to his biography, at one point those close to the Madman of Tsang came to suspect that someone had tried to poison him. Such was the great earnestness of these concerns.[5]

It is said that one occasion Sangyé Gyeltsen arrived in Lhasa during the course of a long and distressing drought. When he announced that the relief they yearned for would soon come, some people questioned how rain could be made to fall from a cloudless sky and called him a "fake yogin" (*rnal 'byor pa zog po*). It rained that very night, and everyone was moved to faith.[6]

We can see that during their lifetimes, Künga Zangpo and Sangyé Gyeltsen had doubters and critics who were skeptical of their spiritual accomplishments or disapproved of their lifestyles. There would have been an even larger population who remained uncertain or ambivalent about the madmen—not to mention those who simply never heard of them. The record does not support the view that Künga Zangpo or Sangyé Gyeltsen at some point achieved a highly realized state, after which their holiness was objectively clear to all others. Rather, what they had or had not achieved spiritually was always open to disagreement. For this reason, it is more accurate to think of one's level of spiritual accomplishment not as a characteristic, but as an attribution: it was a quality that existed not in the medium of the yogin's own person, but in that of public opinion within his society. And public opinion was divided, complex, and perpetually shifting, as it always turns out to be. Like saintly figures of any religion, during their own lifetimes the holy madmen remained incomplete, their holiness just as unstable as the mercurial opinions of their contemporaries. As the anthropologist Guillaume Rozenberg has concluded from his study of saintly figures striving for recognition as *arhats* in modern-day Burma, "if from the point of view of the theologian, sainthood is an individual state—that of spiritual perfection—from the point of view of the ethnologist [and, let us add, the historian], it consists of a system of culturally determined representations and social relations."[7] Rozenberg is careful to refer to the saintly figure during his or her lifetime as an "aspiring saint," since a living person, always still subject to doubt, can never unequivocally achieve such a state.

As Künga Zangpo or Sangyé Gyeltsen were always saints still in the making, during their lives the mad yogins and their supporters were engaged with the task of making the case for their enlightenment and the value of their ways, through a variety of means. Künga Zangpo and Sangyé Gyeltsen themselves did the most to foster the notion that they had achieved enlightened states and enacted a true form of Buddhism. What they truly thought of their own spiritual accomplishments we can never know, but clearly both took on activities that had the effect of fostering the perception that they were or could be highly realized. This included their spending many years in meditative retreat and performing the Practice of the Observance, which may have functioned as a ritual enactment of enlightenment. Near the end of his life, some would interpret Sangyé Gyeltsen's success in overseeing the renovation of the Swayambhūnāth stūpa as proof of his *siddha*hood.

Also involved in making the case for the madmen's respective spiritual accomplishments were their circles of supporters. By the simple fact of being a yogin's disciples they helped attest to his holiness, since Tibetans of the day would have seen the number of disciples a master attracted as to some extent indicative of his level of attainment. Something similar could be said of a yogin's patrons: the more patrons he had, the more illustrious they were, and the more resources they put at his disposal, the more spiritually accomplished he would have seemed. But these supporters also fostered the perception of Künga Zangpo and Sangyé Gyeltsen's spiritual worth through more active measures as well. The madmen's biographies reveal the important roles their followers played in bearing witness to the miracles they supposedly performed. Meanwhile the madmen's patrons actively promoted them by sponsoring the carving of woodblocks for their biographies.

Of foremost importance in Künga Zangpo's and Sangyé Gyeltsen's respective circles of supporters were the authors of their biographies. Since the time they were printed, these texts have done more than anything else to attest to the yogins' spiritual accomplishments. For one thing, the madmen's biographers plainly state that they achieved great spiritual states. The very title of the Madman of Ü's biography describes him as a "preeminent *siddha*." The biography asserts him to have become a *siddha* at a specific moment, and he is casually referred to as a *siddha* throughout.[8] These statements are made in the first part of Künga Zangpo's biography, which was in circulation throughout the last thirty-eight years of his life. The Madman of Tsang was also referred to as a *siddha* in all three of his hagiographies, which were printed after his death. Götsang Repa calls the Madman of Tsang "a *siddha* without rival" in a short encomium written on the occasion of finishing his version of the *Life*, which circulated independently of it.[9]

Another means by which the biographers make an argument for the yogins' great levels of spiritual advancement is asserting them to have performed a great many miracles. At times the Madmen of Ü and Tsang are both said to have walked across rivers, flown through the air, lifted impressively large rocks, gone fearlessly among wild beasts of prey, and miraculously made water appear, as well as to have made their bodies disappear, or to have emanated multiple bodies at once. Both are attributed with having been able to generate such great yogic heat that the snow surrounding their dwellings would melt. Their biographies are filled with depictions of how they withstood ferocious attacks from lords' guardsmen, angry villagers wielding swords, axes, poison arrows, and the ubiquitous "rain of stones." But no matter how severe these attacks were—at times so severe that everyone who witnessed them was certain the yogin had died, we are told—the Madmen of Ü and Tsang always survived without a scratch. These miracles are put forth as evidence of the *siddhis* or worldly superpowers Künga Zangpo and Sangyé Gyeltsen achieved in the course of their spiritual development.[10]

The biographies also use less overt means to foster the perception that Künga Zangpo and Sangyé Gyeltsen had achieved greatness. This includes the authors' decisions to include certain details of the madmen's lives while glossing over others. To exemplify this, let us consider two portrayals of the relationship between the Madman of Ü and the Sakyapa Śākya Chokden. *The Life of the Madman of Ü* tells of Künga Zangpo's visiting Śākya Chokden at his monastery, Serdokchen, on two occasions, during which he received teachings from the scholar-monk and had him write a few texts on his behalf. Meanwhile, the *Life of Śākya Chokden* tells of the Madman of Ü's encountering (or almost encountering) the great scholar on three occasions. On the latter two of these, Śākya Chokden imparted teachings to and composed texts for Künga Zangpo. During these meetings, the Madman of Ü acted subserviently toward Śākya Chokden, even letting the monk rest his feet on his long hair, laid out upon a deerskin. *The Life of Śākya Chokden* tells of another occasion, a year before the two first met, when Künga Zangpo waited an entire week outside Serdokchen, hoping to have an audience with the great scholar. Śākya Chokden had one of his disciples bring the yogin a piece of brown sugar and ask him to leave.[11]

There is overwhelming evidence that the Madman of Ü and Śākya Chokden did in fact meet. The two biographies agree concerning the teachings transmitted by Śākya Chokden to the Madman of Ü, as well as the treatises the scholar composed on the yogin's behalf. These compositions can be found in the *Collected Works* of Śākya Chokden; some of their colophons even identify them as having been written at the request of the Madman of Ü.[12] But there are other aspects of this story about which we are much less certain. Was the Madman of Ü in fact spurned on an early visit to Serdokchen? It is easy to imagine why the Madman of Ü's biographer would have found it preferable to leave this embarrassing detail out of the story of his master's life. We may also entertain doubts about the story of the Madman of Ü's assuming such a demonstratively subservient position by letting Śākya Chokden put his feet upon his hair—precisely the same manner in which the ninth-century Tibetan king Relpachen is reputed to have shown his reverence for the monks of his day. This could be an exaggeration inserted into the story by Śākya Chokden's biographer, or his taking poetic license in describing the relationship between the scholar and the yogin.

This one case exposes the fact that the biographies of the Madmen of Ü and Tsang are products of a purposeful process of selection and representation: from their titles to the words they use to characterize things, to the choices about what to include or exclude, these biographies were written with the strategic intent of making an argument for the greatness of their subjects. They must be read with a degree of caution, seen neither as all-out fictions nor as infallible records of historical events as they actually occurred.

The degree to which the public at large was willing to perceive them as holy men was also a factor in the sanctification of the Madmen of Ü and Tsang. Some citizens of central and western Tibet would have encountered Künga Zangpo or Sangyé Gyeltsen directly, perhaps catching glimpses of their noteworthy behavior in a marketplace somewhere. But even when the yogins' exploits were performed away from population centers, there was often a crowd of witnesses. When the Madman of Ü ate the brains of a corpse while traveling in Tsang, we are told that everyone present was sickened by the sight, indicating that an audience was on hand to witness the feat.[13] After each yogin's initial rise to prominence, he was rarely alone. In truth they were highly exposed, allowing a good many Tibetan citizens to witness their exhibitionistic activity firsthand.

But fifteenth-century Tibetans did not have to encounter the great yogins directly to know of their eccentric behavior. Word of their exploits spread far and wide, and as quickly as any form of information traveled during their day. The epigraph to this chapter gives a sense of how the Madman of Tsang's reputation preceded him: as a small boy, Götsang Repa heard of the yogin's odd lifestyle and was moved to faith. Later in his autobiography, Götsang Repa records having become ecstatically deranged as a teenager when someone arrived bearing news of the Madman of Tsang, "a true *vajradhara*," an enlightened master.[14] That teenager would grow up to become one of the Madman of Tsang's biographers. Just as he experienced goosebumps of faith by hearing word of the Madman of Tsang from these informal messengers, Götsang Repa would be responsible for spreading an understanding of the yogin's greatness to countless others through his version the yogin's biography. Whereas the biographer Nyukla Penchen was first impressed by exploits of the Madman of Ü that he had observed directly, the case of Götsang Repa shows how awareness of the provocative yogins' actions also spread by word of mouth. Nyukla Penchen was also aware of the way news of the Madman of Ü's greatness spread orally: after the yogin is said to have tied a sword into a knot, he writes that "people got goosebumps of faith just hearing about it."[15]

As people heard tell of the Madmen of Ü and Tsang's exploits, they would have responded in a wide variety of ways. Some were moved to faith, taking the stories of the yogins' miracles as proof of their enlightenment. Others remained skeptical, perhaps thinking that although there had been real *siddha*s and enlightened beings in times past, they were not to be found in the impure time in which they now lived. Many would have remained unsure, or half-convinced—relieved, perhaps, that they were not in a position of having to commit themselves to one view or the other.

Those close to the madmen were very much aware of these dynamics of popular renown. Their biographers, for example, make consistent mention of their fame and how it was spread, marking the progress of each madman's rise to holiness. *The Life of the Madman of Ü* states that after Künga Zangpo survived a savage beating by the guards of the king of Ngari Gungtang, the name "'the Madman of Ü' was renowned in and pervaded every direction" for the first time. (Götsang Repa's *Life of the Madman of Tsang* also identifies this as the point at which Künga Zangpo's fame as the Madman of Ü began.) Later, after the Madman of Ü survived another

fierce attack from some soldiers, his biography says that the "white banner of his fame became visible as far as the ends of the earth."[16] In each
of these cases, the Madman of Ü's fame increased after he did something
seemingly miraculous.

The same awareness of the workings of notoriety is displayed in the
Madman of Tsang's biography, since Götsang Repa makes numerous
mentions of the spread of the yogin's fame, which in nearly every case is
said to be a direct result of the yogin's own actions. The epigraph to the
introduction asserts that it was on account of Sangyé Gyeltsen's smearing
himself with ashes and blood and doing shocking things before the people
of Tsari that he was unanimously praised as the Madman of Tsang, soon to
be as universally known among humanity as the sun itself.[17] In one chapter of his *Life* of the Madman of Tsang, Götsang Repa even goes so far as to
suggest that the yogin purposefully endeavored to become more famous,
saying that it was owing to "his diligence in sounding the drum sound of
his fame in every direction" that he "became renowned in the three realms
as a *mahāsiddha* without rival."[18]

The Madman of Tsang's own words reveal his awareness of the relationship between his actions and the public's perception of him. In a song
of instruction to one of his students, he is recorded as having sung:

> If you do the Observance for the sake of fame,
> the jealousy of your "karmic *ḍākinī*" [i.e., consort] will
> cause various adverse circumstances in this life
> and you will be reborn in Vajra Hell in the next.
> Do not do the Practice of the Observance
> for any reason other than obtaining buddhahood.[19]

In this passage a man who had become famous through his exhibitionistic
Practice of the Observance brings up the possibility that one might use the
Practice of the Observance to become famous. Although the yogin is here
admonishing his disciple *not* to do the Practice for any worldly reason, this
implies, of course, that people might be expected to do just that.

After the Madman of Ü endured his famous attack at Nyukla, some
repentant individuals offered to carry him indoors. According to his biography, the yogin responded by saying, "If you carried me, it would damage
my image as a realized yogin."[20]

Furthermore, both madmen played significant roles in the production of the biographies that would so strongly argue for their greatness.

As Nyukla Penchen states, the Madman of Ü told him "again and again" that he should compose a biography of him. Surely Künga Zangpo had a sense of the effect this document would have in spreading his fame and shaping how others perceived him. The Madman of Tsang also told his biographers about experiences and visions he had had, so that they could be recorded for posterity.[21] Perhaps the strongest evidence of the madmen's awareness of the dynamics of representations and holiness is the Madman of Tsang's composing and altering the life stories of other saints of the Kagyü tradition, discussed in chapter 5.

Some of the Madmen of Ü and Tsang's contemporaries also saw them as highly aware of the effects their activity would have on people's perceptions of them. Some even went so far as to say that their eccentric behavior was motivated by their desire for fame, and the wealth and influence that would come with it. Perhaps the most vocal of these critics was the most famous of all the holy madmen, Drukpa Künlé. As will be discussed in chapter 6, Drukpa Künlé was very concerned about the various forms of hypocrisy he observed in the religious culture of fifteenth- and sixteenth-century Tibet. He had strong misgivings about certain religious practitioners who made public displays of the practice of tantra, especially those who went so far as to dress in the garb of the Heruka. As Drukpa Künlé caustically charges in a passage in his *Miscellaneous Writings*:

> You who adorn yourselves with the pure ornaments for the practice
>   of Secret Mantra
> —the topknot, bone ornaments, *khaṭvāṅga*, and tiger-skin skirt—
> you donkeys who cover yourselves with lions' hides—
> it seems to me that you are disclosing secret things for the sake of
>   putting food on the table![22]

Those who dressed in the manner for which the Madmen of Ü and Tsang were famous were (timid, unrealized) donkeys who covered themselves with the hides of (heroic, enlightened) lions. In Drukpa Künlé's view, their taking up this lifestyle was sometimes motivated by material concerns. Elsewhere Drukpa Künlé addresses certain tantric masters who perform empowerment rituals in order to make money, who sing mantras in the marketplace, who are willing to draw a maṇḍala anywhere—all while saying that it is dangerous to reveal such secret things.[23] Throughout his *Miscellaneous Writings*, Drukpa Künlé expresses his concern that certain people who have created tantric personas for themselves are "selling" the dharma—teaching it, appropriating it, and using it for their own benefit.

When making these criticisms, Drukpa Künlé may at times have had the Madmen of Ü and Tsang in mind, since on a few occasions he singles them out specifically as those who have employed tantra for worldly ends. In a composition included in the third volume of his *Miscellaneous Writings*, Drukpa Künlé writes,

> I am not one realized in Cutting, which involves disturbing malicious spirits and the mental continuum—
> I am a yogin for whom all appearances appear as the divine body.
> I am not a masked dancer, a mantrika distributing Secret Mantra in the marketplace—
> I am a yogin who understands all of existence in the maṇḍala.
> I am not the Madman of Tsang, who hypocritically [or superficially] puts on a tiger's skin—
> I am one with a relaxed mind, who tenderly cares for his woman.[24]

In saying that it was improper for the Madman of Tsang to have taken on his distinctive form of dress, Drukpa Künlé is asserting that he did not have the proper level of realization to justify his taking on this lifestyle (an issue that will be returned to later in this chapter), suggesting a more worldly motivation for his doing so. The earlier lines of this passage may also be in reference to Sangyé Gyeltsen.

On another occasion someone asked Drukpa Künlé what he thought about the Madman of Tsang, which may suggest that he was the subject of some controversy at the time. In response, Drukpa Künlé describes the life of the Madman of Tsang in this way:

> First, by means of practicing the text of the *Two-Parted* [*Hevajra Tantra*] while staying in the Gurpa college [within the Pelkhor Chödé monastic complex in Gyantsé], and in particular by wearing the ornamented Heruka garb, he illustrated the chapter on the Practice [the sixth chapter of the first book of the *Hevajra*]. In addition, he took great joy in virtuous activity, practice, and so on. His activities for the time being were good. He was good, except for the fault of his monks' and disciples' aspirations to wealth.[25]

It seems that Drukpa Künlé knew a fair amount about the life of Sangyé Gyeltsen. He clearly understood that the yogin's seeming eccentricity arose from his attempt to enact a literal reading of the late tantras' descriptions of the Practice of the Observance. Although Drukpa Künlé leveled the criticism of being overly desirous of wealth at the Madman of Tsang's followers, we can probably take this censure as extending the great yogin himself. As we have no evidence that Drukpa Künlé ever met the Madman of Tsang, it is likely that he formed this opinion from information about the yogin that was being spread by word of mouth.

Drukpa Künlé also singled out the Madman of Ü for similar criticism. In the course of an autobiographical song, Drukpa Künlé mentions that he once met the Madman of Ü, then launches a scathing attack on the yogin's activities. According to Drukpa Künlé, the Madman of Ü used to rouse demons as enemies, cause others to lose faith, and would "teach the Practice to beggars." Directly after this, Drukpa Künlé turns to the Madman of Tsang, accusing him of, among other things, "showing off his wealth" and "making a profit from his wrathful activity."[26] The relationship between Drukpa Künlé and his two madman peers was not limited to these criticisms, however, as he also formally praised the Madman of Ü at times.

In the previous chapter the distinctive lifestyle assumed by the Madmen of Ü and Tsang was described as a form of religious practice, as commonly understood, assuming that the primary purpose behind this activity was the yogins' striving toward enlightenment. It would seem that Künga Zangpo and Sangyé Gyeltsen's concerns were not so narrowly delimited. Their activities had an important outward-facing component, and the madmen show themselves to have been quite aware of the sort of effect their actions would have in shaping others' perceptions of them, and the worldly ramifications those perceptions might engender. In the eyes of some of their contemporaries—including one of their "holy madman" peers—they may have been motivated to take on this lifestyle by a desire for self-aggrandizement, perhaps even greed. Drukpa Künlé's criticisms show that Tibetans themselves have long harbored suspicions about the motivations of their famous religious figures. There is no single traditional Tibetan view on the "holy madmen," but a wide range of highly divergent ones.

The Repertoire of *Siddha* Behavior

Tibetans and Western scholars and popular commentators have often attempted to explain the eccentric behavior of Tibet's "holy madmen" by making analogies to the Buddhist *mahāsiddhas* ("great accomplished ones") of India.[27] It may be almost inevitable that the holy madmen should be compared to the *mahāsiddhas*, given their respective reputations for eccentricity and high levels of meditative achievement.

Separate from the issue of whether or not Künga Zangpo and Sangyé Gyeltsen actually achieved a state of *siddha*hood is the question of how they may have been influenced by the stories and images of famous *siddhas* who preceded them. Were Künga Zangpo and Sangyé Gyeltsen inspired by the great tantric saints of India in their decisions to take on their distinctive lifestyle? From the evidence presented in their biographies, it is clear that the *mahāsiddhas* were a touchstone for the behavior of the Madmen of Ü and Tsang in a number of ways, including some beyond the most immediately obvious.

During his lifetime, the Madman of Ü had various points of connection with the famous *siddhas* of India. He received and gave teachings derived from the *mahāsiddhas* (especially the *Dohās* of Saraha and the yogic practices of Nāropa), visited holy sites associated with them in Nepal, and is purported to have had visions of some of them. The Madman of Tsang also had visions of the *mahāsiddhas* and received and gave teachings derived from them.[28] All of this is relatively conventional, since most meditators of the Kagyü sect would have had similar connections with the Indian saints from whom they believed their lineage derived. But there is also evidence suggesting that Künga Zangpo and Sangyé Gyeltsen may have consciously modeled their behaviors on those of the *mahāsiddhas* of India. In chapter 2 it was shown that, when attacked as unorthodox by some scholar-monks of the Geluk sect, Sangyé Gyeltsen cited the eighty *mahāsiddhas* as a precedent for his ways. According to another of his biographies, at one point the Madman of Tsang decided to perform a meditation by means of which he reanimated a half-rotten corpse. He was inspired to do this because the "*siddhas* of the past" also used to do "corpse practices" (*ro spyod*). (After having a harrowing encounter with the zombie, Sangyé Gyeltsen was finally able to subdue it again.)[29]

For his part, toward the end of his life the Madman of Ü is purported to have proclaimed, "I am the granddaddy [*spyi mes*] of the eighty [*mahā*]*siddhas* [of India]!" Later he entered a state in which he had magnificent visions and said, "I am the granddaddy of the eighty *siddhas*, and thus I remain surrounded by those *siddhas*."[30] Although it is uncertain what precisely Künga Zangpo meant by these statements, he clearly wished to foster the association between himself and the Indian Buddhist *siddhas* of centuries past.

Of special importance here is the question of on what grounds Künga Zangpo and Sangyé Gyeltsen may have seen themselves as following the precedent established by the *mahāsiddhas* of India. When making his case for why readers should have faith in the Madman of Ü at the end of his part of the *Life*, Nyukla Peṇchen describes how the great yogin had achieved deep meditative realization, then submitted himself to extreme austerities. Nyukla Peṇchen then instructs the reader, "Do not think that the amazing stories of all the *mahāsiddhas* of India differ from this [biography of the Madman of Ü] except in terms of distance"—suggesting that the Madman of Ü is equal to them in all things, save for geographic or temporal location.[31] Here the specific criterion on which Nyukla Peṇchen compares the activities of the Madman of Ü to those of the Indian *mahāsiddhas* is their taking on great austerities in the course of their yogic training. In the same vein, earlier, when the young Künga Zangpo was developing the conviction to become a monk, Nyukla Peṇchen depicts his thought process in the following manner:

> The food and possessions you think you need to gather [in a house-holder's life] are no more your own than the honey of powerless bees, so why amass what you do not need? These temporary joys and pleasures are like the show you see in a dream—recognizing this uncertainty, where should one stay? The superior *siddhas* of the past subjected themselves to extreme difficulties and turned them into dharma practice—they didn't just have the thought of doing so. The dharma is not to be practiced in pleasant and peaceful settings. From now, even if heaven and earth were turned upside-down, I will fearlessly and authentically practice the holy dharma![32]

For Künga Zangpo, the *mahāsiddhas* exemplified an extreme asceticism that he sought to match. In contrast, most commentators today who explain the behavior of the holy madmen by making reference to the Indian *siddhas* make the connection based on the perception that they all embody a natural eccentricity that comes as a result of having transcended worldly concerns and limitations.

Künga Zangpo and Sangyé Gyeltsen may also have sought to imi-tate the *mahāsiddhas* of India insofar as they lived lives dedicated to the Practice of the Observance. Today it is often thought that the eccen-tric behavior for which the Indian Buddhist *siddhas* living between the eighth and twelfth centuries became well known was an expression of a general enlightened eccentricity. It has more recently been suggested that we should revise our understanding of the *siddhas'* behavior, to see it as resulting specifically from their enacting the Practice of the Observance. For example, the collection of songs that constitutes our key body of information on the famous Buddhist *mahāsiddhas* of India is known as the *Caryāgiti*. Although this is often taken as meaning "songs of practice," it should probably be understood as "songs of the Practice."[33]

The special association between the Indian *mahāsiddhas* and the Practice of the Observance was still intact in fifteenth-century Tibet. Nāropa in particular was strongly associated with the Secret Practice. In biographies written in the late fifteenth century, including the Madman of Tsang's *Life of Milarepa*, it is said that when Marpa returned to India to get some further teachings from Nāropa, he could not find him, for he had "gone off to do the Practice."[34] Nāropa is portrayed as dressing in the garb of the Heruka. According to the Madman of Tsang's account, his bone ornaments would come into the possession of Marpa, and eventually play an important role in Milarepa's story. The *khaṭvāṅga* staff itself carried potent connotations, as the *mahāsiddha* Padmasambhava is usually depicted as carrying one. Other *mahāsiddhas* are depicted wearing ornaments of bone and tiger-skin skirts, with pierced ears and long hair bound in a topknot, carrying skull cups, and so on.

As a further indication that the holy madmen may have been influenced by the *mahāsiddhas* on the grounds of being especially dedicated to the Practice of the Observance, when Künga Zangpo first assumed his distinctive lifestyle, his biography cites Saraha's *Dohā Trilogy* as motivating his behavior, along with the tantras. Saraha's *Queen Dohā* contains a description of the Practice of the Observance, including the sorts of women appropriate to take as consorts, actions to be performed in both crowded and haunted places, dancing and dressing in the manner of the Heruka, behaving like a mad elephant or a dumb person, and so on. (Herbert Guenther, not fully realizing that this was a description of a specific practice, took *brtul zhugs spyod pa'i rnal 'byor pa* as referring to an "eccentric" yogin.)[35]

Distinct from the issue of Künga Zangpo's and Sangyé Gyeltsen's being inspired by the *mahāsiddhas* of India, explicit and implicit comparisons between the holy madmen and those earlier *siddhas* are made throughout this body of literature, making for a complex interplay of representations. In chapter 2, it was shown that Karma Trinlepa flatteringly praised the Madman of Ü as an "emanation of father Tilopa." Nyukla Penchen would compare the Madman of Ü with the next great *siddha* in the lineage, saying that when the young Künga Zangpo met his first guru Chuworipa, it was like Nāropa's first meeting with Tilopa. According to the biography, the Madman of Ü would later say that his second guru, Drakchokpa Rinchen Zangpo, was in fact Cakrasaṃvara, that Chuworipa was Tilopa, and that other of his masters were actually (emanations of?) Nāropa and Padampa Sangyé. The Madman of Ü's biography also contains a tale of the yogin's magically pinning the moon in place in the sky, until he decided to release it—very similar to the one told about Virūpa's seizing control of the sun.[36] The Madman of Ü's disciples were keen to explain his life in terms of the mythology of the tradition, and to allow the great yogin's identity to interpenetrate those of the past masters of the lineage.

In Götsang Repa's version of the *Life of the Madman of Tsang*, it is said that a man named Yamchilwa once had a dream in which he saw a yogin wearing the bone ornaments of the charnel ground, striking dancing poses, and carrying a *ḍamaru*, thighbone trumpet, and *khaṭvāṅga*. Yamchilwa wondered, "Who is this?" He was thereupon told by two women, "It's lord Tilopa, returned to benefit beings." When Yamchilwa awoke, he told his attendants to wait and see if such a yogin would appear. That day the Madman of Tsang arrived, playing a *ḍamaru* and blowing a thighbone trumpet, dancing like a deity, and singing tantric songs. Yamchilwa told the Madman of Tsang that he was "like an emanation of noble lord Tilopa." The Madman of Tsang responded by stating that although he was certainly one who upheld Tilopa's lineage, he could not say whether or not he was an emanation (*sprul pa*) of him. A number of significant things take place in this passage. For one, the passage asserts that dressing as and imitating the Heruka were not unique or novel to the Madman of Tsang, but had a strong precedent in the tradition. What's more, the Madman of Tsang is asserted to be the equivalent of or a stand-in for Tilopa, in part, it would seem, because of their shared Practice of the Observance.[37]

The Madman of Tsang would be put forth as the equivalent of Tilopa in other ways as well. At one point, according to Götsang Repa's version of his *Life*, the Madman of Tsang was instructing a disciple who was a *geshé* with great textual learning. In the process of imparting to him an instruction on the Mahāmudrā, the yogin tried to teach him the nature of the mind. The disciple simply was not getting it, so the Madman of Tsang hit him in the head, which later led to his attaining high realization. Here

Sangyé Gyeltsen is implicitly compared to or equated with Tilopa, who five hundred years earlier had imparted a great teaching to Nāropa by hitting him in the face with a sandal.[38]

The relationship between the Madmen of Ü and Tsang and the famous Buddhist *siddha*s of India was complex and multidimensional. Künga Zangpo and Sangyé Gyeltsen may have hoped to match the kind of extreme asceticism for which the great *siddha*s were famous, or their lifestyles defined by the Practice of the Observance. Künga Zangpo and Sangyé Gyeltsen were compared to or even asserted to be emanations of those *mahāsiddha*s, and may have actively encouraged the association.

It is far too simplistic to say that the Madmen of Ü and Tsang were merely imitating the *siddha*s, however. This would be to suggest that Künga Zangpo and Sangyé Gyeltsen did so entirely unselfconsciously, without any consideration of how their taking after the *siddha*s would be seen or thought of by others. This runs counter to the sort of self awareness these holy madmen displayed throughout their lives. Rather than saying that Künga Zangpo and Sangyé Gyeltsen imitated the famous Buddhist *siddha*s of India, it is more accurate to say that they took on modes of speech, dress and behavior that caused their contemporaries to associate them with those famous *siddha*s. Another way of saying this is to observe that the popular fifteenth-century Tibetan understanding of the lives of the Buddhist *siddha*s of India was part of the repertoire of saintly behavior from which Künga Zangpo and Sangyé Gyeltsen drew.[39] The *siddha*s were widely thought to have dressed, acted and spoken in certain ways—ways that exemplified their enlightenment. These notions about the *siddha*s were passed down through time in the body of cultural knowledge we can term the Tibetan *imaginaire*.[40] By taking on comparable styles of dress, behavior, and speech, Künga Zangpo and Sangyé Gyeltsen effectively raised the possibility in the minds of others that they might also be *siddha*s.

Evincing this dynamic, when Sangyé Gyeltsen arrived in Lhasa wearing the Heruka attire, some people wondered out loud if he was a *siddha*. Similarly, after Künga Zangpo was beaten by the guards of the king of Ngari Gungtang, and he triumphantly arose saying *hūṃ* and *phaṭ* and dancing like a deity, all decided that he must be a *siddha*. One means toward being perceived as a *siddha* was to act and dress as famous *siddha*s of the past were thought to have done. As will be shown in chapter 5, the relationship between the holy madmen and the earlier saints of their tradition is further complicated by the fact that the holy madmen had a direct hand in creating the identities of these earlier saints as we now know them.

There is one more potential source of influence on the lifestyles assumed by the Madmen of Ü and Tsang that must be considered. In the late fifteenth and early sixteenth centuries, Indian yogins occasionally made their way to Tibet. Two of these yogins—a Tilmarwa of Bodhgaya and a Jaharbhi, also known as Mitrayogi, who is said to have been renowned as a *siddha* who had achieved a state of immortality—would visit the Madman of Ü at his monastery in the latter part of his life.[41] Künga Zangpo and Sangyé Gyeltsen would have encountered Indian yogins like these at various moments in their careers, in Tibet, Nepal, and the area of Mount Kailash, an important pilgrimage and meditation site for Śaivite ascetics. The Indian ascetics who visited Tibet may have been Nāths or of some other lineage or sect that blurred the boundaries between Buddhist and non-Buddhist. And they may well have espoused modes of dress— carrying a skull cup, smearing themselves with ashes—similar to those adopted by the Madmen of Ü and Tsang. But we have no indication that Künga Zangpo and Sangyé Gyeltsen's decisions to take on their distinctive lifestyle were at all influenced by these contemporary South Asian yogins. Never in suggesting why Künga Zangpo and Sangyé Gyeltsen took on this lifestyle do the holy madmen or their biographers make any reference to the Indian ascetics of their day, instead citing tantric scripture or the *siddha*s of their own tradition from centuries past. It remains a possibility that they may have been inspired to take up this lifestyle in part because of seeing or hearing of contemporary South Asian ascetics dressing and acting in this way, but the records at our disposal give no specific evidence to that effect.

Performing Enlightenment

Among those who knew of the Practice of the Observance in fifteenth-century Tibet, it was generally agreed that one ought to have some degree of religious accomplishment before entering into it. In chapter 2, we saw how one of the Madman of Tsang's disciples asked him "how much experiential realization and what good qualities must one have on the inside" before taking on the garb of the Heruka and beginning the Practice.[42] In his response, Sangyé Gyeltsen suggested a rather lax set of requirements, saying that it would not be improper for someone to take on the garb of the Heruka as long as he maintained his tantric vows, was pure of intention, and worked for the benefit of the dharma. Other Tibetans at the time held the view that only a person who had achieved a very high level of meditative realization ought to engage in the Practice. For them, to adopt this lifestyle was, in effect, to assert oneself to have achieved such an elevated state.

This belief is thoroughly exemplified in the writings of Drukpa Künlé. Regarding those who assumed the external appearance of a tantrika, Drukpa Künlé is recorded in his *Miscellaneous Writings* as having said, "As for living in the manner of a realized one [*rtogs ldan byed pa*], one should have realization about the nature of reality [*gnas lugs rtogs dgos*]. For one to assume this appearance without understanding reality is like covering a donkey with the skin of a leopard." In Drukpa Künlé's understanding, there are those who have a high level of realization and can thereby justifiably take on the appearance of a tantrika—and then there are those who do not. Drukpa Künlé says that because he could not claim to have this level of realization, he would have been ashamed to be spotted wearing the tantric regalia.[43]

Elsewhere, in a verse listing his various disappointments with the religious culture of his day, Drukpa Künlé laments:

> Being a monk without maintaining the vows,
> doing the Observance without having realization,
> teaching the dharma without thinking about cause and effect—
> seeing these three things has made me oh so sad.

Showing how persistent a concern this was for Drukpa Künlé, in another verse he ironically proclaims,

> I prostrate to those who wear the Six Ornaments without realization
>   of reality!
> I prostrate to those who wear monks' robes without maintaining
>   the three sets of vows![44]

Drukpa Künlé was skeptical of many men who lived as monks during his time because he thought it unlikely that they actually observed the vows that in theory made them worthy recipients of the generosity of laypeople. He was similarly skeptical of those who made careers out of their reputations as tantrikas by doing the Practice and dressing in the bone ornaments of the Heruka, suspecting that they had not achieved a level of realization that would justify their doing so.

In another verse Drukpa Künlé observes,

> Asserting yourself to be Heruka,
> you ask the hosts of evil spirits for refuge,
> [but] do not know appearances to be a product of the mind—
> a life like that has been taught by the Sage to be a contradiction.[45]

Here Drukpa Künlé criticizes those who associate themselves with the deity Heruka, as it in some cases leads them to adopt an attitude toward the phenomena of the world that the Buddha has rejected as misguided. Elsewhere, Drukpa Künlé voices a criticism of those who went in for "crazy behavior":

> Speaking of "one taste," this is what you get:
> you eat a mixture of excrement and urine,
> and take enjoyment in clothes from a corpse, and human flesh,
> doing the crazy behavior of whatever happens—
> do not take that as the meaning of "one taste"![46]

In this passage and elsewhere, Drukpa Künlé seems concerned that certain individuals were making a show of norm-overturning behavior like eating filth and dressing in human remains, and referring to this as the practice of the yoga of "one taste" (*ro snyoms*). In Drukpa Künlé's view, doing such things would not be the way of one who truly viewed and experienced all phenomena with equanimity. In making a show of such a behavior, these individuals expose the fact that they have *not* achieved such a state.

In a long missive addressed to various members of the Tibetan religious community, Drukpa Künlé addresses those called "Destroyers [of Illusion]" (*zhig po*, short for *'khrul zhig*), a long-standing category that has a lot of overlap with the term "madman":

> To you all phenomena appear like a dream, like an illusion:
> with your mind to which gold nuggets and clods of dirt are the same,
> in the moment, you address things in the manner of a madman.
> But others abandon the victory banner of the maroon robe,
> and confuse dharmic and worldly activities.
> Treating everything with your senselessness, you take nothing into
>   account.[47]

Here Drukpa Künlé makes a clear distinction between, on the one hand, legitimate "Destroyers," who truly embody the ideal of regarding all phenomena as being of a single taste, whose activities look like those of a madman—and, on the other hand, those who are basically fakes. These misguided individuals have abandoned monasticism and taken on a life of questionable moral character, letting their "religious" activity become just another vehicle for their worldly pursuits.

Drukpa Künlé's comments provide a window into what some contemporaries may have thought about the eccentric behavior of Madmen of Ü and Tsang. Since we know that Drukpa Künlé criticized the Madmen of Ü and Tsang for various things, it is likely that they are included among those he means to chastise here.

Drukpa Künlé most often articulates his understanding of what kind of realization one should have before taking on the garb of the Heruka as "realization about the nature of reality" (*gnas lugs rtogs*). This refers to a deep realization about the fundamental nature of existence, which thereby releases one from the laws of karma—liberating awareness, what is often meant by the English term "enlightenment." In Drukpa Künlé's view, only the most spiritually advanced of people, who were extremely rare, would be justified in taking on this lifestyle.

Because of the widely held view that adopting the Practice of the Observance should be reserved only for the most highly realized, we can say that the dress and lifestyle of the Practice was part of the repertoire of enlightened behavior operative in fifteenth-century Tibet. To act in ways drawn from that repertoire was to put oneself forward as a liberated being. The repertoire of *siddha* behavior would have existed within this broader repertoire of enlightened behavior. If challenged on this matter, Künga Zangpo and Sangyé Gyeltsen could defend themselves by pointing to tantric scriptures and commentaries maintaining that one only needs to achieve "heat" before taking on the Practice, which is not full liberating awareness, but an early precursor to it. It may be that Künga Zangpo and Sangyé Gyeltsen were trying to shift people's perceptions about when it was appropriate to take up this form of practice. In the meantime, they benefitted from the common perception that only an enlightened being would or should take on this appearance and lifestyle—while simultaneously invoking the ire of others for this same reason.

In some ways this comes down to a question of whether the lifestyle of the Practice was viewed as an expression of one's nondual gnosis, or a means of achieving such a state. If focusing on the perceptions of the individual practitioner, we could say that those two things collapse into one: in the moment of performing this activity, he is enlightened. But if we take into account how other observers might have thought about this behavior, the issue can no longer be resolved so easily, since each person would have interpreted and responded to this activity in a different way.

The questions of what enlightenment was, how it was achieved, what kind of behavior would indicate its having been achieved, and so on, were debatable and always open to contestation. Because of this, when trying to reconstruct what it meant to be a *siddha*, to have had achieved liberating awareness, to be enlightened—however one phrases it—the historian must treat this as existing in the eyes of various beholders, rather than within the being of the saintly figure him- or herself.

"To Spread and Increase the Teachings of the Kagyü"

Throughout the biographies of the Madmen of Ü and Tsang there is much talk of their actions being undertaken for the benefit of all sentient beings or for the teachings of the Buddha in general. There are also many indications that the holy madmen felt partial to their own Kagyü sect, with a special interest in protecting its integrity and securing its future, which may have involved defining the sect in a particular way.

In the course of his career, the Madman of Ü showed himself to have had a strong sense of corporate identity, that he was part of some larger entity that ought to be perpetuated. He founded a series of centers dedicated to the practice of meditation, including the monastery that he passed on to his nephew. After a few of Künga Zangpo's close disciples died relatively young, he became concerned that his spiritual lineage might fizzle out. This motivated him to teach more actively, in hope of fostering his lineage. The Madman of Tsang had an even stronger sense of corporate identity, which is best understood through a consideration of the literature he composed and printed.

The affiliation most often expressed by the Madmen of Ü and Tsang is to the Kagyü sect in general. In many cases they refer to the sect as the Dakpo Kagyü, meaning the tradition that passed from Milarepa to Gampopa (who hailed from Dakpo), and branched outward from there. This term is used interchangeably with "Kagyü" throughout much of the literature. For example, a lama Namkha Wangpo once asked the Madman of Tsang, "What is your dharma tradition [*chos rgyud*]?" The great yogin replied, "My tradition is the one renowned as the Dakpo Kagyü." When the Madman of Ü instructed Nyukla Penchen to undertake the printing of some texts, he is quoted as having said that the student would thereby "faultlessly protect the teachings of the Buddha in general, and in particular the teachings of the peerless Dakpo Kagyü."[48]

More numerous than the madmen's making open declarations of allegiance to the Kagyü are instances where their biographers describe their activities as being undertaken for the purpose of benefitting the sect in some way. When the Madman of Ü laid down his monks' robes and took on the garb of the Heruka, Nyukla Penchen says that he did so for the purpose of benefitting the Kagyü, among other things. When the yogin sent some disciples to do virtuous works in different places across Tibet, this was, according to Lhatong Lotsāwa, to "spread and increase the teachings of the Kagyü."[49]

The same kind of concern is displayed in the various versions of the *Life of the Madman of Tsang*. In the earliest version of the *Life*, by Ngödrup Pembar, on a few occasions it is said that the activities of the Madman of Tsang and his disciples would make the teachings of the Kagyü "shine like the sun." Götsang Repa's version of the *Life* relates a dream in which the Madman of Tsang was visited by the Five Long Life Sister goddesses, who assured him that his compiling and printing of the *Life* and *Songs* of Milarepa would directly benefit the Kagyü teachings. The Madman of Tsang also received a letter from the Seventh Karmapa, Chödrak Gyatso (1454–1506) in which he was thanked for his various activities that helped to "spread and increase the teachings of the Kagyü."[50] For Künga Zangpo, Sangyé Gyeltsen, and those close to them, there was no question that a special concern to protect and promote the Kagyü played a role in motivating their undertakings.

Since their deaths, it has become somewhat commonplace to refer to the Madmen of Ü and Tsang as having been members of the Drukpa subsect of the Kagyü. The famous scholar Pema Karpo, the fourth of the Drukchen incarnation lineage (1527–1592), composed in 1575 a history of the Drukpa Kagyü in which he states that the Madman of Ü was, among the tripartite division of the Drukpa Kagyü into Upper, Middle, and Lower branches, part of the Upper branch (*stod 'brug*), which began with the famous yogin Götsangpa Gönpo Dorjé (1189–1258). The Madman of Tsang is listed in a grouping that would be considered the Middle branch (*bar 'brug*), associated with Ralung monastery.[51] Showing how unstable such affiliations can be, in his history of the Kagyü sect, the twentieth-century scholar Troru Khenpo Tsenam names the Madman of Ü, the Madman of Tsang, and the Madman of the Drukpa as among the amazing *siddhas* of the Middle Drukpa.[52]

The Madmen of Ü and Tsang received and passed on teachings that were or would come to be especially associated with the Drukpa Kagyü. What's more, the Madman of Tsang and his close disciples wrote and published biographies of many figures who were (or would be) specifically connected with the Drukpa Kagyü tradition. The early members of the lineage about whom they wrote—Vajradhara, Tilopa, Nāropa, Marpa, Milarepa, Gampopa, and Pakmodrupa—were all part of the lineage shared by most of the Kagyü subsects. But the later figures about whom they wrote—Lingrepa, Tsangpa Gyaré, Götsangpa, Yanggönpa, Shara Rapjampa, and so on—are not shared between all the Kagyü subsects, and are most strongly associated with the Drukpa Kagyü.

Although Künga Zangpo and Sangyé Gyeltsen were associated with the Drukpa Kagyü sect in various ways, there is no indication in their biographies or writings that they paid any special allegiance to it. In fact, the term Drukpa, in the sense of the Drukpa Kagyü, is hardly even used in their biographies.[53] In the more than one thousand extant pages of the Madman of Tsang's writings on the Aural Transmission, not once does the he mention any personal allegiance to the Drukpa Kagyü, instead expressing his allegiance in terms of the Kagyü in general or to the Aural Transmission itself. For these reasons, although the Madmen of Ü and Tsang would most often be labeled as Drukpa Kagyüpas by later Tibetans, there is little reason to think that they conceived of themselves as taking active part in something called the Drukpa Kagyü.

It may be worth mentioning the Tibetan adage:

Half of the people are Drukpa [Kagyüpas];
half the Drukpas are beggars;
half the beggars are *siddhas*.

This saying is attested to as early as Pema Karpo's 1575 history.[54] Although a sect that has been perceived in this way by so many Tibetans might seem a natural home for our madmen, they do not seem to have thought of themselves as members of a Drukpa subsect of the Kagyü. Part of the reason why Künga Zangpo and Sangyé Gyeltsen have come to be so strongly associated with the Drukpa Kagyü is people's connecting and to some extent conflating them with Drukpa Künlé, the "Madman of the Drukpa."

In a similar manner, although the Madmen of Ü and Tsang had connections with religious life at Drikung Til and Taklung monasteries, and
with the Karmapa and the Red Hat, their biographies bear no evidence
that they paid particular allegiance to something they perceived as the
Drikung, Taklung, or Karma subsect of the Kagyü, nor the Shangpa or
Pakmodrupa subsects.

It has also been suggested that the Madmen of Ü and Tsang should
be thought of as members of a particular subsect of the Kagyü, called the
Rechung Kagyü.[55] This is because they were intimately involved with a set
of teachings called the Aural Transmission (*snyan rgyud* or *snyan brgyud*),
which expand on the rituals and meanings expressed by the *Cakrasaṃvara
Tantra*. The transmission was passed from Milarepa to three of his disciples, but the most potent transmission was that which passed through
Rechungpa, and for this reason the entire body is sometimes referred to
as the Aural Transmission of Rechungpa. The Madman of Ü's biography mentions his having received Aural Transmission teachings on four
separate occasions. Later in his career, he would often transmit the Aural
Transmission to his disciples.[56] The degree to which Künga Zangpo's religious career was marked by these teachings is suggested by the fact that
one of the two texts composed by Drukpa Künlé for the Madman of Ü was
a praise of the Aural Transmission lineage.[57] The Madman of Tsang also
received the Aural Transmission teachings, then later transmitted them
on a number of occasions to disciples and lay patrons.[58] The Madman
of Tsang's special interest in the Aural Transmission teachings must
have been public knowledge, since we are told of how a man heard about
the Madman of Tsang as one who was "very learned in the *Two-Parted
[Hevajra Tantra]* and the Aural Transmission of Rechungpa" before ever
having met him.[59] Most importantly, the Madman of Tsang compiled a
massive collection of texts on the Aural Transmission, many of which he
wrote himself.

Although the Madmen of Ü and Tsang may have been integral in passing on the Aural Transmission teachings, we should nevertheless refrain
from thinking of them as having had a special allegiance to a Rechung
Kagyü, which term is never used in any of their biographies, and of which
the Madmen of Ü and Tsang show no evidence of having thought themselves a part. The biographies and writings of the Madmen of Ü and Tsang
strongly suggest that their primary allegiance was to what they put forth as
the Kagyü sect itself, rather than any subsect thereof. Rather than pigeon-
holing themselves as representatives of only one subsect of or lineage

within the Kagyü, they hoped instead to be seen as speaking for and representing the sect as a whole.

It also seems that through their larger activities and the rhetoric they employed, Künga Zangpo and Sangyé Gyeltsen set out to characterize the Kagyü tradition in a rather specific way. According to the *Life of the Madman of Ü*, Künga Zangpo's main guru, Drakchokpa Rinchen Zangpo, told him that he had become a master of the teachings of the Meditation Tradition (spelled *sgrub rgyud* or *brgyud*), and thus should stay in retreats and monasteries high above villages, away from those mired in the concerns of this life. Later, when establishing Tsimar Pel monastery, one of Künga Zangpo's students raised an objection, saying that instead of settling in one locale they should continue meditating in the mountains, moving from place to place as they had before. The great yogin assured him that they were establishing this monastery so that it may become "a shining example for the teachings of the Meditation Tradition."[60] In a text praising the transmission of Saraha's *Dohās*, which he wrote at the request of the Madman of Ü, Drukpa Künlé describes the yogin in the midst of that lineage in the following way:

> I supplicate the Madman of Ü, the Heruka,
> who rests at the peak of the lofty snow mountain of the Meditation
>   Tradition,
> descending in the ten directions in the unending streams of the
>   Aural Transmission,
> filling the whole sky with the crops of virtue.[61]

In the biography of the Sakyapa master Doring Künpangpa, Künzang Chökyi Nyima (1449–1524), written in 1538, the Madman of Ü, "who has reached the very pinnacle of the lords of yogins," is referred to in association with both the Meditation Tradition and the Dakpo Kagyü.[62]

Sangyé Gyeltsen also had a special concern for what he labeled the Meditation Tradition. He closes one of his compositions on the Aural Transmission by stating his hope that any virtue that may arise from his composing the work should go toward spreading the Meditation Tradition. In another composition he refers to the lineage from Tilopa all the way down to Shara Rapjampa as those who have maintained the Meditation Tradition. In the Madman of Tsang's version of the *Life of Milarepa*, he has Marpa refer to his teachings as part of the Meditation Tradition.[63]

The term also appears in the latter two iterations of the Madman of Tsang's biography. In Götsang Repa's version, the holy site of Lapchi is described as the "foundation stone for the excellent house of the teachings of the Meditation Tradition."[64] In Lhatsün Rinchen Namgyel's version, early in his life Sangyé Gyeltsen reflected on the impressive perseverance displayed by the great masters of Buddhism:

> On the banks of the Niranjana river, [Śākyamuni Buddha] practiced the "water austerity" for six years. In like manner, Peṇchen Nāropa, even though he had become learned in the five sciences, pleased his guru by performing many difficult tasks for twelve years. Like that, by performing difficult tasks, noble Mila accomplished whatever his guru said; by means of difficult tasks, he fulfilled his pledge of equating his very life with his practice, and spread the teachings of the Meditation Tradition. I, too, should accomplish the supreme *siddhi* in this lifetime by performing difficult tasks with fierce diligence.

Elsewhere in Lhatsün Rinchen Namgyel's version of the *Life*, Sangyé Gyeltsen is praised for having "made the teachings of the Meditation Tradition shine like the sun during a degenerate age."[65]

Over the years, many Tibetan Buddhists have relied upon the idea of a Meditation Tradition, often contrasted with an Expository Tradition (*bshad brgyud*), to characterize different trends within the religion and to explain their histories. The Indian masters who helped transmit the *Vinaya* (the code of monastic conduct) to Tibet are discussed as being members of either the Meditation or Expository traditions.[66] One master of the practice known as the Pacification [of Suffering] (*zhi byed*) purportedly instructed his disciple, "You stay in a mountain hermitage and propagate the Meditation Tradition. I will stay at Nyendo monastery and propagate the Expository Tradition." These examples suggest that meditation and formalized study (and teaching) of the dharma were seen as partially separable but equal pursuits.[67]

The term Meditation Tradition would also be appropriated by Kagyüpas as a way of referring to their sect specifically. According to Gö Lotsāwa's *Blue Annals*, one Kagyüpa instructed his disciple, "This tradition of ours is the Meditation Tradition, so meditation is more important [than study]. So apply yourself foremost to meditation." It is in this sense, as roughly synonymous with "Kagyü," that the Madmen of Ü and Tsang used the term.[68] To refer to the Kagyü sect as the Meditation Tradition is to foster the perception of its being the branch of Buddhism that places a greater emphasis on practice than on learning, the branch that prioritizes meditative experience as a source of truth over the speculations of reasoning and logic.

Künga Zangpo and Sangyé Gyeltsen both certainly dedicated a lot of effort to meditation, and can fairly be thought of as part of any Meditation Tradition that may have existed. (In his opening homage to the Madman of Tsang, Lhatsün Rinchen Namgyel describes the yogin as "the sun of the Teachings, who primarily teaches the Meditation Tradition from among the *expository* and *meditation* traditions.")[69] But their activities were by no means limited to the personalized act of meditation. Both actively participated in various ways in a competitive religious culture in which innovations were proposed, traditions were appealed to, and innovations were represented as old traditions. They engaged in these concerns through both their actions and the rhetoric they employed, on the registers of their interpersonal encounters and the broader battle of representations. The question of the terminology they used to refer to their beloved sect is one small example. This brings us to the question of how, as "madmen," Künga Zangpo and Sangyé Gyeltsen positioned themselves vis-à-vis other religious groups, and what larger struggles their distinctive lifestyles may have been meant to redress.

Tantric Literalism in Context: Competing Models of Buddhist Holiness

The trajectories of the lives of Künga Zangpo and Sangyé Gyeltsen suggest that celibate monkhood and their tantric literalist lifestyle were mutually exclusive pursuits. Before Künga Zangpo could undertake the Practice, it was necessary that he first give up his vows and robes. Sangyé Gyeltsen had been a monk for more than a decade before dramatically and vociferously renouncing that mode of religious life. What's more, after taking up their distinctive lifestyles, the two ascetics would have numerous dramatic encounters with monks who disapproved of their ways or doubted their spiritual worth. There are so many of these confrontations that they must be read not as chance encounters, but as indicative of how the Madmen of Ü and Tsang's lifestyles positioned them in relation to other religious groups of their day.

The monks with whom the Madmen of Ü and Tsang are shown having these confrontations are usually not ordinary monks, but those who have achieved an advanced degree of learning. In most cases they are referred to as *gewé shényen* or *geshé* (*dge ba'i bshes gnyen, dge bshes*). The Tibetan term *gewé shényen* is a translation of the Sanskrit *kalyāṇamitra*, which is often translated into English as "virtuous friend." In earlier Tibetan usage, it meant a good exemplar of Buddhist values upon whom one relied as a spiritual guide. In the late fifteenth century, the term was used in the Sakya and Geluk sects to refer somewhat generically to monks who had accumulated a lot of institutionalized learning.[70] It would still be some years before the term *geshé* would take the form we are familiar with today, specifically denoting one trained in the Geluk (or Bön) system who has passed a series of exams on a specific body of texts.

On one rather typical occasion, the Madman of Ü is said to have encountered a *geshé* while traveling through Kongpo. This *geshé* harbored doubts about the yogin, but pretended to have faith in him. He called for a tantric feast and invited the yogin to spend the night in the monastery. According to his biography, the Madman of Ü knew that the monk secretly doubted him, so he announced that he would not stay, and left, walking unimpeded through a solid wall on his way out. Upon seeing this miracle, the *geshé* became filled with faith, and Künga Zangpo's fame spread.[71]

Since Künga Zangpo never had a comprehensive clerical education, there are no stories about his debating with learned monks. Instead he would respond to their questions, criticisms, or doubts by performing a miracle, as a sign of his meditative accomplishment—and by extension, of the value of the tradition he represented. For example, a monk referred to as Jozang Sthavira once demeaned the Madman of Ü, charging, "All of this crude behavior of yours does harm to the Teachings. In particular, it is sickening that you should drink so much alcohol." The yogin responded, "You are not the only one who gets to say and recognize what is the Buddha's teaching. I wonder if any of us upholds the essence of the Victor's teachings? I do not harm the Teachings. You be careful!" He continued, "If you are so sickened by the consumption of alcohol, let's see if it is I, the yogin, who has been drinking alcohol, or you, Jozang." The Madman of Ü then made the monk vomit forth a large amount of alcohol, while a small bowl's worth of milk issued from his own mouth.[72]

In contrast, Sangyé Gyeltsen did have a thorough clerical education before taking on his tantric literalist lifestyle, and showed himself fully capable of engaging learned monks in debate. On one occasion the Madman of Tsang found himself arguing with four *geshés* "arrogant about their learning," regarding his views, meditation, and lifestyle, and how they related to scripture and reasoning. Although Sangyé Gyeltsen gave faultless answers to all their queries, the *geshés* still insisted that he was wrong. In frustration he charged that the *geshés* did not heed the valid means of knowing (*tshad ma*; in Sanskrit, *pramāṇa*) constituted by the word of the Buddha, direct perception, or the experience of a yogin, and as such they were refusing to play by the rules of the discursive game they themselves had initiated. So the Madman of Tsang handed spears to the scholar-monks, saying, "Stab me with these until you get tired. Otherwise, I'll stab you each one time." Terrified of the prospect, the *geshés* threw down the weapons and prostrated themselves before the great yogin. The reader cannot but form a very negative impression of the stubborn and hypocritical *geshés*—polar opposites of the brilliant and just Madman of Tsang.[73]

A key encounter between the Madman of Tsang and representatives of monastic learning was described in chapter 2. *Geshés* from Sera and Drepung monasteries—both of the Geluk sect—charged that the Madman of Tsang's manners of dressing and behaving were not actually Buddhist. When he defended his ways by referring to Buddhist deities, the eighty *mahāsiddha*s, and the tantric scriptures, the *geshés* charged that the age they lived in was not a time to be practicing tantra in so literal a manner. When he asked where that was written, they were unable to say.

Another encounter with a representative of the Geluk system is even more revealing. While staying near Mount Kailash, the Madman of Tsang held a gathering at which there arrived a representative of the Geluk system, known as a "Master of the Ten Texts of Ganden" (*dga' ldan bka'* [sic] *bcu pa*), accompanied by fifteen of his students. The scholar-monk did not partake of the *chang* that was being served at the gathering, which compelled the Madman of Tsang to ask, "Have you received tantric initiation? Have you studied and contemplated the ways of the tantras?" The Gelukpa related how he had become a monk at a young age, studied the great philosophical texts, the tantras and their commentaries, and had since done some amount of tantric practice. The Madman of Tsang asked the monk:

> Then why is it that, when sitting here in a profound tantric assembly at a holy place described in many of the *sūtra*s and tantras, you do not partake of the *samaya* substances [referring to alcohol and other sacramental substances consumed in the course of a tantric ritual]? Does that not constitute the second downfall of contradicting the word of the Sugata, and the thirteenth downfall of not upholding one's *samaya* vows?[74] If one commits a root downfall,

one will fall into Vajra Hell—isn't that taught in the tantras that you studied, like the *Guhyasamāja* and so on?

The scholar-monk's response was to say that the historical age they lived in was not a time to practice tantra literally, and that in Tibet there were no legitimate tantric gatherings (*tshogs 'khor, gaṇacakra*). The Madman of Tsang pushed him further, asking, "In what authentic tantra or treatise does it say that? If now is not the time to practice tantra [literally], when is?" The Gelukpa restated the fact that he was a monk adhering to the *Vinaya* and one who took after lord Tsongkhapa and his disciples, and would not, therefore, be drinking any alcohol. Three days after this encounter the scholar-monk vomited blood and died.[75]

Regardless of whether these stories are dramatizations or descriptions of actual events, they show how the tantric fundamentalist behavior of the Madmen of Ü and Tsang was meant to position them in the religious culture of their day. Clearly, Künga Zangpo and Sangyé Gyeltsen were positioned as polar opposites to the *geshés*, who represent a more scholarly and monastic form of Buddhism. The Madmen of Ü and Tsang are not so consistently portrayed as having this kind of adversarial relationship with any other group of religious practitioners—not other meditators, nor Nyingmapas, nor Bönpos or other non-Buddhists (although there are rather fantastic stories about the Madmen of Ü and Tsang converting Hindus during their visits to Nepal). It would seem that there was a special urgency to establish that the yogin embodying tantric fundamentalism stood as a direct foil to the *Vinaya*-following *geshé*, and that the most central point of difference between the madmen and the scholar-monks of their day was the question of how to interpret and enact the tantras—an issue their tantric literalist lifestyle brought unavoidably into the foreground.

Of special importance here is the fact that in many of these encounters, the monks or *geshés* with whom the holy madmen contended are specifically identified as members of the Geluk sect. The Geluk was founded by Tsongkhapa Lozang Drakpa at the beginning of the fifteenth century and spread quickly from then onward, rising to dominate Tibetan religious culture by the middle of the seventeenth century. Much more will be said about the rise of the Geluk sect in chapter 4. Here I shall restrict myself to discussing some of their views. Tsongkhapa's new Buddhist system placed great emphasis on the transformative power of reason, which served as the primary vehicle of spiritual advancement. For most monks, it was only after years of tirelessly refining his understanding of

the Madhyamaka presentation of emptiness that his emphasis would shift
to meditation and tantric practice. Gelukpa education consisted largely of
sustained exegesis on a circumscribed body of philosophical texts, often
mediated through textbooks (*yig cha*). Tsongkhapa's system also placed
great emphasis on conventional morality and was modeled on the gradualist path of the bodhisattva. Monasticism played a major organizing role.
Tsongkhapa prioritized reinstituting the Buddhist monastic code, the
Vinaya, which had been somewhat neglected in Tibet in the centuries that
preceded his time.[76] Gö Lotsāwa writes in his *Blue Annals* that there had
been a preponderance of derelict monks (*dge slong lhod pa*), but, thanks to
the example established by Tsongkhapa and his followers, "the teachings
of the *Vinaya* were made to shine like the sun in this land of Tibet."[77]

Tsongkhapa had great faith in the power, even the necessity of tantra
for the achievement of spiritual perfection. But for the vast majority of
the Geluk's career practitioners, maintaining the monks' vows was to take
precedence over an unreserved pursuit of tantric practice. It is often stated
in Geluk circles that if tantra were to become widely practiced, it would
end up being performed by some who were not thoroughly prepared for it,
which would lead to immorality and mistaken understandings, ultimately
bringing more harm than good. The Gelukpas held that the principle of
cause and effect was immutable, even in light of the ultimate emptiness of
all phenomena. Because of this, conventional morals still hold sway over
a tantric practitioner's actions. In his commentary to the chapter on ethics
in Asaṅga's *Bodhisattvabhūmi*, called *Basic Path to Awakening*, Tsongkhapa
specifically addresses and refutes the view that the tantric commitments
supersede the "lower" monk's and bodhisattva's vows. He even goes so far
as to say that those who hold that view "pollute the Teacher's dispensation
with the sewage of their sordid preoccupations. We who desire something
better should avoid them as we would poison."[78]

Although many basic tantric practices would be performed by monks
within the Geluk system, the more transgressive practices that would
endanger their vows would not. (Some even say that Tsongkhapa, in
order to avoid breaking his vow of celibacy, waited until he entered the
dream-like intermediate state after death, the *bardo*, before practicing the
sexual yoga needed to achieve ultimate liberation.) In Tsongkhapa's system, the aspects of tantric practice that would have caused one to break
one's monastic vows would be carried out symbolically, through visualization, or not at all.

As an example of this approach to the practice of the Unexcelled Yoga Tantras, in his *Fundamentals of the Buddhist Tantras*, Khedrup Jé Gelek Pelzang (1385–1438), one of Tsongkhapa's two closest disciples and a key figure in the establishment of the Geluk sect, shows how the transgressive elements of tantric practice that cannot be forgone could be visualized rather than performed literally. Khedrup Jé describes how, during the Secret Empowerment that opens the door to advanced tantric meditations, the guru should visualize his body as filled with deities and maṇḍalas, then have intercourse with the consort (the "awareness," *rig ma*; in Sanskrit, *vidyā*). After ejaculating, the guru is to scoop a bit of semen mixed with vaginal fluids out of the vagina and place the mixture onto the tongue of the disciple. This empowered substance produces in the disciple an understanding of the union of bliss and emptiness. But then Khedrup Jé clarifies, stating that "in our current age" (*da lta'i dus su*), the initiation can be performed in such a way that if the disciple is able to produce in himself the *conviction* that a substitute substance he is about to receive on his tongue is the product of the guru's copulation with the consort, the effect will be had, even if it is not actual semen derived from intercourse. Later, Khedrup Jé explains how during the Wisdom Empowerment the disciple would have traditionally had intercourse with the consort, which produces the four types of joy that help to deepen his understanding of the union of bliss and emptiness. Khedrup Jé then flatly states that during our historical age, no fully qualified (*mtshan nyid tshang ba*) fellowship of guru, disciple, and consort was to be found, and therefore the rite should be performed with the disciple only visualizing himself joining with the consort, which, if carried out with certitude, would have the desired transformative effect.[79]

In both Khedrup Jé's commentary and the passages cited from the *Life of the Madman of Tsang*, we have seen Gelukpas restate the view that different phases in the history of the world require different types of Buddhist practice. Although it may once have been appropriate to follow the tantras in a literal manner (when people and the age they lived in were more pure), that time has passed. What the current age calls for is a return to the unifying dictates of the *Vinaya*, which ensure moral behavior. The view expressed by Khedrup Jé represents but one of a variety of ways of enacting the tantras offered by exegetes of the Geluk, and was by no means new or unique to their system. But it gives a clear sense of how for most career practitioners of the Geluk, tantra was to be practiced within the confines of the behavioral expectations imposed by nontantric Buddhism. To enact tantra more literally, ungoverned by the monks' vows, was to expose one-self to great risk.

The holy madmen stood in contrast to all scholar-monks to some extent, but their contrast with the Gelukpas—who claimed that unfettered tantra was for a different period of world history, that tantra was to be con-fined to monasteries designated for that purpose, that it should be put off until after one had finished one's conventional education—was the stark-est. In their attempt to obey the letter of the tantras without compromise, remorselessly leaving the monks' vows to the wayside, the Madmen of Ü and Tsang embodied the very antithesis of the Geluk approach. It could be said that the model of the pious, *Vinaya*-following monk, which was the very cornerstone of the Geluk system, was the norm, the "sanity" against which the insanity of the Madmen of Ü and Tsang was defined.

Throughout the *Lives* of the Madmen of Ü and Tsang, scholar-monks and renunciants more dedicated to the practice of meditation are often listed as being of two different categories. When the Madman of Tsang gave teachings to a crowd of over five hundred people, it is said that this group included "*geshés*, male and female yogins, and so on." Throughout Götsang Repa's version of the *Life*, these different groups are often men-tioned as "lamas and *geshés*."[80] In the *Life of the Madman of Ü*, they are referred to as "*geshés* and ascetics."[81] The authors of these texts recognized that in the religious culture of their day, the lifestyles of career Buddhist practitioners were based on differing models of asceticism.

The holy madmen and their *geshé* foils are best thought of as distillations of two much broader competing trends. Geoffrey Samuel has suggested that Tibetan Buddhist culture should be understood as characterized by a "shamanic/clerical" divide. Benjamin Bogin has suggested that we think in terms of a "monk/*ngakpa* dichotomy," while Janet Gyatso has offered the categories of "exegetes" and "visionaries."[82] The adversarial interac-tions between the Madmen of Ü and Tsang and the representatives of monastic learning can be seen as an instantiation of these deep and long-standing tensions within the tradition. In Indian and Tibetan Buddhism there have always been two basic approaches, which are in some ways at odds with one another: is the primary vehicle to liberation formalized study, or meditation? Is logic to be our foremost guide, or experience? Do we place our faith in the didactic language of texts, or disregard it in its imperfection? At the heart of each approach is a specific understanding of the nature of truth—what that highest truth is, how it is established, and how an individual can come to see it. In Buddhism, where "the truth" is the means to liberation from the realm of rebirth in which we are all trapped, this concern is of paramount importance.

No school or sect of Tibetan Buddhism embodies either of these basic approaches fully, and any real-world religious formation will contain elements of both. As Carl Yamamoto is surely correct in pointing out, addressing this dichotomy as it stood in twelfth-century Tibet, this "issue is one of emphasis, and this is all the more reason to speak in terms of a conflict of *style*, not doctrine."[83]

Each of these basic understandings of truth was related to a whole complex of beliefs, practices, and institutions. Each model of truth led to the creation of certain institutions. Those institutions would then propagate their respective styles of Buddhism. Because of this dynamic, it is most accurate to think of these formations as competing "regimes of truth," as articulated by Michel Foucault. As Foucault puts it, " 'Truth' is to be understood as a system of ordered procedures for the production, regulation, distribution, circulation and operation of statements. 'Truth' is linked in a circular relation with systems of power which produce and sustain it, and to effects of power which it induces and which extend it. A 'régime' of truth."[84] The competing ideas of truth and enlightenment within the Buddhist tradition that so many scholars have referred to do not exist in the ether, but in relation to specific institutional structures—sects, lineages, monasteries, political orders, and the individuals who comprise them—that are invested in sustaining those ideas, and whose very existence or livelihood depends on those ideas of truth having currency.

In fifteenth- and sixteenth-century Tibet, some saw the scholar-monk as representing one distinct way, and the holy madman representing another—and the two were fundamentally, antagonistically different. The Gelukpa scholar-monks of the time were the epitome of one regime of truth, fully invested in reasoning, philosophical texts, and conventional morality. This was a regime of large-scale monasticism based on the *Vinaya*, and dedicated to the Geluk sect itself as a corporate entity. The Madmen of Ü and Tsang made themselves the epitome of an alternative regime of truth. As part of their Kagyü-centric program, they insisted that the dictates of the Unexcelled Yoga tantras superseded those of the *Vinaya*. They saw little use in the scholarly practices of memorizing texts, debating, and so on. Instead, they emphasized the need for meditation—hence their self-definition as the Meditation Tradition—and the literal application of the tantras. This regime was based on the model of the rare virtuoso practitioner, who abandons all to take on heroic ascetic trials, rather than the much laxer asceticism of the monastery-dwelling monk.

In the same way that the Madmen of Ü and Tsang's efforts to embody tantric fundamentalism should be seen as their adopting a rhetorical stance, rather than something more absolute, their antimonastic and antischolastic stance should also be seen as rhetorical in nature. Künga Zangpo and Sangyé Gyeltsen supported various monastic institutions through their endeavors, aligned themselves with prominent scholars, and had disciples who were monks. But publicly they embodied an identity that constituted a challenge to the ideals of monasticism and scholasticism. In the same manner, the Geluk was by no means purely dedicated to rationality and monasticism, and contained elements of the other approach within it. The difference was about emphasis, and what guiding metaphors were relied upon by each system.

Conclusion

In his compositions and their colophons, Sangyé Gyeltsen referred to himself by many different epithets: "the carefree madman," "the Heruka," "the yogin adorned with ornaments of bone," "the one who wanders in charnel grounds," "the king of the blood drinkers," and so on. Sometimes he referred to himself as "the yogin known by many different names."[85] This suggests—as of course there is no reason to doubt—that the Madman of Tsang had a complex understanding of the nature of his own identity: that he was not any one of these things, but all of them at once; that he would be the many different things people conceived of him as being.

In chapter 2 we considered Künga Zangpo and Sangyé Gyeltsen's eccentric lifestyle as it pertained to their personal religious practice, as a means to enlightenment. In this chapter we have begun to consider the social and this-worldly effects of their decisions to take on this lifestyle. This opens the door to a very different way of thinking about the holy madmen, one that considers the actual lived dynamics of sainthood as well as the specific historical situation in which their lives played out.

For one, Künga Zangpo and Sangyé Gyeltsen were public figures. They were only rarely in total withdrawal from society, and even then such withdrawal was only ever temporary, as they would eventually come back into contact with their (potentially) adoring public. There is much to suggest that Künga Zangpo and Sangyé Gyeltsen each had a strong sense of the sorts of ramifications his actions would have in the social sphere.

Moreover, Künga Zangpo and Sangyé Gyeltsen never acted in a vacuum, but in a rich cultural environment, where images, actions, and statements often carried palpable associations. Within the culture of their day, in the minds of their contemporaries, there were ideas of saintliness. To act in ways that associated oneself with those ideas was to draw from the repertoire of saintly behavior. Those various ideas of saintliness were not static or agreed upon by everyone; rather, they were perpetuated and contested by individuals and institutions affected by their relative levels of currency. Behind these divergent models of holiness were regimes whose very existence depended on them. The articulation of competing mythologies, through the creation of narratives of saints' lives and other literatures, was one means through which their competition in the real, embodied world was played out.

Having reached this point, we can address some of the meanings of Künga Zangpo and Sangyé Gyeltsen's "madness." Draped with bone ornaments and smeared with filth, cracking open the skulls of corpses and eating the brains, Künga Zangpo and Sangyé Gyeltsen were, to many who had trouble making sense of their behavior, walking freak shows— "madmen." To others, their behavior and the titles they assumed were expressive of having achieved a state of transcendence—they were "mad" insofar as they no longer lived according to the sorts of distinctions by which we ordinary, worldly people orient our lives. They were also "mad" as the Heruka was mad, placing them within a long tradition of "mad" or "intoxicated" deities and practitioners in the South Asian tradition. At the same time, in assuming this lifestyle and the title "mad," Künga Zangpo and Sangyé Gyeltsen were calling into question the Geluk model of religious practice that they had dramatically chosen to forgo. There is no reason to think their "madness" did not express a degree of playfulness, even irony. Künga Zangpo and Sangyé Gyeltsen's "madness" was also informed by a broader rhetoric of madness in Tibetan Buddhism, which will be explored in chapter 7. For Künga Zangpo and Sangyé Gyeltsen, their "madness," in name and behavior, meant many different things to many different people, and all of these things at once.

We should observe that the mere fact of taking on such an epithet, beyond the question of what it "meant," was an act of great significance— if the reader will allow it, even genius. By taking on the personas of "madmen," Künga Zangpo and Sangyé Gyeltsen were able to become much more than mere mortals. This epithet gave them each a potent one-word framework on which to hang a distinctive and memorable persona. During the time in which they lived and for the five hundred years since, Tibetans have imagined and ascribed a great many meanings to their "madness," making them the subjects of perpetual speculation and fantasy. The Madman of Tsang and the Madman of Ü both caught the attention of the Tibetan people—and in recent decades, many more besides—in ways they surely never could have had they remained simply Sangyé Gyeltsen and Künga Zangpo.

The next two chapters will further explore how Künga Zangpo and Sangyé Gyeltsen's decisions to base their public personas on a literal enacting of often-neglected chapters of the Unexcelled Yoga Tantras played out in the environment of exchange and intense competition—given shape by competing models of holiness, and by various worldly and other-worldly concerns—that was fifteenth-century Tibet. But first we will briefly digress to examine the relationship between Sangyé Gyeltsen and Künga Zangpo during the time in which they lived.

Intermezzo

THE RELATIONSHIP BETWEEN THE
MADMEN OF Ü AND TSANG

When dharma lord Möntsepa [Künga Lekzang, a close disciple of the Madman of Tsang] went to Drakar Taso, lord Madman of Ü was also there, and the two stayed together for a long time. Möntsepa praised the precious master [the Madman of Tsang] for his various good qualities, including being learned and accomplished in meditation, and especially for being very learned in the *Two-Parted*. This made the master from Ü want to study the *Two-Parted* under him.

The master from Ü arrived at Kangtsuk cave the day after they had completed a New Year's Eve offering. He asked for an audience, but the precious master was busy giving a teaching to Chödzé Abhaya. An attendant . . . hosted the dharma lord from Ü, along with some patrons who happened to be there. The dharma lord from Ü was offered a single ball of dough, while the patrons were given meat, *chang*, and the like. Angry, he tossed his dough ball down on the plate, snapped his fingers, gave his thighbone trumpet a fierce toot, and left. Some said, "Their connection [*rten 'brel*] as master and student is not good."

GÖTSANG REPA, *The Life of the Madman of Tsang*[1]

CONCERNING THE RELATIONSHIP between Künga Zangpo and Sangyé Gyeltsen, the available sources tell the following tale, which is both rich and mysterious.

According to Götsang Repa's *Life of the Madman of Tsang*, the first meeting between the two men occurred when Sangyé Gyeltsen and some of his students were traveling in western Tibet. At that time Sangyé Gyeltsen encountered the "'dharma lord of Ü,' at that time not yet famous as 'the Madman of Ü,'" whom some called "the Lama of [Densa] Til" or "the Mountain-Dwelling Lama." Sangyé Gyeltsen himself was already quite renowned by this time, since the king of Ngari Gungtang knew of him as a "mad yogin who could not be harmed by any weapon."[2]

When Sangyé Gyeltsen arrived at Dzongkar, the capital of Ngari Gungtang, he went to the king's palace. There he was attacked by weapon-wielding guards. He entered a profound meditative state and generated the divine pride of seeing himself as Hevajra, with eight faces and sixteen arms, trampling the four demons with his four feet. With his right hand raised high in the air, holding his *khaṭvāṅga* in his left, he leapt and danced about. All who saw him in this state became frozen in place. The yogin passed unimpeded into the palace, where he found the king asleep with his head resting on his queen's lap. The yogin stalked up to them unnoticed and slapped the king, waking him with a start. The queen, cowering in a corner, informed the king that a *siddha* had arrived. Unable to see in the darkness, the king felt the yogin's body with his hands and exclaimed that it felt like the body of a ghoul (*srin po*). The king offered the Madman of Tsang a gift of ivory earrings, and he and his entire retinue became devotees.

According to Götsang Repa's account, while the Madman of Tsang was staying at the palace, Künga Zangpo arrived, but was refused admittance. The guards kicked him and he began bleeding from his nose. People crowded around to see. The king announced that if this other yogin were equal to the Madman of Tsang, he should be able to prove himself impervious to weapons and fire. Therefore, he should be hit with swords and staffs, and burned with fire. If he came out unharmed, the king would receive him.

At this point the Madman of Tsang intervened, saying, "Regardless of whether or not he can endure such hardships, it is in principle inappropriate for you, a dharma king, to act in this way." Getting up to leave, he added: "In particular, nothing could be more shameful than for an ascetic [*bya bral ba*] to be killed outside while I am residing here. So I will not stay." In light of the Madman of Tsang's displeasure, the king rescinded his previous order and commanded that Künga Zangpo be let in and offered *chang. The Life of the Madman of Tsang* states that from then on the name "the Madman of Ü, Künga Zangpo, was renowned in every direction."[3]

This same occasion is described very differently in the *Life of the Madman of Ü*. In this version of events, after Künga Zangpo had exchanged his monks' robes for the attire of the Heruka, he spent some time meditating at important sites along the Tibet–Nepal border. Then he decided to "overpower with his glory" the king of Ngari Gungtang, reasoning that if he subdued this one lord, all the gods, demons, and people of Tibet would also come under his sway. So, wearing the garb of the Heruka, Künga Zangpo went directly into the king's palace, showing no fear of the guards, eunuchs, or dogs. He was absorbed in a meditative *samādhi* called "overpowering *saṃsāra* and *nirvāṇa*, all of phenomenal existence, with glory." Too shocked and terrified to move, no one was able to touch him. He went directly into the king's presence. After coming to their senses, some guards rushed in and threw Künga Zangpo out into the courtyard, where he was savagely beaten. He did not suffer any harm, meditating throughout the attack, uttering *hūṃ* and *phaṭ* and performing a ceremonious dance. The king and all his ministers and subjects recognized this remarkable sight as a sign of the yogin's meditative accomplishment and apologized for having attacked him. He was received in all their homes and was henceforth renowned everywhere as "the Madman of Ü."[4]

The Life of the Madman of Ü makes no mention of Sangyé Gyeltsen's being present in Dzongkar at the time. The similarities and differences between the ways the biographies of the two madmen describe this event, and the relationship between the yogins in general, will be returned to below.

The next point of contact between the two ascetics, according to Götsang Repa's *Life of the Madman of Tsang*, was the event described in the epigraph above. After hearing of the Madman of Tsang's accomplishments from one of his disciples, Künga Zangpo wished to study the *Hevajra Tantra* under him. But after Künga Zangpo perceived a slight in the way he was treated by one of Sangyé Gyeltsen's attendants, he left in a huff. People commented on the strained relationship between the two men.

Künga Zangpo and Sangyé Gyeltsen's relationship was not beyond repair, however. According to Götsang Repa's version of the *Life*, not long after this the Madman of Tsang held a special teaching session in order to heal a student who had become ill due to a blockage in the movement of the drops circulating in his yogic body. Sangyé Gyeltsen's bestowal of teachings and empowerments had the desired effect and the student was cured. But during this gathering, a pernicious spirit-being seized another of the attendees. Various attempts to exorcise the entity through ritual were unsuccessful. The lama Menlungpa was asked to perform a wrathful fire ritual (*sbyin sreg*; in Sanskrit, *homa*), which proved ineffective. The Madman of Ü was then asked to give a benediction. His blessing entailed beating some people, tossing about the provisions stored in the lower part of the house, and breaking all its pottery. He beat the afflicted man almost to death. But alas, it did not help. So the Madman of Tsang himself was asked to give a verbal blessing. The short, cryptic prayer he recited includes some lurid images—"tight vagina," "erect penis," and bees or donkeys rushing to crowd around an anus—interspersed with fragments of Sanskrit. After this the bedeviled man recovered. It was said that the fire ritual was unsuccessful because at that time the pernicious spirit was hiding in the riverbank, and that the Madman of Ü's violent blessing failed to have an effect because the spirit was then hiding behind a door.[5]

Götsang Repa's version of the *Life* tells of one last significant moment in the relationship between the two men. Sangyé Gyeltsen had sent some of his disciples on pilgrimage to the Swayambhūnāth stūpa in Nepal. When they returned from their pilgrimage, the students reported that they had had a fight with some of the Madman of Ü's disciples. Members of the two sides had exchanged insults and grown increasingly angry with one another. The friction between the two groups escalated until finally they clashed physically at a gathering while drunk on *chang*. The fight resulted in deaths on both sides.

Hearing this, the Madman of Tsang began to weep, lamenting that in the degenerate age in which they lived, even the representatives of the dharma lacked self-control. He was very upset for some time, crying often, unable to sleep. Then news arrived that six of the Madman of Ü's monks had harassed a group of about fifty of the Madman of Tsang's followers for many days, and that although they had practiced restraint and done nothing to retaliate, one of the Madman of Ü's disciples had stabbed and killed one of them. Killing people was not the way to uphold the teachings of the Buddha, Sangyé Gyeltsen insisted, and ordered his students not to kill anyone in retaliation.[6]

It seems that this spelled the end of the relationship between the two madmen, as Götsang Repa makes no further mention of any interaction between them. They may, however, have continued to share disciples.[7]

According to the most detailed version of the *Life of the Madman of Tsang*, the relationship between the Madmen of Ü and Tsang followed a winding and ultimately tragic course. In nearly every point of contact between the two yogins, the Madman of Tsang is portrayed as the superior of the two: more famous and respected, more learned and patient, more spiritually powerful. This text's version of things suggests that Sangyé Gyeltsen influenced his younger counterpart to take up the tantric literalist lifestyle, since Sangyé Gyeltsen was the first of the two to become established as a "madman," and it was only following an encounter with the Madman of Tsang that Künga Zangpo began to perform the Practice. The Madman of Ü is not mentioned in either of the other two versions of the *Life of the Madman of Tsang.*

The biography of the Madman of Ü is completely silent on these matters, for it does not make a single mention of the Madman of Tsang anywhere in its 150 folios. This raises a number of intriguing possibilities. Was it that the authors of Künga Zangpo's *Life* were resentful of the fame and success of the Madman of Tsang, and were thus moved to excise him from the history of their guru? Was it that Künga Zangpo had long tried to emulate the Madman of Tsang, and his loyal biographers were loath to admit this source of influence on the ways of their beloved master? Was Sangyé Gyeltsen written out of Künga Zangpo's story because of lingering bitterness over the dispute that had led to their students' murdering one another? Did they simply prefer to leave this embarrassing matter out of the historical record they were creating? Or was the Madman of Tsang removed from the story for some other reason entirely? It is unlikely that we shall ever be able to say for sure. This case serves as a perfect example of what it is these hagiographical texts tell us, what they do not tell us, and what the things they do not tell us might in fact reveal.

If Künga Zangpo and Sangyé Gyeltsen had hoped to spark a larger tantric literalist movement, they must be seen as having failed in the endeavor. Perhaps the outcome would have been different if they or their followers had been able to work more effectively together. As it stands, the story of the two madmen's relationship shows the individuals involved to have been perfectly, tragically human, all too human.

Civil War, Strategic Alliances

THE MADMEN OF Ü AND TSANG IN FIFTEENTH- AND
SIXTEENTH-CENTURY TIBET

In the Tiger year [1434] when I was twenty-seven,
the Pakmodrupa troubled times erupted.
The levies of the armies of Ü and Tsang
in a large sense divided Döl and Zhung in two.
The route of march for both the Great Army [of the Pakmodrupas]
and the Tsang army came through Bari Gang.

All the houses and homesteads were put to the torch;
the farming settlements were turned into cattle enclosures.
All the subservient were slaughtered on the knife;
ordinary folk were turned into beggars.

The powerful slew and were slain by the sword;
the weak perished upon the knife of hunger.
Villager was thrashing villager. At such a time,
ties of father and son and brother and brother were of no consequence.

Back and forth raged bitter feuds and defiling vendettas.
No wergild was extracted for the slaughter of men;
no pursuit was organized to follow the looted property.
Time passed in looting, banditry, and murder.

MÖNTSEPA KÜNGA PELDEN (1408–75), *The Story of External
Difficulties Endured*[1]

IN THE LONG history of those renowned as holy madmen in Tibet, no
period has been more significant than the second half of the fifteenth century, which included the activities of the three most famous such figures,
all born in the central Tibetan regions of Ü and Tsang between 1452 and

1458. This chapter explores why it was at this time that the phenomenon achieved its greatest level of prominence.

The verses quoted here give a sense of the destruction and violence that occurred as a result of the protracted struggle for control of central Tibet between the Pakmodru and the Rinpung political regimes—and their many allies and proxies—which played out over the course of a century, beginning in 1434. The Pakmodrupas, based in Ü, lost their position as the de facto rulers of central Tibet for some eighty years, then regained it. The rebel Rinpungpas, based in Tsang, rose up from beneath the Pakmodrupas, dominated them for some time, then underwent a swift decline. The battle between these two factions was fought primarily through political maneuvering and military campaigns. But this battle was also fought in the cultural sphere, as each faction supported certain Buddhist individuals and institutions that were in various ways aligned with their respective agendas, and which were in competition with one another. These interconnected struggles—between warring families, between the regions of Ü and Tsang, between Buddhist sects, and between the different interpretations of Buddhism put forth by those sects—created the circumstances amid which Künga Zangpo and Sangyé Gyeltsen rose to prominence via their tantric literalist lifestyles.

The Pakmodru–Geluk Partnership

The Pakmodru regime was established in the middle of the fourteenth century when a man named Jangchup Gyeltsen (1302–1364) headed a successful rebellion against the ruling Sakyapas. The Khön family at the center of the Sakya sect had been ruling Tibet on behalf of the Yüan dynasty (Mongols who had conquered China). From his appointment as provincial governor (*khri dpon*) of the Nedong district, Jangchup Gyeltsen formed strategic alliances and fought openly with the Sakyapas. In the 1350s, he became the dominant political force in Tibet, outstripping the Sakyapas after their Yüan backers entered a period of decline. In 1354, Jangchup Gyeltsen was awarded the title of *Tai Situ* ("chief minister") by the Mongol emperor of China in recognition of the overlordship he had achieved.[2]

After the time of Jangchup Gyeltsen, the dynasty descended to other members of the Lang clan. The seat of their worldly power was at Nedong, near modern-day Tsetang in the district of Lhokha, south of Lhasa. Generation after generation, this family held the abbacy of nearby Densa Til monastery, which was the seat of the Pakmodru subsect of the Kagyü. They also controlled nearby Tsetang monastery. The political regime was referred to as the Pakmodrupas, named after the subsect of the Kagyü they were all-but synonymous with, since they drew much of their moral authority from their association with the venerable Densa Til.[3] Early on, the head of the Pakmodru government was referred to as the *desi* (*sde srid*), meaning something like "regent" or "governor"; later he was called *gongma* (*gong ma*), "superior one," which carried the meaning of "emperor." Most of these successive rulers lived for some time as celibate monks, before or during their rule. Most also served as abbot of Tsetang or Densa Til monastery, before, during, or after their tenure as rulers. The Pakmodru dynasty would remain the titular, de jure rulers of Tibet until the establishment of the Tsangpa Desi regime in Shigatsé in the 1560s. However, by the mid-1430s their authority was being severely undermined by their former vassals, the Rinpungpa family.

Before experiencing this decline, the Pakmodru regime had been instrumental in the establishment of the Buddhist sect that would come to be known as the Geluk. Tsongkhapa Lozang Drakpa came to central Tibet from Amdo in 1372. The brilliant monk studied the existing sects under some of the most learned masters of the time. His primary allegiance was to the Kadampa tradition, which was then nearly defunct. As a new system based on Tsongkhapa's writings and personal example took root, it was sometimes called the New Kadampa, but also the Gandenpa or Gendenpa, and later the Geluk (*dge lugs*), which means "Virtuous Tradition."

The Pakmodru regime took a shine to Tsongkhapa and played a decisive role as patron of the overachieving monk and his disciples, effectively bringing a new sect to life. As has been widely observed, there seems to have been a strategic intent behind this relationship. Tsongkhapa's conservative religious system appealed to the Pakmodrupas as a means to promote a rule of law based on Buddhist morality. As Matthew Kapstein has summarized, "The emphasis in Tsongkhapa's teaching on strict adherence to monastic regulations and to the ethical guidelines of the Mahayana comported well with [the Pakmodrupas'] desire to reinforce clerical and public mores. In short, Tsongkhapa was a living exemplar of the very values the Pakmodrupa regime sought to uphold."[4]

Gongma Drakpa Gyeltsen (1374–1432) helped propagate the Geluk approach by commanding the printing of Tsongkhapa's works, and even forcing some members of other sects to study Geluk philosophy.[5] Even more instrumental to the rise of the Geluk was the Pakmodru regime's direct financial support. The Pakmodrupas' patronage commenced in 1409, when Tsongkhapa instituted the annual Great Prayer Festival in Lhasa. *Gongma* Drakpa Gyeltsen served as a patron for this undertaking, along with one of his ministers, Namkha Zangpo, the local administrator (*rdzong dpon*, "official in charge of the fort") of Neudzong, whose domain included Lhasa. He had been appointed to this position by *gongma* Drakpa Gyeltsen himself. Collecting taxes on behalf of his sovereign would have made up a large part of his duties.[6] Later in 1409, Tsongkhapa founded Ganden monastery, thirty-five miles east of Lhasa. The main patron for this venture was Drakarwa Rinchen Pel, local administrator of the Taktsé district in which the monastery was located, with *gongma* Drakpa Gyeltsen also providing financial support. Ganden quickly grew into an important center of religious activity, with five hundred monks in residence by the end of its first year.[7] Drepung monastery (which would become the largest monastery in Tibet) was founded just outside Lhasa in 1416 by a disciple of Tsongkhapa's, made possible by patronage again from Namkha Zangpo.[8]

In 1418, the ruler of the town of Gyantsé, Rapten Künzang Pak (1389–1442), sponsored the expansion of the Pelkhor Chödé monastic complex to include a Geluk section. He had served as chamberlain (*gzims dpon*) under *gongma* Drakpa Gyeltsen and still held some official position in the Pakmodru administration. He was a major supporter of Khedrup Jé, one of Tsongkhapa's main disciples.[9] The Pelkhor Chödé now housed schools for the study of the Geluk, Sakya, Kālacakra, and other systems; it was within a Sakya subcollege focusing on the *Hevajra Tantra* that Sangyé Gyeltsen studied before leaving to pursue his more ascetic lifestyle.

The last of the "Three Seats" (*gdan sa gsum*) of the Geluk sect, Sera monastery, was established near Lhasa in 1419 by another of Tsongkhapa's disciples, Jamchen Chöjé Śākya Yeshé (1354–1435). The available records are unclear regarding the early patrons of this monastery, but it seems Namkha Zangpo was likely a major contributor. The establishment of the monastery was also enabled by riches Jamchen Chöjé had received during his visit to the Ming emperor in Beijing. He had been sent there on behalf of Tsongkhapa when he was invited around 1408.[10]

The Geluk sect continued to expand rapidly throughout the fifteenth century, thanks in large part to support from Pakmodru lords and their allies. The Gyümé and Gyütö institutes for the study of tantra were founded in Lhasa in 1433 and 1474.[11] Beyond these, in the fifteenth and early sixteenth centuries in Lhasa and nearby areas—Taktsé, Medro Gungkar, Penyül, Tölung, and Chushül—there were at least thirteen other new Geluk monasteries and three nunneries, and at least ten monasteries and nunneries that were converted to the Geluk from other systems.[12] By the early sixteenth century, there were at least thirty-six Geluk institutions within fifty miles of Lhasa. The Gelukpas were also founding monasteries in other areas of Ü, Tsang (Tashi Lhünpo was founded in Shigatsé in 1447, by the posthumously recognized First Dalai Lama, Gendün Drup, 1391–1474), Kham, Amdo, and even Beijing, where Jamchen Chöjé founded the Huangsi or "Yellow Temple" during his stay.[13] The Geluk was also expanding in the western quarters of the Tibetan world, and quickly grew powerful enough to supplant the Drikung Kagyü as the main religious force in Ladakh, converting Kagyü monasteries to their system.[14] One Tibetan scholar has counted fifty-eight monasteries founded or converted by Tsongkhapa and his direct disciples in Ü, Tsang, and western Tibet; twenty-six in Kham; and three in Amdo. If we were to include monasteries founded or converted by Tsongkhapa's grand-disciples or other associates, these numbers would be much higher. Within a century of the founding of Ganden there were well over a hundred Geluk monasteries and nunneries across Tibet. The meteoric rise of the sect would continue: at the time of writing his *Yellow Beryl* in the late seventeenth century, Desi Sangyé Gyatso (1653–1705) counted 173 Geluk monasteries in Kham alone.[15]

This rough accounting gives a sense of the fervor with which the Geluk sect spread. The historian Hortsang Jikmé has noted that even though the Tibetan religious world was already suffused with the Nyingma, Sakya, Kagyü, Jonang, and other sects, the expansion of the Geluk in central Tibet, Kham, Amdo and even Mongolia was as dramatic as a "wave of fire hitting a store of gasoline."[16]

It seems that the Pakmodrupas understood their support for the budding Geluk sect as a means to achieving a number of goals, beyond fostering a general moral order. For a few centuries leading up to this time, Lhasa had been gaining in importance as the center of the Tibetan world. By aligning themselves with a new sect based in that city, and by directly sponsoring large monasteries in and around Lhasa, the Pakmodru regime would gain a significant foothold there. What's more, the annual Great Prayer Festival initiated by Tsongkhapa brought citizens from all over Tibet to Lhasa for a shared experience of Buddhist teachings, ritual and celebration, and would serve as an effective means for the Pakmodru regime to promote unity and make a symbolic assertion of its hegemony. Running the Great Prayer Festival also had implications for the year-round administration of the Jokhang temple, which housed the Jowo Śākyamuni statue. This holy object was of immense symbolic importance, at the very heart of Lhasa and the entire Tibetan world.[17]

The monastic tradition initiated by Tsongkhapa and his disciples also offered the Pakmodru administration a means to expand its reach, both literally and symbolically, across the whole of Tibet. The religious system formulated by Tsongkhapa was easily institutionalizable and inherently institutionalizing. The Geluk was doctrinally more systematic and streamlined than other sects operating in fifteenth-century Tibet. Whereas the other sects had accreted disparate texts and interpretations over long periods of time, the Geluk curriculum was formulated relatively quickly, based on writings by Tsongkhapa and his direct disciples, and their interpretations of classical Indian and Tibetan treatises. Because the Geluk system prioritized formal study over meditation or spiritual charisma passed on through familial or guru–initiate relationships, it was less dependent on the charisma of a certain place or individual (living or dead) for its spiritual vitality. It could thus be scaled up more easily than other models of Buddhist praxis. Scholars have noted that the rapid spread of the Geluk sect was facilitated by recent innovations in printing. During the time of Tsongkhapa, the use of woodblocks to mass-produce works of literature was in the process of becoming widespread. This technology greatly expedited the implementation of the Geluk's textual curriculum.[18]

Key to the early spread of the Geluk was the organization of their monastic network and their missionary zeal. Small and mid-sized monasteries were formally affiliated as "branch" (*yan lag*) institutions of one of the Three Seats. The brightest monks of small, village-level monasteries would transfer to regional centers, and the most capable among those would move on to Lhasa for further study. After completing their education in Lhasa, monks were encouraged to return to their native areas and found new monasteries. Because of the relative homogeneity ensured by the standardized curriculum and uniform monastic regulations, exchange between these monasteries was highly fluid. Within the larger monasteries there were regional houses—dormitories in which all the monks from a particular region would live. This guaranteed that monks arriving from afar would have ready-made networks of support and would be surrounded by individuals who spoke their same dialect of Tibetan. In a monastery's more official settings, the highly formalized system of debate gave all Geluk monks a means of communicating with one another, regardless of their often having mutually incomprehensible mother tongues. The Geluk monastic network spread outward from its hub in Lhasa and soon covered most of Tibet.[19]

In these various ways the Geluk was substantially different from the other Buddhist sects operating in fifteenth-century Tibet. The Kagyü was fragmented into many subsects and transmission lineages, and its emphasis on meditation over exegesis prevented it from developing into a unified large-scale institution. The Sakya was tied to the charisma of its founding family, and had been in decline since Jangchup Gyeltsen's rebellion and the loss of its Yüan backing. The Nyingma had little corporate identity or structure. In contrast, Tsongkhapa's system offered the possibility of a vastly more unified religious tradition, and was well poised to expand. It offered a new (but not sui generis) way of understanding the world, and with it a new set of power relations. Whether or not the Pakmodru rulers were consciously aware of the sorts of outcomes supporting the Geluk would make possible, they entered into a strategic, symbiotic relationship with the sect, which would expand their sphere of influence in central Tibet and beyond. The Pakmodrupas continued to support branches of the Kagyü— the Pakmodru, Taklung, and Karma—but in a greatly diminished fashion.

Within a century of its founding, the Geluk sect achieved an enormous market share in the Tibetan religious world, symbolically and materially. First, there was the ongoing competition between the sects to position their particular brand of Buddhism at the center of Tibetan religious culture. As the Geluk sect became more prominent, it put forth its ideals, stirring up debate over which was the supreme model of Buddhist religiosity. The other sects were forced to conform to or rebut the assertions made by the newcomers, but either way the conversation increasingly took place on the Gelukpas' own terms. Second, the rise of the Geluk caused declines in the material fortunes of the other sects. The construction of so many Geluk monasteries and the upkeep for these legions of monks were possible only through a huge influx of resources. Money, land, labor, building materials and food supplies were all required. Little grows on the high-altitude Tibetan plateau, in the immense rain shadow of the Himalayas, so the margins of subsistence there are always thin. The intense pooling of resources in the service of one sect had a palpable negative effect on the material well-being of the others.

The swift rise of the Geluk was most threatening to the Kagyüpas, especially the Karmapas themselves, who had the most to lose in the central Tibetan religious world. At least six Kagyü monasteries in the Lhasa area were converted to the Geluk during this period—only the tip of the iceberg in terms of sectarian tension.[20] *The History of the Drikung Kagyü* (written in 1803) asserts that during the fifteenth century, the Drikung Kagyü order came under threat and went into decline: beyond the fact that some of its monasteries in Amdo, Kham, Ü, Tsang, and western Tibet were formally converted to the Geluk, it is said that during the fifteenth century, some of their teachers were led to neglect the Meditation Tradition. In his later retelling, the historian Rasé Dawa Könchok Gyatso inserts a comment (perhaps hyperbolic) that during this time, their "dharma tradition" (*chos rgyun*) was becoming like that of the Geluk, so that the excellent dharma of the Kagyü was on the verge of dying out at many of the important seats of the Kagyü, including Densa Til, Tsurpu, Drikung Til, and Dakla Gampo monasteries.[21]

Note should be made here of the importance of patronage from abroad. One factor motivating the jockeying between the Buddhist sects at this time was the prospect of gaining the attention and favor of powerful, wealthy patrons outside Tibet, and maintaining those relationships once established. Tibetan religious hierarchs or their emissaries would travel to the Chinese capital to give blessings and teachings and to bestow gifts. The gifts they received in return were disproportionately large. These richly-laden caravans traveling between China and Tibet were sometimes attacked by bandits. Throughout the fifteenth century, the Karmapas had enjoyed the favor of the emperors of the Ming dynasty. Between 1436 and 1450, the Sixth Karmapa, Tongwa Dönden (1416–1453), sent eight of these missions, which were so costly to the Chinese emperors that in 1453 they issued a decree limiting their frequency. As invitations started to be extended to members of the Geluk sect, there must have been a perception that an important source of funding for the Kagyü might soon be lost. The fact that there has been some debate over whether a mission sent by the Chinese emperor at the beginning of the sixteenth century was meant to invite back to Beijing the Eighth Karmapa or the posthumously recognized Second Dalai Lama, Gendün Gyatso (1475–1542), may be indicative of the rivalry between the two camps at the time.[22]

The Rinpung Revolt

The family that would come to be known as the Rinpungpas was of the Ger clan, which proudly traced its history as a source of reliable government ministers back to the time of earliest kings of Tibet. Around the turn of the fifteenth century, *gongma* Drakpa Gyeltsen appointed one of his faithful subordinates, Namkha Gyeltsen, to be local administrator of the Rinpung district in Tsang. The family would hold the position for generations, and took Rinpung as a name.[23]

After the death of Drakpa Gyeltsen in 1432, there was an internal dispute among the Pakmodrupas over who should assume the throne. Two years later the issue boiled over, so that 1434 came to be called "the year of the collapse of the house of Pakmodru." The event was also called "the great revolt of the tiger year" in later histories.[24]

Seizing upon the Pakmodrupas' weakness, the Rinpungpas began to defy their superiors. They expanded their holdings in Tsang, taking control of some minor districts near their home territory. Other powerful families in Tsang broke with the Pakmodrupas and aligned themselves with the Rinpungpas. At some point between the late 1430s and the mid-1440s, the Rinpungpas took control of Shigatsé, one of the three main cities of central Tibet, which would be key to the expansion of their influence. As the Gelukpa historian Sumpa Khenpo (1704–1788) dryly states in his *Chronological Tables*, in the year 1435 "the Pakmodrupas lost the Tsang region to the Rinpungpas."[25]

Historians writing about the time period all recognize that from the mid-1430s on, most of the political power in central Tibet was held by the Rinpungpas. But the Rinpungpas never received official recognition from the Ming emperor. Throughout this period, Chinese ambassadors continued to visit Nedong, renewing the Pakmodrupas' official mandate by granting the title of *wang* (rendered in Tibetan as *dbang* or *wang*) to the successive *gongma*s. Nevertheless, at times the *gongma* could not even travel to visit the territories officially under his domain in Tsang.[26]

Despite their de facto sovereignty, the Rinpungpas were never powerful enough to entirely dismantle the Pakmodru administration. Instead, they sought to maintain a shell of the Pakmodru government at Nedong while exercising real power from their stronghold in Tsang. Throughout these years the Rinpungpas took various measures to weaken the Pakmodrupas by dividing them, and to keep an ineffectual or very young *gongma* on the throne. Meanwhile the Pakmodrupas bided their time until they could close ranks, reestablish alliances with third parties, and strike back against their usurpers.

The positions held by Rinpungpas in the Pakmodru administration and the ambivalent marriage ties between the two great families give a sense of the complex relationship between the two factions. Despite the Rinpungpas' making war on the Pakmodrupas and their allies, they continued to serve in the Pakmodru government, as they had prior to their rebellion. When historical records list the important ministers during the reign of each Pakmodru *gongma*, members of the Rinpungpa family are always prominent among them. The Rinpungpas are described in the *Song of the Queen of Spring*, written by the Fifth Dalai Lama, Ngawang Lozang Gyatso (1617–1682), as "those who steered the great chariot of the *gongma desi's* [i.e., the Pakmodru *gongma's*] government."[27] The most significant member of the Rinpung family working within the Pakmodru government was Tsokyé Dorjé (1450–1510/13), great-grandson of Namkha Gyeltsen, who was first appointed local administrator of Rinpung. When the *gongma* Ngaki Wangpo (1439–1491) died, his son Ngawang Tashi Drakpa (1488–1563/64) was still a baby. For the next eight years or so, Tsokyé Dorjé ruled as regent on the child's behalf, a situation histories refer to as "using the seal, [i.e.] replacing the master." Ngawang Tashi Drakpa assumed the throne in 1499, amid a great ceremony put on by the Rinpungpas. The young *gongma* would be a pawn in the hands of the Rinpungpas for some years, until other players in central Tibetan affairs—both noblemen and religious figures—aligned themselves with his family's cause in order to check the influence of the Rinpungpas, who some feared had become too powerful.[28]

Throughout the fifteenth century, the Rinpungpas formed various marriage ties with the Pakmodrupas. To describe just a few of these, shortly after Künga Lekpa (1433–1482/83) had become *gongma* in 1448, at the age of fifteen, he married Chöpel Zangmo of the Rinpung family. There was perpetual tension between the *gongma* and his wife, which drove the politics of the region for some years, as various noble families sided with the *gongma* or his wife during their many disputes and took advantage of the Pakmodrupas' weakness to expand their own influence. Chöpel Zangmo and her son died rather suspiciously in quick succession around 1476.[29] After the Rinpungpas invaded Nedong, Künga Lekpa was forced to abdicate in 1481. A few years after Ngawang Tashi Drakpa was placed on the throne by the Rinpungpas in 1499, he married a daughter of the most infamous of the Rinpungpas, Dönyö Dorjé.[30]

These marriage ties drew the Rinpungpas ever closer to the seat of official power. They created divisions among the Pakmodrupas and gave the Rinpungpas further grounds on which to demand official appointments. There were other powerful noble families who acted as independent agents throughout this conflict, including those who administered Neudzong, Chongyé, Yargyap, Samdé, and other areas. At times they loyally supported the Pakmodrupas, at others aligned with the Rinpungpas. The exchange of women was one means through which the shifting relationships between these groups played out.

While this maneuvering between the Rinpung and Pakmodru regimes was going on, the Rinpungpas conducted a series of military campaigns, whose violence profoundly affected the lives of many common people and laid the foundation for the Rinpungpas' power. We can best understand the regime's military endeavors by looking at the career of the Rinpungpa Dönyö Dorjé (1463–1512), great-great-grandson of Namkha Gyeltsen and the most important supporter of the Madmen of Ü and Tsang.

In his youth, Dönyö Dorjé received a good education, showing an aptitude for military, political, and religious matters. He also served as a sort of apprentice, working in various forts or administrative centers (*rdzong*) controlled by his family. As an adult, he would sire children with a noblewoman of Samdé; with the wife of the provincial governor of Nakartsé (whose company it seems he purchased with extensive gifts); and with a third woman.[31]

This was a chaotic period and the received histories disagree on some details concerning the military campaigns of the Rinpung faction under Dönyö Dorjé. To simplify matters, the presentation of events given here will for the most part follow the description offered by Peṇchen Sönam Drakpa (1478–1554), an influential thinker of the Geluk sect and a member of the Lang clan, in his *New Red Annals*, a history of Tibet from its earliest kings to the time it was written in 1538. Peṇchen Sönam Drakpa relates the history of the late fifteenth and early sixteenth centuries by telling the stories of the families that controlled the major districts of central Tibet, noting their shifting relationships with the Pakmodrupas and the Rinpungpas throughout.

According to the *New Red Annals*, in 1480, at the age of about seventeen, Dönyö Dorjé led an army of the Rinpungpas' and their allies' troops into the heart of Pakmodru territory, entering the Yarlung valley and seizing the seat of the Pakmodrupas' power. A great meeting of noblemen was held at Nedong, officially recognizing the Rinpungpas' new position of dominance. Tsokyé Dorjé was named, "chief minister" (*blon chen*; this was ten years before he became regent). This year or the following one, *gongma* Künga Lekpa and other Pakmodru officials were removed from their positions. The young Ngaki Wangpo was placed on the throne as the next *gongma*. Because Ngaki Wangpo was the last remaining heir to the Pakmodrupa line, the dynasty found itself in a precarious position. During this campaign, the Rinpungpas also seized some holdings near Lhasa, including Lhünpo fortress in Chushül and estates belonging the lord of Neudzong.[32] Some sources state that during this campaign, Dönyö Dorjé's troops also attacked Ganden monastery, but they were turned back because of rituals performed by its abbot, Mönlam Pelwa (1414–1491).[33]

In 1485, the Rinpungpas attacked the town of Gyantsé in Tsang. *The New Red Annals* state that the rulers of Gyantsé had provoked the Rinpungpas into attacking them by raising an army and boasting of their strength.[34]

In 1492, some of the nobles in the Yarlung area became unhappy with Tsokyé Dorjé's administration as regent, which did not involve consulting with other powerholders. In response, Dönyö Dorjé again invaded Ü, taking control a few more districts. The campaign ended with a peace agreement.[35]

In 1498, Dönyö Dorjé, supported by troops supplied by Tashi Dargyé of the Ja district, invaded Lhasa. They seized holdings of Sera and Drepung monasteries, as well as those of the lord of Neudzong and other noblemen in the area. Some nobles fled, while others chose to defect to the Rinpungpas' side. The Rinpungpas would maintain control of Lhasa for the next twenty years, staying in an encampment near town. During this period, the Rinpungpas assumed responsibility for the public good at such trying times as 1500, when the area was hit with drought, famine, and epidemics. The Fourth Red Hat, one of the highest-ranking reincarnations of the Karma Kagyü, also performed a ritual consecrating the local water dikes. The Rinpungpas and the Karma Kagyü were not just occupying Lhasa, but attempting to establish themselves as the rightful and legitimate rulers of the area.[36]

In 1499, Dönyö Dorjé was in Nedong, where he played an important role in the installation of the twelve-year-old Ngawang Tashi Drakpa as *gongma*.[37] In 1509, having come of age, Ngawang Tashi Drakpa began to assert himself. He picked a quarrel with an ally of the Rinpungpas (the father of one of Dönyö Dorjé's wives) in a way that he would not have done in an earlier time. A wedge was growing between the *gongma* and the

Rinpungpas. Tsokyé Dorjé died in 1510. Around this time, Tsokyé Dorjé's son attacked an independent estate, apparently alienating some of the Rinpungpas' allies is the process. The Red Hat, who had been growing closer to the *gongma* and was somewhat estranged from the Rinpungpas, ordered that the Rinpungpas make restitution. To this end, Dönyö Dorjé arranged a formal meeting, during which he made displays of homage and devotion to the *gongma*. He offered the *gongma* a minor estate and some gifts of small value, which constituted an obvious slight. As an expression of his displeasure, the *gongma* began giving these gifts away to other nobles, which offended Dönyö Dorjé. With the conflict still unresolved, the great warlord died in 1512.[38]

Historical records refer to Dönyö Dorjé by a variety of titles, some of which recognize that he was the de facto ruler of central Tibet for some years.[39] As an indication of Dönyö Dorjé's status at the peak of his power, the second of the Pawo incarnation lineage, Tsuklak Trengwa (1504–1564/66), refers to Dönyö Dorjé in his history, the *Scholar's Feast* (written in 1545), as "the lord of the four horns of Ü and Tsang." The biography of the Seventh Karmapa included in the *Scholar's Feast* shows a glimpse of Dönyö Dorjé at the height of his glory: when Dönyö Dorjé invited the Karmapa for tea in what was likely 1501, it is mentioned that the "worldly protector" (*sa skyong*) Dönyö Dorjé had seized Lhasa, controlled Ü and Tsang for some years, and had become like a *cakravartin*, a king who sets in motion the wheel of the Buddhist teachings.[40] The second Pawo may not be the most objective commentator on these matters: he had been raised by Dönyö Dorjé in the early years of his life as a sort of foster child, and had received patronage from the Rinpungpas during his previous incarnation.[41]

After the deaths of Tsokyé Dorjé and Dönyö Dorjé, the Rinpungpas entered a period of decline. The faction would be led in succession by Ngawang Namgyel (1470/82/94–1554?), who was Dönyö Dorjé's cousin (Tsokyé Dorjé's son); Zilnön Dorjé, Dönyö Dorjé's son; and then Ngawang Namgyel's sons, Döndrup Tseten Dorjé and Ngawang Jikdrak, the latter being a famous man of letters.[42] The Rinpungpas continued their belligerent ways in the years after Dönyö Dorjé's death, but the tide had turned against them. The young Eighth Karmapa and the Red Hat had begun to align themselves with the Pakmodru *gongma*, which greatly bolstered his position.[43] The Rinpungpas' territories started to slip away from them. The resurgent *gongma* launched a countercampaign, regaining Lhasa, Chushül, and other strategic holdings around 1518. The Rinpungpas lost Gyantsé around the same time. On a number of occasions up to the 1540s, the Rinpungpas would attempt to regain their former glory and reassert themselves into the affairs of Ü. But these campaigns failed, and their real influence was confined to Tsang.[44]

Dönyö Dorjé's military career must be understood as devoted to gaining control of certain strategic locales throughout Ü and Tsang, the most important of them being Gyantsé and Lhasa (with Shigatsé already under Rinpungpa control). Some versions of this history maintain that it took Dönyö Dorjé and the Rinpungpas at least two attempts to conquer Gyantsé, and two to take Lhasa as well, suggesting how important the Rinpungpas considered them to the expansion of their domain.

Priestly Alliances and Sectarian Aggression under the Rinpungpas

The Rinpungpas pursued their political ambitions through diplomatic maneuvering, strategic marriages, and military action. They also employed the more indirect means of capitalizing on and further exacerbating the competitiveness between Buddhist sects. In various ways the Rinpungpas worked to limit the influence of the Geluk sect, who were so symbiotically aligned with the Pakmodrupas. At the same time, they supported certain Kagyüpas and Sakyapas, who represented an alternative to the Gelukpas in the broader religious marketplace.

Dönyö Dorjé was responsible for a number of overt attacks on the Geluk. During Dönyö Dorjé's first military campaign into the Lhasa area, he may have launched a direct attack on Ganden monastery. Later, the Rinpungpas would seize estates that provided for the upkeep of Sera and Drepung. During the twenty years the Rinpungpas controlled Lhasa, Geluk monks were barred from participating in the Great Prayer Festival, which was instead run by members of the Kagyü and Sakya sects. The administration of the Jokhang temple was also taken out of the hands of the Gelukpas.[45] Some historical accounts state that during this period the Rinpungpas and their allies made life difficult for Geluk monks around Lhasa.[46]

Throughout the latter half of the fifteenth century, the Rinpungpas were closely aligned with the Seventh Karmapa (also referred to as the Black Hat), Chödrak Gyatso, and the Fourth Red Hat, Chödrak Yeshé, who were the two most important hierarchs of the Karma subsect of the Kagyü. Many Tibetan historians assert Dönyö Dorjé's military adventurism into the Lhasa area to be attributable to his close relationships with the two hierarchs. For example, Sumpa Khenpo's history, *The Excellent Wish-Fulfilling Tree*, states that the Red Hat and the Karmapa encouraged (*bskul*) Dönyö Dorjé's aggressive policies, and he then led an army of ten thousand troops into Ü around 1480. The twentieth-century historian Dungkar Lozang Trinlé goes so far as to say that the attack was "incited" (*ngan skul byas*) by the Fourth Red Hat. Others say that the attack was "advised" or "commanded" (*bka' bkod gnang*) by the Red Hat.[47] Some Tibetan historians maintain that it was the Seventh Karmapa who gave Dönyö Dorjé and the Rinpungpas the idea of forbidding Geluk monks from the Great Prayer Festival.[48] It is not only the later histories that portray the two Karma Kagyü hierarchs in this way, for in the verse mentioned in chapter 2, in which Drukpa Künlé states that there was "no rivaling the Madman of Tsang or the Madman of Ü in the Observance," he also states that there was "no rivaling the Red or Black Hat in militancy."[49] Sources penned by other Kagyüpas tend to portray the Fourth Red Hat and the Seventh Karmapa in a more positive light, as bringers of peace.[50] Dönyö Dorjé had the same kind of dual legacy: depending on the perspective of the author, he was either a benevolent protector and patron or a ruthless warlord. The fact that these figures were portrayed in such starkly contrasting ways is an indication of the seriousness of the sectarian and political conflicts they were involved in.

These statements from various commentators also show that the conflict between the Rinpungpas and the Pakmodrupas was widely understood by fifteenth-century Tibetans to be closely related to the competition between the Kagyü and the Geluk. For example, in the *New Red Annals* it is recorded how in the central Tibetan territory of Gyama, one lord "opposed the Pakmodru *desi*, drove away the Gendenpas [i.e., Gelukpas] and destroyed a statue of the precious lord, [Tsongkhapa]."[51] It was apparent to central Tibetan lords at the time that one way to undermine the Pakmodrupas was to attack nearby Geluk monks and monasteries, who were in a sense proxies of the Pakmodru regime. Dungkar Lozang Trinlé describes the situation at the time in the following manner: "In Ü and Tsang there was a great struggle between the Karma Kagyü and the Gelukpas. The provincial governor of Ja, Tashi Dargyé, and Dönyö Dorjé of Rinpung instigated a great disturbance intended to destroy the Geluk, so that its very name would not even exist."[52]

The Rinpungpas' financial support of the Kagyü was funnelled through the Karmapa, the Red Hat, the Drikung Kagyü, the Taklung Kagyü, the Madmen of Ü and Tsang, and many others.[53] They also gave to the Sakya, as will be expanded upon in the next section. In addition to supporting individual monks and ascetics of the Kagyü and the Sakya, the Rinpungpas sought to strengthen those sects' monastic networks, which increased their symbolic presence in a given area, and gave the Rinpungpas an enduring, physical network from which to exercise their power. This is best exemplified in the struggle for military and religious control of the Lhasa area.

The Kagyüpas had for some time wanted to establish a greater foothold in Lhasa, as suggested by the following story from the biography of the Seventh Karmapa included in Pawo Tsuklak Trengwa's *Scholar's Feast*. It is said that in the late 1470s, the Karmapa on three occasions heard a prophecy from the future buddha Maitreya about how the Jowo Śākyamuni statue in the Jokhang temple should be surrounded by a pure monastic community, which would revitalize the Buddha's teachings in Tibet. This was an implicit statement that there was something fundamentally wrong with the Gelukpas, who had been in control of the Jokhang for some years. The Karmapa goes further, lamenting how in this degenerate age, those responsible for the site (the local Gelukpas) pretended to practice religion, but were concerned only with amassing wealth in the manner of householders; although they wore the garb of monks, they were perpetually making preparations for war.

So the Karmapa approached the local administrator of Neudzong for permission to establish a new monastic community in Lhasa. It was not granted. The Karmapa did not give up, feeling that a command from Maitreya should not be treated so lightly and certain that his project was for the greater benefit of the Teachings. The passage suggests that the Karmapa and his followers were at the time in a position to try to forcibly take control of Lhasa, but decided not to do so because of their Buddhist principles. Meanwhile an army of five hundred [Geluk] monks descended upon the Kagyüpas' camp. According to the text, they wore their bowls as helmets and used their cushions as banners. Fortunately, all those in the Seventh Karmapa's camp obeyed his order not to fight back, and nobody was harmed.[54]

This story suggests that the Kagyüpas had an interest in establishing a stronger presence in Lhasa before Dönyö Dorjé took control of the area and made their doing so a real possibility.[55] We should also observe that Tsuklak Trengwa portrays the Karma Kagyü as having a divine mandate for their presence in Lhasa, only to be blocked by the pig-headed allies of the Pakmodrupas and the Geluk. This story would help justify the Rinpungpas' seizing of Lhasa and the Jokhang in 1498.

While Dönyö Dorjé and the Rinpungpas occupied Lhasa, they spon-sored the construction of a handful of monasteries for the Seventh Karmapa and the Fourth Red Hat. Although the records at our disposal are unclear regarding the names, locations and histories of these mon-asteries, the little we do know is telling of the tensions of the day. First, it seems that the Karmapa sought to establish a monastery on top of Marpori, the steep outcropping in the center of town that would become the site of the grand Potala palace in the seventeenth century, during the time of the Fifth Dalai Lama and Desi Sangyé Gyatso. Dönyö Dorjé was skeptical about the prospects of building a full monastery there, citing strong opposition from the local Gelukpas, so only a more modest resi-dence was built. This edifice is mentioned in the biography of the Fourth Red Hat, when he consecrates the structure and later visits it with Dönyö Dorjé.[56]

Second, a more substantial monastery was built on behalf of the Karmapa. Popular history maintains that this monastery was razed by a mob of monks from the nearby Geluk monasteries not long after it was established. The Fifth Dalai Lama, in his *Song of the Queen of Spring*, gives only a veiled description of this, stating that "because nothing could stop certain karmic forces, [the monastery] did not last long." Sources suggest that this monastery was called Tupten Chökhor and was built in the east-ern part of Lhasa, not far from the Barkor. It was commonly known as the "New Karma monastery" (*karma dgon gsar*).[57]

Third, Hugh Richardson and Giuseppe Tucci both suggest that there was another Karma Kagyü monastery built during this time, on the west side of town, closer to Drepung.[58] This institution could not have lasted very long.

Many of the received histories state that these Kagyü monasteries were built with the intention of countering or suppressing (*kha gnon*) the Lhasa-area Geluk institutions.[59] Sumpa Khenpo goes so far as to say that two Karma Kagyü monasteries were built on the east side of Lhasa "with the intention that they would naturally eliminate Sera and Drepung." Sumpa Khenpo writes that around this time, the Karma and Drukpa Kagyüpas together led a band of troops, converted some small Geluk monasteries, and stole some estates from Sera and Drepung. Because of all this, "the Karma and the Geluk were [at odds], like a bat and the light of day."[60] It was thus widely understood that Geluk and Kagyü monasteries could not coexist in Lhasa on an equal footing, but were necessarily in competition with each other in a zero-sum struggle.

Dönyö Dorjé sponsored the construction of another monastery, which, not falling under the sway of "certain karmic forces," had a long and stable history. This was Yangpachen monastery, which became the new seat of the Fourth Red Hat when it was finished around 1503.[61] Dönyö Dorjé granted the land and some local inhabitants as serfs to support the monastery, and designated some 2,800 nomadic families to supply the butter to keep the monastery's lamps burning.[62] When we compare the circumstances surrounding the founding of Yangpachen and the three Lhasa-area Kagyü monasteries on the one hand, and the pattern adhered to in the founding of the Geluk monasteries of Ganden, Drepung and Sera on the other, Dönyö Dorjé's aim in sponsoring these Kagyü monasteries comes into relief. First off, whereas Ganden, Drepung, and Sera were all sponsored by government officials whose seats were quite close to the monastery in question, Yangpachen and the three Kagyü monasteries in Lhasa were nowhere near the base of the Rinpungpas' power in Tsang. Second, Ganden, Drepung, and Sera were all built for Buddhist masters who did not already have monasteries. Yangpachen and the Lhasa-area Kagyü monasteries were built for the Red Hat and the Karmapa, both of whom already had monasteries in the Tölung valley, making these new monasteries in a sense redundant.[63]

Clearly, part of the motivation for the founding of these Kagyü monasteries in Lhasa was to increase the Kagyüpas' and the Rinpungpas' presence in the largest and most important town in Tibet, and to counter the Gelukpas' and the Pakmodrupas' dominance in the area. The strategic significance of Yangpachen is less obvious and requires consideration of the geography of central Tibet. In the fifteenth and sixteenth centuries, there were three main travel routes between Lhasa and Shigatsé, the capital of Tsang and Tibet's second-largest town: there was the central route alongside the Tsangpo river; the southern route passing through Nakartsé and Gyantsé; and the northern route through the Uyuk valley. The central route had long been under the control of the Rinpungpas, as it went right past the Rinpung district. The southern route came under the control of the Rinpungpas when they conquered Gyantsé in the 1480s. This left only the northern route, which was actually the most convenient way of traveling between the Lhasa and Shigatsé. Yangpachen monastery was built directly on this northern route, at its juncture with the main track leading north to Damzhung. It thus seems that Yangpachen was built for tactical reasons, giving the Rinpungpa faction control over the third and final route between Lhasa and Shigatsé and a base of operations within striking distance of Lhasa. It would be inhabited by a Red Hat who was very much in the Rinpungpas' debt.[64]

The Kagyüpas had little success establishing monasteries in Lhasa proper, because of the entrenched strength of the Gelukpas there. But they increased their presence nearby, especially in the hilly areas to the north of town. The Madman of Ü was himself a participant in this trend, for after spending many of his adult years in Tsang and western Tibet, it was in Penyül, just northeast of Lhasa, that he established a monastery and settled for the last thirty years of his life. We can also see the Kagyüpas' concern to establish a presence in the Lhasa area expressed in the call by Karma Trinlepa to Dakpo Rapjampa Chögyel Tenpa (1449–1524) to take control of the Drak Yerpa retreat caves, as recorded in the *Scholar's Feast*.[65]

Further indicating the sectarian and political tensions of the day, in 1494 the Second Dalai Lama was forced to leave Tashi Lhünpo in Shigatsé and go to Drepung, where his safety would be assured. Then after 1498, when the Rinpungpas took Lhasa, he had no choice but to leave Drepung and travel to different places in eastern Ü, away from the reach of Dönyö Dorjé and his allies. The Dalai Lama would not return to Lhasa until the Rinpungpas were pushed out.[66]

This summary gives a sense of how in fifteenth- and early sixteenth-century Tibet, struggles between opposing political factions were played out in part in the religious realm. Meanwhile high-ranking religious figures used these worldly struggles to the advantage of their respective sects. Religious and secular affairs were inseparable. Because the various religious groups defined and positioned themselves against one another around the central issue of truth, their philosophical views were very much connected to real-world outcomes. The beloved author Döndrup Gyel (1953–1985) was led to conclude that during the second half of the fifteenth century, "If one looks at them from the outside, it would appear that the disputes between the tenet systems of the different sects were about defending the teachings of the Buddha. But in reality, the dispute was also about their fighting over material wealth and political power."[67] Taking a similar view, Yaroslav Komarovski has described the situation as follows:

> Weakening of a centralized state power structure, constant conflicts among rival political groups, and [a] struggle for centralization dur-ing the course of the fifteenth century provided a fertile ground for the flourishing of sects and religious figures whose legitimization

and support were sought by political leaders. It comes as no surprise, then, that in tandem with political clashes, the fifteenth century also witnessed an explosion of intra- and inter-sectarian polemics on questions of perception, scriptural authority, and other topics concerning authority, validity, and reality with clear parallels to political affairs and disputes. Rivalry in the political arena was thus accompanied by rivalry in the religious sphere, and inter- and intra-sectarian polemics became a distinguishing feature of the intellectual landscape of fifteenth-century Tibet.[68]

When varying religious views—including those concerning how truth is verified—are so directly linked to material power relations, we must question how religious "religious" formations really are. Even philosophical positions of the most refined and esoteric sort can be seen as impinging on and being impinged upon by tangible relations of worldly power.

Sakya, Kagyü, and Rinpungpa Affairs

The Rinpungpas' patronage of the Karmapa, the Red Hat, and other representatives and subsects of the Kagyü already established in Ü must be seen as attendant to their adventurism into that region. Throughout this period, the Rinpungpas also supported various Sakya endeavors, the locus of whose power had always been in Tsang. Dönyö Dorjé's father and grandfather had sponsored various Sakya institutions in their home region, including the construction of the Jamchen monastic complex in Rong (founded in 1427), as well as its giant, nine-story Maitreya statue (completed in the 1460s). (A man who served as abbot of this monastery would be said to be a reincarnation of a Rinpungpa lord.)[69] They sponsored the Dreyül Kyemö Tsel monastic complex, the foundation for which was laid in 1437, which may have been meant to rival the state of institutional learning at Sakya, Tsetang, and Gyantsé. They also gave patronage to Gorampa Sönam Sengé (1429–1489), Künkhyen Sangyé Pel, and other Sakyapas.[70] Through supporting these institutions and individuals, the Rinpungpas created religious merit, shored up the legitimacy of their rule, and supported a religious tradition that had long been synonymous with the greatness of Tsang itself.

The relationship between the Rinpungpas and the Sakya sect highlights the fact that the conflict between the Rinpungpas and the Pakmodrupas was to some extent a battle between Tsang and Ü.[71] After a stretch of time in which Tsang dominated central Tibetan affairs during the reign of the Sakyapas (supported by the Mongolian Yüan dynasty), they may have chafed at being under the control of a regime based in Ü. A degree of regional pride may have encouraged the Rinpung revolt, and likely motivated other chiefs in Tsang to join their cause. (A degree of competition between Ü and Tsang has often been an important factor in Tibetan politics, as seen in the struggle between the Fifth Dalai Lama and the Tsangpa Desi in the early seventeenth century, and in the struggle between the Thirteenth Dalai Lama and the Ninth Penchen Lama in the early twentieth.)[72]

Tibetans living in the fifteenth century perceived the conflict between the Pakmodrupas and the Rinpungpas as in part a battle between Ü and Tsang. *The Life of the Madman of Ü* relates how sometime around 1514, the yogin was upset over the "civil war that arose between Ü and Tsang."[73] The epigraph to this chapter also suggests that this was seen as a conflict between Ü and Tsang. Thus, in addition to playing out on political and religious registers, the great conflict that so dominated fifteenth- and early sixteenth-century Tibetan affairs was tinged with an element not of nationalism but of regionalism.

It seems that certain Sakyapas were in a way thrown into a partnership with the Kagyü, and that their shared interest in countering the Geluk was a significant factor in bringing them together. This is suggested by the career of the Sakyapa scholar-monk Śākya Chokden. He had close relations with the Rinpungpas, from whom he received financial support. (The Rinpungpas would later use Śākya Chokden's funeral as an opportunity to make a display of their power.)[74] He was also very involved with the Kagyü, as he received extensive teachings from the twelfth abbot of Taklung and had various contacts with the Madman of Ü.[75] Śākya Chokden was quite close to the Karma Kagyü, especially the Seventh Karmapa, who it is said he took as his root lama. *The Scholar's Feast*, then later the *Garland of Biographies of the Karma Kamtsang* by Situ Penchen and Belo Tsewang Künkhyap, both include very favorable biographies of Śākya Chokden.[76] Some even considered Śākya Chokden to share a mind stream with the Karmapas.[77] It would seem he was thought of as an honorary Kagyüpa.

As for Śākya Chokden's position vis-à-vis the Geluk, he was one of Tsongkhapa's most ardent critics, systematically disagreeing with the great founder on issues of defining importance. As Komarovski has shown, Śākya Chokden found Tsongkhapa's approach much too narrow and rationalist, overemphasizing the necessity for Madhyamaka syllogisms as a means to realizing ultimate reality. He felt Tsongkhapa's system was in fact a dangerous break from tradition. Śākya Chokden himself admitted more room for other means to gaining ultimate realization, including meditation and tantric practice.[78]

The differences between Śākya Chokden and Tsongkhapa were not purely philosophical in nature. As Komarovski understands it, Śākya Chokden thought that the Sakya and other sects had become endangered by the swift rise of the Geluk, and he thus felt compelled to formulate a strong alternative. During his years of training, Śākya Chokden had apparently for some time been forced to study the teachings of Tsongkhapa by an official decree issued by the Pakmodru *gongma*. Śākya Chokden expressed great displeasure over this, which he considered an abuse of political power. In short, "The growing influence and popularity of the Geluk system, together with its support by Pakmodru rulers, contributed to the bitterness with which Shakya Chokden approached its philosophical positions."[79]

Whatever the complex of reasons behind his grievances—intellectual, personal, political—Śākya Chokden became an outspoken critic of the Geluk system. His critiques of the sect were so bold and incisive that the Gelukpas outlawed his writings after they rose to near-absolute power in the seventeenth century.[80]

"A Mutual Understanding": The Patrons of the Madmen of Ü and Tsang

A layman's decision to support a religious figure would have had a variety of consequences in fifteenth- and sixteenth-century Tibet. For one thing, it was believed that by giving to a religious figure, a layperson accrued merit (basically, good karma), which would assure him health, prosperity, and success in his endeavors in this lifetime, and a better rebirth than could otherwise be expected in the next. The patron would also gain access to religious instructions that he might put into use personally, if he had the time and interest. Moreover, the patron would receive blessings through tantric empowerment and other rituals, and might employ the lama to perform salvific or life-protecting rituals to benefit himself, his family, or his subjects.

Entering into a relationship with a respected religious figure would also bring a degree of standing and renown to the layman. We could describe this as the patron's exchanging some of his material capital for cultural capital. For someone like Dönyö Dorjé, convincing people that he was a liberal supporter of Buddhism garnered a degree of goodwill, which helped solidify his rule in an uncertain political world. This may have been especially important to the Rinpungpas, whom some saw as politically illegitimate usurpers.[81]

Lastly, as we have seen throughout this chapter, a patron's relationship with an eminent monk, yogin, monastery, or broader religious group could have direct or indirect political ramifications. The purposeful distribution of religious offerings in some cases served as a means to pursue worldly agendas.

For his part, the religious figure would receive various benefits from entering into a patron–preceptor relationship with a layman. Firstly, he would receive material support—foodstuffs, currency, precious metals, silks, tea, land, the labor of serfs—which could be used to feed himself and his disciples, to support religious communities, build new edifices, print texts, and do other pious works. The currency and goods would be funneled through the ascetic to touch upon the lives of many others in his immediate spiritual community and beyond.

This patronage was also tantamount to the layman's recognition of an elevated spiritual status in the religious figure, which would further legitimize the monk or lama in the eyes of the broader public—imparting to him a degree of cultural capital. Receiving the favor of eminent laymen was a significant means through which the holiness of a religious figure was established. The patron might also use his influence to aid the cleric in other ways, by arranging introductions, protecting him, and advocating on his behalf. We see this exemplified in the way members of the Rinpungpa family told others of the accomplishments of Künga Zangpo and Sangyé Gyeltsen, which facilitated their rise to prominence. Patron and practitioner became in some ways allies, their fates interrelated for the course of their relationship and after.

The biographies of the Madmen of Ü and Tsang show the full course of their relationships with some of their powerful lay patrons. In many cases these relationships were initiated early on in Künga Zangpo's and Sangyé Gyeltsen's ascetic careers and continued over a span of decades. These relationships would shift somewhat as the yogins' lifestyles changed: after the Madman of Ü settled at Tsimar Pel at the age of about forty-four, his patrons would travel there or send emissaries bearing gifts and good tidings. The more itinerant Madman of Tsang would continue to visit his patrons throughout his life, although he sometimes sent disciples to request funds on his behalf. In the cases of both madmen we see that the yogins' lay patrons played integral roles in their careers, since they enabled them to support communities of adoring followers and to complete their various good works. These patrons also played essential roles in memorializing the madmen after their deaths.

The Madman of Ü's most significant patrons were the Rinpungpa family. Over the years he would meet with Dönyö Dorjé, his older brother, his father, and his uncle, Tsokyé Dorjé. He would also receive a letter of praise along with some offerings from Ngawang Namgyel, Tsokyé Dorjé's son.[82] A woman of the Rinpung family, who was probably Dönyö Dorjé's aunt, also played an important role as a patron, as she is the only donor listed for the fabrication of a jeweled reliquary to hold the Madman of Ü's remains after he was cremated. Her son, Nyukla Penchen, would have been Dönyö Dorjé's cousin.[83]

The Madman of Ü met Dönyö Dorjé at least five separate times. The first occasion was at Shangdrön Gang (the same place the Madman of Tsang would also first meet Dönyö Dorjé), not far from the family's estate at Rinpung. It is said that on this occasion, Künga Zangpo tied two ferocious guard dogs to one another and urinated on some barley that had been set out to dry, thus frightening and overwhelming all who were present. Shortly after this, it is likely that Dönyö Dorjé sponsored a center for meditation established by the yogin in Pelnam.[84] The yogin had other early encounters with Dönyö Dorjé in eastern Tsang, during a religious gathering at Zambulung in 1488, and shortly thereafter at nearby Renda. On this latter occasion, there was said to be "a mutual understanding between the patron and preceptor" (*yon* [*bdag*] *mchod* [*gnas*] *thugs mthun*). What sort of matters—worldly or religious—they found themselves in agreement about we can only imagine.[85]

The Madman of Ü met Dönyö Dorjé for the fourth time when the warlord was staying at Lhünpo fortress in Chushül, at the confluence of the Tsangpo and the Kyichu rivers, west of Lhasa, strategically located at the junction of some important routes, including the main one between Lhasa and Nedong. The Rinpungpas had taken control of this fortress during Dönyö Dorjé's first major military campaign into Ü around 1480. While staying at the fortress, Dönyö Dorjé paid daily visits to receive teachings from the yogin. Their final meeting took place at Dreyül Dzongkar, near Rinpung.[86] In the *Life of the Madman of Ü*, Dönyö Dorjé is often referred to as "the protector of the earth, great lord among men" (*sa skyong mi dbang chen po*), or some variant thereof.

Another steadfast patron of the Madman of Ü's was Tashi Dargyé, provincial governor of Ja in southern Tibet, near the holy mountain of Tsari. Tashi Dargyé is widely viewed as a significant antagonist in the ongoing conflict of the day. He was strongly aligned with the Rinpungpas against the Pakmodrupas, an ardent supporter of the Kagyü, and, in some people's estimation, an enemy of the Geluk. His son, Jamyang Chökyi Drakpa (1478–1523), would be chosen as the Third Drukchen incarnation, which further solidified the alliance between this family and the Drukpa Kagyü sect. Tashi Dargyé was also an important patron for the printing of the Kagyü-centric history the *Blue Annals* in 1478. *The Life of the Madman of Ü* mentions a handful of the yogin's meetings with Tashi Dargyé, who was said to have been his primary benefactor for some time.[87]

The Madman of Ü received gifts from many other patrons across Tibet, including lesser lords in the areas north of Lhasa. The printing of the first half of his biography in 1494 and the second half in 1537 were both sponsored by Tamdrin Tseten of Nyukla, likely a relative of Nyukla Peṇchen (and perhaps associated with the Rinpungpas).[88] It was with the central Rinpungpa family and Tashi Dargyé, however, that he had the most enduring and significant relationships.

The Madman of Tsang's main patrons fall into three groups: the petty kings of western Tibet, Tashi Dargyé, and the Rinpungpas, with Dönyö Dorjé being the most important among them. Sangyé Gyeltsen spent much of his career in southwestern Tibet, at Lapchi, Chubar, and other sites of special significance for Kagyüpas along the modern Tibet–Nepal border. Over many years he regularly visited Dzongkar, the seat of the Ngari Gungtang kingdom, often on his way to and from Nepal. King Tri Namgyel Dé (1422–1502) and his sons Norbu Dé (1450–1485) and Samdrup Dé (1459–1505), who were seen as descendants of the early Buddhist kings of Tibet, helped sponsor some of the Madman of Tsang's printing projects, as well as the restoration of the Swayambhūnāth stūpa. He sent them a copy of the *Life of Milarepa* when it was complete. The *Collected Songs* of the Madman of Tsang contain the record of his lengthy correspondence with Samdrup Dé, who it seems harbored severe doubts about the yogin, but was won over in time.[89] One of the Madman of Tsang's principal students and biographers, Lhatsün Rinchen Namgyel, was a member of this family, perhaps another son of Tri Namgyel Dé.[90] One can imagine a young Lhatsün Rinchen Namgyel being intrigued by the eccentric yogin who arrived from afar to meet with the older members of his family. Rinchen Namgyel would later use a share of his family's power and wealth to print texts, establish a monastery at Drakar Taso, and do some further work on the Swayambhūnāth stūpa.

Sangyé Gyeltsen had a similarly close relationship with the kings of Lowo Möntang, whom he visited on a number of occasions, mostly while traveling to and from Mount Kailash and Chubar. They also supported the reconstruction of the Swayambhūnāth stūpa and received a copy of the *Life of Milarepa*. For some years Lowo Möntang and Gugé Purang were mired in a bloody conflict, in which the yogin tried, without success, to mediate.[91] He had less substantial contacts with the lords of Gugé and Tsamda.[92]

The Madman of Tsang first came into contact with Tashi Dargyé during an early visit to Tsari. The two would meet a few more times over the years, with the patron providing the yogin and his disciples with provisions whenever they stayed near Tsari. On one occasion the two are said to have drunk together from a skull cup filled with *chang* and human brains, which cemented the metaphysical connection (*rten 'brel*) between them.[93]

According to the yogin's biography, the first meeting between the Madman of Tsang and Dönyö Dorjé occurred when the powerful lord invited him to Rinpung, where he lavished gifts upon the ascetic. During this meeting Dönyö Dorjé requested that the yogin send him a copy of the *Life of Milarepa* when it was finished, along with the accompanying paintings. Dönyö Dorjé would remain a supporter of the yogin for the rest of his life, giving him gifts of gold, silver, and silk. He also supported the Madman of Tsang in his restoration of the Swayambhūnāth stūpa and interceded to grant the yogin control over one of Milarepa's former hermitages, where the yogin established a retreat center that would remain active after his death.[94] Dönyö Dorjé spent a lot of time with the great yogin near the end of his life. During one of these late meetings, in the Shang valley, Dönyö Dorjé is purported to have said to the Madman of Tsang:

> It has been a long time since I have seen the lord of yogins. Because people have been saying that you have become stooped over with age, I thought your hair and complexion would have turned white and you would be weakened by old age. But it is clear that you have not aged at all since we first met as patron and preceptor [*yon mchod*] at Shangdrön Gang.

The Madman of Tsang responded:

> It is just so. I thought that because of the king's consuming the enjoyments of all of Ü and Tsang, he would have become an old man who has lost his teeth. And it is clear that you certainly have grown old!

This made everyone laugh.[95] The exchange gives a sense of the warm relationship between the two men. From there they went to Shigatsé and stayed together for some time. Dönyö Dorjé left for Ü, but furnished the Madman of Tsang and 150 of his students with excellent hospitality for ten days. Shortly before the yogin's death in 1507, the two spent time together in Lhasa, during which the yogin gave various teachings to the warlord. One morning Sangyé Gyeltsen mentioned having had a dream suggesting that they would not meet again in that lifetime as patron and preceptor. The Madman of Tsang left the place where they had been staying and died shortly thereafter. Dönyö Dorjé is mentioned as foremost among the high-ranking officials who traveled to Chubar to participate in rites honoring the Madman of Tsang after his death.[96]

As for what sort of influence the Madman of Tsang might have had on Dönyö Dorjé, Götsang Repa's version of the *Life* maintains that at one point, the great yogin heard that the Rinpungpas had amassed 80,000 troops in preparation for an attack on a lord of southern Latö. Out of his compassion for living beings, the yogin sent a few of his students to deliver a letter reminding Dönyö Dorjé that this kind of military activity was a sin and a cause for bad rebirth, and requesting that he not cast Ü and Tsang into such disorder and instead work more constructively for people's well-being throughout the realm. The ruler took the yogin's advice and dispersed his troops. It is recorded that later the Madman of Tsang again interceded to prevent Dönyö Dorjé from dispatching a body of troops, this time to Dzongkar in Ngari Gungtang, the seat of some of the yogin's loyal supporters.[97]

In reality, none of these campaigns could have possibly involved 80,000 troops. What's more, according to the *Scholar's Feast*, it was because of the Fourth Red Hat's input that Dönyö Dorjé decided against his campaign to southern Latö, not the Madman of Tsang's.[98] The idea that the Madman of Tsang might have had such influence over Dönyö Dorjé is likely a pious exaggeration by his devoted followers. But if it is true that Dönyö Dorjé traveled all the way to Chubar to attend the great yogin's memorial services, this would suggest a deep commitment between the two men.

The Madman of Tsang also had contacts with other members of the Rinpung family at various points in his career. Götsang Repa's *Life of the Madman of Tsang* expresses a sense of gratitude to the Rinpungpas for all they had done for the yogin. It is said that when the Madman of Tsang's activities came to the attention of the Seventh Karmapa, it was because of the kind things that were being said about the yogin at Rinpung. Götsang Repa's version of the *Life* was published thanks in part to one of Dönyö Dorjé's successors.[99] The earliest version of the Madman of Tsang's biography and his *Collected Songs* had been printed a year after his death, thanks to the sponsorship of his consort Küntu Zangmo.

To round out our consideration of the issue of patronage, we should consider what sorts of connections, if any, the Madmen of Ü and Tsang had with the Pakmodru regime. Near the end of his life, the Madman of Tsang received an invitation from the Pakmodru *gongma*, Ngawang Tashi Drakpa, who had recently come of age, to visit him at Nedong. Stating that the yogin was tired, and that "the dependent connections [*rten 'brel*] for his going were not right," he refused the invitation. At this time the Madman of Tsang did, however, meet with the *gongma*'s wife, who was Dönyö Dorjé's daughter.[100] It is impossible to say whether or not the Madman of Tsang was snubbing the head of the Pakmodrus, but he had no significant contacts with the regime during his career.

The Madman of Ü's position with respect to the Pakmodru regime was more complex. Throughout his life Künga Zangpo maintained a connection to Densa Til monastery and especially the forest retreats nearby, where he underwent much of his early training. It seems that early in his career, Künga Zangpo was in fact known as "the lama from [Densa] Til." But although Künga Zangpo spent a good deal of time at Densa Til and the areas around Nedong, there is no record of his having met with the *gongma* or any other representative of the Pakmodru regime. Around 1514 he received some offerings and a letter from *gongma* Ngawang Tashi Drakpa, in which he was praised as a "lord of yogins" and a "preeminent *siddha*." Then in 1522, he received an offering of three bricks of tea from the *gongma*.[101] In the course of his life, Künga Zangpo had only limited contact with representatives of the Pakmodru regime.

This consideration of their careers has given a sense of how Künga Zangpo and Sangyé Gyeltsen were enmeshed in tight and overlapping webs of interpersonal relations. They had their patrons, their followers, and their biographers and associates, many of whom were connected with one another through familial, political, geographic, religious, or other ties. Although it would be a mistake to read too far into any of these individual contacts or apparent snubs, taken together they clearly suggest that the Madmen of Ü and Tsang had close relationships with certain individuals on the Rinpungpas' side of the conflict (including Tashi Dargyé of Ja) and had at best fleeting contact with political figures on Pakmodru side.

Conclusion

Tibet in the fifteenth and early sixteenth centuries was dominated by intensely interrelated political and religious conflicts. The question remains: what effect, if any, did these circumstances have on Künga Zangpo's and Sangyé Gyeltsen's decisions to leave conventional monasticism, don the garb of the Heruka, and enact key dictates of the Unexcelled Yoga Tantras that many of their contemporaries would have performed only very figuratively, if at all? What effect, if any, did these circumstances have on Künga Zangpo and Sangyé Gyeltsen's rise to prominence?

One possibility is that there is no significant connection between the lifestyles assumed by Künga Zangpo and Sangyé Gyeltsen and the historical moment in which they lived. Künga Zangpo and Sangyé Gyeltsen were striving for enlightenment and took on their literalist tantric lifestyle because they understood it to be the most effective means of reaching that goal. Certain powerful laymen saw intrinsic value in Künga Zangpo and Sangyé Gyeltsen, and thus chose to support them. In this view, Künga Zangpo and Sangyé Gyeltsen may not have been particularly self-aware or concerned about how others would respond to their actions. Nor are holders of worldly power necessarily moved by strategic considerations when making decisions about which spiritual guides to support.

Another possibility is that Künga Zangpo's and Sangyé Gyeltsen's respective decisions to take on their literalist tantric lifestyle were a creative response to certain real-world conditions they perceived. This view assumes that Künga Zangpo and Sangyé Gyeltsen were quite aware—either consciously or semiconsciously—of what this lifestyle would represent in the perceptions of others, and how people might treat them as a result. This view also assumes that laymen like Dönyö Dorjé were somewhat strategic in making decisions about which religious figures to patronize. During a time when the ideal of a scholarly, *Vinaya*-based monkhood was becoming the norm and the Gelukpas were rising to prominence, and when the present and future prospects of the Kagyü sect were threatened, Künga Zangpo and Sangyé Gyeltsen made the decision to articulate and embody a distinctive alternative of what a Buddhist renunciant might look like. Instead of retiring permanently to mountain retreats in pursuit of anonymous religious practice and transcendence of worldly affairs, Künga Zangpo and Sangyé Gyeltsen lived their tantric fundamentalism in a demonstrative and public manner. They acted out an ideal of the hermit-meditator that was in some ways the polar opposite of the scholar-monk. The pivot around which these different identities were articulated was the question of how tantra was to be regarded and enacted. The particular model of Buddhistness and Kagyüness embodied by Künga Zangpo and Sangyé Gyeltsen helped them gain the attention and favor of the Rinpungpas and Tashi Dargyé. The Rinpungpas and Tashi Dargyé supported a variety of religious groups and individuals—the Karmapa and the Red Hat, the Drikungpas, various Kagyü ascetics, the Sakya, and others—each of whom constituted an alternative to the Gelukpas in the religious marketplace. Offering money and influence to support these endeavors was an attempt to chip away at the growing strength of the Geluk sect in the cultural sphere and at the standing of the Pakmodru regime in the political one. This is not to say that in taking on their distinctive lifestyle, Künga Zangpo and Sangyé Gyeltsen were pandering to the wishes of powerful lords. There is no evidence to suggest that. But receiving their patronage and support may have encouraged Künga Zangpo and Sangyé Gyeltsen to maintain this distinctive lifestyle, allowing them to support larger circles of followers and to realize their various projects. The existence of these willing channels of patronage helped propel the Madmen of Ü and Tsang into a more central and influential position within the Tibetan cultural world of their day.

To assume that Künga Zangpo and Sangyé Gyeltsen were unaware of or unconcerned about the larger dynamics of the time in which they lived, or of how their attention-grabbing activity would position them relative to those dynamics—culturally, politically, financially—is to portray them as somewhat naïve, blind to the workings of their own society and culture. This may be taking their "madness" too literally. On the other hand, to assume that Künga Zangpo and Sangyé Gyeltsen were concerned about what secondary ramifications their taking on this lifestyle might entail is to portray them as somewhat strategic, even calculating in their self-presentation to the world. Similarly, to assume that Dönyö Dorjé and other powerful laymen were unaware of the real-world ramifications of their patronage decisions is to portray them as rather shortsighted. The other alternative is to view their decisions about religious patronage as strategic in nature.

It remains an open question, about which the reader will have to decide for him- or herself, which one of these views offers the most accurate portrayal of the reasons behind Künga Zangpo and Sangyé Gyeltsen's distinctive behavior, if not a different view entirely. Was their tantric literalism a sincere form of striving toward enlightenment? Was this the perfect activity of bodhisattvas, enacted for the benefit of other beings? Was it that their greatest concern was for society as a whole, and that they understood the lifestyle they assumed as being the most effective way of spreading and fostering a true form of Buddhism for the greater good of all? Was their activity intended to help support their sect somewhat indirectly, by offering an alternative model of Buddhistness from that of the Geluk? Was it intended to help their sect more immediately through the patronage it would bring? Were Künga Zangpo and Sangyé Gyeltsen motivated by desires for their own enrichment and advancement, as suggested by Drukpa Künlé? Was it a combination of these concerns? Which of these concerns are mutually exclusive, if any? How much credit should we afford Künga Zangpo and Sangyé Gyeltsen as creative, independent agents? How much self-awareness should we think they possessed? How "religious" should we assume they were?

We have arrived at the limit of what religious studies, history, or any academic discipline can tell us. Beneath any pattern of behavior they may have performed, beneath any rhetoric they may have employed, the innermost workings of the minds and hearts of anyone dead five hundred years remain a closed book, ultimately unknowable. Although we may make the Madmen of Ü and Tsang the ostensible subjects of our debate, in truth we would be debating the nature of religion. And such views on religion ultimately rest on key assumptions about human nature itself. Rather than seeking to convince readers of my opinions on these grand matters based on the cases of Künga Zangpo and Sangyé Gyeltsen, I propose their lives for inclusion in any ongoing debates we might have.

Let me close this chapter with a quotation from E. Gene Smith, who translated its epigraph, and whose efforts at preserving and making Tibetan literature available to readers all over the world have played an enormous role in making the research for this book possible. In 1969 he wrote of the fifteenth-century "holy madmen":

> The *smyon pa* [nyönpa, madman] is the antithesis of the scholastic monk; yet to view the phenomenon simply as a reaction against monastic reforms and Gelukpa rationalism misses much of the point. The *smyon pa*, too, represented a force for reform. Just as the movement of Tsongkhapa attempted to reorient the Kadampa tradition toward the fundamental contribution of Atiśa—the Graduated Path (Lam rim), with its emphasis on the exoteric as an indispensable foundation for the esoteric—so the *smyon pa* represents an

attempt to re-dedicate the Kagyüpa sects to old truths and insights that were being forgotten. . . .

The evidence is fairly conclusive that the *smyon pa* phenomenon was at least in part a reaction against the great prestige and wealth of the hereditary lineages. It was an attempt to re-invest the Kagyüpa tradition with some of its former religious fervor, to re-kindle the incandescent spirituality of the early yogis. The chief symbol for this movement was Milarepa: a mystic poet who had founded no monastery or school and had never been a monk, a saint who remained a legend.[102]

I agree with most aspects of Smith's assessment, but would add an important qualification. As we will see in the next chapter, the famous fifteenth-century holy madmen were not simply "re-dedicating" the Kagyü sect to a static set of truths and insights. Rather, through their writing and publishing, they actively created a particular vision of the Kagyü, of which their activity as "madmen" then became an expression. The creation of the Madman of Tsang's particular portrayal of Milarepa was a central part of this process.

5

Making History

THE LATER PROJECTS OF THE MADMEN
OF Ü AND TSANG

Over time I have heard about the way you, the holy lord of yogins, the Madman of Tsang, have created woodblocks for printing the *Life* and *Songs* of glorious Laughing Vajra [Milarepa]; how you have established meditation centers at the three holy mountains [*gnas gsum*; Tsari, Lapchi, and Mount Kailash]; and completed other works to spread and increase the teachings of the Kagyü. I was thereby delighted and overjoyed. More recently, you have taken on the responsibility of spreading the Teachings by renovating the Swayambhūnāth stūpa in Nepal, establishing meditation centers at Chubar in Drin, and so on. I myself shall do whatever I can to assist you. Do not give up! May the world be adorned with gloriously blazing auspiciousness!

Letter sent to the Madman of Tsang by the
SEVENTH KARMAPA, CHÖDRAK GYATSO[1]

IN THE LATTER parts of their careers, the Madmen of Ü and Tsang's provocative behavior and itinerancy gave way to more sedate pursuits. Künga Zangpo established monasteries that took the ideal of meditation as their central concern. Meanwhile the Madman of Tsang became known for overseeing meditation communities, renovating the Swayambhūnāth stūpa, writing down the Aural Transmission, and creating a remarkable body of Kagyü biographical literature that would prove the most important facet of his legacy. This chapter considers the ways these projects continued the agendas the madmen earlier pursued through their distinctive asceticism and identity creation, but now through different means, to more enduring effect, reaching wider audiences, and enabled by what they had achieved in the intervening years.

As we have seen throughout this study, a good deal of what we know about the "holy madmen" has been mediated through a process of selective representation by their biography-writing disciples. This chapter will show how the Madman of Tsang was himself an active participant in the selective and purposeful portrayal of earlier saints of the Kagyü, suggesting that he was highly self-aware of the process of identity formation—a master of the dynamics of representation, rather than their mere prisoner.

The Projects of the Madman of Ü and His Disciples

In the course of his career, Künga Zangpo was involved with the establishment of three religious institutions. In his late twenties, he founded the Fortress of the Expanse of Being in the Lower Nyang (*myang smad*) area of Tsang. A few years later, he established Liberation Park in Kharak, on the border between Ü and Tsang. Dönyö Dorjé was likely the primary sponsor behind one of these, if not both. Referred to as *drupdé* and *drupdra* (*sgrub sde*, *sgrub grwa*), these centers were specifically dedicated to meditative training and retreat. The yogin's association with these institutions was short-lived, and we are told of his visiting each only a handful of times.

Then in 1502, Künga Zangpo took control of a monastery north of Lhasa called Tsimar Pel. The great yogin would remain there for the last thirty years of his life. To some of Künga Zangpo's followers, his settling down in this fashion seemed to be in contradiction with the lifestyle upon which he had built his reputation. When Künga Zangpo first charged one of his students with acquiring the place by gaining the favor of the local lords, the disciple balked, saying, "Wouldn't it be better if we, teacher and students, stayed in whatever mountains, as we did in the past?" The Madman of Ü answered by saying that there were different ways of working for the benefit of sentient beings, and that this monastery would serve as a "shining example for the teachings of the Meditation Tradition."[2]

The rift between the ways in which the Madman of Ü and his disciple thought about the potential value of this monastery suggests that the disciple took his master's rhetoric of renunciation and itinerancy very literally, more literally than the yogin intended. Künga Zangpo, seeing a bigger picture, was attuned to the effects their meditation would have in the social sphere, and was comfortable with the irony of building a monastery dedicated to upholding the Meditation Tradition.

In the years that followed, Künga Zangpo would take on an almost inconceivable asceticism. From 1502 to 1512, he remained in a strict retreat that would serve as the capstone to his spiritual career. For much of this time he was literally sealed inside his chamber, interacting with the world only through a small window. When Künga Zangpo announced the end of his self-imposed isolation, people all over Tibet heard about his remarkable feat of renunciation and flocked to Tsimar Pel to make offerings, receive his blessing, and learn under him. This was the Madman of Ü at the peak of his fame and influence. Meditation, and people's awareness of its practice, was at the heart of this expanding community.

In stark contrast to the Madman of Tsang, we have no record of the Madman of Ü's ever having composed a single text.[3] He was, nevertheless, fully aware of the power of texts, especially printed ones. In his mid-thirties, Künga Zangpo encouraged Nyukla Penchen to compose a biography describing the events of his life up to that point. Woodblocks were soon carved and copies of the text put into circulation. Then in 1509, Künga Zangpo instructed this same disciple to make printings of Saraha's *Dohā Trilogy*, a text on the Secret Practice of India, and the *Life* and *Songs* of Milarepa, perhaps using the woodblocks completed by the Madman of Tsang twenty-one years earlier. Nyukla Penchen would also compose the biography of another Kagyü master. Later, Lochen Gyurmé Dechen (1540–1615)—a disciple of Lhatong Lotsāwa Shényen Namgyel, the Madman of Ü's other biographer—would compose the most significant version of the *Life of Tangtong Gyelpo* (see chapter 7).[4] Although they did not become a major force of literary production, members of the community surrounding the Madman of Ü did take an interest in immortalizing masters of the Kagyü through literature.

The Literary School of the Madman of Tsang

From the late nineteenth century to the middle of the twentieth, European and American Tibetologists were aware of the famous *Life of Milarepa* but misunderstood who its author was. In 1881, the Moravian missionary H. A. Jäsche referred to the text as "Milarepa's autobiography." In the succeeding decades, other scholars took the text as having been written by Milarepa's disciple Rechungpa. It was not until the 1960s that Garma C. C. Chang and Herbert Guenther showed that the author who identified himself as "the yogin who wanders in charnel grounds, wearer of the bone ornaments" was the Madman of Tsang. Since then our awareness of the vast literary corpus produced by the Madman of Tsang and his close disciples has increased. In recent decades this body of literature has been the subject of a good deal of scholarly research.[5]

The literary school of the Madman of Tsang included not only the great yogin and his biographer-disciples Ngödrup Pembar, Götsang Repa, and Lhatsün Rinchen Namgyel, but also Wangchuk Gyeltsen, Śrī Lopen Repa Jampel Chö-lha, and the grand-disciple Sangyé Darpo, who wrote a history of the Kagyü tracing a lineage from the Buddha down to the Madman of Tsang, referenced in chapter 2. This "school" got its start at the time of the Madman of Tsang's printing the *Life* and *Songs* of Milarepa in 1488 and continued until around 1570.[6]

The two most prolific members of this school were Lhatsün Rinchen Namgyel and Götsang Repa. Although Lhatsün Rinchen Namgyel's biography's claim that he was responsible for the printing of four thousand folios of text may be a pious exaggeration, we can count at least twenty-eight works edited or composed by him over a period of twenty years, most of which were printed in 1550s, and totaling over fifteen hundred folios. Lhatsün Rinchen Namgyel worked mainly at Drakar Taso, the hermitage near Gungtang—his natal home—where Milarepa is held to have achieved enlightenment. Götsang Repa worked mainly at Rechung cave, where Rechungpa once meditated and where the Madman of Tsang passed away, located near Nedong and Densa Til in central Tibet. Götsang Repa is responsible for publishing at least twelve works, totaling over seven hundred folios.

Some of the texts that bear their names were compiled or written by Götsang Repa and Lhatsün Rinchen Namgyel themselves. On other texts they functioned as overseers—like editors or executive producers—guiding the work of writers, scribes, and woodcarvers. These writing and printing projects could involve contributions from scores of individuals, thus requiring a singular oversight and vision. Among the many works printed at Rechung cave and Drakar Taso, we have no evidence of there ever being alternate printings of the same text, which suggests that there was ongoing communication between the two hubs. Götsang Repa and Lhatsün Rinchen Namgyel both wrote biographies of the Madman of Tsang, however.

The productivity of this circle was remarkable. At least fifty-five texts written and printed by this school are extant today. They likely produced other works that were never printed, or which have since been lost. The majority of the texts produced by this school were biographies and poetry collections of individuals that together tell a history of the Kagyü lineage from its origins outside time and space to its Indian masters and their Tibetan disciples, who fostered those teachings in the snowy land to the north. A primary concern of this literature is to tell the story of how the teachings of the Kagyü were transmitted from one generation to the next, shoring up the Kagyüpas' claim that their teachings were of authentic Indian origins. The main lineage described in this body of literature runs as follows: the buddha Vajradhara, Saraha, Tilopa, Nāropa, Marpa, Milarepa, Gampopa, Pakmodrupa, Lingrepa, Tsangpa Gyaré, Götsangpa, and Yanggönpa (figure 5.1). After a gap of more than a century, the narrative resumes with Shara Rapjampa, followed by stories telling about his disciple the Madman of Tsang, Lhatsün Rinchen Namgyel, Götsang Repa, and others. This is in effect a single story, a single history, told over the course of these many biographical texts. That the biographies produced by the Madman of Tsang and his school would become the standard accounts of these figures' lives is remarkable, given how long after the fact they were written in many cases. That the Madman of Tsang remained for so long unknown to the Tibetological world as the author of the *Life of*

FIGURE 5.1   "The learned and accomplished Nāropa. The *mahāsiddha* Tilopa. The translator Marpa."

Milarepa indicates just how successful he was in removing himself from the horizon of the text. In the minds of many, this is a record of history, not a story shaped by later hands.

In creating these new versions of the *Lives* of past masters, the authors working in this school drew from an earlier set of narrative traditions, keeping what was useful to them, discarding what was not, reordering events, changing details, and improving the narratives' literary styles through more effective plotting, stronger thematic development, and more uniform language. The discernable stamp put upon this body of literature by these authors ranges from the very words they used to their decisions about how to characterize past masters, to the question of what and what not to take the trouble of writing and printing. Through the production of this literature, the Madman of Tsang and his school strategically shaped the Kagyü, as a means of responding to challenges it faced during their day. In the process, they created much of what we "know" today about the history of the Kagyü sect. By looking more closely at the Madman of Tsang's creation of the *Life of Milarepa*, the next section will give a sense of roles they played in selectively shaping the past and affecting the present.

Writing and Printing the *Life of Milarepa*

The Madman of Tsang's personal literary corpus consists mainly of the *Life* and *Songs* of Milarepa, the *Life of Marpa*, and the *Compendium of the Aural Transmission*.[7] There is also a volume of songs and poems attributed to the Madman of Tsang, which was compiled and printed by his followers in the year after his death. It seems that Sangyé Gyeltsen came to think of his literary production as the most important task of his life. According to Ngödrup Pembar's version of his biography, shortly before his death the yogin said that he had taken this human form solely for the purpose of creating the *Life* and *Songs* of Milarepa, and a physical, written copy of the *Compendium of the Aural Transmission*. With those projects finished, his life's work was complete.[8]

Sangyé Gyeltsen first wrote about Milarepa around the age of thirty-two, when he composed a brief biographical praise of the saint after visiting the village where he was born. This text, which was probably in verse, divides Milarepa's life into twelve great deeds.[9] A few years after this, Sangyé Gyeltsen would undertake the composition and printing of his full versions of the *Life* and the *Collected Songs* of Milarepa. According to Lhatsün Rinchen Namgyel's version of his *Life*, the Madman of Tsang's decision to take on this project was precipitated by a vision of Nāropa, while staying at Dröpuk, a cave associated with Milarepa. While Sangyé Gyeltsen was in a dream-like state, Nāropa appeared before him, in a giant form, wearing the six bone ornaments. The Madman of Tsang asked Nāropa to impart to him his Six Dharmas. When Nāropa responded speaking in Sanskrit, a translator appeared and told the Madman of Tsang that the great Indian *siddha* was instructing him to compile the biography and the songs of Milarepa, carve the texts into woodblocks, then print and distribute copies of them. The Madman of Tsang's immediate response was to say that he did not have the material resources to make such a project possible. Nāropa pointed in the direction of Lowo Möntang, Ngari Gungtang, and southern Latö, assuring the yogin that patronage would arrive from those places. Then the Madman of Tsang protested that he did not have the capacities to complete such an undertaking, which would require preparing wood and supervising scribes and carvers—tasks in which he had no prior experience. Nāropa indicated five women sitting nearby—goddesses—who vowed to help the Madman of Tsang in the endeavor.[10]

Götsang Repa's version of the *Life of the Madman of Tsang* does not tell of his having such a vision, but states that one morning the Madman of Tsang awoke inspired to compose and print a version of the *Life of Milarepa*. Andrew Quintman translates Götsang Repa's description of the Madman of Tsang's thoughts (which expands on a passage from Ngödrup Pembar's earlier version of the *Life*), suggesting the various concerns that motivated him to take up the project:

> At present in this snowy land there exist numerous biographies and collected songs of Jetsün Zhepa Dorjé [Milarepa]. However, the [transmission of] his extraordinary biography has been interrupted. I should rectify this, teach the profound and vast Dharma and instructions to my worthy disciples, and then bring them to liberation; indeed that is what [such a work] does. All agree on the need to accumulate merit. Yet from the king, too busy for the proper activity of authentic Dharma, ministers, and important leaders full of arrogance, to the majority of common people, all are proud of their Dharma activity; and even if they have time to practice and do so, they don't know how to practice the profound key points. Rather than stirring up bubbles of technical jargon, [such a biography] would be a wish-fulfilling gem, an exceptional means for leading them to buddhahood in one lifetime. It would thus awaken the

inner potential for virtue in arrogant *geshe*s who are on the verge of becoming non-Buddhists.

If this biography of Jetsün Zhepa Dorjé were available to be seen, for those attached to sense pleasures and their own lives it would become a support for enduring the hardships of ascetic practice. For those who take pleasure in distraction, it would become a support for practicing one-pointedly. For those who doubt the possibility of attaining buddhahood in one lifetime or say they have no time for meditation on the profound, it would serve as a perfect example of those very things. They would have confidence in the authentic Dharma of definitive meaning, and the most capable individuals would be liberated in their lifetime or in the intermediate state at the moment of death. People of intermediate ability, even though they have no personal experience, would develop faith and devotion in experienced individuals and provide them material support. They could make pure aspirations, enter retreat, and based upon practice in future lifetimes they would reach liberation. Even the least capable would abandon perverted views and engender exceptional faith and then develop certainty that they would reach the limits of life's round [*saṃsāra*]. Once this printing is finished it will benefit limitless beings.[11]

Since these words were penned by the great yogin's disciple (or, in fact, by the combined efforts of two of them), we must be careful not to assume that they express the Madman of Tsang's thoughts with perfect accuracy. But the Madman of Tsang did clearly pursue many of the ideals mentioned here in creating his version of the *Life* of Milarepa, which would serve not only as a testament to the power of meditation and the possibility of achieving liberation in a single lifetime, but as a salvo against those who marginalized the practice of tantra and posited a more gradualist model of the Buddhist path, especially the arrogant *geshé*s overconcerned with philosophical wrangling. All of this while creating a version of the *Life* more accessible to the public—whether literate or illiterate—than any prior version had been.

Milarepa had been very popular in Tibet since decades after his death. Sangyé Gyeltsen capitalized upon and dramatically expanded this notoriety.[12] In creating his versions of the *Life* and *Songs* of Milarepa, the Madman of Tsang drew extensively from many existing stories and songs about or attributed to the yogin, some of which were written down, while others circulated orally. Quintman's research on the versions of the *Life* of Milarepa that preceded the Madman of Tsang's has allowed us a better understanding of how Sangyé Gyeltsen drew and diverged from preexisting accounts. For example, many of the most noteworthy passages in the Madman of Tsang's version of the *Life* are lifted directly from earlier versions. The hilarious moment when, after his death, Milarepa's disciples discover a letter he left behind, which reads, "Whoever said that Milarepa possessed gold, fill his mouth with shit," was drawn from a twelfth- or thirteenth-century version of the biography commonly known as the *Twelve Great Disciples*. Much of the Madman of Tsang's portrayal of Milarepa's death is also drawn from this text, including the exquisite passage describing the rain of flowers that fell on the day of Milarepa's funeral.[13] The Madman of Tsang recognized great literature when he saw it. In creating his version of the *Life* of Milarepa, the Madman of Tsang also drew from versions written by Gampopa, Gyeltangpa Dechen Dorjé, and others, as well as from the text known as the *Black Treasury*.

The Madman of Tsang's version of the *Life* was thus a composite that drew from a rich hagiographic tradition. Nevertheless, the great yogin put his own distinctive mark on the text through the way he put these pieces together. As has been observed many times, the Madman of Tsang's *Life* of Milarepa is an outlier in the genre of Tibetan spiritual biography. Usually such a text takes the form of a chronological listing of events, its narrative driven almost entirely by its subject's linear journey from birth to enlightenment to death. What sets the Madman of Tsang's version of the *Life* apart is his concern for storytelling, which makes the final product in some ways more like a novel than a typical Tibetan Buddhist biography.

One means by which the narrative is given added richness is the unique sense of time conveyed by the Madman of Tsang. The story is tightly constructed, with a good deal of foreshadowing, symbolism, repeated tropes, thought-provoking parallels and reversals, and bits of dialogue that echo throughout the text. Together, these devices give the narrative a special temporal texture. For example, a prospective student's going before a new lama and making a request of "food, clothing, and dharma" occurs a number of times in the story. Through the lamas' varying responses to this question, the Madman of Tsang is able to starkly differentiate them from each other and establish their contrasting characters. Similarly, early in the story, Milarepa's biological mother threatens to kill herself if he does not succeed in winning them revenge. Later, once Milarepa has left his earthly family and entered into his spiritual one, Marpa's wife dissuades the young man from the idea of killing himself. In this way the author has established a telling contrast between the two women, and the realms, worldly and religious, with which they are associated. This kind of narrative depth makes the events of the *Life* feel like the unfolding of an affair of great consequence, rather than one mere thing happening after another.

The most fundamental change the Madman of Tsang made to the *Life* of Milarepa was to "fictionalize" it in this way, in the sense of creating a highly crafted narrative.[14] He also made other significant changes to the form and content of the text. One of his most important stylistic innovations was to divide the Milarepa literature into two separate texts: the *Life* and the *Collected Songs*. The *Collected Songs*, made up of short episodes relating songs Milarepa sang to his disciples on various occasions, are more than twice as long as the *Life*. Moving these out of the main narrative enabled the Madman of Tsang to create a more streamlined and entertaining story.[15]

Another significant innovation of the Madman of Tsang's was his framing the *Life* as an oral account. The text is presented as a transcription of Milarepa's own telling of his life story to his disciples at Rechungpa's request (leading some Western Tibetologists to understand the text as Milarepa's autobiography or a composition by Rechungpa). This added an immediacy to the narrative, making it feel like real history. This also helped mask the role played by the Madman of Tsang as the author of the text.[16]

Beyond these stylistic innovations, the Madman of Tsang also made changes to the content of the *Life* and *Songs* of Milarepa. These range from minor details to important historical "facts," to how specific concerns are portrayed. In an earlier version of the *Life*, there is a story about Milarepa's mistaking a burning lamp for a special meditative experience. When creating his version, the Madman of Tsang reworked this story, now making it about a lamp being put on Milarepa's head and miraculously never going out.[17] The Madman of Tsang also chose to portray Milarepa as physically invulnerable.[18] Through making small changes like these, the Madman of Tsang portrayed Milarepa in a more perfect light than earlier versions had.

The Madman of Tsang also does many small things that together have the effect of portraying Milarepa as equivalent to the Buddha. The text begins with the phrase that opens all Buddhist *sūtras*: "Thus have I heard." The dialogue format makes the *Life* similar in form to a *sūtra*, with Milarepa occupying the role of the Buddha, and his disciples Rechungpa and Ngendzongpa filling the roles of Śāriputra, the interlocutor, and Ānanda,

FIGURE 5.2 "Rechungpa Dorjé Drakpa. Homage to noble Milarepa. Ngendzongpa."

who had perfect memory (figure 5.2). After Milarepa's death, his disciples are unable to light a fire to burn his corpse until Rechungpa arrives, which is reminiscent of the way traditional accounts say the Buddha's body could not be burned until his disciple Mahākāśyapa got there. The Madman of Tsang also divided Milarepa's story into twelve chapters, mimicking traditional accounts of the life of Śākyamuni Buddha as comprised of twelve great acts. Through these changes to the form and content of the narrative, the Madman of Tsang directly and indirectly suggests that Milarepa is to be thought of as on par with the Buddha himself.[19]

At the same time that the Madman of Tsang made these changes to emphasize the amazing status Milarepa achieved during his life, he also took specific measures to assert that Milarepa was not an emanation of a deity or the reincarnation of an enlightened master, but was born an ordinary person. Earlier versions of the *Life* had stated that Milarepa was an emanation of the Indian saints Nāgārjunagarbha or Mañjuśrīmitra. The Madman of Tsang's version of the *Life* insists that Milarepa started off as an ordinary human, which makes his achieving enlightenment all the more impressive. This Milarepa truly exemplifies how a common man—even a great sinner—can achieve enlightenment in a single lifetime through the practice of tantra. The whole of the *Life* is made into a testament to the potency of the specific spiritual tradition Milarepa was a part of, in keeping with Götsang Repa's statement that the Madman of Tsang hoped this text would serve to change the minds of "those who doubt the possibility of attaining buddhahood in one lifetime."[20] This intention may even be obliquely signaled by the Madman of Tsang within the body of the *Life*. When Ngendzongpa asks Milarepa who he was an emanation of, the great yogin responds: "To suggest . . . that [a highly realized] individual is an emanation of a buddha or a bodhisattva is a sign that you lack conviction in the short path of Secret Mantra."[21]

Of particular interest is the question of how the Madman of Tsang chose to portray Milarepa vis-à-vis the religious culture of his day. This is a major theme in the tenth chapter, which describes the years of the yogin's most austere asceticism. While living in a cave, with no possessions, Milarepa is visited by Dzesé, a childhood friend to whom he had once been betrothed. She observes that Milarepa's genuine renunciatory lifestyle is very different from that of other Buddhists of their day. Milarepa explains his position:

> There are those who once fell prey to worldly pride and then, having learned to preach on a few religious books, took pleasure in their own gains and in the defeat of others. Such people call themselves dharma practitioners and wear golden robes, all the while seeking as much wealth and fame as possible. I turn my back on all such people and always will.

Dzesé says that she has never before seen a religious practitioner take on austerities the way Milarepa has, and that he appears to be worse off than even a beggar. She observes, "Your practice and manner of dress and theirs are exactly the opposite. It seems one of them is not the dharma. Were they equally the dharma, I would still prefer theirs."[22] This exchange establishes the idea of there being two distinct ways of practicing religion: there are those who study books, wear nice robes, and amass wealth, and then there are those like Milarepa who embody true asceticism. It cannot be the case that both constitute the highest ideal.

As Milarepa continues his austerities, he becomes as thin as a skeleton and his skin turns green, the color of the nettles that are his sole source of sustenance. His clothes wither away, leaving him naked. Eventually his sister Peta finds him meditating at Drakar Taso. On her way there, she had seen one lama Bari Lotsāwa, dressed in fine silk garments and sitting upon a throne, surrounded by people plying him with *chang*, tea, and offerings.[23] When Peta finds Milarepa, she suggests that he try to achieve something like Bari Lotsāwa. Crying, she says that even if Milarepa were to become the lowest of Bari Lotsāwa's monks, his life would be incomparably better than it is now. What is the purpose of Milarepa's putting himself through so much hardship, when other religious practitioners can live a life of much greater ease?

In response, Milarepa questions the thinking behind Peta's suggestion, asking if she is ashamed of his nakedness. Milarepa asserts that his nudity is no cause for shame: the real cause for shame is committing sin. Living off temple offerings and the lama's wealth is a cause for shame. Milarepa states that he has chosen his life of extreme austerities because he is so disgusted with the ways of worldly people. He quotes his master Marpa, who told him, "Abandon the frivolous distractions of the eight worldly concerns. Renounce food, clothing, and conversation. Wander in isolated places. And above all else, practice with a fierce intention to renounce this life." In a song, Milarepa restates his decision to renounce worldly pleasures, including the joys of monastery life, which brings the perquisites of eloquent discourses to listen to, tasty butter tea, and young monks eager to serve.[24]

One telling and very pointed change the Madman of Tsang made to the *Life* concerns the circumstances surrounding the great yogin's death. In earlier versions of his biography, Milarepa is said to have died after being poisoned by a Bönpo priest with whom he had had an argument. The Madman of Tsang changed this, substituting a jealous scholar-monk—a *geshé*—for the Bönpo priest.[25] Evidently Sangyé Gyeltsen did not hold as inviolable or sacred the narrative traditions he received.

According to the Madman of Tsang, the relationship between Milarepa and the *geshé* proceeded in the following manner. When the wealthy and influential *geshé* Tsakpuwa first met Milarepa, he prostrated to him, as was customary. But Milarepa, having only ever prostrated to his own lama, did not return the courtesy. This incensed the *geshé*. He then handed Milarepa a text on Buddhist logic and asked for a word-by-word explanation. Milarepa responded by saying that the *geshé* himself knew the conceptual meaning of the text, but not the inner meaning, which is that one should abandon worldly attachments and meditate. Milarepa then sang a song based on a series of pairs with starkly contrasting elements: having meditated on his tutelary deity, he had forgotten the world of the senses. Having done tantric meditation, he had forgotten the books on dialectics. Having taken the Teachings into his mind stream, he had forgotten to engage in doctrinal polemics. Having dwelt in the unaltered state of naturalness, he had forgotten the ways of hypocrisy. Having made a monastery inside his body, he had forgotten the monastery outside. (The Madman of Tsang was acutely aware of the relationship between models of knowledge and the physical institutions to which they symbiotically relate.)

Frustrated that Milarepa would not engage him in debate, the *geshé* pitted their respective discourses against each other. "The tradition of meditators may be as you describe it, but if I were to pursue the matter using logical reasoning, your dharma talk would lead nowhere," he said. The patrons, however, took Milarepa's side, telling the *geshé*, "However learned you may be in the dharma, the world is filled with religious people like you. You are not equal to even a single pore on the Jetsün's body. So take a seat at the head of our assembly and quiet down. Do what you can to increase your wealth. You do not have even the smell of dharma."[26]

Following this, the *geshé* thought angrily:

Milarepa, who acts like a know-nothing madman [*smyon pa*] with his nonsense, his lies, and deceit, is a disgrace to the teachings. He confuses people and then lives off their charity. But although I have such extensive learning and am the wealthiest and most influential man in the region, in religious matters I am not even respected as much as a dog. I must do something about this.[27]

The reader knows there is no truth to the *geshé's* claim about Milarepa's wealth. After it is revealed that the *geshé* has secret plans to marry a woman (another jab at the monastic tradition), he has some poison mixed with curdled milk, which he gets her to give to Milarepa. The omniscient Milarepa knows that the food is poisoned, but eats it anyway, out of compassion for the unfortunate messenger, who would have been ashamed if she did not complete her mission. Facing death on account of the poison, Milarepa exhorts his followers not to build a reliquary for his remains and not to set up a monastery, but rather to imitate his detached religious lifestyle and meditate in solitary places in the mountains. He assures them that in the course of practicing in this way, even if they go against the words of some religious texts, they are not opposing the real intention behind the Buddha's teachings.[28]

Shortly before Milarepa's death, he wins *geshé* Tsakpuwa over with his miraculous abilities and the two are reconciled. Then after some last miraculous displays to his disciples, and some more final teachings—"Be humble in conduct. Wear ragged clothes. Renounce all thoughts of food, clothing, or conversation. Practice while enduring physical hardship and mental adversity," echoing Marpa's instructions to him—and prefiguring what Shara Rapjampa will later say to the Madman of Tsang—Milarepa passes away.[29]

The Madman of Tsang formulated his incredibly rich versions of the *Life* and *Songs* of Milarepa with a number of specific agendas in mind. He intended his version of the *Life* to function on one level as a polemic against institutionalized and scholastic forms of Buddhism, which relied on a gradualist model of spiritual development and downplayed the trans- formative power of tantra. The conflict between Milarepa and the *geshé* is about two mutually exclusive discourses within the world of Buddhism. The *geshé*'s is the discourse of philosophers; Milarepa's, that of medita- tors. The *geshé*'s discourse is pedestrian. Milarepa, on the other hand, represents something exceptional. Milarepa's entire style of Buddhism, the regime of truth of which he is a representative, is a threat to the sys- tem embodied by the *geshé*. The difference between the two discourses is ultimately about competing understandings of the true meaning of the teachings of the Buddha. The tense encounter between Milarepa and *geshé* Tsakpuwa is extremely similar to ones the Madman of Tsang is said to have had with *geshés* of the Geluk sect. This suggests a continuity of concern between the events of Sangyé Gyeltsen's life as a tantric literalist ascetic and the hagiographic literature he composed.

A lesser portion of the ire expressed by the Madman of Tsang's *Life of Milarepa* may be seen as directed at the institution of reincarnation lin- eages, which were becoming an increasingly important feature of Tibetan Buddhist culture with each passing decade.[30] In this system, spiritual mas- tery tended to be perceived and embodied in individuals who were essen- tially born into positions of holiness—a charisma of office. In the religious system articulated by the Madman of Tsang in the *Life of Milarepa* and his other works, an individual's relative holiness should be based on the potency of the lineage he has been initiated into and what he has achieved through meditative practice.

The Madman of Tsang's purposeful re-presentation of Milarepa's life was thus a salvo in the battle over what Tibetan Buddhism should be, and, consequently, where the Kagyü would stand within it. The great pur- pose to which the Madman of Tsang hoped to put the *Life* and *Songs* of Milarepa is suggested by his concerted effort to blockprint and distribute copies of the texts—even if that effort was somewhat misunderstood by his followers.

Woodblock printing was an emerging technology in fifteenth-century Tibet, having been used in the region for sixty or so years before the Madman of Tsang published his *Life* and *Songs* of Milarepa.[31] Before that time, every copy of every text had to be written by hand, which resulted in relatively unstable literature of very limited reach. To suddenly have the means to create thousands of exact duplicates of a text was a change so drastic that it is difficult to fully appreciate. This new technology made it possible for certain texts to circulate across the whole of Tibet. Access to texts would no longer be the exclusive domain of the elite.

But making the woodblocks to print a text was a costly undertaking. First, one needed to amass a stockpile of wood—a precious commodity in central Tibet—and have it cut into thin, rectangular blocks. Then workers would painstakingly carve a mirror image of each page of text onto a woodblock. Mistakes—especially hard to avoid when carving text in reverse—were not easily repaired. The upkeep and perhaps salaries for these carvers (up to thirteen for a single text) would have to be paid for the duration of the project.[32] Once all of the woodblocks were carved, ink and costly paper would be needed for each printing.

Because of the great resources it required, at the same time that woodblock printing democratized *access* to certain texts, the *production* of religious discourse was to some extent de-democratized. The select few texts that were blockprinted would have an oversized influence, while representations still produced the old-fashioned way became marginalized by sheer force of numbers. The emergence of this new communications technology constituted a major tipping point in Tibetan religious culture. Tsongkhapa's well-funded school benefitted from the application of this technology, since from early on the Pakmodrupas and their appointed ministers sponsored the printing of Geluk texts. The Madman of Tsang clearly understood the implications of this new technology and enthusiastically embraced it. The great success of the Madman of Tsang and his literary school is in large part attributable to the ardor with which they embraced woodblock printing.

The story of the Madman of Tsang's production of the *Life* and *Songs* of Milarepa exemplifies the great cost and the great potential of this new technology. The prohibitive expensiveness of printing was felt palpably by all involved in the project. According to legend, when Nāropa visited the Madman of Tsang to tell him to make a *Life* and *Songs* of Milarepa, the yogin's foremost concern was about who would pay for the undertaking. The actual project began with the Madman of Tsang's sending disciples all over Tibet, from Ngari in the west to Kongpo in the east, to gather the existing stories and biographies about Milarepa, as well as the many songs attributed to him, which were circulating in oral and written forms. This was accomplished at a substantial cost to the Madman of Tsang, who is said to have "made use of his material possessions without hesitation" to sponsor the search. According to Götsang Repa's version of these events, the Madman of Tsang was personally engaged in collecting offerings of money and materials. He is even said to have fallen ill on account of the effort he exerted in begging.[33]

The ambitious project nearly bankrupted the Madman of Tsang and his community. According to Götsang Repa, midway through the carving of the woodblocks, some of the Madman of Tsang's disciples complained that all of their assets had already been exhausted. Moreover, military conflict in southern Latö meant that an important source of funding could no longer be relied upon. Some of the Madman of Tsang's disciples suggested that they should all abandon the project and go into meditative retreat, with the hope achieving realization. The Madman of Tsang's response was unequivocal: "You all shut up!" He scolded these quarrelsome students and told them to get back to work.[34]

The near-mutiny and the Madman of Tsang's response to it are instructive. In maintaining that they should have been in meditative retreat instead of wasting their precious human lives producing mere literature, the great yogin's disciples were trying to adhere to the stated ideals of the Kagyü tradition, and the central message of the very text they were in the process of printing. But Sangyé Gyeltsen had a different understanding of the task at hand. He saw that printing and distributing large editions of the *Life* and *Songs* of Milarepa would have a greater impact, then and in the long term, than if he and his disciples were to spend all of their time in meditation. The yogin's greatest concern at this point in his life was not for the salvation of his relatively small circle of followers, but in shaping Tibetan religious discourse as a whole. He knew full well that commodifying and reasserting the ideals of renunciation and meditation through a body of printed literature would ultimately be of greater consequence than if he and his disciples were to live out the remainder of their individual lives in meditative retreat.

The Madman of Tsang brought the printing project to completion is 1488, two years after it began. The group began sending copies of the text to people and communities of significance all over Tibet. They also made sets of *tanka*s illustrating the life of Milarepa, which would accompany copies of the text sent to important patrons like Dönyö Dorjé. These visual depictions greatly expanded the reach of the *Life*, making it more easily accessed by the illiterate majority of Tibetans at the time. This was fully in line with Sangyé Gyeltsen's stated intention of spreading the story of Milarepa to a wider audience. Quintman has characterized this project as "one of Tibet's first concerted multimedia approaches to life writing." The fact that the Madman of Tsang wanted as many people as possible to have access to his *Life* of Milarepa through one means or another is significant, given that biographies of Milarepa created prior to this time were usually meant to be kept secret and were specifically not for public consumption.[35] The Madman of Tsang was not only printing copies of his new text, but making a dramatic shift in how the biography was to circulate and be conceived of. The community around the Madman of Tsang also formulated a verse of prayer and a guru worship ritual featuring Milarepa. The *Life*, the *tanka*s, and these ritual materials together helped create a potent and comprehensive cult of Milarepa.

The Madman of Tsang's versions of the *Life* and *Songs* of Milarepa were immensely popular from the very start. So many copies of the *Life* and *Songs* were made that the woodblocks wore out. After a few decades, new ones had to be made—then again, then again, and once more. A total of five sets of woodblocks were carved for the *Life* and *Songs* of Milarepa within a period of about seventy years.[36] Given the cost of producing each set of woodblocks, this is truly remarkable. Although a few of the earlier versions of the *Life of Milarepa*, such as the *Twelve Great Disciples* and the *Black Treasury*, would continue to be distributed and read by a few members of the tradition, the Madman of Tsang's version became the standard one, marginalizing all others.[37] Five hundred years on, it continues to be the best-loved Tibetan spiritual biography ever written. Its effect in shaping understandings of the Kagyü, the "holy madman" phenomenon, and Tibetan religious history as a whole cannot be overstated.

Milarepa the Madman, the Madman as Milarepa

The mythology of Milarepa has had a major impact on the way Tibetans today think about the holy madman phenomenon. This is despite the fact that Milarepa is not commonly referred to as a "holy madman" (*grub thob smyon pa, rnal 'byor smyon pa*, or *bla ma smyon pa*) in the same way that

Künga Zangpo, Sangyé Gyeltsen, and Drukpa Künlé are. Complicating the matter, during his lifetime and since, the Madman of Tsang's identity has to some extent merged with that of Milarepa—a Milarepa partially of his own creation. Their identities inflect and interpenetrate each other so deeply that they cannot be fully separated. In the next few pages I will tease out a few strands of their knotty association, toward better understanding the influence this image of Milarepa has had on perceptions of "holy madmen."

One particular moment from the mythology of Milarepa has been especially instrumental in shaping how Tibetans tend to think about the "holy madmen." In the depths of his retreat, Milarepa was living alone in a cave, so absorbed in meditation that he lost all concern for anything else. When his sister Peta came to visit, she was shocked to find him bone-thin and naked. Peta left her brother with a length of fabric to make a loincloth out of, for the sake of modesty. When Peta returned some time later, she found that Milarepa had not made a loincloth but crude sheaths for his fingers and penis, which barely covered anything at all. Furious, Peta said that Milarepa was no longer human and did not know what shame was, and chastised him for wasting the cloth she had worked so hard to acquire. Milarepa responded by saying that he, as a yogin dedicated only to the practice of virtue, had nothing to be ashamed about. He regarded all parts of his physical self with equanimity, so what was there to cover up? The naked body is a natural thing. On the other hand, the ones who should be ashamed were worldly people, who never ceased to engage in sinful activity. Milarepa's asceticism was for the purpose of practicing religion, and he refused to be judged by the conventions of a system that was ultimately dedicated to all the wrong things.[38]

Tibetans often refer to this story in support of their interpretation of the title "madman" as suggesting that in fact we are the ones who are truly mad, not the great saints who may appear crazy to our conventional, deluded ways of thinking.[39] (According to the biographical record of his life, the Madman of Tsang once used this story to teach what it meant to be without shame, *ngo tsha*, but did not connect it to his "madman" behavior.)[40] The yogin's seeming eccentricity results from and indicates his transcendence. When retelling this story, Tibetans sometimes quote a line supposedly from the mouth of Milarepa that goes something like, "The world sees Mila as crazy, but Mila sees the world as crazy." There is no line in the Madman of Tsang's version of the *Life* that closely resembles this.[41] Oral tradition may have inserted this statement into the mythology of Milarepa. (There is, however, an episode in Lhatsün Rinchen Namgyel's version of the *Life of the Madman of Tsang* in which the great yogin is questioned by a religious teacher: "They say there's a mad renunciant around—is it you?" Sangyé Gyeltsen replies, "If you look at it from a different perspective, it is you who is crazy.")[42]

Another story Tibetans sometimes reference when explaining the nature of holy madness is Milarepa's meeting with Padampa Sangyé (died in 1117), an Indian yogin who traveled many times to Tibet. This tale is told in the Madman of Tsang's version of Milarepa's *Collected Songs*, but was likely in circulation before then. As the story goes, Padampa Sangyé said that Milarepa was "like one who acts crazy" after he sat in such a way that his penis was exposed.[43] Milarepa responded by singing the song of the "crazy tradition" (*smyon lugs*). After a formulaic supplication, he begins:

> Others say of the yogin Milarepa,
> "Is he crazy? Is he crazy?"
> I too wonder if I am crazy,
> so I'll explain the crazy tradition of the crazy one.

He goes on at length to say that everything his tradition rests upon is "crazy":

> The father is crazy, the son is crazy, the lineage is crazy.
> The fount of the lineage, great Vajradhara is crazy.
> The great-grandfather Tilopa, wise and good, is crazy.
> The grandfather Nāropa, the great *paṇḍita*, is crazy.
> My old father Marpa the translator is crazy.
> I, Milarepa, am also crazy.

The next few lines elaborate on why this is so. Each of these integral members of the Kagyü lineage was made "crazy" by a negative force (*gdon*), but one of an assuredly benevolent nature. Vajradhara was made crazy by the "negative force" of the four "bodies" of buddhahood; Tilopa by the "negative force" of the Mahāmudrā; Marpa, by the four classes of the tantras; and Milarepa himself by the yogic winds and mentation (*rlung sems gnyis*). Nāropa was made "crazy by the 'negative force' of the Awareness Observance" (*rig pa brtul zhugs gdon gyis smyo*).

Milarepa then comes to the exegetical climax of the song:

> The unbiased view is crazy.
> Nonreferential, naturally luminous meditation is crazy.
> Nongrasping, self-liberating activity [*spyod pa*] is crazy.
> The result, free of expectation or fear, is crazy.

The enigmatic reversals continue throughout the remainder of the song. Milarepa declares that he punishes demons with the master's teachings; that the Mahāmudrā hurts his back, while the Great Perfection hurts his chest; that he catches illnesses through doing vase-breathing in meditation; that the fever of wisdom and the cold of meditation afflict him. After hearing this song, Padampa Sangyé observes, "Your kind of craziness is very good." In this song in which good is bad and bad is good, the intended meaning seems to be that although Milarepa's behavior may appear crazy to other people (as it did to Padampa Sangyé and Peta), it is in line with an approach that has long characterized his venerable spiritual tradition. Their "madness" simply shows that they have transcended delusory understandings of the spiritual path.

The Mongolian scholar Ngawang Khedrup (1779–1838), abbot of the Hevajra Practice College of Urga, wrote an eleven-folio text titled *Dispelling Insanity: A Commentary on the Crazy Song Sung by Lord Mila, Laughing Vajra*, which shows the kind of meaning the Tibeto-Mongolian tradition has long found in this song. As Ngawang Khedrup says, Milarepa needed only nettles and water to sustain himself, could get by wearing only a single piece of cloth, and spoke true things that did not concur with the way people usually thought. For these reasons, "people saw him as a crazy person who did not accord with the ways of the world."[44] But it is in fact the people of the world, trapped lifetime after lifetime in *saṃsāra*, who are the truly mad ones. Ngawang Khedrup continues, explaining that figures in the lineage from Vajradhara down to Milarepa were all "mad" in this same basic way: they appeared crazy because they embodied wisdom in a deluded world. Vajradhara was "crazy" because his efforts to liberate beings were misrecognized by them. Tilopa was made crazy by a pure wisdom derived from the Mahāmudrā. Nāropa's "craziness" resulted from his practice of the Awareness Observance: the great *paṇḍita* was the wisest of scholars and a monk of pure conduct, but abandoned that life to take on the Practice. He removed his clothes, tied up the plaits of his hair, adorned himself with human bones, wandered from place to place, and coupled with a slender-waisted woman. In the perception of common people, it seemed he had been made crazy by a malevolent force. Marpa, in turn, was "crazy" because of the effort he put into collecting the tantric teachings in India, because in the eyes of worldly people, paying so dearly for something you cannot eat or wear might be seen as pointless. As for Milarepa, through his practice he obtained omniscience and supernatural powers, enabling him to do things that appeared to people like a magician's tricks or the behavior of a madman.[45]

Beyond these two stories, there is a further, rather limited rhetoric of madness sprinkled throughout the Madman of Tsang's mythology of Milarepa. In a song found in the *Life*, Milarepa says, "look at my conduct, like that of a madman." The evil *geshé* Tsakpuwa says that Milarepa "acts like a know-nothing madman."[46] But the Madman of Tsang was restrained in his use of a rhetoric of madness in the *Life*, and he may even have downplayed it in comparison to authors of earlier versions. For example, in a thirteenth-century biography of Milarepa written by Gyeltangpa Dechen Dorjé, when a man plowing a field with his son sees Milarepa flying around, showing off his yogic superpowers, he calls him a "madman." When this story is repeated in the Madman of Tsang's version of the *Life*, the word "madman" is no longer included.[47]

The Madman of Tsang and his school may have made a more concerted effort, however, to inject into the history of their tradition a rhetoric and symbolism derived from the Unexcelled Yoga tantras and the deity Heruka. In the opening line of the *Life*, the Madman of Tsang introduces Milarepa as "the great Heruka." At the very moment when Milarepa arrives to train under Marpa's disciple Ngok Lotsāwa, he was just then reciting some key lines from the *Hevajra Tantra* in which the deity describes himself. Ngok proclaims this to be an excellent sign.[48] The Madman of Tsang also portrays the guru Marpa as the deity Hevajra in a number of ways. Marpa's wife is named Dakmema, which is the name of Hevajra's consort (Nairātmyā in Sanskrit). At one point Marpa reveals his body as that of Hevajra or Cakrasaṃvara. According to the Madman of Tsang, after his death, some would see Milarepa's body in the form of Cakrasaṃvara, Vajravārāhī, or another deity. Nāropa's set of bone ornaments are among Marpa's most prized possessions, and play a recurring role in the story. When in a vision Rechungpa travels to a more enlightened realm, everyone is wearing ornaments made of bone.[49] A sensitive reading of the *Lives* of Milarepa, Marpa, and other fathers of the Kagyü would likely reveal myriad implicit and explicit suggestions that there was a special relationship between these earthly figures and the supreme deities of the *Hevajra* and *Cakrasaṃvara* tantras. It would seem that in composing this literature, Sangyé Gyeltsen sought to establish a relationship of identity—explicitly or implicitly—between the deity Heruka and the great luminaries of the Kagyü sect. Since the Madman of Tsang also presented himself as Heruka, his characterization of the past directly affected the way he was perceived in his own time.

When Tibetans use what they know of Milarepa to explain the phenomenon of "holy madness," they do so based on an underlying belief that the "madness" later enacted by Sangyé Gyeltsen and other "holy madmen" was essentially of the same nature as the seeming eccentricity of the great saint Milarepa. Clearly the Madman of Tsang and the Milarepa portrayed by him both lived as individuals embodying a form of religious life that was rare (or at least said to be rare) in their respective times. They defined themselves against mainstream norms, and thus had analogous positions vis-à-vis the greater religious cultures they lived within. And for this reason they were both "mad." But the tantric fundamentalist "madness" enacted by the Madman of Tsang was very different the "madness" of Milarepa. While Sangyé Gyeltsen was labeled "mad" in large part because of his dressing like Heruka and fashioning a public identity based on the Practice of the Observance, Milarepa is not portrayed as having dressed like Heruka or taken on the Practice of the Observance at all—not even in Sangyé Gyeltsen's portrayal of him. The fact that the differences in their respective lifestyles have escaped from memory over the past few centuries is a testament to the extent to which the *Life of Milarepa* came to speak for the Madman of Tsang, and for many other holy madmen as well. This is in large part because of the way the Madman of Tsang collapsed his identity with that of Milarepa, which has affected understandings of the nature of "holy madness" ever since.

During his lifetime some people regarded the Madman of Tsang as a reincarnation or an emanation of Milarepa. At the very outset of his version of the *Life* of the Madman of Tsang, Götsang Repa states explicitly that Sangyé Gyeltsen was the rebirth of Milarepa. Later in the biography, one Lodrö Tashi hears from a merchant about a "powerful lord of yogins, the Madman of Tsang, an emanation [*sprul pa*] of lord Mila."[50] This would indicate that the Madman of Tsang was reputed to be an emanation of Milarepa even during his lifetime.

Significantly, there are indications that the Madman of Tsang may have fostered this belief himself. According to the earliest version of the

Madman of Tsang's biography, composed a year after his death by Ngödrup Pembar, while on his deathbed the great yogin congratulated his followers and patrons on having had such good fortune to "truly meet Milarepa during this degenerate age." According to Götsang Repa's later version of the *Life* of the Madman of Tsang, when the woodblocks of the *Life* and *Songs* of Milarepa were being consecrated, some people asked the Madman of Tsang who he was an emanation of—was it Rechungpa or Ngendzongpa, or someone else? The Madman of Tsang told them to look at the footprint at Rechen cave in Lapchi, where they would find their answer. Milarepa was believed to have left in solid rock the footprint in question, which the Madman of Tsang had had gilded some years earlier. This would constitute an implicit admission on behalf of the Madman of Tsang that he was in fact an emanation or a reincarnation of Milarepa.[51]

These accounts suggest that the Madman of Tsang was renowned as an emanation of Milarepa during his lifetime, and that he himself probably played an active role in fostering this notion. With this relationship established, anything the Madman of Tsang might subsequently assert in his writings about Milarepa, he was also, in a way, saying about himself. Quintman has gone so far as to argue that the Madman of Tsang thought of himself *as* Milarepa, and writing the *Life of Milarepa* was ultimately an act of autobiography.[52] Regardless of whether or not Sangyé Gyeltsen truly thought of himself as Milarepa, their identities have become conflated in many people's understandings. By fostering his personal association with Milarepa, the Madman of Tsang turned the version of the *Life of Milarepa* he wrote into another means through which he could project an identity for himself into the world.

It is sometimes maintained that the Madman of Tsang modeled his lifestyle on Milarepa's.[53] We have seen in this book that Sangyé Gyeltsen embodied a form of asceticism and an identity very different from Milarepa's. But this popular misunderstanding is extremely instructive, insofar as it shows how circular the relationship between the Madman of Tsang and Milarepa has become: each is in some way a reflection of the other, and each has an effect on how the other has been understood. The Madman of Tsang's biography of Milarepa has probably contributed more to current understandings of Tibet's "holy madmen" than the details of their actual lives.

In composing his version of the *Life of Milarepa*, the Madman of Tsang carefully removed any suggestion that Milarepa was a reincarnation of some past master, choosing instead to portray him as an ordinary human who achieved greatness through his own diligence and the power of the teachings on which he relied. In light of this it may seem surprising that the Madman of Tsang would have encouraged the thought that he himself was an emanation or reincarnation of Milarepa. Perhaps Sangyé Gyeltsen encouraged this association between himself and Milarepa in order to accrue further credibility for the model of Buddhistness and Kagyüness that he chose to enact. In so doing, he would have been participating in the commodification of the idea of Milarepa—now conceived of, known of, and worshipped as never before—around which a stable and better-defined Kagyü could be formed.

In the Madman of Tsang's version of him, Milarepa rails against those who make outward displays of religiosity. Was anyone more guilty of this than the Madman of Tsang, who walked around Tibet dressed in the attire of the enlightened? Although in his version of the *Life of Milarepa*, Sangyé Gyeltsen portrays scriptural exegesis as a fruitless endeavor, did he not rely on quotations from scripture to defend his own lifestyle? The penniless Milarepa is set up as a foil to the rich and evil *geshé* Tsakpuwa. But wasn't the Madman of Tsang more like the *geshé* than Milarepa in financial matters? In the Madman of Tsang's version of things, one of Milarepa's disciples praised him: "Lord, when you faced material wealth / You were like mercury hitting the ground, / A yogin unsullied by taint."[54] Sangyé Gyeltsen could not be praised in similar terms. It is not the case that the Madman of Tsang really wanted all members of the Kagyü sect to "Do without food, clothing, and fame," as Marpa had instructed Milarepa, and Milarepa his many disciples, and as the Madman of Tsang was instructed by his own teacher. Quite to the contrary, the Madman of Tsang worked to commodify the ideals of meditation and asceticism, as embodied in the story of Milarepa, in order to position the Kagyü sect strategically in the competitive marketplaces of fifteenth- and sixteenth-century Tibet, and beyond.

The Madman of Tsang's fate was inextricably tied to Milarepa's on a number of different levels, from the most abstract to the most concrete. Versions of the Madman of Tsang's own biography would often be printed alongside the *Life* and *Songs* of Milarepa. Sangyé Gyeltsen's personal fame, then and forever after, was pegged to the success of his literary creation.[55]

Putting the Aural Transmission to Paper

Between his creation of the *Life* and *Songs* of Milarepa in 1488 and his renovation of the Swayambhūnāth stūpa in 1504, Sangyé Gyeltsen's main project was to gather and compose texts elucidating a body of teachings known as the Aural Transmission (*snyan rgyud, snyan brgyud*), which he referred to as the quintessence of the *sūtras* and tantras, the most profound of all the Teachings.[56] These instructions offer dedicated students the promise of buddhahood in one lifetime—or even a single instant. The chapter of Götsang Repa's version of the *Life* describing this project refers to Sangyé Gyeltsen's efforts as "putting the Aural Transmission in writing," signaling that the crux of the endeavor was the creation of a physical copy of this body of teachings.[57]

The Aural Transmission teachings, which ultimately explicate the *Cakrasaṃvara Tantra*, were believed to have passed from the buddha Vajradhara to Tilopa and through the early fathers of the Kagyü. By the time of the Madman of Tsang, they were in disarray. As Götsang Repa explains, these teachings—"the secret words of the *ḍākinīs*, which are like the essence or the heart of all the profound dharmas of the precious Kagyü"—had been referred to and transmitted separately as the Saṃvara Aural Transmission, the *Ḍākinī* Aural Transmission, the Rechungpa Aural Transmission, the Ngendzongpa Aural Transmission, the Dakpo Aural Transmission, and so on. But these various names and transmissions all ultimately refer to the same body of very secret, very profound teachings.[58]

Over a period of years, the Madman of Tsang collected various written Aural Transmission texts, put on paper some that had been circulating orally, and composed new texts of his own. This was undertaken with the intention of unifying the disparate threads of the transmission and creating a more definitive version of the whole. According to Ngödrup Pembar's version of the *Life*, the yogin was motivated to make this collection out of fear that the teachings might be lost.[59]

The product of the Madman of Tsang's labor was a twelve-volume *Compendium* (*yig cha*) of Aural Transmission texts, only fragments of which are extant today.[60] The most important of the original texts composed by the Madman of Tsang is a long commentary on the *Vajra Verses on the Aural Tantra* (*snyan rgyud rdo rje'i tshig rkang, Karṇatantravajrapada*), the brief tantra that serves as a sort of root text for the whole of the Aural Transmission.[61] Sangyé Gyeltsen's commentary includes a history of the Aural Transmission lineage told through biographies of its individual members; instructions on the Six Dharmas of Nāropa, including the yogic practices of inner fire, illusory body, dream yoga, the yoga of "clear light," controlling the way the consciousness exits the body at death, and projecting one's consciousness into a corpse; sexual yoga; Mahāmudrā meditation leading to the realization of the emptiness of all phenomena; the processes of death, traversing the intermediate state, and rebirth; deflecting the negative influence of demons and other obstacles to religious progress; the various stages of spiritual accomplishment; and much more. The other Aural Transmission texts composed by the Madman of Tsang cover a remarkable range of concerns. He discusses major topics like empowerment rituals and the Secret Practice (as summarized in chapter 2), as well as minor details, such as at which point in the creation of a religious statue the eyes should be painted on, and what exact prayers must be recited when restoring a stūpa. One text explains the various yogic postures (*'khrul 'khor*), while another describes how to initiate women into the higher tantric practices.[62] This collection is a comprehensive presentation of tantric practice, covering a wide range of rituals—often in their full, intermediate, and abbreviated forms—and showing Sangyé Gyeltsen to have been a consummate *vajra* master. Sangyé Gyeltsen composed most of his own Aural Transmission texts in the mid-1490s, working at Chubar, Lapchi, and Mount Kailash. The *Compendium* also included texts penned by other masters, like Marpa, Barawa Gyeltsen Pelzang (1310–1391), and Zhaluwa Gelong Khyenrap (1436–1497).

The real significance of this project can only be understood by taking into account the mode in which the Aural Transmission had circulated prior to this time. In India and Tibet, advanced tantric teachings and practices were traditionally of restricted access. A potential practitioner could gain entry into the instructions only after undergoing a special initiation ritual. That ritual would be performed only for a student who had proven himself dedicated and worthy, and who was willing to pay a fee. Once thus empowered, the practitioner would in time be able to initiate others. Advanced tantric teachings were thus a valuable commodity for those to whom they had been entrusted. Some teachings were never written down, so that access to them could be more closely controlled, since they would have to be received directly from someone who had memorized them. Other teachings were written down but remained incomprehensible to those who did not have the oral teachings that functioned as a cipher. Secrecy, orality, and encodedness helped to maintain the division between the initiated and the uninitiated.

The Aural Transmission was held to have been, since its very beginning, of a particular type of secret teaching: the single-transmission lineage (*gcig brgyud* or *chig brgyud*). A master holding these teachings was supposed to give them only to one particularly gifted and trustworthy disciple, and that disciple to only one student of his own. It is said that the *ḍākinīs* had commanded that the Aural Transmission teachings be treated in this way. If one broke this "seal" (*rgya*) by giving the teachings to multiple students or to the uninitiated or unworthy, one would face ghastly repercussions: a brief text included in the Madman of Tsang's collection—asserted to relate instructions written down (*yi ger bkod*) by Marpa after he received them from Nāropa—threatens that if one were to reveal these teachings to a person not formally initiated into the Aural Transmission, then Mahākāla and the *ḍākiṇīs* should split one's head open.[63] The Aural Transmission's being a single-transmission lineage and an oral or aural lineage were closely related, for many have interpreted the injunction of a single-transmission lineage to mean an exclusively oral one as well. Perhaps we can glean an insight into the purpose this command of strict secrecy served historically when in the colophon to one of his texts the Madman of Tsang states that the teachings of the *ḍākiṇīs'* Aural Transmission "had a strict seal of orality . . . to ensure that they would not be given to those who would sell them for material wealth." The mystique of exclusivity made the teachings only more valuable.[64]

The mythology of the tradition maintained that the "seal" with which the Aural Transmission had been stamped stipulated that it must be kept as a single-transmission lineage for thirteen master–student generations from the time it was imparted to Tilopa by the buddha Vajradhara. This is stated in the final verse of the *Vajra Verses on the Aural Tantra*. A variation of this is repeated in the Madman of Tsang's version of the *Life of Milarepa*: when Marpa instructs Milarepa in the ways of the Aural Transmission before imparting them to him, he tells Milarepa that he should give the most essential teachings to only one most competent disciple, and must never teach them for the sake of wealth.[65] Milarepa is said to have given the most essential of the Aural Transmission instructions to his disciple Rechungpa, who gave them to Gampopa. But the mythology also suggests that Milarepa gave some of these teachings directly to Gampopa, and to Ngendzongpa as well. (The history of the transmission of these teachings is especially messy and unclear.) All three would pass the teachings on to disciples of their own, resulting in there being multiple separate transmissions by the time of the Madman of Tsang.[66]

If Tilopa was the first in the lineage, then according to the history given by the Madman of Tsang, the mandate of the single-transmission lineage would have expired by some point between the time of Milarepa and that of Shara Rapjampa (the lineage is enumerated differently in different accounts).[67] By giving parts of the Aural Transmission to three of his disciples, Milarepa may have technically broken the seal of the single-transmission lineage. But according to the mythology established by the Madman of Tsang, Milarepa had been given special permission to do just that. As told in an episode his *Collected Songs*, Milarepa was visited by Vajrayoginī, who gave him permission to loosen the stipulation of the single-transmission lineage somewhat. In his telling, Götsang Repa adds to this account, saying that Vajrayoginī also imparted to Milarepa some teachings on the Aural Transmission; that she gave him permission to write down some of the Aural Transmission, which he did; and that Rechungpa, Ngendzongpa, and Gampopa all wrote down parts of the teachings as well. According to Götsang Repa, some subsequent holders of the lineage would also write a little bit about the Aural Transmission, but as these writings were not widely disseminated, the seals of orality and single-transmission were nevertheless maintained in principle.[68]

The Madman of Tsang's concerted effort to bring together into a single collection the various Aural Transmission teachings was an attempt to reunify the Aural Transmission, to bring the branches stemming from Milarepa back together again, and thus restore the instructions to a state they were in—at least purportedly—during an earlier time. In creating his textual collection of the Aural Transmission, the Madman of Tsang was also responsible for a major shift in how those teachings circulated. No longer an exclusive, amorphous body of teachings shrouded by a veil of mystery, the Aural Transmission would be clearly defined and laid out in a physical textual collection. This physical text could then be read and reread, shared and copied, worshipped and preserved.

The "seal" of the *ḍākinīs* having technically expired at some point before his time, the Madman of Tsang should in theory have been free to disseminate the Aural Transmission teachings more widely without provoking the displeasure of its divine protectors. But it seems that the great yogin's putting these teachings on paper was still a potentially controversial undertaking, for which he felt the need to apologize, and which his disciples were careful to defend. At the beginning of his version of the *Life of the Madman of Tsang*, Götsang Repa includes a cryptic five-line prophecy given by Tilopa. Through some impressive hermeneutical gymnastics, Götsang Repa interprets these lines as referring to the Madman of Tsang, who would come seventeen master–student generations after Nāropa (the members of which he enumerates); who would gather the essential teachings of the *ḍākinīs*, the Aural Transmission; and who, the seal ensuring their secrecy having expired, would then spread those teachings and give them to innumerable students.[69] In this presentation, the Madman of Tsang's gathering and promulgating the Aural Transmission were preordained.

Throughout the Madman of Tsang's biographies, there are other instances where it is asserted that he was divinely inspired to carry out this project. According to Götsang Repa, at one point the Madman of Tsang was considering writing a commentary on the *Hevajra Tantra*, during which time he was visited by Vajrayoginī, who told him that there were already many commentaries on that tantra, and he should instead focus his efforts on explicating the meanings of the Aural Transmission. The next day he considered that he "needed to explicate and spread" the *Vajra Verses of the Aural Transmission*. Shortly after this, he began writing about the Aural Transmission and putting its oral texts on paper.[70] Just as the Madman of Tsang had included a story of Milarepa's getting divine permission to distribute the Aural Transmission a bit more widely, the Madman of Tsang's own biographer would seek to justify his doing so in precisely the same manner.

The wrathful protector deity Mahākāla, who was considered a protector of the Aural Transmission teachings, also played a significant role in these affairs. According to Götsang Repa's version of the *Life*, one night while staying near Tsari, the Madman of Tsang had a vision in which he was visited by a black man who identified himself as (an emanation of) four-armed Mahākāla, the "protector" (*srung ma*) of the Aural Transmission (figure 5.3). The apparition promised to be his personal protector in dharmic activities from then on.[71] During his visits to Kathmandu years later, the great yogin would on at least three occasions visit a famous stone statue of Mahākāla known as "the Protector of the Tibetan Field." During two of these visits, the great yogin was seen by the local populace holding hands and dancing with the deity, which is said to have resulted in the widening of his fame in the region. On another visit to the statue—here referred to by Götsang Repa as the guarantor or patron (*chos bdag*) of the Aural Transmission—the great yogin thanked the deity for ensuring that there would be no obstacle to his setting the teachings to paper, now that the seal demanding that they be preserved as a single-transmission lineage no longer applied.[72]

It seems that having the blessing of the deities was not enough to dispel all of Sangyé Gyeltsen's concerns, since he continued to defend and apologize for his writing down the Aural Transmission. In a two-folio text titled the *Profound Transference of Consciousness*, he states that "although

FIGURE 5.3 "Homage to the glorious four-armed protector"

it is generally inappropriate to put the profound meanings of the Aural
Transmission onto paper," he has done just that, because of the benefit
it will bring to other practitioners, and because a wisdom ḍākiṇī had
appeared and given him permission to do so. The end of the text reads,
"Set [to paper] by the Madman of Tsang, the Heruka, for the sake of others." We also see this kind of defensive language in other texts Sangyé
Gyeltsen wrote about the Aural Transmission, suggesting that the issue of
how these texts ought to circulate had not been fully resolved.[73]

After the Madman of Tsang and his disciples had finished gathering,
composing, and editing the texts of the *Compendium*, creating copies
of it became a pressing concern. The yogin's hope of a copy written in
gold went unfulfilled, which he expressly regretted before his death. He
also voiced a wish to have copies sent to the great meditation sites of the
Kagyü.[74] It does not seem that there was any plan to carve woodblocks for
the collection during the great yogin's time.

The notion that the Aural Transmission existed as a single-transmission
lineage or in purely oral form at any time after its earliest days is a pious
exaggeration, since the tradition itself recognizes multiple streams of

transmission, and that some of the teachings had been written down even as early as Marpa's time. Nevertheless, the Aural Transmission had long defined itself by those related ideals. The Madman of Tsang's putting this body of teachings into textual form constituted a dramatic departure from tradition. This could have led to a decline in the perception of these teachings' potency. But it seems that Sangyé Gyeltsen hoped to maintain the charisma of secrecy and orality, despite the changes he was responsible for. Exemplifying this, in the colophon to a text laying out teachings of the Aural Transmission, the Madman of Tsang writes, "May the assembly of mother and sister *ḍākinīs* tolerate my having put in writing the unwritten secret words of the *ḍākinīs* for the sake of clarifying the oral instructions of the Aural Transmission!"[75] The great yogin is intent upon having it both ways at once: in spite of their being written down and available to a broader audience, he still characterizes the teachings as strictly oral and secret.

The Madman of Tsang also sought to bolster the Aural Transmission's charisma of secrecy and orality through writing his biographical history of the lineage. The history told through the biographies composed by the Madman of Tsang and his disciples served to prove the efficacy of the Aural Transmission, and established its prior secrecy and orality so unassailably that it no longer needed to be kept particularly secret or oral. The biographies of the lineage had long played this kind of role in supporting the Aural Transmission teachings, since early versions of Milarepa's biography were included as introductory material to some teachings associated with the Aural Transmission, and even in Gö Lotsāwa's *Blue Annals*, Milarepa's life is recorded, not in the context of Marpa's main lineage, but in the section recounting a history of the Aural Transmission.[76]

Exemplifying the relationship between these Aural Transmission texts and the biographies of the lineage, the Madman of Tsang's biography of Tilopa, contained within his long commentary on the *Vajra Verses*, tells of Tilopa's encounters with a king, a butcher, a magician, a singer, an alcohol seller, and so on, each of whom he turns to the dharma through his teachings. A separate text contained in the *Compendium of the Aural Transmission*, titled the *Inconceivable Mahāmudrā*, relates the full teachings (originally oral, but since then written down) given by Tilopa in each of those encounters. The biography provides a context and a historicity for these songs, and asserts their indisputable orality—regardless of what form they now circulate in.[77]

In creating his *Life* and *Songs* of Milarepa, the Madman of Tsang brought together disparate narrative traditions of the famous poet-yogin and created a new, more comprehensive and streamlined version that would be accessible to a much wider audience. His work in formulating and making a textual version of the Aural Transmission instructions was comparable in many ways. These biographical and Aural Transmission literatures would serve to legitimate one another in a reimagined Kagyü sect centered on this most potent body of teachings. In a moment of turmoil and uncertainty, the great yogin's setting the Aural Transmission to paper would, in the estimation of Ngödrup Pembar, make the teachings of the Kagyü "shine like the sun."[78]

Renovating the Swayambhūnāth Stūpa

In the summer of 1504, the Madman of Tsang was staying at a retreat site called Onjung, near Lapchi and Chubar, along the border of Nepal and Tibet. The site had had a colorful history in the years since Milarepa was believed to have meditated there, with various Kagyü groups vying for control over its caves. When the Madman of Tsang asked the local lord for permission and support to build a residence there, he was denied, it was said, because of his being a fallen monk and because the lord did not have faith in the Kagyü, preferring instead the Ngorpa subsect of the Sakya. When the Madman of Tsang's community began construction work anyway, the lord tried to stop them. Some of the great yogin's disciples suggested they use black magic to coerce the lord to change his mind. Some students suggested they abandon the project, since "this meaningless building work" was distracting them from their individual religious practice. Others suggested the Madman of Tsang petition Dönyö Dorjé, because "there was nobody who would not listen to him."[79] The yogin chastised his students for thinking mainly about their own lives and the current moment, arguing that the work of spreading the Teachings required a more expansive vision, including past and future lifetimes.

The situation dragged on for a while. Some students grew concerned that if the yogin did not succeed in this endeavor, people would lose faith in his miraculous abilities. Eventually, Dönyö Dorjé came to know of the situation and from Rinpung issued a command that the Madman of Tsang should be given possession of the site. As if by the intercession of a divine protector, all was immediately resolved. For some time the Madman of Tsang also controlled a meditation cave near Mount Kailash called

Serkyi Jakyib, which he wrested away from the Gelukpas.[80] The Seventh Karmapa's letter suggests that the yogin helped foster meditation sites in other holy places as well.

The following winter, the Madman of Tsang would oversee the renovation of the Swayambhūnāth stūpa in Kathmandu, which was the last major undertaking of his life. Although this project did not have the same long-term impact as his literary production, it was a matter of enormous significance at the time. Many across Tibet, Nepal, China and the greater Buddhist world saw the state of the grand monument as an indication of the state of Buddhism on earth.[81] Its being in disrepair reflected poorly on the Buddhists of the entire region. Overseeing the collective effort of the stūpa's renovation would be the capstone to Sangyé Gyeltsen's remarkable career, building upon his previous accomplishments, and confirming his status as a realized and powerful being.

The Swayambhūnāth stūpa, standing atop a hill on the western side of Kathmandu, dates from before the eleventh century, although its early history is unclear.[82] The stūpa is held sacred by Buddhists and Hindus alike, with a rich mythology imbuing it with significance. Tibetans have believed the stūpa to contain relics of the Buddha or of his disciple Kaśyapa, that it was the site of Nāgārjuna's hair cutting, that the stūpa was not manmade but arose spontaneously during an earlier world age, and so on.[83] The Kathmandu valley had long been an important destination for Tibetan traders and pilgrims, who liked to make the trip during the winter months. Meditators would also visit caves and charnel grounds around the valley, some of which were believed to have been blessed by visits from great Indian *siddhas* like Nāropa. The holy madmen, their followers, and many in their wider circle of Kagyüpas would visit the Kathmandu valley and the Swayambhūnāth stūpa in the fifteenth and sixteenth centuries.

Over the years, the stūpa has fallen into disrepair many times—afflicted by the ravages of time, struck by lightning, and occasionally attacked by invaders of the Kathmandu valley. Between 1370 and 1817, the stūpa was rebuilt at least eleven times, and enlarged in the process; at the time of the Madman of Tsang, it was visibly smaller than it is today.[84] Many of these renovations, both before and after the Madman of Tsang, were overseen and sponsored by Tibetans, many of whom were associated with the Kagyü.

The significance of the Madman of Tsang's renovation project is brought into relief through a consideration of the one that preceded it.

In 1412 or 1413, the Indian Śākya Śrī Śāriputra (1335–1426) oversaw a total reconstruction of the monument. Years earlier, Śāriputra had renovated or rebuilt many of the temples at the site of the Buddha's enlightenment in Bodhgaya, of which complex he then became abbot. The main sponsor for his renovation of Swayambhūnāth was the king of Kathmandu, Jyotirmalla, supported by additional funds Śāriputra gathered from various regional rulers in Tibet, including the Pakmodru *gongma* Drakpa Gyeltsen. After completing the renovation, Śāriputra spent some years in Tibet, then traveled to Beijing, where he eventually died, but not before imparting to the emperor designs for a new temple based on the one celebrating the Buddha's enlightenment at Bodhgaya.[85] The fact that the Madman of Tsang would be the next person invited to oversee work on the stūpa suggests that he was a similarly respected and trusted figure in the northern Buddhist world.

The Madman of Tsang had visited the Swayambhūnāth stūpa during two earlier stays in the Kathmandu valley. It is said that on his first visit, he sat cross-legged in meditation on one of the brass rings atop the stūpa for seven days. Despite an earthquake, he did not waver from his meditation, which greatly impressed the locals. During his second visit to the valley, while staying at a temple near the stūpa, it is said that Sangyé Gyeltsen was visited by the god Ganesh, who requested that he renovate the monument and pledged his assistance. On this second visit, he had a coat of whitewash applied to the stūpa.[86]

Götsang Repa's version of the *Life* of the Madman of Tsang devotes an entire chapter to the restoration project.[87] According to this account, via Tibetan pilgrims returning from visits to Kathmandu each year, the Madman of Tsang had for some time been receiving requests from king Ratnamalla of Kathmandu (reigned 1484–1520) and his ministers, as well as other Nepalese and Tibetans, that he undertake the restoration of the stūpa. He acquiesced after receiving an especially urgent request while staying at Chubar in 1501. Around this time, the populace of Nepal would have been mainly Buddhist, with the royal families of Kathmandu increasingly employing the services of Śaivite priests, although still continuing to sponsor Buddhist activities. Most laymen would not have made much of a distinction between Buddhist and non-Buddhist, leaving such concerns to the professionals whose livelihoods depended upon them.[88] Seeing to the renovation of the stūpa was especially important to Ratnamalla's reign. He promised to provide upkeep for the yogin and eighty followers until the project was finished.

When the Madman of Tsang gathered his students to begin making preparations, some voiced concerns about taking on the project. Some spoke about the risk of failure, and the loss in prestige that such an outcome would entail. Some thought it could be done, but would take three or four years. Some feared that it would be too wearying for the Madman of Tsang, who was nearly fifty years old. Some were concerned that the undertaking would be a distraction from their religious practice. Some worried about how many of them would die, since spending time in the relative lowland of Nepal was a dangerous prospect for Tibetans. A pressing concern was the question of who should be dispatched to do the fund-raising: some thought the more famous of the Madman of Tsang's disciples should be sent, while others thought that they would not gather enough donations unless the great yogin went personally. He ended up sending his students to visit potential donors, equipped with a letter of request. Lords, ministers, and former students of the great yogin now staying in places as far away as Tsari in the east and Mount Kailash in the west were petitioned for support.

Fund-raising and initial preparations took about three years. Once everyone had regathered at Chubar in 1504, some departed for Nepal with the yogin, while others stayed behind, performing rituals to ensure the success of the project. After a grand reception in Kathmandu, the party settled at the stūpa site. Rituals were performed, after which the upper part of the holy monument was disassembled, inaugurating a time of inauspiciousness. Fearing disease, many of the Tibetans returned home. Among the disciples of the great yogin who stayed, some oversaw work teams, while others performed rituals and meditated. We are told that working on the project there were seventy-two carpenters; six hundred and forty wood preparers; a hundred and thirty wood cutters; twelve blacksmiths; twenty-five metal beaters; twenty-five coppersmiths; twelve goldsmiths; and eight hundred people conscripted (*'u lag*) to haul wood each day.[89] Since they did not tear down the bulbous part of the stūpa and worked only on its outside, this was a relatively small-scale project. A good deal of the manpower must have been put toward raising the necessary scaffolding. They replaced the thirteen brass rings, the canopy atop them, and various other adornments. In the course of the renovation, the Madman of Tsang made some slight alterations to the form of the stūpa, such as adding a copper parasol. The work on the stūpa was completed in two months and thirteen days; the yogin's visit to the Kathmandu valley would last a total of three and a half months.

The project was a joint Newari–Tibetan undertaking. In true ecumenical fashion, many of the key rituals would be performed in the Newari style, then in the Tibetan style.[90] The Madman of Tsang had a dual role in the project. For one thing, he was the chief foreman, directing everyone working beneath him. The account notes that the Nepalese tended to work slowly. In particular, the man serving as translator between the Tibetans and the Nepalese was extremely lazy and spent much of his time drunk, which delayed their progress. In a skillful and passive-aggressive manner, the Madman of Tsang guilted him into improving his conduct, which suggests that it took managerial talent and interpersonal skills to keep the project moving forward.[91]

The Madman of Tsang also served as a sort of spiritual foreman, as he was responsible for rituals performed before, during, and after the renovation, to ensure that work progressed safely and that the completed stūpa would be just as holy and efficacious as the previous one had been. But Sangyé Gyeltsen's spiritual potency would also be called upon outside of these formal rituals. When fire had caused a dangerous mishap, he made a pronouncement, blinked his eyes, and snapped his fingers, after which conflagrations were a problem no more. Rain had been impeding their work, so he made a successful supplication that it should not rain again until the project was finished. He also magically protected his workers from a swarm of angry bees. The account thus suggests that if the Madman of Tsang had been any less of a *siddha*, the project would not have been accomplished. The account also states that from start to finish, the project was blessed and aided by various spirit-beings—Ganesh, Viśvakarman, the *ḍākiṇīs* and dharma protectors—which testifies to the yogin's divinely favored status.[92]

The successful completion of the project was taken by many as an indication of the Madman of Tsang's spiritual potency. It is said that at the time some people exclaimed, "If [Sangyé Gyeltsen] is not a *siddha*, who is?"[93] In the view of others, he was nothing short of a deity himself. The biography describes how the Tibetans and Newaris present at the time reflected on how amazing it was that the project was completed so quickly. Some of them had visions of the Madman of Tsang, in some cases seeing him as Guru Śāntikara (who had once renovated the stūpa and remained a divine presence there) or glorious Heruka.[94] Some of the Nepalese, unable to wrap their minds around this great accomplishment, said, "Your guru is not human. He is Mahākāla himself."[95]

The great pomp with which Sangyé Gyeltsen was treated during his stay in the valley also suggests the importance of the project and his role within it. We are told that when the yogin arrived in Kathmandu, he was grandly received by king Ratnamalla and his ministers, people from all classes of society, musicians of every stripe, and hundreds of beautiful women. During the course of the renovation, offerings were brought to him. At the consecration ritual and on his departure from the valley, Sangyé Gyeltsen had audiences with the king, during which gifts of clothing and gold jewelry were lavished upon him. Newaris accompanied him for a long way when he left, tearful at seeing the great master go.

After Götsang Repa's description of the renovation project, he repeats three folios of text apparently written by the Madman of Tsang himself. This passage begins with a long versified list of the many donors for the project and the amounts of gold, silver, bronze, horses, silk, salt, and tea they had each given. This is followed by a calculation of the cost of the project: a total of 2,751 *zho* of gold was expended on gold and copper, payments to workmen, board for the Madman of Tsang's retinue, and the sending of letters and gifts before and after the restoration.[96] The Madman of Tsang then describes what work was done to the stūpa and thanks Guru Śāntikara and the god Viśvakarman for allowing the project to come to completion. Lastly, he states that his purpose in writing this letter was to ensure that in future times, all the Tibetans who came to the stūpa—monks, nuns, yogins, yoginīs, and householders—could be informed of the facts of its renovation.

This would not be the end of the Madman of Tsang's care for the stūpa. A few years after the renovation project, he traded some of his possessions for gilded copper, which he had his students apply to the four pillars supporting the upper part of the monument. It also seems that he had hoped to establish an endowment for regular whitewashings of the stūpa, but was unable to accomplish this.[97]

The connection between the Madman of Tsang's lineage and the great stūpa did not end with his death. In the 1520s the stūpa was damaged by invaders, who tore off the copperwork and tried to set fire to the monument. The person who took responsibility for dismantling the stūpa and completely reconstructing it from its central pillar was Lhatsün Rinchen Namgyel. According to Rinchen Namgyel's biography, the Madman of Tsang appeared to him in a dream and requested that he restore the monument. The work was carried out over the course of ten years, being completed by one of Rinchen Namgyel's disciples in 1572.[98]

The renovation of the Swayambhūnāth stūpa at the beginning of the sixteenth century was a considerable task. It required the oversight of an individual well connected with the powerful lords of Nepal and Tibet, and organized enough to oversee a team of hundreds of workers speaking a variety of languages. He also needed to have close relationships with the powerful figures of the spirit world, and enough spiritual potency of his own to ensure the success of the undertaking. The fact that Sangyé Gyeltsen was invited to take up this project shows the great respect with which he was regarded; the fact that he completed it successfully served to prove and justify his enlightened status. The son of a humble family from a small village in Tsang now stood at the highest peak of the Himalayan religious world.

Conclusion

When the Madman of Ü expressed his intention of settling down at a more permanent monastic establishment, it seemed to some of his followers that this would be to abandon the kind of religious life they had been pursuing for decades. A similar dissension emerged among the ranks of the Madman of Tsang's disciples when he drew them into compiling and printing the *Life* and *Songs* of Milarepa, when he was working to establish a retreat center at Onjung, and again when he undertook the renovation of the Swayambhūnāth stūpa. Wouldn't these projects be a distraction from the individual meditative practice they had for so long made the defining feature of their version of the Kagyü religious program?

These disagreements expose a difference in thinking between the madmen and their followers. Toward the ends of their careers, Künga Zangpo and especially Sangyé Gyeltsen each came to understand the potential effects of their actions in a new way. Each took an interest in pursuing projects that would effectively transubstantiate their individual asceticism, and that endured by the forefathers of their sect, into something that would touch upon the lives of the greater Tibetan public and revitalize and strengthen their version of the Kagyü in a time of great change. During a lifetime of meditation and asceticism—even of the most shocking and attention-grabbing sort—one can accomplish only so much. But there is virtually no limit to the kind of effect that one can have by building an institution based on the idea and rhetoric of meditation and asceticism. This can come in the form of a monastic center, or a more abstract institution, constructed through the writing and printing of a new history. Of more enduring effect than changing from within is shifting the religious discourse around oneself.

In taking on their tantric literalist asceticism in the early parts of their careers, neither Künga Zangpo nor Sangyé Gyeltsen had much of an impact on the religious culture of their day. Since his death, the Madman of Ü has been all but forgotten, for most Tibetans have never heard his name. The Madman of Tsang, on the other hand, has become one of the most influential Tibetans of all time, and it is without question because of his literary production that he has achieved this immortality (figure 5.4). Whereas earlier on in his career Sangyé Gyeltsen had endeavored to turn himself into a powerful symbol, he later turned to creating even more powerful and enduring symbols through literature. Half a millennium later, the Kagyü sect is still profoundly shaped and animated by his version of the *Life of Milarepa*.

In putting Künga Zangpo and Sangyé Gyeltsen forward as *siddhas*, their faithful followers described them as men who saw all phenomena as empty of their own inherent existence. The madmen were like magicians, with the ability to manipulate appearances. Waking life was as insubstantial as a dream. In time, Künga Zangpo and Sangyé Gyeltsen each proved this estimation to be true. Knowing the self to be an illusion, they

FIGURE 5.4 "Homage to the Madman of Tsang, the Heruka"

fashioned new selves for the world to see. Knowing conventional realities to be subjective, they made themselves different men for different people at different times. Sangyé Gyeltsen, not limited by the conventions of what was known, created a new past, present, and future by rewriting the history of his sect. Each madman took control of our world of false appearances, and, rather than remaining subject to its falsity, transcended unreality by using it to his advantage.

6

Who Was Drukpa Künlé?

The biographies of lamas in which everything is too ordered tend to read like a creditor's account book, in which it says, "In this year and month, on this day, I made a loan for this amount, and I shall collect this many measures of barley or peas in return . . ." It's much too narrow. "In this year he began his training . . ." Then if it's a major lama: "Someone made an offering of this horse . . ." If it's a minor lama: "Someone offered this much felt to make hats out of, and this much grain . . ." What is the use of writing such things? It's like, "During the warmth of the day, he ate this kind of food . . . At night, he took this kind of a shit . . ." Doesn't it make you laugh?

DRUKPA KÜNLÉ, *Miscellaneous Writings*[1]

THE MOST FAMOUS of all the Tibetan "holy madmen" is Drukpa Künlé (born in 1455), often referred to as Druknyön (*'brug smyon*), taken as meaning "the Madman of the Drukpa [Kagyü sect]" or, somewhat mistakenly, "the Madman of Bhutan."[2] Because of Drukpa Künlé's great popularity over the past few hundred years, his legacy has had a disproportionately large influence in shaping the way Tibetans today think about the tradition of "holy madness." In more recent decades, his image has also greatly influenced the way many non-Tibetans think about "holy madmen," and Tibetan Buddhism in general.

By contrasting more recent and popular depictions of Drukpa Künlé with the information that can be gleaned from his *Miscellaneous Writings* and other fifteenth- and sixteenth-century sources, this chapter will show that the popular image of Drukpa Künlé is a wild caricature of the historical individual, who emerges as sober, thoughtful, and in some ways rather conservative. As a result, understandings of "holy madness" based on the popular image of Drukpa Künlé must be thoroughly reevaluated.

Drukpa Künlé has long been famous across the whole of the Tibetan cultural world, including Bhutan, in whose religious culture he has come

to occupy a central place since the Drukpa Kagyü sect's rise to prominence there in the seventeenth century. In this chapter, when I use the
words "Tibet" and "Tibetan," this in some instances includes Bhutan and
the Bhutanese as well, since they were long part of a contiguous cultural
sphere, Bhutan's having become its own state separate from Tibet only in
recent centuries.

Popular Depictions of Drukpa Künlé

Drukpa Künlé is among the most prominent figures in Tibetan oral traditions. For many Tibetans, he is the first person who comes to mind upon
hearing the term "mad *siddha*" or "mad lama." Among the short tales
often recounted about Drukpa Künlé, one maintains that he once killed
a herd of animals by chopping off their heads. Then, using his magical
powers, he reanimated them. As they were coming back to life, the large-
bodied animals picked up the heads of smaller ones, and vice versa, resulting in the creation of a species of oddly proportioned animals, the takin,
which still live in the Himalayas today. Other popular stories speak more
to Drukpa Künlé's famous irreverence. One tale relates how, when staying
as the guest of a family, Drukpa Künlé instructed the father to recite something resembling a Buddhist prayer, but including sexual references of the
most vulgar type. Despite his family's understandable shock, the old man
persisted in his recitation of the prayer, and because of the strength of his
faith in Drukpa Künlé, achieved a rainbow body at the time of death. Some
stories show Drukpa Künlé performing magical feats, which serve as a testament to his status as an enlightened *siddha*. In his legacy as a trickster,
he assumes a role similar to that of the Tibetan folk hero Akhu Tönpa.
Because of the similarities between them, Akhu Tönpa has at times been
included in discussions of "holy madmen," and the two figures are sometimes conflated, with certain stories attributed to either Drukpa Künlé or
Akhu Tönpa in different tellings.[3]

Oral renderings of Drukpa Künlé's exploits have always been the most
important source for Tibetans' understandings of him. These oral tellings have a complex relationship with the various collections of stories
about Drukpa Künlé that have been put on paper and printed over the
past five centuries. Much of the written literature about Drukpa Künlé
was based on oral recitations; once included in written collections, those
stories achieved canonical status and became even more influential. As
this chapter will show, the relatively free exchange between the textual

and oral literature concerning Drukpa Künlé has made his image highly adaptable—putty in the hands of later generations.

Many of the stories popularly told about Drukpa Künlé (including the two related above) are contained in a textual collection often referred to by Tibetans as Drukpa Künlé's "dirty stories" (*gtsog gtam*) or his "secret biography" (*gsang ba'i rnam thar*).[4] This short text has been published under a variety of titles, including *The Life Story of the Protector of Beings, Künga Lekpa, Telling of his Activities in Mön, Paro, and Other Places; The Southern Cycle of the Extensive Life Story of the Dharma Lord Drukpa Künlé;* and the simpler but misleading *Autobiography of Drukpa Künlé.*[5] I shall refer to this text, in its variant forms, as the *Southern Cycle.*

A note at the beginning of the text states that it was compiled at Tago monastery in Bhutan by a descendent of Drukpa Künlé, the dharma lord Tsewang Tenzin. Bhutanese tradition asserts that Tsewang Tenzin (1574–1643/44) was a grandson of Drukpa Künlé.[6] We should be cautious about accepting this, however, for there are varying accounts of Drukpa Künlé's progeny, as discussed below.

The *Southern Cycle* is made up of a series of disconnected episodes, which are not organized into a coherent narrative. These episodes involve stories of Drukpa Künlé's singing dirty songs, coupling with many women, grabbing a giant demoness by her breasts, and so on. There is no account of Drukpa Künlé's familial origins, birth, youth, or death. There are no essential elements of the story that carry over from one episode to the next, save for a geographic continuity: the stories are grouped in such a way that as we read them we travel with Drukpa Künlé from various places in Tsang south to Yamdrok Tso, to areas that are today part of Bhutan and other southern Himalayan regions, and then back to central Tibet, ending with tales about Drukpa Künlé at Taklung and Sakya monasteries.

Much of the content of the *Southern Cycle* is derived from oral traditions. The phrase used to describe the compiling of the collection is *brjed tho bkod,* which means "to record," in the sense of writing what one has heard. The inclusion of these stories in a print collection helped ensure their continued circulation in the oral tradition.

The contents of the *Southern Cycle* have also reached innumerable others around the globe in an alternate form. In 1966, the Bhutanese scholar-monk Drakpuk Geshé Gendün Rinchen (1926–1997), commonly known as Geshé Chapu, published a text with the title *The Essence of the Ocean of Stories about the Protector of Beings, the Dharma Lord Künga Lekpa, which is Meaningful to Behold.* This text was translated by Keith Dowman and printed under the title *The Divine Madman: The Sublime Life and Songs of Drukpa Kunley.* Dowman's translation of Geshé Chapu's work has been printed four times in English. There have also been two editions in German translation, two in Spanish, two in French, and one in Romanian.[7] These many translations and editions have made Geshé Chapu's work remarkably widespread and well known in the Western world. Its influence in shaping how readers of European languages have come to think about Drukpa Künlé, about "holy madmen," and Tibetan Buddhism in general cannot be overstated.

In composing his version of the *Life* of Drukpa Künlé, Geshé Chapu used the entirety of the *Southern Cycle,* save for a few pages. The material drawn from the *Southern Cycle* takes up a little more than a third of Geshé Chapu's text. Geshé Chapu divided up and reordered passages from the *Southern Cycle,* at times interspersing them with passages drawn from elsewhere.[8]

Other tales Geshé Chapu included in his version of the *Life* are of local character, drawn from more recent Bhutanese oral traditions. For example, Geshé Chapu interrupts a passage taken directly from the *Southern Cycle* to insert a story about how Drukpa Künlé built a stūpa in a particular place in order to subdue the local malevolent spirits. The origins of other holy objects are also explained, such as when Drukpa Künlé urinated on a *tanka* (the urine turned to gold, of course) which, according to Geshé Chapu, could still be seen at Tago monastery at the time of his writing. Many of the tales incorporated into the *Life* explain the origins of remarkable natural phenomena, including how a fresh water spring came into being, why one place has a very scarce water supply, and the origin of some strange rock formations. In Dowman's translation of Geshé Chapu's version of the *Life,* the iconoclastic refuge prayer Drukpa Künlé imparted to the old man reads:

> I take refuge in an old man's chastened penis, withered at the root, fallen like a dead tree;
> I take refuge in an old woman's flaccid vagina, collapsed, impenetrable, and sponge-like;
> I take refuge in the virile young tiger's Thunderbolt, rising proudly, indifferent to death;
> I take refuge in the maiden's Lotus, filling her with rolling bliss waves, releasing her from shame and inhibition.

Here the story is employed to explain the construction of a stūpa and later a monastery—the place still blessed by its fleeting contact with Drukpa Künlé long ago. There are also stories explaining how certain places around Bhutan got their names thanks to Drukpa Künlé's at times irreverent intervention.[9]

Geshé Chapu incorporated many local legends into the life story of the great saint (although for every legend he included, there are surely many more that he did not). It is not difficult to imagine the process through which, over time, stories would be formulated associating the highly revered Drukpa Künlé with the origins of remarkable objects, places, and place-names, in parts of Tibet and especially in Bhutan. For many readers, Geshé Chapu's including these local legends in his version of the *Life* cemented them as historical fact.[10]

In addition to using almost all of the *Southern Cycle* (which was largely based on earlier oral traditions) and oral traditions then current in the Tibetan cultural areas in and around Bhutan, Geshé Chapu also drew from another text, the *Miscellaneous Writings* of Drukpa Künlé (discussed at length below). Approximately one-sixth of Geshé Chapu's text is drawn from the four volumes of the *Miscellaneous Writings*. Geshé Chapu's version of the *Life* retains the flavor and the style of the *Southern Cycle* and feels only minimally influenced by the *Miscellaneous Writings*.

Geshé Chapu's version of the *Life* is a series of disconnected episodes—reflecting the fact that it drew from disparate oral traditions and two textual collections that are themselves made up of disjointed episodes—with some minor steps taken toward adding narrative structure to the story. Drukpa Künlé's wanderings are now framed as a search for the finest alcohol and the most beautiful women. And although Geshé Chapu rearranges somewhat the order of the episodes taken from the *Southern Cycle*, he still traces the same basic route for Drukpa Künlé's travels, from central Tibet to the southern regions and back again. Geshé Chapu also includes a brief account of Drukpa Künlé's familial origins based on that given at the beginning of Drukpa Künlé's *Miscellaneous Writings*. Geshé Chapu makes brief mention of the yogin's death, stating that he died in 1570 at the age of 115.[11]

Despite these motions toward creating a more coherent narrative of Drukpa Künlé's life, by at least giving it a unifying theme and a beginning and an end, many details that would make Drukpa Künlé seem a more embodied historical being are absent from Geshé Chapu's version of the *Life*. We never hear tell of Drukpa Künlé learning from a lama or doing ordinary religious practices. There is almost no mention of his family, save for stating that he lost his father at a young age. Many of the episodes read like fantasies, such as Drukpa Künlé's encounters with Tsongkhapa and Sakya Paṇḍita, both of whom died well before Drukpa Künlé was born.[12] Because of the impossible, miraculous, and extremely unlikely events described therein, Geshé Chapu's version of the *Life* gives one the sense of a Drukpa Künlé largely disembodied from the realities of his own life and from history.

The themes of alcohol and sex are present from start to finish in Geshé Chapu's presentation. Drukpa Künlé retires to *chang* houses to enjoy himself between his exploits. In one song, he says that because of the great fondness he feels for the sweet nectar of alcohol, he must have been a bee in a previous life.[13] In this version of the *Life*, Drukpa Künlé is said to have had five thousand consorts. Some of the women who became his sexual partners were drawn into a spiritual life because of the experience. One story relates how Drukpa Künlé met a woman bearing the signs of a *ḍākiṇī*, and, after having sex with her, allowed her to leave her husband and follow him. Later, Drukpa Künlé uses the guilt the woman felt for having left her husband to encourage her to meditate diligently. In another story, Drukpa Künlé refuses to stop copulating with a woman even though a crowd has gathered to watch them. Through this shaming, the woman receives some religious benefit. At one point he even threatens to have sex with his own mother—this was, of course, with the intention of teaching her a lesson and helping her overcome her faults. The theme of sex is so ubiquitous that it even descends into the egregious, with Drukpa Künlé smashing a pernicious demon in the mouth with his penis and incapacitating a demoness by covering her with his giant foreskin.[14]

Another repeated theme in Geshé Chapu's version of the *Life* is Drukpa Künlé's criticizing the various religious communities of his day. In one song he exclaims that the Kagyüpas waste their time drinking, the Sakyapas splitting doctrinal hairs, the Gelukpa monks looking for boyfriends, and so on. Much fun is poked at Ngawang Chögyel (1465–1540), Drukpa Künlé's younger cousin and the abbot of Ralung monastery.[15] This Drukpa Künlé often derides people for being too full of themselves. He takes pleasure in pointing out hypocrisy, especially in the monastic community.

Although Drukpa Künlé voices criticisms of representatives of all the major sects, his most pointed barbs are reserved for the Gelukpas. He is said to have once brought a donkey into an assembly at Drepung monastery. As the monks chased him out, he shouted, "You people care more about chanting than meditation!" Two of those Drepung monks later ask him, "What crime did you commit that hell wasn't deep enough for you?" Drukpa Künlé responds that the road to hell "was blocked by monks from Sera monastery." A strong criticism of the Geluk is articulated when Drukpa Künlé tries to visit Tsongkhapa, who was then residing at Ramoché temple in Lhasa. The monks ask Drukpa Künlé what he has to offer the great master. He suggests that he make an offering of his testicles. After being turned away, Drukpa Künlé manages to gather some gold, and when he returns, he is promptly granted a meeting with Tsongkhapa, who gives him a knotted thread to wear for protection. Drukpa Künlé then ties the thread around his penis and goes into the marketplace, shouting, "If you have fifty pieces of gold you can gain audience with the Buddha Tsongkhapa himself! He may even give you one of these!" He wagged his genitals with the thread attached.[16]

The Drukpa Künlé presented by Geshé Chapu is a licentious trickster. There is nothing serious about him, save for his dedication to enjoying himself and his underlying drive to lead people to the dharma through whatever means necessary. At times it seems these stories attempt to portray Drukpa Künlé as one of the most scatological persons ever to have walked the earth. There is no doubt that these stories would have provided great entertainment for those hearing and retelling them. A storyteller caught up in the moment might exaggerate a story even further to increase its comedic or pedagogical effect.

In Geshé Chapu's presentation (most of this holds for the *Southern Cycle* as well), Drukpa Künlé is called a "madman" as a natural result of his great irreverence and scatological behavior. When visiting Pelkhor Chödé monastery in Gyantsé, Drukpa Künlé would not prostrate to the great stūpa or the monks, but only to a beautiful woman seated nearby. At this the monks exclaimed, "Oh my! How disgusting! This Drukpa Künlé is truly crazy!" His "madness" could even rub off onto other people: when Drukpa Künlé instructed the old man to recite the dirty prayer quoted above, his wife asked him, "Are you crazy?"[17] In this world Drukpa Künlé is an enlightened *siddha* who can do whatever he pleases. His eccentricity and craziness are indulged in because they indicate above all else that he is enlightened.

Drukpa Künlé's *Miscellaneous Writings*

Our most important source for understanding what sort of person the historical Drukpa Künlé was is a four-volume collection of writings, many of which seem to have originated from Drukpa Künlé himself.

The first volume (which makes up nearly half the collection and was translated into French by R. A. Stein in 1972) is labeled the biography (*rnam thar*) of Drukpa Künlé. Although it begins and ends with accounts of Drukpa Künlé's early life and death, most of the text consists of discrete episodes in no apparent order, with no overarching narrative. Since the first volume is presented in the first person, it is sometimes called Drukpa Künlé's autobiography (*rang rnam*). The titles of the other three volumes, containing further teachings, letters, and poetry, describe their contents as derived from or fragments of his biography, or his miscellaneous writings. Sometimes the entire four-volume collection is referred to as the biography (*rnam thar*) of Drukpa Künlé, which is misleading, as the second, third, and fourth volumes are not presented in the manner of a biography, and even the first volume would be an outlier in the genre. The four volumes are best understood as Drukpa Künlé's "miscellaneous writings" (*gsung 'bum 'thor bu*), as the fourth volume is titled.[18]

The colophons to the first and second volumes suggest that the first three volumes were gathered into their current form by one called the Mad Monk of Mön, who was regarded as a reincarnation of Drukpa Künlé.[19] The Mad Monk of Mön claims to have taken great care in gathering manuscripts relating the life and writings of "the great mad *siddha*" or "mad *mahāsiddha*"(*grub smyon chen po*), and for this reason the contents of these volumes should be accepted as genuine. "We have no reason to doubt that [in the *Miscellaneous Writings*] we are dealing with a collection of oral songs and narratives, written down perhaps in part by 'Brug-pa Kun-legs [Drukpa Künlé] himself, but mostly by his disciples and patrons," John Ardussi concludes based on his own research.[20]

There are a few instances in the first volume of the *Miscellaneous Writings* where Drukpa Künlé talks about the task of writing. The epigraph to this chapter is part of Drukpa Künlé's response to someone who asked him why his biography (*rnam thar*) was so disordered. He describes how he wrote down bits and pieces of his life story based on what he could remember, which has resulted in this haphazard collection. After criticizing the manner in which some other lamas' biographies are written, he states that his aim has been to write things that might be of some religious benefit to others, rather than to record the details of his life. This passage, which so perfectly exemplifies the kind of reasoned and insightful irreverence expressed at moments throughout the *Miscellaneous Writings*, may have been written by Drukpa Künlé himself, or inserted by a later editor seeking to justify the atypical form of this "biography."[21]

There is much that remains uncertain regarding the history of these texts. A verse of praise included at the end of the first volume mentions an earth-female-ox year, which likely refers to 1529 or 1589. The woodblocks for the first three volumes were carved at Driu Lhé monastery in Nyel, central Tibet, in a water-dragon year, which could refer to a date anywhere between the sixteenth and nineteenth centuries. The woodblocks for the fourth volume were carved at a later time. A more detailed investigation of the history of these materials is overdue, but outside the scope of this book.[22]

The many episodes that make up the four volumes of the *Miscellaneous Writings* include transcripts of purported conversations, correspondence with contemporaries, poems, editorials, expositions on issues relating to Buddhist philosophy, conduct, and much more. Although the *Miscellaneous Writings* are similar to the *Southern Cycle* and Geshé Chapu's version of the *Life* in that they all have a disjointed episodic structure, the contents of the *Miscellaneous Writings* are very different in nature. The episodes contained in the *Miscellaneous Writings* are on the whole much less entertaining than those in the more popular collections. There are fewer obviously fictional elements (there is no mention of Drukpa Künlé's interacting with Tsongkhapa or Sakya Paṇḍita, for example). There is much less crude language. This is in effect the "clean" version of Drukpa Künlé's *Life*, and his "public" rather than "secret" biography, even if traditionally few were familiar with its contents. The *Miscellaneous Writings* contain no stories formulated for the purpose of explaining the existence of odd natural phenomena or place-names. Often the compositions that make up the collection are put one after another with no clearly marked transition between them. In some instances, a flimsy context is given for a piece of writing. For example, one episode begins, "A *geshé* once said to me, 'Sing a song about the proper view, meditation, and conduct using examples from the behaviors of wild animals!'" This is followed by a transcript of the song Drukpa Künlé purportedly sang in response.[23] The story is certainly far-fetched. Rather than having occurred as described, it seems more likely that this poem was written or dictated by Drukpa Künlé, then at a later point someone (an editor or perhaps Drukpa Künlé himself) constructed this context for the composition in an attempt to incorporate it into a narrative of his life. As one progresses through the first volume and into the other three, well-ordered and properly (or shoddily) introduced compositions give way to completely decontextualized fragments—or as is more likely, fragments for which no context has been constructed. It seems that whoever put together this collection—the Mad Monk of Mön or someone who preceded him—began with the intention of weaving the many writings attributed to Drukpa Künlé into something resembling a biography, but quickly grew weary of the task.

Supporting the view that many of these compositions originate from Drukpa Künlé himself is the fact that they record his interactions with other figures living at the time. Nyukla Penchen seems to have been one of Drukpa Künlé's most consistent and significant conversation partners, with the *Miscellaneous Writings* containing records of their meetings and full transcripts of letters they exchanged.[24] We also see Drukpa Künlé meeting with and passing comment on other important figures of the day, like Dönyö Dorjé (see further below). Some of what is related in the *Miscellaneous Writings* is corroborated by other documents from the fifteenth and sixteenth centuries. The second part of the *Life of the Madman of Ü*, written in 1537, describes Drukpa Künlé's coming to meet the great yogin at his monastery in Penyül in 1512 or 1513. It is said that on this occasion Drukpa Künlé offered the Madman of Ü a praise (*gsol 'debs*) of the Aural Transmission that he had composed. The third volume of Drukpa Künlé's *Miscellaneous Writings* contains the text of this praise, including the detail that he composed it at the request of the Madman of Ü.[25]

The amount of material shared between the *Miscellaneous Writings* and the *Southern Cycle* is negligible. Based on this, we can be certain that the two collections developed independently of one another.[26]

The Trajectory of Drukpa Künlé's Life

From the biographies of the Madmen of Ü and Tsang, we know many of the details of their lives: where they went, what kind of lifestyle they assumed, and so on. But we rarely see things from the madmen's own perspectives, since everything is mediated through their biographers. With Drukpa Künlé, the situation is completely the reverse. His *Miscellaneous Writings* tell us very little about the basic events of his life, but a vast amount about his thoughts and opinions, giving us a much more intimate understanding of the man.

As for biographical details, after the opening supplications, the first volume begins: "Now I shall tell a little about the story of how I, Drukpa Künlé, was born . . ."[27] Drukpa Künlé—or an author assuming the guise of Drukpa Künlé—states that he was born into the Gya clan, as a descendant of Tsangpa Gyaré (1161–1211), the founder of Ralung monastery, who was considered to be a reincarnation of Nāropa. It says that Drukpa Künlé had been enjoying a happy childhood until his father Rinchen Zangpo, who held the position of *nangso* (*nang so*), was killed in the course of a dispute with his brother—Drukpa Künlé's uncle—over some inheritance or the succession of the family line. This happened when the boy was thirteen years old. Members of the Neudzong faction (*snel pa phyogs*), who governed the Lhasa area under the auspices of the Pakmodrupas, were involved in the killing in some way. After this the uncle married Drukpa Künlé's mother, perhaps dispossessing him of his inheritance.

As a result of these tragic events, Drukpa Künlé's life was turned upside-down. He was made the responsibility of his paternal aunt, who sent the boy to work in the service of Rinpungpa Küntu Zangpo, the father of Dönyö Dorjé. (This is similar to the way Dönyö Dorjé would care for the young Tsuklak Trengwa, the second Pawo.) Speaking in the first person, Drukpa Künlé says that he was not happy living with Küntu Zangpo. But because the Rinpungpas were at the time being attacked by many factions on all sides, he had no choice but to remain in their service. It is not clearly stated why this was so.

Having stayed with the Rinpungpas for six years in Tsang (from around 1467 to around 1473), at the age of nineteen or so Drukpa Künlé developed the urge to practice the dharma and left for Ü. He gave his few belongings to his sister and his uncle, and set off. Later in the first volume, there is a song Drukpa Künlé sang on the occasion of his mother's death, in which he again mentions his sister, who apparently was a nun.[28]

The story goes on to describe the young man's studies under a handful of masters throughout Ü and Tsang. These include the likes of Lhatsün Künga Chökyi Gyatso; the Seventh Karmapa; and the Second Drukchen, Künga Penjor (1428–1476), who was probably a cousin of Drukpa Künlé's. It is said that during this period Drukpa Künlé became a monk, taking his novice vows at Nyingro Menchukha in Nenying, southeast of Gyantsé. (An episode later in the first volume states that he went on to take full ordination at Zhalu monastery.)[29] After these few pages, all narrative continuity comes to an end and we can no longer be certain to which period of Drukpa Künlé's life the various short compositions are meant to pertain. Toward the end of the first volume, Drukpa Künlé's death in the area of Nakartsé is described as an event surrounded by many miracles, attesting to the yogin's greatness. The cremation of his corpse generated many relics, which were placed inside a silver reliquary housed at Lampar mon-astery in Tölung (in Bhutan), and watched over by his son, Zhingkyong Drukdrak.[30]

It seems that for most of his life, Drukpa Künlé traveled around with no fixed residence. He turned down various opportunities to head monastic communities. When offered an estate connected with Ralung monastery, he said that taking control of any lands during this degenerate age could only lead to more suffering, citing the death of his father in a dispute over some property as an example.[31]

One of the key features of Drukpa Künlé's character in the popular Tibetan imagination is his voracious sexual appetite and his use of sex as a means to propel women along the spiritual path. The picture of Drukpa Künlé that we get from the *Miscellaneous Writings* is a much tamer one. At some point he must have given up his monks' vows, for in the *Miscellaneous Writings* there is mention of his having a wife (*yum chen*) named Tsewang Dzom (although we should not assume that they were formally married in a modern Western sense) and a son named Zhingkyong Drukdrak. There is no mention of a second wife named Norbu Dzom (also known as Pelzang Butri) or the son Drukpa Künlé is asserted to have had with her, named Ngawang Tenzin. Based on other sources, E. Gene Smith seems quite confident that Ngawang Tenzin was in fact the son of Drukpa Künlé, sired when the saint was in his fifties. The son of Ngawang Tenzin, Tsewang Tenzin, is listed as the compiler of the *Southern Cycle*. The family line would die out, but the reincarnations of Tsewang Tenzin's son, Tenzin Rapgyé (1638–1696)—Drukpa Künlé's great-grandson, who served as the Fourth Desi, the temporal ruler of Bhutan—continue to be recognized to this day. The fact that neither Ngawang Tenzin nor his mother is men-tioned in the *Miscellaneous Writings* casts doubt on the claims that he and his progeny in Bhutan were actual descendants of Drukpa Künlé.[32]

Drukpa Künlé's other or perhaps only son, Zhingkyong Drukdrak, is mentioned many times in the course of the *Miscellaneous Writings*. We get a tantalizing glimpse into their domestic lives when one episode begins with Drukpa Künlé's complaining that his son would not listen to him, which the boy's mother said was Drukpa Künlé's fault: evidently he had spoiled the boy. This leads to a long excursus on human nature. A differ-ent episode begins with Drukpa Künlé's relating how some people once said to him, "You Drukpa [Kagyüpas] put too much effort into caring for women and children." In response, Drukpa Künlé explains how taking care of women and children is a good way to practice the Six Perfections that are the foundation of Mahāyāna Buddhist morality—generosity, ethics, patience, diligence, concentration, and wisdom. The *Miscellaneous Writings* give record of a song Drukpa Künlé sang describing a ritual to be used to prolong the life of Zhingkyong Drukdrak, who must have been ill at the time. Another passage in the first volume records a letter of safe passage (*lam yig*) he wrote for his son; it contains requests that people help Zhingkyong Drukdrak in his journeys, as well as advice for him.[33] Given how often Zhingkyong Drukdrak is mentioned in the *Miscellaneous Writings*, it is suspicious that Ngawang Tenzin is not mentioned at all.

Drukpa Künlé is forthright about how his having a wife and son affects his position within Buddhism. One passage relates how some people asked Drukpa Künlé to give a teaching in order to establish a dharmic connection between them. He responds by saying that because he had a wife and child, he was not faultless, and therefore should not teach the dharma, since for him to do so would anger the buddhas. (On this occasion Drukpa Künlé observes that the great translator Marpa also had a child, but since he was Hevajra incarnate, he surely had perfect control over his emissions, and his son would thus not have been conceived in the ordinary worldly fashion.) At times in the *Miscellaneous Writings* Drukpa Künlé refers to himself as a "monastic householder" (*ser khyim pa*).[34] He does not seem regretful about his domestic obligations. Rather, he comes across as a committed family man. Despite his having at least one sexual partner and a child, there is no reason to believe he was the kind of sexual libertine he is commonly thought to have been. He would be considered a rake only if held up to the standard of celibate monasticism. Over time, this aspect of his identity was exaggerated, so that he would be considered a profligate—coupling with five thousand women!—by anyone. Below we shall see more examples of how some characteristics of who Drukpa Künlé was got exaggerated and distorted over time, resulting in the creation of the wilder popular image of him.

One last passage, pertaining to Drukpa Künlé's attitudes toward women, is worth mentioning here. There are many interesting and creative think pieces in the *Miscellaneous Writings*, most of which are presented as records of conversations. One begins with Drukpa Künlé's mentioning how some people had been saying that in the degenerate age we live in, women had become more powerful than men in some contexts, which they regarded as a bad thing. Relying on an interesting line of reasoning, Drukpa Künlé expresses his own thoughts on the matter, which are that the current state of affairs in which women are sometimes the more prominent half is nothing new: since time immemorial, in the pairings of various things, the feminine counterpart has often been the dominant one. He offers as an example the sun (which in Tibetan, *nyi ma*, bears a feminine linguistic marking) and the moon (*zla ba*, which bears a masculine marking): when the sun comes up, the moon disappears. A ewe's wool is softer and better than that of a ram. The primacy of the feminine aspect holds not only in the worldly domain but in the religious as well. There is a mother goddess of the Perfection of Wisdom, but there is no father god of the Perfection of Wisdom. In the realm of tantra, the resting place of the body, speech, and mind of all the buddhas is the vagina of the Vajra Queen (*rdo rje btsun mo*); there is no male equivalent. The word lama, *bla ma*, has a feminine marking, but there is no masculine equivalent, *bla pho*. And so on. In some of the examples he lists in this passage, Drukpa Künlé is using linguistic evidence to suggest a long-held unconscious recognition of the superiority of the feminine. We should not read too far into this brief essay to assume that Drukpa Künlé espoused modern liberal attitudes about gender, but it does show him to be more thoughtful than the way he is usually portrayed.[35]

Drukpa Künlé's Position in Politics

There are a number of places in the *Miscellaneous Writings* where Drukpa Künlé addresses the central Tibetan political situation of the time. In the tense conflict between the Pakmodrupas and the Rinpungpas, Drukpa Künlé found himself conflicted, caught in the middle, since he had good reasons to support both opposing factions.

In one episode Drukpa Künlé is asked by an unnamed interlocutor to explain the reasons for his loyalty to the Pakmodrupas. As becomes clear from his response, this is a question of his supporting the Pakmodrupas instead of the Rinpungpas, whom some of his contemporaries assumed he would have supported, given his other affiliations. (The fact that Drukpa Künlé went to live with the Rinpungpas after the death of his father may suggest there was a standing relationship between the two families.) Drukpa Künlé begins by stating a few reasons why he has remained loyal to the Pakmodrupas, who are in a sense the rightful rulers of Tibet and have always been associated with the Kagyü. He criticizes the Fourth Red Hat for not doing more to put an end to the conflict between the Pakmodrupas and Rinpungpas. In the course of this exposition, Drukpa Künlé mentions the complexities of Ralung monastery's position in these matters. As Ardussi has described, the Ralungpas had long-standing ties with the

Pakmodrupas, but were geographically much closer to the Rinpungpas' main holdings. This put Ralung in a position of not wanting to alienate either faction.[36]

On another occasion, Drukpa Künlé makes similar comments about the conflict between the Pakmodrupas and the Rinpungpas, adding that the Rinpungpas are worthy of his allegiance because of the fact that they would be faithful servants of the Pakmodrupas if it were not for their being agitated by demons—by "demons" he could mean any number of things, as shown below—and also because of the fact that they had cared for him after his father was killed.[37] It is worth noting here that there is no indication that Drukpa Künlé blamed the Pakmodrupas for the role their representatives in Neudzong played in his father's death.

In the third volume of the *Miscellaneous Writings* there is a fascinating letter of request, offering further insight into Drukpa Künlé's thoughts on the political situation of the day. The first half of the letter is addressed to heads of the Pakmodru and Rinpung political regimes, as well as some lesser lords. In the opening verse, Drukpa Künlé expresses his hope that the Pakmodru and Rinpung factions can *both* emerge victorious. He again states the validity of the authority of the Pakmodrupas. Then he describes how the ambitious Rinpungpas seized their share of power by sowing discord among the various ministers through murder and so on. Having laid out the situation, Drukpa Künlé turns to the possibility of finding a solution that would bring an end to hostilities. He suggests that a border be established between the areas controlled by each side, and that the Rinpungpas "should reassume their previous position of subservience to the *gongma*." He then addresses the other parties involved in the political affairs of central Tibet—the families ruling Gongkar, Yargyap, Taktsé, Drikung, Nakartsé, and so on.

At this point the document takes a curious turn, leaving behind political affairs to address the people of Tibet more generally. Drukpa Künlé humbly requests reforms in the behavior of sorcerers ("mantrikas propitiating deities, reciting mantras, and setting up maṇḍalas should not cast spells or cause hailstorms"), monks, meditators, and nuns ("if a nun should get pregnant, she should not remain with the man"), before moving on to people in society following secular vocations, including merchants, servants ("servants should assume a lower position and behave in the manner of servants"), and the like. The letter ends with his saying, "If all of this is done, I shall be thankful. If not, everyone will experience some hardship." This letter is dated the third day of the third month of the

monkey year, dispatched from a place called Pelgyé, and signed by Künga
Lekpa, the Madman of the Drukpa.[38]

When Drukpa Künlé entered the household of Rinpungpa Küntu
Zangpo at the age of thirteen, Dönyö Dorjé would have been about six years
old. They may well have known each other while young. Nevertheless,
Drukpa Künlé would criticize the actions of Dönyö Dorjé as an adult.
At one point Drukpa Künlé mentions Dönyö Dorjé in passing, opining
that in "attacking everyone," his military campaigns exemplify the very
opposite of good Buddhist behavior. It is said that Dönyö Dorjé once met
Drukpa Künlé and requested a dharma teaching from him. Drukpa Künlé
did not oblige, saying, "If you're not liberated from your actions, emptiness will not help," which then led to some conversation. Other times
the relationship between Drukpa Künlé and Dönyö Dorjé is portrayed as
amicable, such as when Drukpa Künlé was invited by Dönyö Dorjé while
staying in Kongpo with the Seventh Karmapa, and when Drukpa Künlé
exchanges letters with Dönyö Dorjé, then sings a song for him.[39] Drukpa
Künlé would also visit Rinpung and correspond with other Rinpungpa
lords, as well as with Tashi Dargyé of Ja.[40]

In the end, it seems that Drukpa Künlé had an ambivalent relationship
with Dönyö Dorjé and the Rinpungpas. He had lifelong ties to the family,
but was not above voicing his true opinions about them. The time Drukpa
Künlé spent living among the Rinpungpas may in the end have given him
a platform from which to criticize their ways, somewhat ironically. As
one whose home life was disrupted by the ravages of factional violence,
he surely felt the high cost of such fighting. It seems that Drukpa Künlé
hoped to position himself as a mediator in the greater conflict between
the Rinpungpas and the Pakmodrupas, since he had good reasons, both
ideological and personal, to support either side.

Drukpa Künlé the Critic

In oral tradition, the *Southern Cycle*, and Geshé Chapu's version of the *Life*,
Drukpa Künlé comes across as the ultimate iconoclast. He disseminates
scatological prayers, urinates on religious images, and refuses to show
respect to the monks of Gyantsé. The perception of Drukpa Künlé as an
iconoclast seems to be based on certain characteristics of the historical
individual, but having been taken to an exaggerated degree.

In a passage representative of sentiments he expresses many times
in his *Miscellaneous Writings*, Drukpa Künlé says that he was once asked

if there was anyone practicing the dharma in a pure manner during the time in which they lived. His response is a grand tour criticizing every sector of the Tibetan religious world. He says that he visited a monastery of the Kagyü sect where all the monks were drinking *chang*. He visited a Sakya monastery where the monks deprecated all other religious systems. He visited a Geluk monastery where all the monks were overly attached to their individual colleges. He visited a Nyingma monastery where all they did was masked dancing. He also visited charnel grounds where people practiced Cutting, but left because he was concerned about becoming too caught up with worldly, unenlightened deities. He visited Drukpa Kagyü monasteries, but did not want to get drawn into quarrelling with his relatives. He has visited some yogins in meditative retreat, but all they have to say is, "How many more days?" The lamas he knows are occupied with worldly concerns; their attendants are like tax collectors. The great meditators have consorts, which they justify by saying that they are goddesses. On the other hand, the logicians all have little monks to keep their spirits up. In his uniquely perceptive and acerbic fashion, Drukpa Künlé has found fault with everyone.[41]

In a similar passage, Drukpa Künlé again pans the entire spectrum of Tibetan religious practitioners, and some laypeople as well. There are monks who make pious expressions of faith, with palms joined and eyes closed, but do not actually feel that faith on the inside. There are *geshés* who teach others, but do not incorporate the dharma into their own thinking. Some who take on the appearance of realized ones (*rtogs ldan rnam pa'i spyod pa*) brazenly meditate on themselves as Heruka, but do not actually cultivate the good qualities of the deity. There are great meditators (*sgom chen*) who show fake signs of meditative accomplishment. Some attendants watching over their lamas' treasuries are as rapacious as hungry ghosts. There are worldly lords who hold others to the law, but do not obey it themselves. There are servants who criticize others for not faithfully serving their lords, although they do not either. There are patrons who give gifts only in hope of a return. Some individuals' livelihoods are provided by religious estates, although they shamefully do not maintain their vows. The song ends with Drukpa Künlé's turning attention to his own failings, saying, "It is amazing that I, the yogin Künlé who travels around the country, have abandoned my homeland but have not given up attachment. I'm a liar calling myself a 'renunciant'!"[42]

This kind of denunciation is one of the most consistent themes in the *Miscellaneous Writings*. Sometimes Drukpa Künlé directs his criticisms at the various sects of Tibetan Buddhism. In other places he directs his critical eye at general categories of practitioners. In chapter 3, it was described how Drukpa Künlé condemned nonmonastics who outwardly display a tantric lifestyle. The group he criticizes with the greatest frequency are monks, whom he charges with not actually upholding the vows that in theory make them worthy recipients of the generosity of laypeople. He often expresses his suspicion that older monks are having sexual relations with the younger ones. By giving up the trappings of monkhood upon taking a wife, Drukpa Künlé has absolved himself from criticism of being a false, hypocritical monk.

As a general comment about the state of religion during his day, Drukpa Künlé asserts, "All those who now teach religion sell the dharma for the sake of wealth. They teach the dharma for the sake of getting food and clothing, with no thought of helping anyone, and thereby oppose the word of Śākyamuni Buddha. I hope that he will protect them from punishment in their future lives."[43] In another song Drukpa Künlé ironically sings, "I prostrate to those who exchange the dharma for wealth!" His concern that people are "selling" the dharma, using it for their own advantage, is a persistent theme throughout.

What ultimately drives these criticisms is Drukpa Künlé's distaste for hypocrisy. He has seen firsthand how people benefit from their status as monks or ritualists or tantrikas. But monks who are not actually celibate, ritualists who do not know the meanings of the rituals they perform, and tantrikas who have not achieved genuine realization have all broken their basic contract with the society that supports them. It is this disjuncture between the outward display and the inner meaning that unsettles Drukpa Künlé. He does not condemn people simply for having faults; he seems very open-minded, and accepting of people's mistakes. He often jokes about his own failure to live up to Buddhist ideals. But what irritates Drukpa Künlé is when people pretend to be better than they actually are. For Drukpa Künlé, hypocrisy is not a simple human mistake, but results from people's greed, which is truly the biggest threat to the dharma.

Because of his concerns about hypocrisy and about "selling" the dharma for personal gain, Drukpa Künlé refused to fully participate in the formal trappings of Tibetan Buddhist life, which put him in an ambiguous position with respect to the religious culture of his day. One episode in the first volume of the *Miscellaneous Writings* begins with some people asking Drukpa Künlé about the way he dressed. He says that when he was younger he had the ability to control his yogic winds, and thus could get by wearing just a cotton cloth on his upper body. He used to wear maroon shorts and boots of some type. He traveled with a one-man tent, a flint, a small book, a cushion, and some *tsampa*, and used to carry a *khaṭvāṅga* and a *ḍamaru*. He wore conch-shell earrings and long hair.[44] If we accept this passage as originating with Drukpa Künlé or someone close to him, it would seem that at some point in his life he wore his own distinctive quasi-tantric, quasi-monastic manner of dress. The fact that Drukpa Künlé is referred to as a "covert yogin" in the *Life of the Madman of Ü* may reflect his ambiguous religious status.

Drukpa Künlé's refusal to join or take leadership of a fixed religious community also stemmed from concerns about hypocrisy. In the same way that while living as a monk or a yogin the external form can get divorced from the meaning that is supposed to underlie it, monasteries tend to get entangled with worldly affairs and drawn away from their missions as communities dedicated to the practice of the dharma. There are a number of instances where Drukpa Künlé states that he would prefer not to take control of a monastic community, even when specifically asked to do so. In one passage he says that staying in one place for a long time is not the way of a true religious practitioner, since it inevitably leads to one's becoming attached to a place or to a particular patron. Then an individual will become concerned with the amount of respect shown to him, which can lead to conflicts. Drukpa Künlé goes on to offer his perspective on religious institutions:

When a monastery is first founded, it is held up by the dharma. In the middle, it is maintained through negotiations. In the end, it is taken over by sin [*sdig*]: although it is called a monastery, [its inhabitants] are lazier than worldly people. So why bother founding one? If Śākyamuni Buddha saw the round [i.e., shaved] head [of a monk] resting on the bosom of a woman, what would he say? If one is going to act in that way, it would be better to continue wearing lay clothing.[45]

In Drukpa Künlé's understanding of the way things tend to work in the real world, the ideal of the monastery as a place dedicated to the practice of religion is rarely realized. This is because religious communities invariably end up mired in worldly concerns, and because of the great difficulty of living up to the ideal of perfect celibacy.

Although the *Miscellaneous Writings* do not discuss Drukpa Künlé's having had an extensive education, he shows himself to be quite learned in Buddhist doctrine. He quotes a wide variety of Buddhist texts, including the *Hevajra Tantra*, the songs of Saraha, the *Thirty-Seven Deeds of the Bodhisattva*, works by Sakya Paṇḍita, Tsangpa Gyaré, the words of Milarepa, and so on. The text he cites with the greatest frequency is the *Condensed Perfection of Wisdom Sūtra*. In the course of his pithy response to the question of whether or not the dharma body exists amid conceptuality (*rnam rtog chos sku*), a topic of considerable discussion among fifteenth- and sixteenth-century Kagyüpas, Drukpa Künlé cites the *Suvarṇaprabhāsa Sūtra*. Elsewhere he describes and defends subtleties of the Drukpa Kagyü system on questions of methods and realization. He gives a brief but profound exposition on the ontological status of karma, arriving at the observation that the relationship between karma and conditions (*rkyen*, which we can perhaps take as meaning "materiality") is like that of the chicken and the egg: conditions arise from karma, and karma arises from conditions, so who can say which comes first? (Geshé Chapu's Drukpa Künlé employs the same kind of reasoning when he approaches some monks in the midst of their daily philosophical debate, farts under their noses, then asks, "Which came first, the air or the smell?")[46]

Whereas in the popular versions of his *Life*, we see Drukpa Künlé fighting with giant demonesses with gaping vaginas and hanging breasts, in the *Miscellaneous Writings* he gives a thoughtful explanation of the many different things the word "demon" (*bdud*) can in fact refer to. He states that anything that does not accord with the practice of religion, from the most abstract to the most concrete, can be considered a demon. This includes students who do bad things, masters with no ethical discipline, and those who practice the Observance without having "achieved heat."[47]

Drukpa Künlé was very self-aware of his position as a perpetual critic, a disenchanted observer of Tibetan religious culture. According to a passage in the *Miscellaneous Writings*, someone once mentioned to Drukpa Künlé that in his compositions or the stories about him (*rnam thar rnams*), it seemed that he was always criticizing (*zur 'tshag*) others. Drukpa Künlé responds:

> I have no intention of hurting anyone. In general, this is a degenerate age, and I see no one who lives in accordance with the teachings of the Buddha. As for me, I have no particular talent, so I write whatever appears in my mind. I don't say that people are doing things they aren't doing. I also don't *not* say the things that people *are* doing.[48]

Drukpa Künlé has no good reason to criticize anyone falsely. By the same token, he sees no reason to refrain from describing the disquieting things he sees taking place around him. His is a fresh and honest voice in what he considered a benighted age. We might speculate that Drukpa Künlé's taking such a critical stance on the religious culture of his day had something to do with his being born into religious royalty. Because of his family's association with Ralung monastery, high expectations were placed upon him, which he could never escape from. At the same time, being born into such a position allowed him a behind-the-scenes look at how religion worked in his society. He did not like what he saw.

A reading of his *Miscellaneous Writings* suggests that Drukpa Künlé was highly astute and relatively conventional, even conservative in some ways. He by no means set out to overturn the social order. Although he took a contrarian attitude with respect to certain trends of his day and was critical of much that he saw taking place around him, his criticisms are motivated by his own high standards for how Buddhism should be practiced and how people should conduct themselves. Rather than maintaining an anything-goes attitude, he was a stickler for propriety. Because of the impossibility of living unhypocritically through any of the readily available modes—as a monk or a yogin, as a logician or a meditator, as a lay patron or an abbot—Drukpa Künlé chose not to conform to any of these preexisting categories. In order to avoid slipping into hypocrisy, he kept himself unattached. But over time this understanding of who Drukpa Künlé was would be lost, as his identity as a critic would give way to later representations in which he took a laissez-faire attitude toward everything. Drukpa Künlé's stance as a nonconformist critic would get exaggerated, resulting in stories of his doing the crazy, iconoclastic, scatological things that would become the defining feature of his persona in the Tibetan imagination.

Drukpa Künlé and the Holy Madmen

Geshé Chapu's version of his *Life* includes a brief episode in which Drukpa Künlé, the Madman of Ü, and the Madman of Tsang travel together to Tsari. While at the holy mountain, the Madman of Ü leaves a footprint on a rock and the Madman of Tsang makes a handprint. Drukpa Künlé then says, "Even my dog has that kind of power!" and makes a paw print in solid rock with his hunting dog's leg. According to Geshé Chapu, these three marks could still be seen at Tsari at the time of his writing.[49]

The contents of the *Miscellaneous Writings* suggest a less rosy relationship between Drukpa Künlé and his "madman" peers. As was mentioned
in chapter 2, Drukpa Künlé referred to the Madmen of Ü and Tsang as
unrivaled masters of the Observance. But as shown in chapter 3, he also
made overt criticisms of the two, questioning their motivations, and
whether or not they had the proper meditative realization to justify taking
on their tantric lifestyle.

Contained in Götsang Repa's version of the *Life of the Madman of Tsang*
is a paraphrase of a letter of safe passage written by the Madman of Tsang,
in which he asks people to provide his disciples with lodging and food
while they travel and undertake meditative practice all over Tibet. What
seems to be the full version of this letter is included in the first volume
of Drukpa Künlé's *Miscellaneous Writings.*[50] The Madman of Tsang begins
by claiming that the letter's contents represent an order of the Kagyü
lamas, a command from Hevajra, the speech of the protector deities.
Calling himself "the yogin who wanders in charnel grounds, the king of
the blood-drinkers" (as he signed the *Life of Marpa*), the Madman of Tsang
asks lords, soldiers, citizens, and brigands to not impede the travels of his
disciples as they head into the mountains to raise the banner of meditation. He asks these laymen to give his disciples lodging at night, to give
them food, help them cross rivers, and show them the way to their desti-
nations. He promises these citizens that such meritorious activity will be
rewarded. However, if they disrupt the activities of his students, steal their
belongings, or impede their travels, the Madman of Tsang will unleash his
wrath and propitiate the blood-drinking deities, which will lead to disaster
for those individuals and their descendants, including loss of livestock,
wealth, and even their lives.

Directly following this in the *Miscellaneous Writings* is an alternative
letter of safe passage written by Drukpa Künlé. He calls himself "the
monastic householder, the Madman of the Drukpa" (*ser khyim pa 'brug pa
smyon pa*). He describes his disciples as "monks who are neither lay nor
properly ordained" (*grwa pa skya min ser min*), who reside in their individual monasteries of attachment and aversion, who beg alongside the road,
who think killing someone is an act of dharma, who sell false goods, who
expound upon the scriptures even though they do not know how to read or
write, who give tantric initiations to others without having the empowerments themselves, who claim to have compassion but have no concern for
the lives of animals. Drukpa Künlé requests that people give his disciples
a little *tsampa* and show them where to find water. He requests that people

not chase away the nuns, whether they have decided to kill their babies or to raise them. For those who fulfill his request, he hopes that they will not be deceived by others and they will be well. But for those who do not do as he has requested—those who give *chang* to his students, those who let them reside in their homes, those who bother them, ask them questions about the dharma—he will enter into a meditation of fierce faith and . . . hope that the three defilements of hatred, desire, and ignorance will be completely eradicated, for them and their descendants.

Drukpa Künlé's letter is a satirical takedown of the Madman of Tsang and the seriousness with which he took himself. In direct contrast to the pretension displayed in the Madman of Tsang's letter, Drukpa Künlé is self-deprecating, pointing out the faults of his monks—although we can take this as a commentary, not just on Drukpa Künlé's followers, but on Drukpa Künlé himself and Tibetan religious in general. Some of Drukpa Künlé's more extreme allegations may be directed at the Madman of Tsang's own circle. Drukpa Künlé points out the hypocrisy in the Madman of Tsang's position, in which he threatens to punish people for not acceding to his requests. In direct contrast, Drukpa Künlé purposefully maintains a compassionate attitude toward everyone. It seems that Drukpa Künlé felt compelled to try to take the Madman of Tsang down a few pegs.

The relationship between Drukpa Künlé and the Madman of Ü seems to have been less contentious, perhaps because of the latter's relatively humble status. As mentioned above, the biography of the Madman of Ü states that "the covert yogin, the Madman of the Drukpa, Künga Lekpa," came to visit him at his monastery. Drukpa Künlé gave vast material offerings, as well as a supplication of the Aural Transmission that he had composed. This is said to have pleased the Madman of Ü very much. He then gave Drukpa Künlé some teachings and gifts. Drukpa Künlé's *Miscellaneous Writings* corroborate this account, giving the praise to the Aural Transmission in full. There are also praises of Tārā and of the *Dohā* lineage composed at the request of the Madman of Ü, an imaginative verse in praise of the Madman of Ü himself, and a record of a conversation between the two men about the nature of conceptuality (*rnam rtog*).[51]

It would seem that, as so often happens in our lives, Drukpa Künlé had complicated relationships with his "madman" peers. Although we have no indication that he ever met the Madman of Tsang, Drukpa Künlé was highly critical of the way he carried himself. Drukpa Künlé seems to have had a mostly positive relationship with the Madman of Ü, in spite of certain reservations he had about the yogin's lifestyle.

Sometimes Sangyé Gyeltsen, Künga Lekpa, and Künga Zangpo, all born within a span of six years, are collectively referred to as "the three madmen" (*smyon pa gsum*). This implies that their "madness" can be understood as being of a single type. But if we accept the contents of the *Miscellaneous Writings* as giving a generally accurate portrayal of Drukpa Künlé, we see that he was very different from Künga Zangpo and Sangyé Gyeltsen in terms of the sense in which they were "mad." Drukpa Künlé did not dress in the garb of the Heruka or act out in public, and he was deeply skeptical of those who did. Perhaps calling himself a "madman" was a way for Drukpa Künlé to carve out a space for himself as a wandering, critical outsider who chose not to conform to the categories presented to him by the culture in which he lived. Calling himself a "madman" was a playful act of self-deprecation, an attempt to humble himself while expressing such acerbic criticisms of others. Perhaps Drukpa Künlé called himself a "madman" as nothing more than a pen name, which has a long precedent in Tibetan literary production, as will be described in the next chapter. In taking on the identity of a "madman," Drukpa Künlé may well have been influenced or inspired by the Madmen of Ü and Tsang, who were better known at the time. Perhaps Drukpa Künlé was capitalizing on the popular renown of the Madmen of Ü and Tsang, or hoping to put himself in conversation with them in the broader religious discourse of the day. All three took on the persona of "madman" partially in a spirit of protest. But whereas Künga Zangpo and Sangyé Gyeltsen's "madness" was directed against certain threats to the Kagyü sect they held so dear, Drukpa Künlé was much less devoted to the sect, and his "madness" was instead directed against various aspect of the current state of Tibetan religious culture—including much of what the Madmen of Ü and Tsang themselves stood for.

The Transformation of Drukpa Künlé

Drukpa Künlé exemplifies a phenomenon observable at many times and places in the history of the world's religions: a saintly figure whose rhetoric, behavior, and character become subject to dramatic revision after death, as control over his image passes from himself and a circle of followers into the hands of a much broader public.

At the time of his death, Drukpa Künlé was a minor figure in the Tibetan world—less famous than the Madmen of Ü and Tsang, his relative the Second Drukpa hierarch Künga Penjor, or Śākya Chokden. This is indicated by the rarity of references to Drukpa Künlé in the literature of the time, the fact that no narrative of his life was recorded, that his writings were not collected until much later, and that there are no contemporary visual depictions of him.[52] We do not even know when Drukpa Künlé died. But his unique and interesting persona and his birth into a family at the center of the Drukpa Kagyü sect ensured him a degree of significance that would increase exponentially over time.

Despite the extreme differences between the Drukpa Künlé depicted in Geshé Chapu's version of the *Life* and the historical Drukpa Künlé whose image we are able to reconstruct, there are significant threads of continuity between them. The fact that Drukpa Künlé gave up his monkhood and took a wife (or possibly a few partners) got exaggerated over time, so that he came to be viewed as an irrepressible libertine. His rejection of the monastic norm led to his later reputation as a lover of alcohol. The fact that he expressed insightful criticisms of the religious culture of his day became exaggerated, turning him into the ultimate iconoclast. The historical Drukpa Künlé's remarkable wit, playfulness, and sense of humor are all preserved in later depictions of him, although the vehicle through which they are expressed has been changed completely: while the historical Drukpa Künlé labored over his compositions with a well of ink, the Drukpa Künlé of popular imagination cannot help but express himself through kinetic, bodily activity. The Drukpa Künlé known and loved today is in these many ways a caricature of the original.

This transformation was achieved over the course of generations, through the interventions of uncountable ordinary folk, telling and retelling stories of the "madman's" exploits. Not bounded by even a basic narrative of the yogin's life, tales could be altered or created anew, just so long as they were in keeping with Drukpa Künlé's reputation as a man who observed no limitations.

As Michael Aris has described, Bhutan has long been home to a very colorful body of popular literature. There was once an entire class of bards who made a living by traveling around and reciting these texts. Some were exempted from certain taxes, or even supported by the Bhutanese government directly. They would often tell stories about famous historical and quasi-historical figures, including Buddhist saints, but also trickster and Robin Hood figures like Akhu Tönpa, Wang Drukgyel, and others.[53] Drukpa Künlé figured prominently among them. In the course of their repeated tellings, the image of Drukpa Künlé would be dramatically transformed by these professionals more concerned with entertaining their audience than with fidelity to history.

These Bhutanese bards have also traditionally satirized Buddhist literature by reciting dirty versions of Buddhist liturgies, filled with the language of genitalia, sexuality, and drinking. These are carnivalesque inversions of religious forms. One such text takes the form of a *sūtra*, in which the centrally positioned teacher—"the One-Eyed Buddha," a talking phallus—teaches the "dharma of copulation" (*rgyo chos*), which ultimately leads all involved to consummate bliss. Popular depictions of Drukpa Künlé are clearly influenced by this literature. The verse that constitutes the climactic teaching of the "dharma of copulation" *sūtra* also appears in the *Southern Cycle* and in Geshé Chapu's version of the *Life* of Drukpa Künlé. This proves the overlap and mutual influence between tales of Drukpa Künlé and these other forms of popular literature.[54] Also contributing to the make-up of the popular image of Drukpa Künlé are traditional Bhutanese beliefs about spirit-beings and fertility, many of which predate the arrival of Buddhism in the area.

The fact that the historical Drukpa Künlé was sometimes known as a "madman" served as a catalyst in the transformation of his image. As a "madman," wild eccentricity was expected of him. The fact that he called himself a "madman" somewhat ironically, expressing humility and his position as an outsider and a critic, was lost, buried under tales of compassionate lewdness. He became "mad" in a much more literal sense. In the process, Drukpa Künlé's "madness" was made into a by-product of his enlightenment. The tales of mad behavior that developed over time turned Drukpa Künlé into a *siddha*.

Also feeding into the popular image of Drukpa Künlé was the kind of eccentric activity the other "holy madmen" of his time were famous for. We have no evidence that the historical Drukpa Künlé engaged in public and attention-grabbing behavior like that of Künga Zangpo and Sangyé Gyeltsen. But in the inexactitude of popular memory, aspects of the Madmen of Ü and Tsang's activities became associated with the Madman of the Drukpa. The marketplace, rather than the writing desk, became the venue for his eccentricities. Stories of the Madman of Ü's belligerent blessings and his vulgar iconoclasm in Nepal may have contributed to the creation of tales about Drukpa Künlé's irrepressible antics. The Madman of Ü's carrying a bow and arrow as part of his Heruka costume may have contributed to Drukpa Künlé's reputation for doing the same.

The Madman of Tsang's nude Practice of the Observance may have led to Drukpa Künlé's outrageous protest of Tsongkhapa's corruption. The Madman of Tsang's apparent disobedience while a student at the Pelkhor Chödé monastic complex became Drukpa Künlé's refusal to prostrate before its holies. Perhaps the strange mantra the Madman of Tsang spoke to heal his demon-afflicted student led to Drukpa Künlé's blasphemous prayer. Drukpa Künlé would sometimes be called a Heruka, despite the fact that we have no indication of his ever dressing in the garb of the deity. Although the provocative ascetic lifestyle of the Madmen of Ü and Tsang would be largely forgotten by later generations, it would live on, completely decontextualized and imparted with new intentions, in the tales of Drukpa Künlé's exploits.

This later, composite Drukpa Künlé has come to speak for the entirety of the holy madman tradition, as the sort of madness displayed in later depictions of Drukpa Künlé would be applied to interpreting the behavior and rhetoric of the Madmen of Ü and Tsang, and in fact of all "holy madmen." The understanding that Künga Zangpo and Sangyé Gyeltsen were enacting tantric literalism—which the historical Drukpa Künlé himself fully understood—was lost, and they came to be thought of as enlightened libertines whose actions expressed their transcendence of the world. The popularity of the composite Drukpa Künlé has caused Tibetan and Western commentators alike to gloss over major differences between the activities of the various holy madmen, ultimately obscuring the diversity and creativity they embodied. This exemplifies how understandings of the holy madmen have materialized out of the feedback loop that is described in chapter 7.

Understandings of the behaviors and lives of saintly figures often become subject to revision after their deaths. A case in point is Padmasambhava, who was a minor figure in the Tibetan religious world during his lifetime, but who became a focus of intense cultic activity in the centuries after his death. It is possible to deduce that the images of some saintly figures were transformed in subsequent biographical accounts for a specific purpose. Milarepa was strategically reimagined and reemployed by the Madman of Tsang. With Drukpa Künlé, the transformation occurred more organically. He captured the imaginations of Tibetans and Bhutanese, and they gradually changed him through retellings of his deeds. This dramatic transformation took place through many small increments over a long stretch of time, through the efforts of many unknowing participants all under to the spell of Drukpa Künlé's "holy madness."

7

The Enduring Trope of Holy Madness

Then at the entrance to the bridge at Tedung, [Tangtong Gyelpo] met the lord of Tsamda, Gyeltsen Pel, accompanied by seventeen attendants on horseback.

"Renunciant lama, where have you come from?" they asked.

"I came from behind," he replied.

"Where are you going now?"

"I'm going forward."

"He's a feisty one!"

LOCHEN GYURMÉ DECHEN, *The Life of Tangtong Gyelpo*, "Madman of the Empty Valley"[1]

Other Madmen and Madwomen

Drukpa Künlé was not the only "madman" in his illustrious family. His grandfather's eldest brother, Namkha Pelzang (1398–1425), was renowned as "the Madman of Ralung." As told in a brief biography composed by his younger brother, Namkha Pelzang was born into the family that controlled Ralung monastery, became a monk at about six, then underwent a standard monastic education. In 1413 he ascended to the throne at Ralung, which he would hold until his death. In 1422 he gave up his monkhood and took a wife. Following this, the biography states how, for the sake of teaching sentient beings during the degenerate age in which we live, the Madman of Ralung assumed both peaceful and wrathful modes and was called a "covert yogin." Although his time on the throne is said to have been a period of prosperity and wellness in the area around Ralung, Namkha Pelzang fell ill and died before he reached thirty.[2]

There is no mention of Namkha Pelzang's engaging in antinomian behavior comparable to that of the Madmen of Ü and Tsang. It seems that he was called a "madman" for deviating from the norm of celibacy. Although he assumed various personas and was called a "covert yogin" by some, his lifestyle must have remained at least somewhat conventional, since he was able to remain the abbot of Ralung. In following his own path to becoming a "madman" two generations later, Drukpa Künlé may well have been motivated in part by what he knew of his great uncle.

The turn of the sixteenth century was the moment in Tibet's history when "holy madmen" were most numerous and influential. There was the Madman of the Drukpa, the Madman of Ü, the Madman of Tsang, the Madman of the Charnel Ground, the Madman of Taklung, and the Madman of Üding, all associated most strongly with the Kagyü.[3] Another Kagyüpa, the Madman of Dakla Gampo (1451–1502), Mipam Drakpa Gyeltsen, lived a life very similar to that of the Madman of Ralung. He was born into religious royalty as a member of the Nyiwa clan, entered the monkhood at eight, and became the twelfth abbot of Dakla Gampo monastery at the age of ten. In his late teens he underwent a dramatic change in behavior and abdicated in favor of Drukpa Künlé's cousin, Künga Penjor, the Second Drukchen. Mipam Drakpa Gyeltsen took a consort and acted in ways that seemed strange to others, which put a strain on his relationship with his former community. According to a biography of him contained in a history of Dakla Gampo written in 1662,

> Because of his performing miracles and signs of accomplishment, he was undisputedly renowned as a *siddha*. . . . Because he performed various types of activity [or the Practice, *spyod pa*], in terms of dress and outward display, he was also renowned by the name "the dharma lord, Madman of Dakla Gampo."[4]

At this moment in Tibetan culture, "madman" was a ready category through which a practitioner of the Kagyü might present himself, and through which a community might interpret an ascetic's actions.

There were "madmen" and "madwomen" in Tibet long before the fifteenth century. Most early exemplars of the tradition were associated with the meditative and ritual practices of Cutting (*gcod*) and Pacification [of Suffering] ([*sdug bsngal*] *zhi byed*), both of which were initiated by the Indian yogin Padampa Sangyé. According to the history of Cutting offered in Gö Lotsāwa's *Blue Annals*, there was a Madwoman of Lhasa, who was one of four *ḍākiṇīs*, along with Machik Lapdrön, important in the life of Padampa Sangyé. Padampa Sangyé had a grand-disciple called Mad Beré. Machik Lapdrön's great-grandson was called Samdrup, the Mad Skull Cup. The records also tell of a Madwoman Gyel-lecham, a Madman of Chokro, and a Little Madman of Gya, who was also known as Mad Dönden. All three are connected to the Pacification tradition or its mythology.[5] The Madmen of Ü and Tsang were also involved with Cutting, and with a Secret Practice that was, by their time, partially synonymous with it.

In the nineteenth century, Dharma Sengé, a famous scholar of Tibetan medicine, was known as the Madman of Kham. He was a renowned practitioner of Cutting and wrote biographies of its early masters.[6]

A figure known as the Latsé Madman, or the Latsé Powerful One, or by his proper name, Latsé Khyenrap, lived in Nangchen, Kham, in the 1970s or 80s. As told to me by one who grew up in the area, the Latsé Madman specialized in the practice Cutting. Living in a cave, he wore tattered clothes and kept long hair and a beard. He is said to have had no concern about clean or unclean things, for it was all the same to him. He never washed and did not care about what he ate. When a corpse was left unattended to (because the person had died from an infectious disease or had no family), the Latsé Madman would prepare it for disposal. He had a miraculous ability to heal sick people, taking the disease into his own body and destroying it. He could drink any amount of alcohol and never get drunk. When the villagers gathered for some occasion, the Latsé Madman would do all manner of crazy things, including taking off his clothes, dancing around, sitting where he was not supposed to, drinking excessively, and saying contrary things: if everyone said something was good, the Latsé Madman would say it was bad; if everyone said it was bad, he would say it was good. Many people in the area had great faith in the Latsé Madman. Nevertheless, the local children were afraid of the unpredictable ascetic and tried to avoid the hillside where he lived.[7]

Among the other "madmen" associated with the Kagyü sect not already discussed in this book, there was the Madman of Go, or Karma Sidrel, born in the sixteenth century, who was a famous sculptor. There was also the Madman of Ur, who was the first Chungtsang incarnation of Drikung, Chökyi Drakpa (1595–1659).[8]

A number of Nyingmapas were also known, more or less, as "madmen." Many of these figures were treasure revealers (*gter ston*). Orgyen Lingpa (born in 1323) and Pema Lingpa (1450–1521) referred to themselves, respectively, as "the madman of the treasures" (*gter smyon*) and "the mad treasure revealer" (*gter ston smyon pa*).[9] The Madman of Kongpo

(1597–1650), associated mainly with the Nyingma, and Tangtong Gyelpo, associated with both the Kagyü and the Nyingma, who is believed to have revealed treasures and was sometimes referred to as a "madman," are discussed below. Wensa Madman Chö Dorjé, born in the fourteenth or fifteenth century, was associated with the Kadampa or nascent Geluk sect. A Mad Domchung taught the Mahākaruṇika teachings.[10] Over the centuries there have been scores of other "madmen," many of whom never made it into the historical record.

Among Tibetan Buddhists who were during their lifetimes and after commonly referred to as "madmen," with that term carrying generally positive connotations, we find a great diversity of lifestyles, ranging from true ascetics and tantric literalists to artists and doctors. With regard to some of these figures, we know very little about the lifestyles they adopted or why others felt it appropriate to call them "mad." Among those we know more about, it is clear that there was no single model they adhered to: every "madman" was meaningfully unique. This brief survey also shows that these "madmen" are not dispersed evenly throughout Tibetan Buddhist culture, but tend to be clustered within certain subtraditions of religious performance, including Cutting, treasure revelation, and especially the Kagyü.

The Broader Rhetoric of Madness

A rhetoric of "holy madness"—at times praiseful, at times pejorative—has circulated within Tibetan Buddhist culture from at least the tenth century to the present, both in- and outside the lives of those who have come to be known as "madmen" and "madwomen." Historical records mention a popular religious movement that took place from the middle of the eleventh century to the middle of the twelfth. Its leader was a woman who was said to be possessed by a spirit. She held beliefs about life, death, and causality that did not conform to accepted Buddhist views. Her disciples were known as "the mad ones" (*smyon tsho pa*) or "mad yogins" (*rnal 'byor smyon pa*).[11] The scant literary references to this community do not show whether they embraced the designation "mad" or had it applied to them in criticism.

The yogin Kodrakpa Sönam Gyeltsen (1170–1249) became famous during his time because of his asceticism and realizations. His *Collected Songs* were compiled and printed in the sixteenth century by Lhatsün Rinchen Namgyel, as yet another project of the Madman of Tsang's literary school. Kodrakpa had much in common with Milarepa, in terms of poetic style, emphasis on the primacy of meditation, and inhabiting many of the same places in southwestern Tibet. Kodrakpa even made allusions to Milarepa's words in his songs. Kodrakpa also employed a rhetoric of madness very similar to Milarepa's: he talks about renouncing his home, family, good food, and material comforts as part of his spiritual regimen, toward cultivating his connection with all sentient beings and finding contentment within. Kodrakpa writes of himself that, because of his living in this way:

> Some people say, "He's insane—insane!"
> I wonder whether this beggar has gone insane.[12]

Like Milarepa, Kodrakpa has turned the idea of madness on its head. If worldly conventions define what it means to be sane, he would prefer to be crazy.

Nyakré Sewo (1141?–1201) was born in Kham, but traveled to central Tibet and became one of Pakmodrupa's four main disciples. He would later return to his homeland and found Lé monastery, of the Martsang branch of the Kagyü. Widely regarded as a *siddha*, Nyakré Sewo is reputed to have performed many magical feats. In his writings, he playfully refers to himself as the Madman of Nyak. He writes:

> I, the Madman of Nyak, who does whatever he wants;
> I, the Madman of Nyak, whom nobody wants;
> I, the conceited Madman of Nyak;
> I, the Madman of Nyak, who has attained the twofold goal [for self
>   and others]. . .[13]

Nyakré Sewo also makes reference to "acting like a madman" (*smyon pa'i bya spyod*) and "doing a lot of the Observance, in the manner of a *siddha*."[14]

Urgyenpa Sengé Pel (or Rinchen Pel, 1229/30–1309) is popularly regarded as a *siddha* of the Drukpa Kagyü. After a thorough religious training under Bodong Rinchen Tsemo, Götsangpa Gönpo Dorjé, the Second Karmapa, and other famous figures, he spent the rest of his life traveling through China and South Asia, including Kashmir and the holy land of Oḍḍiyāna (Urgyen in Tibetan), from which he acquired his name. According to his biography, Urgyenpa was called a "madman" on many different occasions. When the yogin arrived at the home of a lord in Ngari wearing a short robe that was in poor condition, the lady of the house wondered to herself if he was a madman or a *siddha*. Knowing exactly what she was thinking, the yogin asked, "Am I the crazy one, or is it you?" Later, a king would exclaim that Urgyenpa was "mad" when he acted out in his presence. In time, he would come to be known by this designation, as a companion referred to him as "Urgyenpa the Madman." According to his biography, when Urgyenpa went to visit Kublai Khan (1215–1294) in China, the latter praised him for how learned he was in the dharma, and explained that although people said Urgyenpa was a madman and a charlatan (*zog po*), because of his wisdom and conduct he was clearly neither of those things.[15]

Sönam Peldren (1328?–1372?), a married nomadic woman with no formal education or religious training, claimed to be an emanation of Vajravārāhī. Many miracles were attributed to her, and she acquired a cult following after her death. Her biography, one of the earliest depicting a Tibetan Buddhist woman, shows the theme of religious "madness" to have followed her throughout her life. Because of her pretensions to being highly realized in spite of her lack of religious training, many regarded her with skepticism. In songs she would address the way others saw her, saying:

Because I am not deluded by ignorance,
the sun of the wisdom of no-self has risen [in my mind].
In the perception of ordinary beings
I am seen as a crazy woman with an ugly mind.

In this same song, Sönam Peldren explains that her various religious accomplishments—not being deluded by ignorance, being fully dedicated to tantra, and so on—are what put her at odds with worldly expectations. In other songs she praises the Practice of the Observance. She is reputed to have acted in ways demonstrating a disregard for social conventions. Once, with other people around, she took off all her clothes. When her husband wondered at how she was not the least bit ashamed (*ngo . . . tsha*) by her nakedness, she explained her behavior as a sort of symbolic teaching.[16]

Shuksep Jetsün, also known as Ani Lochen or Shuksep Lochen Rinpoché (1853–1950), is one of the most famous Tibetan Buddhist nuns of all time. Born in India's Rewalsar (Tsopema in Tibetan), she spent many years meditating in various places throughout the Himalayas before settling at Shuksep hermitage, near Lhasa. Madness is a recurring theme in her biography. Because she at times said and did strange things, some people said she was a *siddha*, while others wondered if she was insane.[17] She writes of herself as being "like a mad person" or being "labeled mad," and is reputed to have sung songs using the term "crazy" (*smyo*) and referring to the Observance (although these may have been composed by a later editor of her biography). She is also said to have sung a song playing with the idea of her being mad.[18] At one point, her lama told her to go naked through the Barkor in Lhasa, but her dharma siblings prevented her from doing so. On another occasion, Ani Lochen's mother jokingly called two of the nun's teachers "mad *siddhas*" (*grub smyon*) because of the way they tended to interrupt her meditation.[19]

Stories are still popularly told of Amgön Rinpoché (1853–1945), a hermit at Drikung Til, who is renowned for his miraculous powers, including the ability to transform himself into a young monk, or to travel in an instant to Lhasa to buy dumplings. Amgön Rinpoché is also fondly remembered for his eccentric behavior. When people brought him offerings, he would not accept them; when people arrived empty-handed, he would ask what they had brought. Refusing to recognize paper money as having value, he plastered the walls of his cell with the currency he received from the faithful. A rhetoric of madness was often used in reference to his eccentric behavior. On one occasion the monastery's disciplinarian said to him, "Amgön, you are crazy." The yogin responded, "I'm not crazy. The crazy one is you. One-upping is crazy." The reason Amgön Rinpoché said this, we are told, is that the disciplinarian had established a sumptuous residence for himself, and Amgön Rinpoché wanted to point out that this was in actuality more problematic than any of the odd things he himself had done. According to the yogin's biography, on another occasion Amgön Rinpoché acted in a disruptive manner, motivated by lines from the sixth chapter of the first book of the *Hevajra Tantra*, which read, "Having achieved some heat, / if you want to do some Practice . . ." In response, Drupwang Tseten Rinpoché said, "[Amgön Rinpoché] is not crazy. It is a sign of his having achieved *siddhis* . . . This is not like ordinary madness."[20]

Popular tradition maintains that Amgön Rinpoché once brought an ox into the assembly hall and put it at the head of the line of monks. Some of them exclaimed, "Now Amgön is crazy! What to do?" Others complained that he was belittling them by placing them all in such a lowly position behind an ox. Others interpreted this as a symbolic teaching: if the retreatants embodied the qualities of renunciation and realization, what difference would it make to them who or what was seated at the head of their line? Drukpa Künlé is storied to have done the exact same thing with a donkey while visiting Drepung monastery four hundred years prior.[21] If we take this story about Amgön Rinpoché as having really happened, it may be that he was imitating a famous madman of the past. If, as seems more likely, the story is a fabrication, it would suggest that those around Amgön Rinpoché who perpetuated this tale were interested in associating him with Drukpa Künlé, or that stories of behaving in this manner were part of a general lore of eccentric yogin behavior from which they drew.

This *Life* of Amgön Rinpoché was compiled by Rasé Dawa Könchok Gyatso in 2003, based on oral traditions. Rasé Dawa has sometimes referred to himself as a madman. He signs this work as "the mad subject of Drikung, Rasé Könchok Gyatso."[22]

Oral tradition maintains that Do Khyentsé Yeshé Dorjé (1800–1866), a famous eastern Tibetan master, was once attacked by two vicious dogs, one black and one white. Defending himself, he chopped the dogs to bits. When he magically put the dogs back together, the pieces got rearranged, so that mixed black and white dogs were created. It is said that because of this, black-and-white dogs can still be found in the area today. There is a widely known story of Drukpa Künlé's doing the exact same thing.[23]

A popular story tells of Dza Patrül Rinpoché (1808–1887)—a disciple of Do Khyentsé Yeshé Dorjé, who called himself "Patrül the Old Dog" (*khyi rgan pha sprul*)—happening upon a monk meditating in a monastery. Patrül Rinpoché asked the monk what he was meditating on. "Patience," he replied. The yogin walked away, came back, and repeated the same question, to which he again responded, "Patience." Patrül Rinpoché kept asking the monk again and again, challenging him to manifest real patience instead of just meditating on it as an abstract quality. Because of stories like this, Tibetans will occasionally bring up Patrül Rinpoché in discussions of "holy madmen." In his famous *Words of My Teacher*, Patrül Rinpoché warns against "mad guides" who are lax in their religious commitments yet "ape the *siddhas* and behave as if their actions were higher than the sky."[24] It is not clear to whom Patrül Rinpoché is here referring.

While Gendün Chöpel (1903–1951) was studying at Drepung monastery in his twenties, one of his teachers jokingly called him a "madman" because of his contrarian views about fine points of Buddhist philosophy. Gendün Chöpel was known for engaging in unpredictable, transgressive behavior during this part of his life, such as getting drunk, stripping off his clothes, and disguising himself as an illiterate bodyguard monk (*ldab ldob*). Later in his career he would be called a "madman" in a more decidedly negative sense. In a vicious response to a philosophical treatise in which Gendün Chöpel had contested many traditional Geluk views, someone called him "Gendün Chöpel the madman" (*dge chos smyon pa*). This author goes further, saying that Gendün Chöpel was an emanation of Māra, sent forth to destroy the teachings of the Buddha. But Gendün Chöpel would also be remembered as "mad" in a more praiseful sense. A recent scholarly book about his views is titled *The Madman's Middle Way*.[25]

In 1969, during the Cultural Revolution, bloody revolts broke out in many districts of Tibet. The most famous of these incidents took place in Nyemo, in the Ü region. Over the course of two days, hundreds of Tibetan villagers attacked local officials and troops of the People's Liberation Army. The villagers were led by a nun named Trinlé Chödrön, who claimed to be possessed by deities. Many people thought she was mentally unstable. In the eyes of others, her madness was a by-product of her having entered an altered state that enabled her to communicate with the gods. Some called her a "madwoman" (*smyon ma*). Her "madness" was open to multiple interpretations.[26]

One mode in which a rhetoric of madness has traditionally been employed in Tibet is as a pen name. "Madman" is in fact one of the most used pen names in the history of Tibetan literary production. The Fifth Dalai Lama sometimes referred to himself as the Mad Mantrika of Zahor. The author of one Tibetan epic calls himself the Madman of Dingchen. This pen name is still used by Tibetan writers today, in Tibet and in exile, and may be more popular than ever before.[27] One of the most active of these writers is "Mad Lu, the Heruka," also known as Yeshé Gyatso Rinpoché.[28] Closely related to the use of "madman" as a pen name is the tradition of calling one's compositions "crazy words" (*smyo tshig*) or "crazy songs" (*smyo glu*).[29] Often the contents of these works have nothing to do with the theme of madness, in spite of their titles.

The use of the word "mad" in this context would seem to express humility, since the author announces his composition to be of no consequence, inviting his readers to disregard his words as the prattle of the insane. But at the same time, there is such a well-established precedent for referring to oneself in this way that to assume the pen name "madman" is to identify oneself with those who have done so in the past. For this reason, assuming the pen name "madman" can be motivated by the very opposite of humility. But the term may carry other connotations as well, such as expressing the author's commitment to challenging convention (but doing so through a highly conventional mode), or homage to those renowned as "madmen" of generations past (or those, like Milarepa, who employed a rhetoric of madness but were never commonly regarded as "madmen"). To use "madman" as one's pen name is to evoke a wide swath of connotations.

We can observe a complex interplay between the use of "madman" as a pen name and its use to refer to accomplished religious figures. Those adopting "mad" as part of a pen name, those employing a rhetoric of madness but not remembered as "madmen," and those who are remembered primarily as "holy madmen" are all on the same continuum of "madness." In calling himself a "madman" in his compositions, someone like Nyakré Sewo invited varying interpretations of his life. He skillfully located himself at multiple places on this continuum simultaneously, since different observers would find different meanings in his "madness."

The rhetoric of madness can be applied to oneself or to another, and can express praise, censure, or ambivalence. In each case, and in the eyes of different observers, it can take on any of a wide range of meanings. Those for whom "madman" became an enduring sobriquet are simply those who became associated with this rhetoric especially strongly. Individual "madmen" and "madwomen," in the various reasons why they were called "mad," represent only some of the possible meanings expressed by this rhetoric.

Influencing Deed and Representation within the Madman Tradition

Throughout this history we find examples of individuals regarded as "madmen" influencing others in their decisions to become "madmen," and of interlocutors applying what they know of one "madman" to making sense of the behavior of someone else. These cases give a sense of the process through which the idea and the rhetoric of holy madness are maintained and transmitted over time.

In his decision to take on the eccentric lifestyle that would lead to his becoming a "madman," Künga Zangpo was likely influenced by the older and better-established Madman of Tsang. This was probably the case with the Madman of Tsang's disciples who became known as "madmen" as well. A few decades later, the Kagyü ascetic Drakpa Tayé (1469–1531) would come of age in a religious culture bearing the full influence of the Madmen of Ü and Tsang. Early in his religious education, Drakpa Tayé went into town to collect alms. There he met a local official who said to him, "You and your master should be like the master Madman of Tsang and the Madman of Ü—will that be so?" The young Drakpa Tayé answered that he intended to be one called the Madman of Chuk (*phyug smyon*). This was probably a joke, conveying that he wanted to be a "wealthy madman." The Madmen of Ü and Tsang were well known at the time, providing a reference point for lay observers and Kagyü ascetics alike. In time, Drakpa Tayé would meet both of these famous holy madmen. While staying at Nyukla, he received the reading transmission (*lung*) for the first part of the *Life of the Madman of Ü* after it was put into circulation in 1494. He also met Drukpa Künlé at Ralung monastery. Drakpa Tayé would go on to do the Practice of the Observance, clothe himself in ashes, and talk of "the Practice of the Mad Observance" in his songs. He would often praise his teacher, Lhatsün Künga Chökyi Gyatso, as "mad Lhatsün." Drakpa Tayé had an especially close relationship with Dönyö Dorjé.[30] Although not considered a "madman," Drakpa Tayé seems to have been directly influenced by the "madmen" of his day.

The Madman of Tsang did not come up with the idea of becoming a "madman" on his own, but was influenced by those who had come before him. One figure likely influencing him was Tangtong Gyelpo, who loomed especially large in the religious culture of the day. Tibetans remember Tangtong Gyelpo as a *mahāsiddha* who lived for 124 years (1361–1485), who built iron bridges all across Tibet, and who founded the tradition of Tibetan opera (*lha mo*).[31] Lochen Gyurmé Dechen's version of the *Life of Tangtong Gyelpo*, published in 1609 and quoted as the epigraph to this chapter, tells of the *siddha*'s staying at the Four-Doored Kakṇi stūpa in the Lhasa Barkor, sitting perfectly still for a year without moving. This or some similar story must have been in circulation during the time of the Madman of Tsang, since all three versions of the *Life of the Madman of Tsang* tell of his staying at the Four-Doored Kakṇi stūpa. Upon seeing him there in his strange attire, some people exclaimed, "It's a demon!" while others said, "It's Tangtong Gyelpo!"[32] If the Madman of Tsang truly did meditate at this stūpa, it may indicate his being aware of the precedent established by Tangtong Gyelpo and his hope to follow in his footsteps—or, to phrase it differently, that the Madman of Tsang sought to draw from the repertoire of saintly behavior established in part by Tangtong Gyelpo. If the people of Lhasa really did confuse the Madman of Tsang with Tangtong Gyelpo (who was most likely deceased by this time), this would indicate the latter's influence on the religious culture of the day, constituting a reference point by which people made sense of ascetics taking on odd forms of behavior. If this story was fabricated by Ngödrup Pembar, author of the first biography of the Madman of Tsang, it would indicate his desire to associate or compare the Madman of Tsang with the famous saint who had preceded him. Whichever is the case, the figure of Tangtong Gyelpo played a significant role in bringing about this story of the Madman of Tsang. In addition, biographies of Tangtong Gyelpo and the Madman of Tsang both tell of their making naked circumambulations of holy objects, in which a similar dynamic of imitation on behalf of the Madman of Tsang, or comparison on behalf of the ascetics' formal or informal biographers, may be discerned.[33]

There are also cases in which we can determine that a certain "madman" was directly influenced by literary or oral accounts of prior ones. In other cases, we can determine that literature about a prior "madman" was recycled, influencing representations of a later one.

As an example of a later "madman's" actions being directly influenced by those of an earlier one, the Madman of Kongpo, commonly known as Namkha Jikmé (1597–1650), was sometimes called a Heruka or a Destroyer of Illusion (*'khrul zhig*).[34] In a text on the Practice of the Observance, he justifies the practice by quoting numerous canonical texts, especially the *Hevajra Tantra*. He mentions wearing the garb of the Heruka and eating repulsive substances like the "five meats" and the "five nectars"; he specifically mentions doing this before the Four-Doored Kakni stūpa in Lhasa. He was confronted in the act by a philosopher-monk (*mtshan nyid pa*), who asked him what he was doing, and where in the Buddha's teachings dressing that way, drinking alcohol, or eating such repulsive things was taught. In response, the Madman of Kongpo questioned the orthodoxy of the monk's own lifestyle, much as the Madman of Tsang did that of the *geshés* of the Geluk. Later in this same text, Namkha Jikmé responds to being called a "madman" by addressing his "madness" in a song. He asserts a connection between his activities and the Aural Transmission of the Madmen of Ü and Tsang, and the life story of Drukpa Künlé.[35] The Madman of Kongpo was thus directly influenced by what was known about the famous fifteenth-century holy madmen, and was self-consciously aware of this fact. In making a point of practicing the Observance at the Kakni stūpa, he was probably also being influenced by Tangtong Gyelpo, perhaps by way of the Madman of Tsang, whether he was aware of it or not.

Many examples of the way certain narratives of earlier madmen were recycled to influence narratives about later ones can be found in the literature surrounding Tangtong Gyelpo. As with Drukpa Künlé, notwithstanding Tangtong Gyelpo's fame and significance in Tibetan religious culture, we know very little about him as a historical figure. A few traditional biographies of Tangtong Gyelpo were composed over the years. The latest was written in 1609, based on earlier accounts. Its author, Lochen Gyurmé Dechen, was believed to be a descendent of Tangtong Gyelpo. He was also a disciple of Lhatong Lotsāwa Shényen Namgyel, author of the second part of the Madman of Ü's biography. Since this biography was the only one cut into woodblocks and widely disseminated, it would become the standard account of the *mahāsiddha* Tangtong Gyelpo's life.

Lochen Gyurmé Dechen's version of the *Life of Tangtong Gyelpo* consistently invokes a rhetoric of madness. According to this biography, Tangtong Gyelpo was first called a "madman" by his father and other inhabitants of their village when he disturbed an earth spirit in the process of subduing a malicious entity that had been causing an epidemic: not believing that his unconventional ritual would be efficacious (which of course it was), people called him crazy. When studying at Sakya monastery, the young man did not take to his studies the same way the other monks did, showing no interest in textual learning. According to Gyurmé Dechen, people said, "This little monk is poor in the treatises." His not being ashamed at this resulted, Gyurmé Dechen asserts, from his enacting the Practice of the Observance. Because of his nonconformity, he began to be known as Mad Tsöndrü, a name that would stay with him for some time.[36] Much later, when he returned to his home village after claiming to have spent the previous eighteen years training in Nepal and India, people called him a madman and a liar. He was called a madman again when he slept on Dölpopa's (1292–1361) throne at Jonang monastery. At one point, however, Tangtong Gyelpo would be visited by some *ḍākinīs*, who gave him five special names, one of which was the Madman of the Empty Valley.[37] When Tangtong Gyelpo was called a "madman" at any point for the rest of his life or after, the term conveyed more praise than insult. Tangtong Gyelpo's "madness" follows a trajectory that can be observed in the biographies of many Tibetan "madmen": early on he acts in odd ways and is called "mad" in a pejorative albeit playful sense. But during the course of his life the meaning of the term "mad" is transformed, taking on a more positive valence.

Gyurmé Dechen's version of the *Life of Tangtong Gyelpo* contains many passages that are very similar to ones found in the biographies of the Madman of Tsang. The *Life* maintains that when Tangtong Gyelpo was staying at Bodhgaya, the locals saw a fire blazing at night. When they came to investigate the cause of it, they saw that it was actually Tangtong Gyelpo generating yogic fire through meditation. According to all three versions of the *Life* of the Madman of Tsang, the same thing happened when Sangyé Gyeltsen was meditating near Kathmandu.[38] There are a few possible explanations for the similarity between these two accounts. It could be that this miracle was originally attributed to Tangtong Gyelpo and widely known at the time of the Madman of Tsang, on the basis of which the story about the latter was told. It could be that the author of the *Life of Tangtong Gyelpo* drew this story from a version of the *Life* of the Madman of Tsang, all three of which had been published long earlier. Or it could be that this was a miracle attributed to many Tibetan yogins, and not original to the Madman of Tsang or Tangtong Gyelpo, or to their respective biographies.

A further example of this sort of borrowing, influence, or drawing from a more general lore is as follows. The epigraph to this chapter is a passage from Gyurmé Dechen's *Life of Tangtong Gyelpo*, in which the yogin gives saucy responses to the questions of where he had come from and where he was headed. This is basically the same as an event included in all three *Lives* of the Madman of Tsang, in which he is asked by an official: "Where do you come from? What knowledge do you have? Where are you going?" The Madman of Tsang answers, "I come from behind; now I go toward what's in front of me." The official then responds, "He's a feisty one!" The word translated as "feisty," *kha gyong*, is exactly the same in the *Lives* of Tangtong Gyelpo and the Madman of Tsang.[39] In the biographies of both figures, there are multiple exchanges based on this same basic line of questioning.

A similar encounter is described in Geshé Chapu's 1966 *Life* of Drukpa Künlé. While traveling along the road, Drukpa Künlé meets five girls (another repeated trope in this literature), who ask him, "Where are you from and where are you going?" He answers, "I come from behind and I'm going on ahead." A variation of this is also included in Karma Trinlepa's version of the *Life* of the Indian *mahāsiddha* Saraha.[40] It will surely be found in other Tibetan biographies of Buddhist ascetics as well.

These passages are too similar to result from mere coincidence. They may represent later biographers' mining earlier biographies for material, or drawing from a general stock of narratives that precedes and exists independently from these individual texts. These passages may also signal that this same basic tale has been attributed to these different yogins in oral tradition, showing how popular perceptions of these figures inflect one another.

The lines of influence traced in this section are circular or looping rather than linear and unidirectional. Neither in deed nor in representation of his deeds is a "madman" ever fully independent of those who preceded him. The various agents of meaning making whose products we are considering here—the "madmen," their general public, and those who have taken up the task of creating formal accounts of their lives—all operate within a rich literary culture saturated with narratives. Regardless of whether or not "holy madness" truly exists as an individualized state of mind, it is clear that the theme of "holy madness" circulates within this literary culture, alongside many other tropes. When employing this rhetoric of madness (whether it be the ascetic himself or someone speaking or writing about him), one is, consciously or unconsciously, drawing from the past history of the term, while also contributing to that history. The repertoire of "mad" rhetoric and behavior is always evolving, looking both at what came before and what might lie ahead.

The Allure of Holy Madness

The Second Dalai Lama, who spent most of his life serving as abbot of a succession of Geluk monasteries, signed many of his writings "the mad beggar Gendün Gyatso." It is quite clear that he intended "mad beggar" to express a playful irony or humility (at least faux humility), as the pen name has long done. But some later interpreters would view his use of the term very differently. As the current Dalai Lama explains:

> The implication of "Mad" here is that when a person gains experience of emptiness, the ultimate mode of existence of all phenomena, his perception is as different from that of ordinary people as a madman's. Due to his or her realization of emptiness, a practitioner completely transcends the conventional way of viewing the world.[41]

A blurb on the back of the book claims that the Second Dalai Lama "was 'crazed' by the wisdom of the nature of reality." Asked to give a gloss on the appellation, Richard Gere states that the Second Dalai Lama's signing his works "the Mad Beggar" "refer[s] to that state beyond all attachment and conventional modes of thought and behavior, the realization of emptiness." We can question whether or not this is the sense in which the Second Dalai Lama used the term "madman" in reference to himself. Would he have unabashedly claimed to be enlightened in this way? (Could we imagine the current Dalai Lama saying such a thing about himself?) Instead, it seems more likely that these commentators have construed the "madness" of the Second Dalai Lama to mean something significantly different from what he originally intended.

The narrative of enlightenment and transcendence leading to a radically different manner of engaging with the world has long proven to be one many audiences find compelling. In recent centuries among Tibetans, and more recent decades among Westerners, the idea of madness-as-enlightenment has become so prominent that it has caused people to lose sight of the other senses in which the term "mad" may originally have been used. This has led to distorted understandings and representations of Tibet's past. The very fact that Glenn Mullin would title his translation of the Second Dalai Lama's poetry *Mystical Verses of a Mad Dalai Lama*—foregrounding and taking completely out of context something that was only a minor aspect of the Second Dalai Lama's mode of being in the world—is a testament to just how strongly people are drawn to the idea of madness-as-enlightenment. Titling the book in this way surely would not have an adverse effect on its sales numbers. The chapter on the Second Dalai Lama's life in Alexander Norman's 2008 *Secret Lives of the Dalai Lama* is titled "A Mad Beggar Monk," showing the traction this way of referring to him has gained.

Further exemplifying the current potency of the idea of "holy madness," while translating the first volume of the *Miscellaneous Writings* of Drukpa Künlé, R. A. Stein encountered a sentence in which the word "I" was missing. In a footnote, Stein explains: "The author voluntarily omits the first person pronoun. The style of a 'mad' saint who wants to eliminate the notion of 'myself.' "[42] Anyone who has studied the Tibetan language, and surely someone as learned as Stein, can tell you that, unlike English, in Tibetan the doer of an action does not need to be stated in order for a sentence to be grammatically complete. More often than not, it is implied by context. Stein has been compelled to read saintly madness into an ordinary sentence.

Lama Zhang (1122–1193), founder of the Tselpa branch of the Kagyü, signed many of his compositions "the crazy beggar-monk of Zhang" (*zhang gi sprang ban smyon pa*). We have no reason to believe that Lama Zhang referred to himself as a "madman" in any way other than as a pen name, in a manner that was playful, self-denigrating, and perhaps ironically boastful at the same time. And yet Ronald Davidson has placed Lama Zhang among other "holy madman" of the Tibetan tradition because of his use of the term. Davidson suggests that Lama Zhang saw his warlike activities in the Lhasa area as being justified because of his high state of realization. Following a more detailed study, Carl Yamamoto has asserted this characterization of Lama Zhang as a scandalous and dangerous figure to be mistaken.[43] The idea of madman-as-enlightened-being can be so compelling that it makes even good scholars misinterpret the past.

These examples are evidence of the kind of feedback loop that has driven the discourse about "holy madmen" for the past five hundred years. The original sense in which a "madman" (or other religious figure resorting to a rhetoric of madness) employed the term gets reinterpreted and distorted by others. This distorted version then drowns out the original meaning of the term. This sort of distortion can occur at any point in the chain of many different agents' individual acts of meaning making, including the "madman," his contemporary public, his biographers, later readers or hearers of his tale, and later commentators on the phenomenon. That distorted understanding can gain its own agency as it goes on to influence other individuals' understandings of "holy madness." By its very nature, the designation "mad" invites romantic speculation. There is always a potential for slippage between what someone means the term "mad" to imply and what others might read into it. This potential increases dramatically over time. Because of this, earlier meanings of "holy madness" tend to get buried, and sometimes can be recovered only through extended acts of excavation.

After his death, people latched onto the idea of Drukpa Künlé's being a "madman," and subsequently generated a new understanding of who he was. This latter understanding of Drukpa Künlé's "madness" now dominates the way people think about "holy madmen" in general. The fact that Künga Zangpo and Sangyé Gyeltsen achieved their reputations as "madmen" primarily through assuming a lifestyle based on the Practice of the Observance has been forgotten, replaced by the notion that the sense in which they were "mad" was mainly about being enlightened. Who among the Second Dalai Lama, the Madman of Ü, the Madman of Tsang, and Drukpa Künlé would have claimed to be completely enlightened? And yet this is the way so many observers, both Tibetan and Western, have interpreted and explained the meaning of their "madness."

In 2006, the Rubin Museum of Art in New York, a world leader in trans-Himalayan art, put on an exhibition titled "Holy Madness: Portraits of Tantric Siddhas." The primary subjects of this exhibit were the famous Indian *siddhas* of the seventh to eleventh centuries. The exhibition's catalog includes ten essays by scholars in the fields of Indian and Tibetan religion and art. A rhetoric of madness was traditionally employed concerning a handful of the Indian and Tibetan mystics—Buddhist, Hindu, Jain, Sufi—addressed in the exhibit and its catalog. But the scope of the exhibition and catalog extended well beyond these few, so that the majority of figures brought together under the title of "Holy Madness" were not traditionally discussed using such terminology.[44]

The process that has led to this application of the idea of "holy madness" is as follows: from at least the tenth century to the present there has been a small subset of religious practitioners in Tibet who through their eccentric behavior, writings, and self-proclamations, have come to be called "madmen" within their own culture. Some of these figures emulated the famous eccentric *siddha*s of India who came before them. Modern-day scholars have so fixated upon their "madness" that "holy madness" has become a commonly referred to category in our work. It has become so ubiquitous that scholars now apply the idea of holy madness back onto other Indian and Tibetan ascetics who traditionally were not referred to in that way. The idea of holy madness has quite literally taken on a life of its own, among scholars and popular commentators alike.

There is no question that the learned curators of this exhibition are aware of these important distinctions. But they are also aware of the great allure of "holy madness"—a sexy, compelling idea sure to generate broader public interest. It is this allure that has brought me to write the current study, and may well have moved the reader to pick it up. Although "holy madness" has carried widely divergent meanings and inflections over time, it continues to persist as a potent and moving category of thought.

Chögyam Trungpa Rinpoché (1939–1987) played an especially important role in bringing about this state of affairs in which Western commentators so readily employ the notion of "holy madness" in making sense of Tibet's (and India's) past. Trungpa was born in eastern Tibet, the eleventh in the Trungpa reincarnation lineage. In 1959 he fled to India, then went to study at Oxford. He emigrated to Canada and then to the United States, establishing centers in Vermont and Boulder, Colorado. He taught in North America from 1970 until his death. His accomplishments during this time were remarkable. He established a vast network of meditation centers, either under the name of Tibetan Buddhism or the quasi-Buddhist "Shambhala International." He wrote thirty books, including the well-known *Cutting through Spiritual Materialism*. By skillfully blending old and new, and by framing Buddhism in the discourse of

modern psychology, Trungpa made himself into one of the most important agents in determining how Tibetan Buddhism has been received by
Westerners.

Trungpa had eccentric tendencies. Late in his life, he took to wearing military uniforms. He established a retinue of guards, who attended an annual
boot camp where they learned to march in formation. He tried to train
some of his American students to speak with an Oxford accent. Sometimes
when traveling by plane, Trungpa would tell the pilot he was the king of
Bhutan and suggest that this be announced to the other passengers.[45]

Trungpa was also a man of more serious controversy. He was a heavy
drinker for most of his adult life—by some accounts an alcoholic—and
sometimes arrived to give teachings visibly drunk. In his twenties he gave
up his monkhood and fathered a son with a nun. Years later he would
get married, but continued to have sexual relationships with many of his
disciples.[46]

Trungpa's disciples and latter-day followers have always readily admitted to these facets of his life. Even so, most do not waver in seeing Trungpa
as an enlightened being, even casting these aspects of his personality in a
decidedly positive light. I was once told by a devoted follower that Trungpa
could give brilliant teachings while "drunk off his ass," and his ability to
be so lucid while intoxicated simply proved how highly realized he was.

Of interest here is the way Trungpa created specific circumstances
ensuring that his behavior would be interpreted in this manner. The most
important factor in shaping how Trungpa's supporters would interpret
his behavior is the idea that, since Trungpa was an enlightened master
who had completely given over his life to teaching the dharma, everything
he did was a teaching. Every gesture, every word was part of Trungpa's
enlightened activity, his attempt to transmit the teachings of the Buddha
to those around him. Once during a business meeting, Trungpa stopped
in the middle of a conversation to ask the nun Pema Chödrön, "Do you
masturbate?" She explains this as having been a deep and profound teaching.[47] As Fabrice Midal states in his 2001 biography of Trungpa, "Certain
surprising things he did can seem shocking today, and may also have
seemed brutal or crazy at the time, but thanks to them the persons they
were aimed at were able to open fully." According to Midal, simply by
helping Trungpa get dressed in the morning one could receive "a powerful transmission." Trungpa's sexual relationships with his female students
were "a very precious communication."[48] In response to the uproar over an
incident in 1975 when Trungpa allegedly had two of his followers forcibly

stripped of their clothing at a party during a three-month retreat, the poet Alan Ginsberg referred to Trungpa's actions as part of a "conscious-making" tradition stretching back thousands of years. Ginsberg said that this was "a traditional Buddhist practice applied in America in as gentle a way as possible." The frightened couple's pleas for someone to call the police were "vulgar."[49] In this view, Trungpa's actions cannot be judged based on our usual conventions, because he was not an ordinary man living in the world, but an enlightened being who lived somehow beyond this world, only doing what he could to help liberate others. For these reasons, Trungpa was perfect and beyond judgment.

These examples give a sense of the atmosphere Trungpa formed around himself, in which his actions would be interpreted in a specific way by his followers. A basic element of this hermeneutical atmosphere was Trungpa's idea of "crazy wisdom." Trungpa was not entirely clear on what he intended "crazy wisdom" to mean. He variously described it as "the action of truth," or as "controlling psychic energies." He described crazy wisdom as "very timid or cowardly," but also as "what characterizes a saint in the Buddhist tradition." Trungpa said that the "essence" of crazy wisdom is "hopelessness." At the same, time Trungpa talked about crazy wisdom as the totality of the good qualities manifested by the eight forms of Padmasambhava. Trungpa also asserted crazy wisdom to be a pedagogical mode, a sort of skillful means or *upāya*.[50]

Trungpa also said that one can experience crazy wisdom only by coming into contact with "the crazy-wisdom lineage." This lineage was passed on to Trungpa by the second Jamgön Kongtrul (1902–1952). Trungpa said that crazy wisdom is especially present in the Nyingma sect and connected with the Great Perfection. (Later, Trungpa's followers would see crazy wisdom as something especially exemplified by the early masters of the Kagyü.) Trungpa said that crazy wisdom could "only be taught in [a] savage count[ry]." In the same way that Padmasambhava once brought crazy wisdom to Tibet, Trungpa was now bringing it to the United States. He encouraged the comparison.[51]

These highly varied comments about "crazy wisdom" were all made by Trungpa in the course of one month in 1972. The transcripts from these teachings show that his students were confused by his presentation, in which crazy wisdom seemed to mean so many different things at once.[52] It would appear that Trungpa himself did not have a fixed idea of what he wanted "crazy wisdom" to mean. Rather, it functioned as a catch-all for a variety of positive qualities. Trungpa could change what it meant from one moment to the next in order to suit his needs. When Trungpa was trying to link himself to Padmasambhava, "crazy wisdom" was a special character-istic of that saint. When he wanted to praise his lama and his lama's lama, "crazy wisdom" was unique to that lineage. Later in his career, Trungpa would state that "crazy wisdom" was the equivalent of a Tibetan term, *yeshé chölwa* (*ye shes 'chol ba*), which I have never come across—not in any of the thousands of pages of Tibetan literature on or by "holy madmen" that I have read, nor in the conversations I have had with Tibetans.[53] (The Dalai Lama has referred to "crazy wisdom" as "new vocabulary.")[54] In artic-ulating his notion of "crazy wisdom" in the course of his career, Trungpa was drawing from various precedents in Indian and Tibetan Buddhism's past. But what he created must be seen as his own formulation, despite his claims that he was merely conforming to tradition.

In time it was accepted as axiomatic by many of Trungpa's followers that crazy wisdom had long been a part of the Tibetan Buddhist tradition, that it was embodied by enlightened beings, that it was a profound teach-ing method, and, most important of all, that Trungpa had it. In 2005, Midal wrote that Trungpa was "a master in the 'crazy wisdom' school." Other devotees casually call Trungpa a "holder of crazy wisdom."[55] A docu-mentary film about his life is even titled *Crazy Wisdom*. Trungpa was thus remarkably successful in creating the very categories through which he would be understood. Through his skillful presentation of certain ideas, he created an environment in which it was not just accepted, but expected that he would act in ways that challenged other people's notions of propri-ety. Perhaps it was the unique set of circumstances, with Trungpa at the forefront of the spread of Tibetan Buddhism to the Western world, that enabled him such freedom in shaping these conceptual categories. With few other representatives of Tibetan Buddhism around, Trungpa was an unquestioned source of authority.

Chögyam Trungpa did not explicitly compare himself with famous "holy madmen" of the Tibetan tradition like the Madman of Tsang or Drukpa Künlé. (Trungpa preferred to compare himself to Padmasambhava, who, he said, embodied his own form of "crazy wisdom.") Nevertheless, after Trungpa had popularized the idea of "crazy wisdom" within his circle, many would come to see him as a latter-day version of the famous holy madmen of Tibet, especially Drukpa Künlé.[56]

One of the most influential books in shaping how the non-Tibetan world thinks about "holy madmen" is Keith Dowman's translation of Geshé Chapu's *Life* of Drukpa Künlé, whose introduction contains the oft-cited line: "If insanity is defined as deviation from a psychological norm, the divine madman is truly crazy; but if a spiritual ideal is used as a yardstick, undoubtedly, it is the vast majority of us who are insane."[57] The explanation of the holy madmen that Dowman offers in this introduction is deeply indebted to Trungpa's presentation, relying on the terms "crazy wisdom," "spiritual materialism," and "neurosis."

Further showing the kind of influence Trungpa has had (often by way of Dowman) is the work of Georg Feuerstein. Feuerstein is by his own admission an advocate of spirituality rather than a scholar of religion.[58] But what he may lack in scholarly rigor, he makes up for in popular appeal and book sales. Unrestrained by indebtedness to traditional Tibetan ways of thinking or to scholarly standards, writers like Feuerstein and Dowman are free to tailor their accounts for modern Western readers.

In 2006, Feuerstein published a five-hundred-page book titled *Holy Madness: Spirituality, Crazy-Wise Teachers, and Enlightenment*, an expanded version of a book first published in 1991. *Holy Madness* offers a survey of eccentric saintly figures from many of the world's religions, including Christian mystics who acted like fools in their humility before Christ, Hindus intoxicated by their devotion to god, and Zen masters of China and Japan, whose teaching methods Feuerstein calls a form of "shock therapy" (a term Dowman employs in explaining the behavior of Drukpa Künlé). Feuerstein also discusses the lives of some modern spiritual masters like Gurdjieff, Aleister Crowley, Osho (Rajneesh), and Adi Da/Bubba Da Free John (Franklin Jones), who were all "crazy-wise" in some way. Throughout the book, Feuerstein casually alternates between the terms "holy madness" and "crazy wisdom."

Much of Feuerstein's chapter on the "Crazy Adepts of Tibet" is actually devoted to the Indian *siddha*s he sees as their precursors, relating stories about Saraha, Kāṇha, and Manibhadrā, and the lineage running from Tilopa to Nāropa to Marpa and Milarepa. Each master in this lineage taught his successor by using unpredictable, sometimes brutal lessons that Feuerstein assures us exemplify "crazy wisdom." Feuerstein also spends some pages on Drukpa Künlé, for which his sole source is Dowman's *Divine Madman*. Feuerstein also discusses the life of Chögyam Trungpa, continually reminding the reader that all of his actions embodied crazy wisdom. He refers to Trungpa as "a modern Drukpa Kunley" because of his sexual exploits.[59]

Feuerstein's writings highlight the fact that Chögyam Trungpa figures in this state of affairs as more than just another mad saint. Although

Feuerstein addresses "holy madmen" in all the major religions, his basic definition of holy madness is based primarily on ideas about the "holy madness" tradition in Tibet articulated by Trungpa and Dowman. Feuerstein credits Trungpa with coining the very term "crazy wisdom."[60] Feuerstein's understanding of holy madness in the Tibetan context creates the category under which the exemplars of "holy madness" of other religious traditions are brought together. This example shows how Trungpa's articulation of the notion of "crazy wisdom" has influenced the way Westerners have understood the whole of the "holy madman" tradition, not just in Tibet or within Buddhism, but in other religious traditions as well.[61]

Chögyam Trungpa was not a passive observer of Tibetan religious culture, but an active participant in its ongoing creation. He acted upon the ways people thought, including how they would interpret his own behavior. He did not simply pass on eternal truths, but purposefully selected from the repertoire of ideas that were available to him, making use of the topics and tropes—each a narrative, or a fragment of one—that seemed most useful in light of the message he sought to convey and the circumstances amid which he tried to convey it. Wisdom, compassion, emptiness, karma, generosity—these tropes are nearly ubiquitous in Buddhist discourse and it is often difficult to see what significance lies in individual instances of their use. But "holy madness" is a trope made use of less often, and it therefore stands out more strikingly when employed.

It is not hard to sense how Trungpa's promotion of the idea of "crazy wisdom" affected the circumstances of his life and the reception of Tibetan Buddhism in the West. But we can only partially reconstruct the purposes to which "madmen" who lived long ago employed the rhetoric of madness. From the turn of the first millennium to the present, Buddhists in the Tibetan cultural world have heard tales of "holy madmen," making such figures part of the Tibetan Buddhist *imaginaire.* Sangyé Gyeltsen, Künga Zangpo, the Madman of Kongpo, the Latsé Madman, and others each decided to take on an identity that his contemporaries would associate with that of "holy madman." Once others started to consider these individuals "holy madmen," they would each play a role in shaping the idea of holy madness, both for their contemporaries and for future generations. At the same time, they influenced how others thought about earlier "holy madmen," actively shaping understandings of history around them. It is in this ever-evolving body of applied understandings that the meaning of "holy madness" is found.

Epilogue

IN 2009, I WAS fortunate enough to meet with His Holiness the Seventeenth Karmapa in Dharamsala to ask his thoughts on the tradition of "holy madmen" in Tibetan Buddhism. Our conversation centered on the Madman of Tsang and Drukpa Künlé, and the reasons why an ascetic of the Kagyü might be moved to smear himself with ashes or eat the brains of a corpse. When we had finished, I asked the Karmapa to grant me a new Tibetan name. I sat in a waiting room until one of his attendants arrived carrying a red card with gold lettering. Inside was written my new name: Karma Drondül Nyönpa—"Karma, Subduer of Beings, Madman."

What did the Karmapa mean by giving me this name? Surely not that I am somehow an enlightened being. Was it a commentary on what he thought of me, or the odd things I had come to ask him about? Did our conversation lead him to perceive in me a reasoned irreverence, or a commitment to exploring new ways of thinking about things? Perhaps he was just being playful.

In my understanding, if I were to use the name "madman" in reference to myself, the combination of meanings it expressed would be entirely unique. Rather than expressing my transcendence of worldly dualities, it would be a knowing homage to those who had taken on this identity in the past. It would express my affection for the Kagyü, and my long-standing interest in the lives of ascetics. It would express the fact that, by virtue of having written this book, I may have some influence on the way other people think about the "madmen" of times past, which in a way places me within that tradition. The meanings expressed by the name would be determined by the narrative of my life and the details of my personal relationship to Buddhism. The epithet would be open to various interpretations by others, based on their individual understandings of me and of the "madman" tradition.

The fact that the Karmapa gave me this name reminds us of the fact that *nyönpa*, "madman," is after all just a word, and can be applied and interpreted in many different ways. Although the meaning of the term is inflected by all the ways it has been used in the past, its every application is nevertheless a fresh act of meaning making, which may inflect meanings expressed in future uses of the term. The loose conventions that determine how the term is used and understood are precipitated out of a feedback loop involving various agents and their individual acts of meaning making. These moments of meaning making are part of the continual fashioning of narratives, about ourselves, others, and the world around us—the production of discourse—through which we convince ourselves and others to accept certain understandings of things, and thereby act within our cultures.

Notes

INTRODUCTION

1. Rgod tshang ras pa, *Gtsang smyon he ru ka phyogs thams cad las rnam par rgyal ba'i rnam thar rdo rje theg pa'i gsal byed nyi ma'i snying po*, ed. Lokesh Chandra (New Delhi: Sharada Rani, 1969), 37.6–38.1. In the notes that follow, this text is referred to simply as Rgod tshang ras pa. For other translations of this idiosyncratic passage, see Andrew Quintman, *The Yogin and the Madman: Reading the Biographical Corpus of Tibet's Great Saint Milarepa* (New York: Columbia University Press, 2014), 123–4; Stefan Larsson, *Crazy for Wisdom: The Making of a Mad Yogin in Fifteenth-Century Tibet* (Leiden: Brill, 2012), 135.

2. According to Sman pa tshe dbang rta mgrin (interview, September 7, 2009), in Tibetan culture traditionally, 60 to 70 percent of all cases of madness would have been considered to result from problems with the psychophysical winds (*rlung gi nad*). Problems can also arise with the channels in which the winds circulate, leading to "channel madness" (*rtsa smyo*). Some cases of "wind disorder" are perceived as having been caused by demonic attack, complicating the question of how they should be classified. See Kim Gutschow, "The Practice of Tibetan Medicine in Zangskar: A Case of Wind Disorder," in *Healing at the Periphery: Ethnographies of Tibetan Medicine in India*, ed. Laurent Pordié (Durham, NC: Duke University Press, forthcoming); John Ardussi and Lawrence Epstein, "The Saintly Madmen in Tibet," in *Himalayan Anthropology: The Indo-Tibetan Interface*, ed. James Fisher (The Hague: Mouton, 1978), 329–31.

3. These terms are spelled *grub thob smyon pa*, *rnal 'byor smyon pa*, and *bla ma smyon pa*.

4. *Bde mchog mkha' 'gro snyan rgyud kyi gzhung 'brel sa gcad dang sbrags pa*, in Gtsang smyon he ru ka, *Bde mchog mkha' 'gro snyan rgyud (Ras chung snyan rgyud): Two Manuscript Collections of Texts from the Yig cha of Gtsang-smyon He-ru-ka*, 1:5–360 (Leh: Smanrtsis shesrig spendzod, 1971), here citing 336.2.

5. Jack Kerouac, *The Dharma Bums* (New York: Penguin, 1986), 186.

6. For more on the ways European and American scholars and practitioner-commentators have approached the question of Tibet's holy madmen, see the chapter "Popular Conceptions, Scholarly Presumptions" in my dissertation, "Subversive Sainthood and Tantric Fundamentalism: An Historical Study of Tibet's 'Holy Madmen'" (PhD diss., University of Virginia, 2011).

7. On Mi la ras pa's dates, see Quintman, *Yogin and the Madman*, 1, 226; Peter Alan Roberts, *The Biographies of Rechungpa: The Evolution of a Tibetan Hagiography* (Abingdon and New York: Routledge, 2007), 81–4.

8. In this book I will not adhere to the distinction between "tantric" and "esoteric" Buddhism suggested by Christian Wedemeyer, although there are other contexts in which doing so is certainly worthwhile; *Making Sense of Tantric Buddhism: History, Semiology, and Transgression in the Indian Traditions* (New York: Columbia University Press, 2013), 9.

9. These comments are based on interviews and less formal conversations with Tibetans regarding the topic of holy madmen. The *bla ma*s, *mkhan po*s, and *rin po che*s I interviewed, many of whom were born in Tibet, are listed in the bibliography. Most are of the 'Bri gung, 'Brug pa, and Karma branches of the Bka' brgyud. Several Rnying ma *mkhan po*s were interviewed. I have also had many less formal conversations with monks of the other sects, and with laypeople with varying degrees of education. Among religious specialists, those with the greatest interest in "holy madmen" tend to be from the 'Brug pa Bka' brgyud. When I mentioned to Chos rgyal rin po che that he seemed to have a special interest in the holy madmen, he replied, "Of course I'm interested in them—I'm a 'Brug pa!"

10. Aviad Kleinberg, *Prophets in Their Own Country: Living Saints and the Making of Sainthood in the Later Middle Ages* (Chicago: University of Chicago Press, 1992); Robert Ford Campany, *Making Transcendents: Ascetics and Social Memory in Early Medieval China* (Honolulu: University of Hawai'i Press, 2009).

11. *chos pa ri la sgom na/ zan gong gyen du 'gril*; Cristoph Cüppers and Per K. Sørensen, *A Collection of Tibetan Proverbs and Sayings: Gems of Tibetan Wisdom and Wit* (Stuttgart: Franz Steiner Verlag, 1998), 90.

CHAPTER 1

1. Smyug la paN chen ngag dbang grags pa and Lha mthong lo tsA ba bshes gnyen rnam rgyal, *Dpal ldan bla ma dam pa grub pa'i khyu mchog phyogs thams cad las rnam par rgyal ba'i spyod pa can rje btsun kun dga' bzang po'i rnam par thar pa ris med dad pa'i spu long g.yo byed*, in *Bka' brgyud pa Hagiographies: A Collection of Rnam Thar of the Eminent Masters of Tibetan Buddhism*, vol. 2 (Palampur, Himachal Pradesh: Sungrab Nyamso Gyunphel Parkhang, Tibetan Craft Community, 1972), 388.1–5. Descriptions of the versions of the Tibetan text used

in this study are given in the bibliography. Unless specified, citations of Smyug la paN chen and Lha mthong lo tsA ba reference the 1972 edition.

2. *dad pa'i spu long g.yo.*

3. Dominick LaCapra, "Rethinking Intellectual History and Reading Texts," *History and Theory* 19, no. 3 (1980): 250.

4. Smyug la paN chen and Lha mthong lo tsA ba, 448.4–6.

5. My approach to using these texts is greatly influenced by Kleinberg, *Prophets in Their Own Country*, chap. 3. For a discussion of the ways some historians have suggested we treat hagiographic texts, see Campany, *Making Transcendents*, 8–22.

6. For a biography of Smyug la paN chen, see Dpa' bo gtsug lag phreng ba, *Chos 'byung mkhas pa'i dga' ston* (Beijing: Mi rigs dpe skrun khang, 2006), 592.12–593.8; repeated in Si tu paN chen chos kyi 'byung gnas and 'Be lo tshe dbang kun khyab, *Bsgrub brgyud karma kaM tshang brgyud pa rin po che'i rnam par thar pa rab 'byams nor bu zla ba chu shel gyi phreng ba* (New Delhi: D. Gyaltshan and Kesang Legshay, 1972), 1:648.3–649.3. In his colophon to the *Life of the Madman of Ü*, Lha mthong lo tsA ba states that he completed his part of the text in 1537, when he was twenty-six years old (in the Tibetan manner of counting), which puts his birth around 1512; 657.2; Cyrus Stearns, *King of the Empty Plain: The Tibetan Iron-Bridge Builder Tangtong Gyalpo* (Ithaca, NY: Snow Lion, 2007), 10.

   For other summaries of Dbus smyon's life based on this same biography, see "The Three Divine Madmen," in *The Dragon Yogis: A Collection of Selected Biographies and Teachings of the Drukpa Lineage Masters* (Gurgaon: Drukpa Publications, 2009), 44–7; Franz-Karl Ehrhard, "The Holy Madman of dBus and His Relationships with Tibetan Rulers of the 15th and 16th Centuries," in *Geschichten und Geschichte: Historiographie und Hagiographie in der asiatischen Religionsgeschichte*, ed. Peter Schalk, 219–46 (Uppsala: Uppsala University Library, 2010).

7. Separate from the issue of Tibetans traditionally counting ages differently from Westerners is the fact that in the first part of Dbus smyon's biography, Smyug la paN chen sometimes expresses an uncertainty, saying, for example, that the boy was "eight or nine" when he started learning to read and write, 392.1.

8. Smyug la paN chen and Lha mthong lo tsA ba, 641.2.

9. Smyug la paN chen and Lha mthong lo tsA ba, 655.5–6.

10. David DiValerio, "Reanimating the Great Yogin: On the Composition of the Biographies of the Madman of Tsang," *Revue d'Etudes Tibétaines* 31 (2015): 25–49. See also Larsson, *Crazy for Wisdom*, which includes descriptions of these biographies and their authors.

    On Rgod tshang ras pa's dates, which are not definitively known, see Franz-Karl Ehrhard, "Editing and Publishing the Master's Writings: The Early Years of rGod tshang ras chen (1482–1559)," in *Edition, éditions: L'écrit au Tibet, évolution et devenir*, ed. Anne Chayet et al., 129–61 (Munich: Indus Verlag, 2010); Roberts, *Biographies of Rechungpa*, 40–44.

For summaries of the life of Gtsang smyon also based on Rgod tshang ras pa's account, see Don grub rgyal, <<Mi la ras pa'i rnam thar >> gyi rtsom pa po'i lo rgyus, in Dpal don grub rgyal gyi gsung 'bum, 3:27–53 (Beijing: Mi rigs dpe skrun khang, 1997); Larsson, Crazy for Wisdom, 324–6; Quintman, Yogin and the Madman, 123–5; Roberts, Biographies of Rechungpa, 60–64; E. Gene Smith, "Introduction to The Life of Gtsang smyon Heruka," in Among Tibetan Texts: History and Literature of the Himalayan Plateau, ed. Kurtis Schaeffer, 59–79 (Somerville, MA: Wisdom, 2001), essay first published in 1969; "Three Divine Madmen," 41–4.

11. nga brgyal [sic], Rgod tshang ras pa, 27.7.

12. Rgod tshang ras pa, 28.5.

13. Larsson translates this passage, Crazy for Wisdom, 107–8. On the three biographies' respective descriptions of Sangs rgyas rgyal mtshan's ordination status, see 78–9.

CHAPTER 2

1. Smyug la paN chen and Lha mthong lo tsA ba, 437.2–440.2. I have left a few words out of my translation, since neither I nor anyone I consulted was able to make definitive sense of them: dam tshig gi rdzas gza' bsrungs la sogs pa bsten par mdzad. The 1494 printing reads the same, 17a2. Read in its existing form, the line might be taken as saying that the samaya-bound implements Kun dga' bzang po adopted were connected to a protector deity like Rāhula. It may be that some words are missing from the text, or that gza' bsrungs is mistakenly used in place of bza' btung. I am also uncertain of my translation of the phrase gzhan snang thabs kyi cha'i bogs dbyung ba (the same in the 1494 printing, 16b1), which I have rendered as "enhance the aspects of my method visible to others."

Cyrus Stearns states that when the Hevajra Tantra is referred to as brtag gnyis or brtag pa gnyis pa, this should be understood as meaning "the second fascicle," because of the story that what remains of the Hevajra Tantra is in fact only the second part of an earlier whole, the first part having been lost; Luminous Lives: The Story of the Early Masters of the Lam 'Bras Tradition in Tibet (Boston, MA: Wisdom, 1996), 236. Complicating the matter, the version of the text that has been utilized in the Tibetan tradition is split into two "books" or "parts." Although some may have understood brtag gnyis as carrying the meaning suggested by Stearns, I believe many more would have understood this as referring to the fact that the text has two parts.

2. Rgod tshang ras pa, 44.5–7, 69.1–70.1; Smyug la paN chen and Lha mthong lo tsA ba, 513.6–514.2.

3. Wedemeyer, Making Sense, 134–6, 156.

4. Zhwa dmar IV, *Dam chos dgongs pa gcig pa'i gsal byed: A detailed explanation of the 'Bri-guṅ Bka'-brgyud Dgoṅs gcig teaching* (Bir: D. Tsondu Senghe, the Bir Tibetan Society, 1992), 64.5–6; Stearns, *King of the Empty Plain*, 60, 486.

5. These translations are offered in Stearns, *King of the Empty Plain*, 59; Christian Wedemeyer, *Āryadeva's Lamp that Integrates the Practices (Caryāmelāpakapradīpa): The Gradual Path of Vajrayāna Buddhism According to the Esoteric Community Noble Tradition* (New York: American Institute of Buddhist Studies, Columbia University Press, 2007), 742; Wedemeyer, *Making Sense*, 137; Larsson, *Crazy for Wisdom*, 216–26. R. A. Stein translates *brtul zhugs* into French as "conduite exceptionnelle"; *Vie et chants de 'Brug-pa Kun-legs le yogin* (Paris: G.-P. Maisonneuve et Larose, 1972), 320.

6. The tantra is known by others names, including *Śrīherukābhidhāna* and *Laghusamvara*. See David B. Gray, *The Cakrasamvara Tantra (The Discourse of Śrī Heruka) (Śrīherukābhidhāna): A Study and Annotated Translation* (New York: American Institute of Buddhist Studies, Columbia University Press, 2007), 4–5.

7. Wedemeyer, *Making Sense*, 149–51. The information provided in the next few paragraphs is drawn from Wedemeyer's chapter "The Practice of Indian Tantric Buddhism." On the meaning of "achieving heat," see Stearns, *King of the Empty Plain*, 60–62. Karma pa III Rang byung rdo rje writes that the indicators of having "achieved the lesser heat" (*cung zad drod . . . thob pa*) include not being distracted by conceptual formations, having destroyed the afflictive emotions, and so on; *Brtag gnyis rnam bshad dri med 'od* (Seattle, WA: Nitartha International, 2006), 144.1–4. I wonder if in Tibet having "achieved heat" was ever understood as meaning having had success in the practice of the inner fire visualization of *gtum mo*.

8. Wedemeyer, *Making Sense*, 145.

9. For more detail on the relationship between Gtsang smyon and Kun tu bzang mo, see DiValerio, "Subversive Sainthood," 119–20; Larsson, *Crazy for Wisdom*, 172. Rgod tshang ras pa mentions Gtsang smyon's giving an empowerment using "an actual consort" (*dngos kyi rig ma*), 131.2.

   The line I take as referring to Kun dga' bzang po's taking a consort reads *rim pa gnyis kyi rnal 'byor spyod pa nye rgyud dang bcas pas mtshams sbyar*; Smyug la paN chen and Lha mthong lo tsA ba, 437.6; 16b1 in the 1494 edition. I understand *nye rgyud* to be a mistake for *nye rgyu*. Neither *nye rgyu* nor *nye rgyud* nor *nye brgyud* is used anywhere else in the biography, so a larger pattern of usage cannot be established; *nye bar len pa'i rgyu* is used twice, in both cases referring the cause of something; 569.2, 592.1. There is also mention of Dbus smyon's mastery of *las rgya'i man ngag*, which likely refers to sexual practices; 403.4.

10. Rgod tshang ras pa, 40.5–6. For an alternate translation, see Larsson, *Crazy for Wisdom*, 139. For a similar passage, see Rgod tshang ras pa, 192.5–6.

11. Rgod tshang ras pa, 48.3–7. For an alternate translation, see Larsson, *Crazy for Wisdom*, 153. For other examples, see Rgod tshang ras pa, 30.6 and 34.7–35.1, the latter describing Sangs rgyas rgyal mtshan's running back and forth amid a crowd of people near Tsa ri, eating brown sugar and feces, while urinating everywhere, which was mentioned in chapter 1; Larsson, *Crazy for Wisdom*, 119–20.

12. The passage running 522.4–524.3 in Smyug la paN chen and Lha mthong lo tsA ba, which will be translated below, mentions Kun dga' bzang po's performing this sort of public norm-overturning behavior; 595.1–596.4 describes the death of his disciple.

13. Smyug la paN chen and Lha mthong lo tsA ba, 452.4–453.1, 506.6–507.6, 565.5–566.3. Dbus smyon is said to perform *drag po brtul zhugs [kyi] spyod pa* on at least eight different occasions, constituting the majority of the instances of the use of the term *brtul zhugs [kyi] spyod pa*. In other places slightly different terminology is used to describe similar behavior, such as at 570.4–6.

14. *blo ma song*; Rgod tshang ras pa, 46.2–5, 126.6–127.3.

15. Sangs rgyas dar po, *Sangs rgyas dar po chos 'byung*, NGMPP L392/14, 79b2–3.

16. Dwags po paN chen bkra shis rnam rgyal, *Dpal kye'i rdo rje zhes bya ba'i rgyud kyi rgyal po'i 'grel pa* (Si khron mi rigs dpe skrun khang, 2002), 193.16–194.5. The practices are listed as: *kun tu bzang po'i spyod pa*; *gsang spyod dam sbas pa'i spyod pa*; *rig pa brtul zhugs kyi spyod pa*; and *phyogs las rnam rgyal gyi spyod pa*, which is more commonly rendered as *phyogs thams cad las rnam par rgyal ba'i spyod pa*. On the "*samaya* substances," see Wedemeyer, *Making Sense*, 145, 239, 245; Wedemeyer, *Āryadeva's Lamp*, 118.

17. This may also have meant something like *tshogs 'khor gyi spyod pa*, "the Practice at/of Gaṇacakras" or "tantric feasts."

18. Karma 'phrin las pa, *Dri lan the tshom mun sel zhes pa khams ri bo che'i dge slong gi zhu lan*, in *The Songs of Esoteric Practice (mgur) and Replies to Doctrinal Questions (dris lan) of karma-'phrin-las-pa*, 210.2–218.4 (New Delhi: Ngawang Topgay, 1975), here citing 211.7–212.1. Stearns, *King of the Empty Plain*, 60, 159, 512. Karma pa III Rang byung rdo rje states that *gsang ba'i spyod pa* is a "prerequisite" (*sngon du 'gro ba*) for *brtul zhugs kyi spyod pa*; *Brtag gnyis rnam bshad dri med 'od*, 143.11–12.

19. More examples are offered in DiValerio, "Subversive Sainthood," 112–36.

20. Wedemeyer, *Making Sense*, 136.

21. . . . *mtshan nyid gang yin pa'ang*; Smyug la paN chen and Lha mthong lo tsA ba, 522.1–2.

22. *rig pa brtul zhugs tshogs kyi spyod pa*, which could also be taken as "the public practice of the Awareness Observance." Rgod tshang ras pa, 230.3–231.3; Larsson, *Crazy for Wisdom*, 189, 224–6.

23. A few of the lamas I spoke with specifically cited the current Dalai Lama as one who lives with excellent monastic conduct (*tshul khrims*) and thereby embodies *kun tu bzang po'i spyod pa*.

24. For a more detailed discussion of how the term gets used, see DiValerio, "Subversive Sainthood," 134–5. The term is occasionally used in reference to nonpractitioners, such as in praising the Rin spungs pa Don yod rdo rje; Smyug la paN chen and Lha mthong lo tsA ba, 510.2, 518.6–519.1.

25. Wedemeyer, *Making Sense*, 136–7, 168.

26. *'brug pa'i khrid chen brgyad*. Dbus smyon is said to have received or taught: *gsang spyod*, Smyug la paN chen and Lha mthong lo tsA ba, 404.2; *mai tri rgya gar gsang spyod che chung*, directly followed by *na ro pa'i gsang spyod*, 410.6–411.1; *rgya gar gsang spyod*, 458.5, 573.2, 580.2; *rgya gar gsang spyod che chung*, 598.2.

27. Smyug la paN chen and Lha mthong lo tsA ba, 592.2–5, 642.1–3.

28. *Dpal na ro pa chen po'i gsang spyod kyi 'khrid*, in Gtsang smyon he ru ka, *Bde mchog mkha' 'gro snyan rgyud*, 1:715–48.

29. On Sha ra rab 'byams pa sangs rgyas seng ge, see Larsson, *Crazy for Wisdom*, 271–3.

30. Rgod tshang ras pa, 24.4–5. For an alternate translation, see Larsson, *Crazy for Wisdom*, 94. His writing about *nA ro gsang spyod* is mentioned at 190.6. His practicing *nA ro gsang spyod* is also mentioned in Dngos grub dpal 'bar's version of the *Life*, 9a6.

31. On *gcod* see Alejandro Chaoul, *Chöd Practice in the Bön Tradition* (Ithaca, NY: Snow Lion, 2009); Giacomella Orofino, "The Great Wisdom Mother and the Gcod Tradition," in *Tantra in Practice*, ed. David Gordon White, 396–416 (Princeton, NJ: Princeton University Press, 2000); Sarah Harding, *Machik's Complete Explanation: Clarifying the Meaning of Chöd* (Ithaca: Snow Lion, 2013); Jerome Edou, *Machig Labdrön and the Foundations of Chöd* (Ithaca: Snow Lion, 1996).

32. *na ro chos drug dang gsang gcod dang snyan rgyud sogs zab khrid rnams*; Rgod tshang ras pa, 142.3. In Smyug la paN chen and Lha mthong lo tsA ba, 520.2–522.2, *gcod* and *spyod* are used seemingly without much care, in a text that is generally free of this kind of mistake. The issue of the relationship between *gcod* and *spyod* is addressed in Chaoul, *Chöd Practice in the Bön Tradition*, 14, and suggested in Edou, *Machig Labdrön and the Foundations of Chöd*, 39–40, 57–63.

33. George N. Roerich, *The Blue Annals* (Delhi: Motilal Banarsidass, 1996), 980–83; 'Gos lo tsA ba gzhon nu dpal, *Deb ther sngon po* (Chengdu: Si khron mi rigs dpe skrun khang, 1984), 2:1139.1–1142.2.

34. Smyug la paN chen and Lha mthong lo tsA ba, 431.2, 601.2–3.

35. Rgod tshang ras pa, 37.3–6. For an alternate translation, see Larsson, *Crazy for Wisdom*, 133–4. The *sbas pa'i sgrub chen bco brgyad* are mentioned at 164.3–4, 190.7–191.1, 207.4, 263.7–264.6.

36. *Bde mchog mkha' 'gro snyan rgyud kyi gzhung 'brel sa gcad dang sbrags pa*, in Gtsang smyon he ru ka, *Bde mchog mkha' 'gro snyan rgyud*, 1:5–360, here citing 184.2. For other examples of how the idea of "behaving like a madman" is discussed in the Tibetan commentarial tradition, see DiValerio, "Subversive Sainthood,"

185–202; included is a discussion of Dbus smyon and Gtsang smyon's performance of "senseless, babbling behavior," *tho cho* or *tho co spyod pa.*

37. *smyon pa lta bu'i tshul gyis gshegs pa*; Rgod tshang ras pa, 41.7–42.2. For an alternate translation, see Larsson, *Crazy for Wisdom*, 137.

38. Smyug la paN chen and Lha mthong lo tsA ba, 522.4–523.4.

39. *ya nga bag tsha rnam rtog med pa smyon pa lta bu*; Karma 'phrin las pa, *Do ha skor gsum gyi Ti ka 'bring po sems kyi rnam thar ston pa'i me long: A commentary on the three cycles of dohā composed by the great Saraha* (Thimphu: Druk Sherig, 1984), 285.6.

40. Mar pa chos kyi blo gros, *'Bum chung nyi ma* (Dehradun: Srong btsan dpe mdzod khang, 2005), 99.3–4; Smyug la paN chen and Lha mthong lo tsA ba, 598.4.

41. *khrag 'thung ba.* Ronald Davidson, *Indian Esoteric Buddhism: A Social History of the Tantric Movement* (New York: Columbia University Press, 2002), 213; Gray, *Cakrasamvara Tantra*, 40.

42. *Snyan rgyud kyi zhal gdams lus dkyil*, in Gtsang smyon he ru ka, *Bde mchog mkha' 'gro snyan rgyud*, 1:819–31, here citing 829.3–830.2.

43. *he ru ka'i chas, he ru ka'i chas brgyad, he ru ka'i cha lugs, dur khrod kyi chas, rus pa'i rgyan, rus pa'i rgyan drug.*

44. For other interpretations of the *Hevajra Tantra*'s list, see Wedemeyer, *Making Sense*, 140; G. W. Farrow and I. Menon, *The Concealed Essence of the Hevajra Tantra, with the Commentary "Yogaratnamālā"* (Delhi: Motilal Banarsidass, 1992), 61–2; David Snellgrove, *The Hevajra Tantra: A Critical Study* (Oxford: Oxford University Press, 1959), 1:63–5. It is not entirely clear what these various descriptors refer to, nor does it seem that traditional commentators were always certain or in agreement about them. On the *Cakrasamvara*'s list, see Gray, *Cakrasamvara Tantra*, 277–8.

45. *Bde mchog mkha' 'gro snyan rgyud kyi rab gnas rgyal ba kun bsdud*, in Gtsang smyon he ru ka, *Bde mchog mkha' 'gro snyan rgyud*, 1:555–641, here citing, 611.2–612.3. For another description of the deity by Gtsang smyon, see 479.1–480.4 in *Bde mchog mkha' 'gro snyan rgyud kyi bum dbang dang 'brel ba'i gdams ngag thun mong yid bzhin nor bu*, in *Bde mchog mkha' 'gro snyan rgyud*, 1:459–519.

46. Rgod tshang ras pa, 231.4–233.6. On the history of this implement, see David Brick, "The Origin of the *Khaṭvāṅga* Staff," *Journal of the American Oriental Society* 132, no. 1 (2012): 31–9.

47. Smyug la paN chen and Lha mthong lo tsA ba, 542.4; 494.2–3, 613.1–615.5; 512.1–3; 645.5–6.

48. Rgod tshang ras pa, 46.5–7; Larsson, *Crazy for Wisdom*, 149.

49. Smyug la paN chen and Lha mthong lo tsA ba, 512.6–513.6, and also 472.3–473.4, 498.5–499.1. Rgod tshang ras pa, 119.3–4, 122.2. Some of this uncertainty arises from ambiguity in the way these instances are described. For example, when Dbus smyon had nearly reached the age of sixty and was quite settled at Rtsi dmar dpal, he received a request from 'Bri gung mthil to perform a consecration

ritual for their new *bkra shis sgo mangs* stūpa. Unwilling to travel there, the yogin *he ru ka'i chas brgyad po legs par sku la bsgos* and recited a prayer accompanied by a dance. This could be read as saying, "having put on the eight emblems of the Heruka . . ." (suggesting that he had not been wearing the costume prior to this moment), or as saying, "wearing the eight emblems of the Heruka . . ." (suggesting that he had been wearing it); Smyug la paN chen and Lha mthong lo tsA ba, 630.3–6.

50. Smyug la paN chen and Lha mthong lo tsA ba, 648.6. The *he ru ka'i cha lugs can gyi thugs sras rtogs ldan nyer brgyad* are mentioned in Rgod tshang ras pa, 83.4–5, 110.5, 164.2, 170.7, 190.7, 207.7, 259.5–262.1. One of Gtsang smyon's students is casually referred to as "Chos mchog dpal bzang who does the Practice of the Observance" (213.5) and "without rival in the Practice of the Observance" (260.1). It is likely that wearing the garb of the Heruka is part of what is expressed by these designations. See other disciples described similarly at 259.4, 260.2, 260.4.

51. Gray, *Cakrasamvara Tantra*, 54–5.

52. One of the first lines of the *Cakrasamvara Tantra* reads, "Union with Śrī Heruka is the means of achieving all desired aims"; Gray, *Cakrasamvara Tantra*, 155 Gray describes how the practitioner achieves union with Heruka by means of "creative visualization" (36). For similar statements in the *Hevajra Tantra*, see Snellgrove, *Hevajra Tantra*, 1:48; Farrow and Menon, *Concealed Essence*, 10.

53. Smyug la paN chen and Lha mthong lo tsA ba, 502.1–3; see also 512.6, 518.5–6. For other examples of his dancing similarly, but described using different terminology, see 442.3–5, 446.4, 449.4–7. For Gtsang smyon, see Rgod tshang ras pa, 54.4–5, 124.3, 149.4. Dancing may have been prescribed within the Practice of the Observance in part because Indian Buddhist monks were forbidden from doing it; Wedemeyer, *Making Sense*, 179.

54. . . . *drag po he ru ka'i brtul zhugs bzung*; Smyug la paN chen and Lha mthong lo tsA ba, 532.1–5. *Drag po* can be a translation of the Sanskrit word *raudra*, which is derived from the word Rudra, which is the name of the wrathful form of Śiva upon whom the Buddhist deity Heruka is modeled; Gray, *Cakrasamvara Tantra*, 228.

55. The first text mentioned is *Bde mchog mkha' 'gro snyan rgyud kyi las byang yid bzhin nor bu*, in Gtsang smyon he ru ka, *Bde mchog mkha' 'gro snyan rgyud*, 2:625–79, here citing 639.7. His receiving the name is described in Rgod tshang ras pa, 36.2–3. He signed the two famous biographies as *dur khrod nyul ba'i rnal 'byor pa khrag 'thung rgyal po* and *dur khrod nyul ba'i rnal 'byor pa rus pa'i rgyan can*.

The association between Gtsang smyon and the term Heruka is ubiquitous. For example, he is referred to as "the Heruka from Tsang" in the titles to versions of his biography and *Mgur 'bum* published around 1508. Dbus smyon's association with the term is attested to in a number of sources, including a verse of praise by 'Brug pa kun legs, *'Brug pa kun legs kyi rnam thar* (Beijing: Bod ljongs mi dmangs dpe skrun khang, 2005), 418.7–8; and in the popular biography of 'Brug pa kun legs translated by Keith Dowman in which Dbus smyon, Gtsang smyon, and 'Brug smyon are referred to as "three Herukas"; *The Divine Madman: The Sublime Life and Songs of Drukpa Kunley* (Varanasi and Kathmandu: Pilgrims, 2000), 110, 184. See also Johan van Manen, "A Contribution to the Bibliography of Tibet," *Journal and Proceedings of the Asiatic Society of Bengal* 18, new series (1922): 485, 513, which shows that among Tibetans in the early twentieth century there was an active tradition referring to Dbus smyon as a Heruka.

56. The first verse of praise runs 78.4–79.3 in Karma 'phrin las pa, *Songs of Esoteric Practice (mgur) and Replies to Doctrinal Questions (dris lan) of karma-'phrin-las-pa*, here citing 78.4–5. The second runs 18.7–20.1, here citing the lines 18.7–19.1, which are grammatically unclear.

57. Rgod tshang ras pa, 4.6, 259.3–4. In his version of the *Life*, Lha btsun rin chen rnam rgyal refers to the yogin in a verse of praise as, "You who are fully perfected in the Practice of the Observance," 53.3–4.

58. 'Brug pa kun legs, *'Brug pa kun legs kyi rnam thar*, 202.6–9; Stein, *Vie et chants*, 320.

59. The *mi khom pa'i gnas brgyad* are: being born in a hell, as a hungry ghost, as an animal, as a god, or as a human in a non-Buddhist place, with faulty faculties, with mistaken views, or in a time when Buddhism is not present in the world.

This description of these events, from his being called a ghoul in Lha sa to the end of the debate, is given in Rgod tshang ras pa, 44.5–46.2. For an alternate translation, see Larsson, *Crazy for Wisdom*, 147–8. In the *dge bshes*'s objections to Sangs rgyas rgyal mtshan's ways, I have taken their use of the word *spyod pa* as referring to his general lifestyle, with the term employed in its generic sense; it could also be taken as functioning as a term of art, referring specifically to Sangs rgyas rgyal mtshan's mode of enacting the Practice.

60. Rgod tshang ras pa, 62.1–3; Larsson, *Crazy for Wisdom*, 163. The lines quoted are *khyod kyis ma byin par yang long / pha rol bud med bsten par byis*; Snellgrove, *Hevajra Tantra*, 1:97, 2:57; Farrow and Menon, *Concealed Essence*, 192. For other instances of Gtsang smyon's justifying his actions as being based on the *Hevajra Tantra*, see Rgod tshang ras pa, 55.1–4, and 172.5–173.1, where he quotes book I, chapter seven, verses 8–9. See also Lha btsun rin chen rnam rgyal's version of the *Life*, 57.7–58.3, where the author describes the yogin's behavior on a particular occasion as similar to that prescribed in the Practice chapter of the *Hevajra Tantra*.

During Sangs rgyas rgyal mtshan's monastic education, it says that he *thugs su tshud* the *Hevajra Tantra*, which could be taken as meaning that he memorized the text (which would have been a normal undertaking in that pedagogical environment), or that he studied it very closely; Rgod tshang ras pa, 27.2.

61. Rgod tshang ras pa, 32.4–33.6; Larsson, *Crazy for Wisdom*, 116–17. This same story is told in Dngos grub dpal 'bar, 8b5–9a3, and in Lha btsun rin chen rnam rgyal, 18.6–19.4.

62. Rgod tshang ras pa, 54.2–55.1.

63. The term **anuttarayogatantra* is not attested to in Indian sources. Rather, this category is typically used by Tibetan scholars attempting to organize Indian tantric texts. See Gray, *Cakrasamvara Tantra*, 5–8, for a concise description of this class of tantras. On the dating of these tantras, see Gray, 11–13, and Ronald Davidson, *Tibetan Renaissance: Tantric Buddhism in the Rebirth of Tibetan Culture* (New York: Columbia University Press, 2005), 40–41.

64. Versions of Atīśa's biography even state that it was specifically in order to bring tantric practice into line with ethical discipline that he was compelled to travel to Tibet in the first place; Roerich, *Blue Annals*, 245–6; 'Gos lo tsA ba, *Deb ther sngon po*, 1:300.14–303.3. On Atīśa's *Byang chub lam gyi sgron me*, see Snellgrove, *Indo-Tibetan Buddhism* (Boston, MA: Shambhala, 2002), 481–4. On Sa skya paNDi ta's *Sdom gsum rab dbye*, see Jared Douglas Rhoton, *A Clear Differentiation of the Three Codes: Essential Distinctions among the Individual Liberation, Great Vehicle, and Tantric Systems* (New York: State University of New York Press, 2002), 23–5. Sgam po pa's approach is summarized in the fifth book of Jamgön Kongtrul's *Shes bya mtha' yas pa'i rgya mtsho*, published in English as *Buddhist Ethics*, trans. International Translation Committee (Ithaca: Snow Lion, 1998), 303–4.

65. For examples of this process of reinterpretation and its history, see Gray, *Cakrasamvara Tantra*, 68–71, 124–31, and elsewhere; and Snellgrove, *Indo-Tibetan Buddhism*.

66. Book I, chapter six, verse 6. See Snellgrove, *Hevajra Tantra*, 1:63, 2:19; Farrow and Menon, *Concealed Essence*, 63; Karma pa III Rang byung rdo rje, *Brtag gnyis rnam bshad dri med 'od*, 143.3–6.

67. Karma pa III Rang byung rdo rje, *Brtag gnyis rnam bshad dri med 'od*, 144.14–145.21.

68. Karma pa III Rang byung rdo rje, *Brtag gnyis rnam bshad dri med 'od*, 162.1–166.21; see also 65.13–16.

69. Book I, chapter six, verses 11–12. Snellgrove, *Hevajra Tantra*, 1:64, 2:19; Farrow and Menon, *Concealed Essence*, 65; Karma pa III Rang byung rdo rje, *Brtag gnyis rnam bshad dri med 'od*, 146.19–147.18. For a similar passage in the same chapter, where the same proccess of reinterpretation is employed with respect to the six bone ornaments, see Karma pa III Rang byung rdo rje, 140.9–141.8.

70. Book I, chapter six, verse 14. Snellgrove, *Hevajra Tantra*, 1:64, 2:21; Farrow and Menon, *Concealed Essence*, 65; Karma pa III Rang byung rdo rje, *Brtag gnyis rnam bshad dri med 'od*, 148.12–21.

71. Mar pa chos kyi blo gros, *'Bum chung nyi ma*, 100.15. On these ten substances, see Wedemeyer, *Making Sense*, 106. For more on how this sort of coded language

works, see Snellgrove, *Indo-Tibetan Buddhism*; Davidson, *Indian Esoteric Buddhism*, 262–9.

72. Karma pa III Rang byung rdo rje, *Brtag gnyis rnam bshad dri med 'od*, 146.2–18, 147.13–15.

73. On the first Dpa' bo, see DiValerio, "Subversive Sainthood," 368–73. On Lha btsun kun dga' chos kyi rgya mtsho, see DiValerio, 374, 383–4. The quotation is from Ma pham rdo rje, *Rnal 'byor gyi dbang phyug grags pa mtha' yas dpal bzang po'i rnam thar mgur 'bum* (Gangtok: Gonpo Tseten, 1977), 3.4.

74. The first quotation is from Henry Munson, "Fundamantalism," in *The Routledge Companion to the Study of Religion*, ed. John R. Hinnells (New York: Routledge, 2005), 351. The second is Martin E. Marty and R. Scott Appleby, "Conclusion: An Interim Report on a Hypothetical Family," in *Fundamentalisms Observed*, ed. Martin E. Marty and R. Scott Appleby (Chicago: University of Chicago Press, 1991), 835. See also Lionel Caplan, "Introduction," in *Studies in Religious Fundamentalism*, ed. Caplan (Albany: State University of New York Press, 1987), 14, 17.

   There has been some debate over the meaning and proper use of the term "fundamentalism": some scholars maintain that it should be used only to refer to the conservative Protestant movement that coined the term; others maintain that the term is too loaded and should not be used at all; others claim that "fundamentalism" is a uniquely twentieth- and twenty-first-century phenomenon, a response to changes in the "modern" world; see Peter Herriot, *Religious Fundamentalism and Social Identity* (New York: Routledge, 2007), 2; Malise Ruthven, *Fundamentalism: The Search for Meaning* (New York: Oxford University Press, 2004), v–vi. I would suggest we use the term more generically, as referring to a phenomenon that can be observed many times and places in the history of world religions.

75. Smyug la paN chen and Lha mthong lo tsA ba, 632.2–633.2.

76. David Kinsley gives an overview of the theme of holy madness in various strands of the Hindu tradition, some of which may be argued to have directly or indirectly fed into the religious identity embodied by Dbus smyon and Gtsang smyon, " 'Through the Looking Glass': Divine Madness in the Hindu Religious Tradition," *History of Religions* 13, no. 4 (1974): 270–305. See also June McDaniel, *Madness of the Saints: Ecstatic Religion in Bengal* (Chicago: University of Chicago Press, 1989).

77. For a discussion of some of this history, see Wedemeyer, *Making Sense*. For a much less accurate exploration of these issues, including some suggestions beyond those that Wedemeyer has made, see DiValerio, "Subversive Sainthood," 202–227.

78. Larsson, *Crazy for Wisdom*, 216–26; Geoffrey Samuel, *Civilized Shamans: Buddhism in Tibetan Society* (Washington, DC: Smithsonian Institution Press, 1994), 302–7; Stearns, *King of the Empty Plain*, 58–80. On modern scholars'

tendency to overlook the importance of the Practice, see Wedemeyer, *Making Sense*, 134, 244–5.

The only lama I spoke with who claimed to have done the practice was Tshangs gsar kun dga' rin po che, who said that during his training in the 'Ba' rom Bka' brgyud in Nang chen, Khams, they would occasionally perform *brtul zhugs*, which meant spending a night at the burial ground (*dur khrod*), and little beyond that. This would be performed late in one's training in *gcod*. In his understanding, the purpose of the practice was to test if one had overcome fear, which would indicate success in *gcod* practice.

CHAPTER 3

1. Rgod tshang ras pa, *Rnal 'byor gyi dbang phyug rgod tshang ras chen pa'i rnam thar tshigs gcad ma dngos grub rgya mtsho*, NGMPP L978/7, 2a7–2b1. Ehrhard offers a translation in "Editing and Publishing," 133. See also Roberts, *Biographies of Rechungpa*, 43; Larsson, *Crazy for Wisdom*, 257.

2. Smyug la paN chen and Lha mthong lo tsA ba, 510.6–518.4. In the account of the life of Smyug la paN chen offered by Dpa' bo gtsug lag phreng ba, it is specifically stated that he first encountered Dbus smyon when he was brutally attacked while doing *rig pa brtul zhugs kyi spyod pa* at Smyug la, then arose unharmed after being pinned under a large heap of rocks; *Chos 'byung mkhas pa'i dga' ston*, 2006, 592.12–593.8; repeated in Si tu paN chen and 'Be lo tshe dbang kun khyab, *Bsgrub brgyud karma kaM tshang*, 1:648.3–649.3.

    In *Chos 'byung mkhas pa'i dga' ston*, accepting physical abuse is here referred to as *mi gcod*, which may perhaps be taken as "human Cutting" or "self-sacrifice"; 592.15. Kun dga' grol mchog also mentions this instance and the great fame Dbus smyon achieved because of it, again using the term *mi gcod*; *PaNDi ta chen po shAkya mchog ldan gyi rnam par thar pa*, in *Collected Works of Śākya mchog ldan* (Thimphu, Bhutan: Kunzang Tobgyey, 1995), vol. 16 (*ma*), 1–234, here citing 178.7–179.1. The term is used in a similar manner in Smyug la paN chen and Lha mthong lo tsA ba, 520.2, 521.1. The same term is used in Rgod tshang ras pa's version of the *Life of the Madman of Tsang* to describe Kun dga' bzang po's being beaten outside the gates of the king's palace in Mnga' ris rdzong dkar, although (mis)spelled as *mi spyod*; 70.6. The phrase *mi gcod drag po* is used in the biography of another contemporary, Dpa' bo chos dbang lhun grub (of whom Dpa' bo gtsug lag phreng ba was considered a reincarnation), to describe his purposefully seeking out physical abuse; Si tu paN chen and 'Be lo tshe dbang kun khyab, 1:661.3. Seeking out physical abuse therefore seems to have come as part of the Practice of the Observance, a topic worthy of further investigation.

3. Rgod tshang ras pa, 70.3–71.3. It seems that the treasure revealer Pad+ma gling pa, living at the same time, once suggested that he and a competing lama should both be thrown into a fire, to see who was true and who false; Michael Aris,

Hidden Treasures and Secret Lives: A Study of Pemalingpa (1450–1521) and the Sixth Dalai Lama (1683–1706) (London and New York: Kegan Paul International, 1989), 65–6.

4. Smyug la paN chen and Lha mthong lo tsA ba, 559.4–5, 524.6–525.4.

5. Rgod tshang ras pa, 165.2–166.3, 156.6–158.2.

6. Rgod tshang ras pa, 117.2–5.

7. Guillaume Rozenberg, *Renunciation and Power: The Quest for Sainthood in Contemporary Burma*, trans. Jessica Hackett et al. (New Haven, CT: Yale University Southeast Asian Studies, 2010), 151.

8. For example, the biography claims that in his early twenties Kun dga' bzang po achieved *siddha*hood, Smyug la paN chen and Lha mthong lo tsA ba, 426.2; the title and opening homage refer to him as a *grub pa'i khyu mchog*, 384.1; the biographer refers to him as *phyir mi ldog pa'i grub pa'i khyu mchog chen po*, 437.2–3, and so on.

9. Rgod tshang ras pa, untitled verse praise of the Madman of Tsang, NGMPP L803/5, 1b3. In his version of the *Life*, Rgod tshang ras pa referes to the yogin as a *grub thob*, 179.5, and 173.4, which is drawn from Dngos grub dpal 'bar, 18a4. The title of Lha btsun run chen rnam rgyal's version of the *Life* refers to him as *grub thob gtsang pa smyon pa*.

10. All three biographies of Gtsang smyon open with quotations from Buddhist scripture that are asserted to prophesize this amazing being, which serve to attest to the yogin's greatness in a manner similar to the descriptions of his miracles. Discussed in Larsson, *Crazy for Wisdom*, 55–7.

11. Smyug la paN chen and Lha mthong lo tsA ba, 509.1–510.1, 549.5–550.1. Kun dga' grol mchog, *PaNDi ta chen po shAkya mchog ldan gyi rnam par thar pa*, 178.3–179.1, 179.1–3, 173.3–6. I thank Slava Komarovski for bringing these passages to my attention. Dbus smyon would be listed as one of ShAkya mchog ldan's disciples in the latter's biography, 229.3; Yaroslav Komarovski, *Visions of Unity: The Golden Paṇḍita Shakya Chokden's New Interpretation of Yogācāra and Madhyamaka* (Albany: State University of New York Press, 2012), 328.

12. On their relationship, see Komarovski, *Visions of Unity*, 35, 46, 328. The three texts are contained in vol. 13 (*pa*) of ShAkya mchog ldan's *Collected Works*: *Brtag gnyis kyi bsdus don bshad rgyud kyi rgyud pa'i rim pa*, 464–7; described in Komarovski, 65; *Dbu ma'i lta khrid/ zhi gnas dang lhag mthong zung du 'jug pa ngo mtshar rgyan gyi phreng ba*, 190–202; described in Komarovski, 35, 58, 69; and *Lam skor brgyad kyi gsal byed bdud rtsi'i thig pa*, 630–40; described in Komarovski, 66. In this last text's colophon, Dbus smyon is referred to by the name given to him by ShAkya mchog ldan, *dbus smyon rdo rje bdud 'dul*, 640.5–6.

13. Smyug la paN chen and Lha mthong lo tsA ba, 507.6–508.6.

14. Rgod tshang ras pa, *Rnal 'byor gyi dbang phyug rgod tshang ras chen pa'i rnam thar tshigs gcad ma dngos grub rgya mtsho*, 4a5. See also Ehrhard, "Editing and Publishing," 136–7; Larsson, *Crazy for Wisdom*, 258.

15. *gtam thos pa tsam gyis kyang dad pa'i pu long g.yos par gyur;* Smyug la paN chen and Lha mthong lo tsA ba, 546.2–3.

16. Smyug la paN chen and Lha mthong lo tsA ba, 443.4, 484.2. See also 475.6–476.3, 546.6–547.3, 549.1–2.

17. Rgod tshang ras pa, 38.1. The spread of his *snyan pa* or *grags pa* is also mentioned at 9.7, 171.4, 229.1–2.

18. Rgod tshang ras pa, 67.1–2. The pertinent part reads: *snyan pa'i rnga sgra phyogs kun du sgrog pa la brtson pas/ srid pa gsum na 'gran zla med pa'i grub thob chen por grags pa'i bskor* [*sic*]. It is possible that the author intends the agent of the verb phrase *sgrog pa la brtson pa* to be taken not as Sangs rgyas rgyal mtshan but his followers. A passage suggesting this latter possibility is given at 33.5–6. If the latter reading is the correct one, the passage still supports my broader contention about the role of the yogin's supporters in making the case for his holiness—and their self-awareness about their significance in doing so.

19. Rgod tshang ras pa, 103.3–4.

20. *khur na rtogs ldan rnal 'byor pa'i bstan pa la gnod;* Smyug la paN chen and Lha mthong lo tsA ba, 517.1.

21. Smyug la paN chen and Lha mthong lo tsA ba, 559.1–2. On the role of Gtsang smyon in telling his own life story, see DiValerio, "Reanimating the Great Yogin."

22. 'Brug pa kun legs, *'Brug pa kun legs kyi rnam thar,* 242.17–20; Stein, *Vie et chants,* 380. 'Brug pa kun legs's words echo king Ye shes 'od's famous edict from around 990, in which he decried those who used tantra to justify moral laxity. See Snellgrove, *Indo-Tibetan Buddhism,* 186–7; Jacob P. Dalton, *Taming of the Demons: Violence and Liberation in Tibetan Buddhism* (New Haven, CT: Yale University Press, 2011), chap. 4.

23. 'Brug pa kun legs, *'Brug pa kun legs kyi rnam thar,* 88.20–89.3; Stein, *Vie et chants,* 156.

24. 'Brug pa kun legs, *'Brug pa kun legs kyi rnam thar,* 435.10–15. I take *spyod yul* as a mistake for *gcod yul; kha lding* as *kha gting;* and *bu mad* as meaning *bud med* or *bu smad.*

25. 'Brug pa kun legs, *'Brug pa kun legs kyi rnam thar,* 473.9–14. The final line reads *grwa bu slob rnams kyang longs spyod don du gnyer ba'i skyon tsam ma gtogs bzang ba 'dug.* This is followed by a comment about Dbus smyon.

26. 'Brug pa kun legs, *'Brug pa kun legs kyi rnam thar,* 367.14–22. The key phrase regarding Dbus smyon is *spyod pa sprang po rnams la bslabs;* those regarding Gtsang smyon are *nor ngom byas* and *drag pa thams cad tshong par song.*

27. In interviews, Mkhan po kun mchog rnam dag, Mkhan po nyi ma rgyal mtshan, and Dbang 'dul rin po che explained the nature of holy madness by making extensive reference to Saraha, Virūpa, Nāropa, and other Indian *mahāsiddhas,* as ones who appeared strange to the world but secretly harbored great wisdom. Dowman compares 'Brug smyon to Saraha, *Divine Madman,* 26. In his chapter on tantric Buddhism within Williams's *Buddhist Thought,* Tribe

cites the Tibetan holy madmen as exemplifying the spiritual ideals of which the Indian *mahāsiddhas* were the utmost embodiment; Paul Williams, with Anthony Tribe, *Buddhist Thought: A Complete Introduction to the Indian Tradition*, New York: Routledge, 2000), 216, 273. Consider also Rob Linrothe, ed., *Holy Madness: Portraits of Tantric Siddhas* (New York: Rubin Museum of Art, 2006), discussed further in chapter 7.

28. Dbus smyon receives transmissions of songs by Saraha, Tilopa, Nāropa, Virūpa, Lohipa, Shawaripa, and other of the eighty *mahāsiddhas*, Smyug la paN chen and Lha mthong lo tsA ba, 410.5–6; gives teachings on these songs, 598.3; visits holy sites associated with the eighty *mahāsiddhas*, 451.4; and sees them in visions, 457.6, 537.6–538.5. Gtsang smyon teaches the *dohās*, Rgod tshang ras pa, 142.3; his teacher, Sha ra rab 'byams pa, is said to be an emanation of Saraha, 8.7, 20.6–7.

29. The story begins at Lha btsun rin chen rnam rgyal, 34.1.

30. *kho bo grub thob brgyad cu'i spyi mes chen po cig yin*, Smyug la paN chen and Lha mthong lo tsA ba, 581.1; *kho bo grub thob brgyad cu'i spyi mes yin pas kho bo la grub thob de dag gis bskor nas yod*, 622.5–6. *Spyi mes* can mean "forefather" or "ancestor." Mkhan po tshul rnams rin po che (September 12, 2009) glossed the term here as meaning the *'byung gnas*, *rtsa lag*, or *gtso bo*. I hope that "granddaddy," in its colloquial sense, expresses the meaning of an ancestor, but also "the most important of all."

31. Smyug la paN chen and Lha mthong lo tsA ba, 525.4–6. In this passage the term *rnam par thar pa* could perhaps also be taken as "the liberations," meaning their respective degrees of meditative accomplishment.

32. Smyug la paN chen and Lha mthong lo tsA ba, 394.5–395.3.

33. Wedemeyer, *Making Sense*, 168.

34. *spyod pa la gshegs pa*; Gtsang smyon he ru ka, *Rnal 'byor gyi dbang phyug chen po mi la ras pa'i rnam mgur* (Xining: Mtsho sngon mi rigs dpe skrun khang, 2005), 107.3; Tsangnyön Heruka [Gtsang smyon he ru ka], *The Life of Milarepa*, trans. Andrew Quintman (New York: Penguin, 2010), 94. 'Gos lo tsA ba, *Deb ther sngon po*, 1:464.18, 485.13–15; Roerich, *Blue Annals*, 383, 401.

35. Herbert Guenther, *Ecstatic Spontaneity: Saraha's Three Cycles of Dohā* (Berkeley, CA: Asian Humanities Press, 1993), 135–9. Sa ra ha, *Mi zad pa'i gter mdzod man ngag gi glu*, in *Dege Tengyur*, vol. shi: 28b–33b; Tohoku no. 2264. In Karma 'phrin las pa's commentary to this text, *Do ha skor gsum gyi Ti ka 'bring po sems kyi rnam thar ston pa'i me long*, he discusses the Practice of the Observance at length in the course of explicating this section of Saraha's verses, exploring different understandings of what Saraha may have meant by referring to outer, inner and secret meanings, quoting the *Hevajra Tantra* numerous times in the course of this discussion; 270.2–286.2.

There is no evidence that Kun dga' bzang po or Sangs rgyas rgyal mtshan took any special inspiration from the Indian *mahāsiddha* Ḍombi Heruka, although Dbus smyon is said to have seen him during a vision that included many other figures; Smyug la paN chen and Lha mthong lo tsA ba, 538.3.

36. Smyug la paN chen and Lha mthong lo tsA ba, 397.1–2, 620.2–4, 575.6–576.5.

37. Rgod tshang ras pa, 131.5–132.5; Quintman, *Yogin and the Madman*, 161; E. Gene Smith, "Introduction to *The Life of Gtsang smyon Heruka*," in *Among Tibetan Texts*, 61–2. In a very similar manner, Sangs rgyas rgyal mtshan once had an encounter with a lord who claimed to have had a dream about Saraha the night before; Rgod tshang ras pa, 46.4–5; Larsson, *Crazy for Wisdom*, 148.

38. Rgod tshang ras pa, 136.4–137.5.

39. The idea of a "repertoire of saintly behavior" is drawn from Kleinberg, *Prophets in Their Own Country*, 37. See also 5, 134.

40. Rozenberg, drawing from Steven Collins's *Nirvana and Other Buddhist Felicities: Utopias of the Pali Imaginaire* (Cambridge: Cambridge University Press, 1998), offers an especially useful description of the idea as it pertains to his study: "the French term *'imaginaire'* refers to the loosely organized yet relatively coherent mental world of the Burmese Buddhists and its functioning, with its reference ideas, images, stories, and their effects on the way things are seen. The *imaginaire* is part of culture insofar as it is a set of representations that may inspire action or whereby action or reality may be given meaning"; Rozenberg, *Renunciation and Power*, 159.

41. Smyug la paN chen and Lha mthong lo tsA ba, 606.1–3, 623.4–624.2.

42. Rgod tshang ras pa, 230.6.

43. 'Brug pa kun legs, *'Brug pa kun legs kyi rnam thar*, 38.16–39.4; Stein, *Vie et chants*, 87. Similar to these concerns, Bogin describes how Yol mo bstan 'dzin nor bu (1598–1644), who cast off his monks' robes to wear white and grow dreadlocks, responded to others' arguments that one should not take on the dress of the Heruka until one has achieved the level of a *vajradhara*; Benjamin Bogin, "The Dreadlocks Treatise: On Tantric Hairstyles in Tibetan Buddhism," *History of Religions* 48, no. 2 (2008): 102–3.

44. 'Brug pa kun legs, *'Brug pa kun legs kyi rnam thar*, 99.19–21, 360.20–21; the first passage is translated in Stein, *Vie et chants*, 172.

45. 'Brug pa kun legs, *'Brug pa kun legs kyi rnam thar*, 167.6–8; Stein, *Vie et chants*, 269. For a similar passage, see 'Brug pa kun legs, 20.9–11; Stein, 63.

46. 'Brug pa kun legs, *'Brug pa kun legs kyi rnam thar*, 228.22–229.2; Stein, *Vie et chants*, 359.

47. 'Brug pa kun legs, *'Brug pa kun legs kyi rnam thar*, 89.18–21; Stein, *Vie et chants*, 157. These words are framed not as 'Brug pa kun legs's own, but those of a diviner. However, we have every reason to read this as 'Brug pa kun legs's own composition; Stein also views the passage in this way, 149.

48. Lha btsun rin chen rnam rgyal, 125.1–2; Larsson, *Crazy for Wisdom*, 184; Roberts, *Biographies of Rechungpa*, 218. Smyug la paN chen and Lha mthong lo tsA ba,

438.5, 592.5. On another occasion, Dbus smyon expresses a special indebtedness to the Bka' brgyud, 527.4.

49. Smyug la paN chen and Lha mthong lo tsA ba, 438.5, 606.5–607.1. Dbus smyon is called *bka' rgyud rin po che'i bstan pa mi 'gyur ba'i srog shing* by his biographer, 555.1; and *bka' rgyud bstan pa'i srog shing chos rje rin po che dbus pa* in a letter he received from a 'Bri gung hierarch, 630.3–4.

50. Dngos grub dpal 'bar, 17a7, 30a1. Rgod tshang ras pa, 139.7. The letter is translated as the epigraph to chapter 5.

51. Pad+ma dkar po, 'Brug chen IV, *Chos 'byung bstan pa'i pad+ma rgyas pa'i nyin byed ('Brug pa'i chos 'byung)*, published as *Tibetan Chronicle of Padma-dkar-po*, ed. Lokesh Chandra (New Delhi: International Academy of Indian Culture, 1968), 594.6, 613.6. On this text, see E. Gene Smith, "Padma dkar po and His History of Buddhism," in *Among Tibetan Texts*, 81–6 (essay first published in 1969). Neither Dbus smyon nor Gtsang smyon had a very strong association with Rwa lung monastery, although Lha btsun rin chen rnam rgyal's version of the *Life* of Gtsang smyon states that he met with a 'Brug pa Bka' brgyud hierarch there; Larsson, *Crazy for Wisdom*, 141, 148.

52. Khro ru mkhan po tshe rnam, *Dpal mnyam med mar pa bka' brgyud kyi grub pa'i mtha' rnam par nges par byed pa mdor bsdus su brjod pa dwags brgyud grub pa'i me long* (Sarnath: WA Na bka' brgyud nyam skyong tshogs pa skabs so bzhi pas dpar skrun zhus, 2007), 103. See also Stein, *Vie et chants*, 9.

53. On a number of occasions Dbus smyon receives or gives a set of teachings called the *'brug pa'i khrid chen brgyad*. Gtsang smyon has a conversation with Chos rje g.yam spyil ba, which is described as *'brug chos rnams dang ras chung snyan rgyud sogs 'grel gtam mang du mdzad*; Rgod tshang ras pa, 132.4.

54. *mi phyed 'brug pa/ 'brug phyed sprang po/ sprang phyed grub thob*; Pad+ma dkar po, *Chos 'byung bstan pa'i pad+ma rgyas pa'i nyin byed*, 580.6; Quintman, *Yogin and the Madman*, 57.

55. Smith, "Introduction to *The Life of Gtsang smyon Heruka*," in *Among Tibetan Texts*, 61. See also Quintman, *Yogin and the Madman*, 152; Larsson, *Crazy for Wisdom*, 29–30, 295; Stefan Larsson, "What Do the Childhood and Early Life of Gtsang smyon Heruka Tell Us about His Bka' brgyud Affiliation?" in *Mahāmudrā and the Bka'-brgyud Tradition: Proceedings of the Eleventh Seminar of the International Association for Tibetan Studies, Königswinter 2006*, ed. Roger R. Jackson and Matthew T. Kapstein, 425–52 (Andiast: International Institute for Tibetan and Buddhist Studies, 2011).

56. Smyug la paN chen and Lha mthong lo tsA ba, 406.2, 408.5, 409.4, 480.6, 582.4, 599.2, 601.6, 622.4, 631.1.

57. Smyug la paN chen and Lha mthong lo tsA ba, 601.3; 'Brug pa kun legs, *'Brug pa kun legs kyi rnam thar*, 412.2–414.13.

58. Rgod tshang ras pa, 24.7–25.3, 130.7, 142.3, 166.4, 172.4–5; Lha btsun rin chen rnam rgyal, 13.1, 92.7, 123.5.

59. Rgod tshang ras pa, 58.1–2.

60. Smyug la paN chen and Lha mthong lo tsA ba, 419.4–420.3; *sgrub rgyud kyi bstan pa mig rkyen bzang po cig 'jog pa*, 585.5–586.3. See also 498.1, 552.5. Scholars tend to translate *sgrub rgyud* as "Practice Tradition." Here I use "Meditation Tradition" to avoid confusion with the Practice (*spyod pa/caryā*).

61. 'Brug pa kun legs, *'Brug pa kun legs kyi rnam thar*, 411.14–17.

62. Tshar chen chos rje blo gsal rgya mtsho, *Rje btsun rdo rje 'chang chen po kun spangs chos rje'i rnam thar ngo mtshar dad pai'i spu long g.yo ba* (Thimphu: National Library of Bhutan, 1985), 8.2–9.4; the date for the composition of the text comes from 152.3. According to this biography, it became "renowned in every direction" that Dbus smyon recognized Kun spangs pa as being an emanation of Phag mo gru pa, indicating the kind of esteem and authority Dbus smyon's word carried during his lifetime. This reference came to my attention thanks to Ehrhard, "Holy Madman of dBus," 240–41. That the two met around 1513 is confirmed by Dbus smyon's own biography, Smyug la paN chen and Lha mthong lo tsA ba, 602.2–4.

63. Gtsang smyon he ru ka, *Snyan rgyud kyi zhal gdams lus dkyil*, in *Bde mchog mkha' 'gro snyan rgyud*, 1:819–31, here citing 831.3. *Bde mchog mkha' 'gro snyan rgyud kyi gzhung 'brel sa gcad dang sbrags pa*, in *Bde mchog mkha' 'gro snyan rgyud*, 1:5–360, here citing 12.1. *Rnal 'byor gyi dbang phyug chen po mi la ras pa'i rnam mgur*, 113.2, 117.16; Tsangnyön Heruka, *Life of Milarepa*, 100, 105.

64. Rgod tshang ras pa, 164.6. See also 11.6–7, 194.4, 198.4.

65. Lha btsun rin chen rnam rgyal, 19.6–20.1, 111.6. See also 38.6, 40.2. The passage translated here is discussed by Larsson, *Crazy for Wisdom*, 122.

66. Roerich, *Blue Annals*, 84–7; 'Gos lo tsA ba, *Deb ther sngon po*, 1:114.5–117.3.

67. *khyed kyis ri khrod du bzhugs nas sgrub brgyud spel ba dang / ngas snye mdor bsdad nas bshad rgyud spel*; 'Gos lo tsA ba, *Deb ther sngon po*, 2:1117.13–15; Roerich, *Blue Annals*, 962.

68. *rang re'i brgyud pa 'di sgrub brgyud yin pas sgrub pa gal che bas sgrub pa la gtso bor gyis la 'bad pa thon*; 'Gos lo tsA ba, *Deb ther sngon po*, 2:740.12–14; Roerich, *Blue Annals*, 630.

   According to *Deb ther sngon po*, Mar pa's lineage was divided into a *sgrub pa'i bka' gzung*, passed down through Mi la ras pa, and a *bshad pa'i bka' gzung*, passed down through some other disciples; 'Gos lo tsA ba, *Deb ther sngon po*, 1:490.10–11; Roerich, *Blue Annals*, 405. In most usages of the term *sgrub brgyud* in the literature surrounding the fifteenth-century holy madmen, the term was used to refer to the whole of the Bka' brgyud sect, rather than in this much narrower sense.

   Bla ma zhang (1123–1193) used *sgrub brgyud* as synonymous with Bka' brgyud; Carl S. Yamamoto, *Vision and Violence: Lama Zhang and the Politics of Charisma in Twelfth-Century Tibet* (Leiden: Brill, 2012), 83–4. Roberts, *Biographies of Rechungpa*, 35, states this to be "an alternative name for the Kagyu." Dan Martin addresses the term, "The Star King and the Four Children of Pehar: Popular

Religious Movements of 11th- to 12th-Century Tibet," *Acta Orientalia Academiae Scientiarum Hungaricae* 49, nos. 1–2 (1996): 187.

69. Lha btsun rin chen rnam rgyal, 3.1.

70. For a sense of how this term was used in late fifteenth-century Tibet, see Komarovski, *Visions of Unity*, 32–3, 314–15.

71. Smyug la paN chen and Lha mthong lo tsA ba, 475.6–476.3.

72. Smyug la paN chen and Lha mthong lo tsA ba, 473.4–474.6.

73. Rgod tshang ras pa, 100.5–101.4. For more examples see 132.5–133.5, 155.5–156.6.

74. The fourteen "Root Downfalls" operative on the level of Unexcelled Yoga Tantra, including the second and thirteenth mentioned here, are described in Jamgön Kongtrul, *Buddhist Ethics*, 256–64. He explains the thirteenth downfall: "*To fail to accept the pledge substances* means to have doubts about and to refuse the pledge substances during any tantric activity due to feeling that one must adhere to monastic forms of conduct, etc." These "pledge substances" include "the outer and inner five meats, five nectars" (264), and so on.

75. *da lta gsang sngags dngos su nyams su len pa'i dus min cing / bod na tshogs 'khor mtshan nyid pa yod yang med. . . . de 'dra'i bzhed pa de rgyud dam bstan chos kyi lung tshad ldan ga nas bshad/ da lta gsang sngags nyams su ma lan na nam nyams su len*; Rgod tshang ras pa, 179.2–180.3.

In Gtsang smyon's *Gsung 'bum* there is described another interaction with people who challenged his approach, saying *spyir gyis da lta gsang sngags dang sgom pa nyams su len pa'i dus ma yin zhing / khyad par lta sgom spyod pa 'di 'dra thub pas ma gsungs pa*; 9b4–5; Larsson, *Crazy for Wisdom*, 171.

In Lha btsun rin chen rnam rgyal's version of his *Life*, Gtsang smyon has an argument with monks from Se ra and Dga' ldan monasteries in the marketplace in Lha sa, which quickly escalates into a physical altercation with swords and rocks; 38.6–39.5.

76. On Tsong kha pa's system and its attitudes toward tantra and monasticism, see Martin A. Mills, *Identity, Ritual and State in Tibetan Buddhism: The Foundations of Authority in Gelukpa Monasticism* (New York: RoutledgeCurzon, 2003), 19, 20, 102–4; Snellgrove, *Indo-Tibetan Buddhism*, 479; Samuel, *Civilized Shamans*, 506–515; Matthew Kapstein, *The Tibetans* (Malden, MA, and Oxford: Blackwell, 2006), 119–20; Giuseppe Tucci, *Tibetan Painted Scrolls* (Rome: La Libreria della Stato, 1949), 1:42–3; Guy Newland, "Debate Manuals in dGe lugs Monastic Colleges," in *Tibetan Literature: Studies in Genre*, ed. José Ignacio Cabezón and Roger Jackson, 202–216 (Ithaca, NY: Snow Lion, 1996); Elizabeth Napper, "Ethics as the Basis of a Tantric Tradition: Tsong kha pa and the Founding of the dGe lugs order in Tibet," in *Changing Minds: Contributions to the Study of Buddhism and Tibet in Honor of Jeffrey Hopkins*, ed. Guy Newland, 107–131 (Ithaca, NY: Snow Lion, 2001); Rachel M. McCleary and Leonard W. J. van der Kuijp, "The Market Approach to the Rise of the Geluk School, 1419–1642," *Journal of Asian Studies* 60, no. 1 (2010):

162; Georges Dreyfus, "Tibetan Scholastic Education and the Role of Soteriology," *Journal of the International Association of Buddhist Studies* 20, no. 1 (1997): 31–62.

77. 'Gos lo tsA ba, *Deb ther sngon po*, 1:113.6–17; Roerich, *Blue Annals*, 83.

78. Translated by Mark Tatz, *Asanga's Chapter on Ethics with the Commentary of Tsong-kha-pa* (Studies in Asian Thought and Religion, vol. 4; Lewiston, NY: Edwin Mellen, 1986), 210–11. See also 37, 94–8, 262. This is Tsong kha pa's *Byang chub gzhung lam*. See also Tatz, "Whom is Tsong-kha-pa Refuting in His Basic Path to Awakening?" in *Reflections on Tibetan Culture: Essays in Memory of Turrell V. Wylie*, ed. Lawrence Epstein and Richard F. Sherburne, 149–63 (Studies in Asian Thought and Religion, vol. 12; New York: Edwin Mellen, 1990).

79. Ferdinand Lessing and Alex Wayman, *Mkhas grub rje's Fundamentals of the Buddhist Tantras (Rgyud sde spyiḥi rnam par gźag pa rgyas par brjod)* (The Hague: Mouton, 1968), 319–25. Throughout Mkhas grub rje's explanation of these rites, the word he uses to express the way these rites were traditionally performed is *dngos su*, meaning "literally" or "in actuality." He is careful to state that in the modified form of the practices he prescribes, the same effect is nevertheless produced *dngos su*, "in actuality." Gtsang smyon's debate with the Dga' ldan bka' bcu pa was over whether or not tantra should be practiced *dngos su* during our historical period; Rgod tshang ras pa, 179.2–180.3.

80. *dge ba'i bshes gnyen dang / rnal 'byor pho mo sogs*; Rgod tshang ras pa, 256.2–3. *bla ma dge ba'i bshes gnyen*, 54.2; *bla ma dge ba'i bshes gnyen rtogs ldan gyi rnal 'byor pho mo rnams*, 171.6.

81. *dge bshes bya bral*, Smyug la paN chen and Lha mthong lo tsA ba, 550.6; in variant forms at 543.3, 548.4, 554.6.

82. Samuel, *Civilised Shamans*; Bogin, "Dreadlocks Treatise," 96; Janet Gyatso, "The Literary Transmission of the Traditions of Thang-stong rGyal-po: A Study of Visionary Buddhism in Tibet" (PhD diss., University of California at Berkeley, 1981), iii–iv. See also R. A. Stein, *Tibetan Civilization*, trans. J. E. Stapleton Driver (Stanford, CA: Stanford University Press, 1972), 156–7. This situation bears comparison to the split between "village" and "forest" monks described by Stanley Jeyaraja Tambiah in *The Buddhist Saints of the Forest and the Cult of Amulets* (Cambridge: Cambridge University Press, 1984).

83. Yamamoto, *Vision and Violence*, 110. See also 103–4.

84. Foucault, "Truth and Power," in *Power/Knowledge: Selected Interviews and Other Writings, 1972–1977*, ed. Colin Gordon, 109–33 (New York: Pantheon, 1980), here citing 133. Interview first published in French in 1977.

85. All references are to texts contained in Gtsang smyon he ru ka, *Bde mchog mkha' 'gro snyan rgyud. gu yangs smyon pa*; *Bde mchog mkha' 'gro snyan rgyud kyi smin lam dbang gi sdom tshig*, 1:361–66, here citing 366.4. *rje he ru ka*; *Bde mchog mkha' 'gro snyan rgyud kyi las byang yid bzhin nor bu*, 2:625–79, here citing 639.7. *rnal 'byor pa rus pa'i rgyan can*; *Snyan rgyud tshig bcad ma*, 2:793–800, here citing 800.3. *dur khrod myul ba'i rnal 'byor pa khrag 'thung rgyal po*; *Bde mchog mkha'*

'gro snyan rgyud kyi sbyin bsreg 'phrin las lhun grub, 1:643–80, here citing 679.5–6; also in *Dpal ye shes mgon po phyag bzhi pa'i rjes gnang*, 1:767–78, here citing 778.2. *rnal 'byor du ma'i ming can*; *Bde mchog mkha' 'gro snyan rgyud yab bskor yum bskor gyi bstod pa bskyed rims gsal ba'i nyi ma*, 1:533–54, here citing 554.5; also in *Bde mchog mkha' 'gro snyan rgyud kyi zhal gdams dpa' bo chig thub kyi gdams ngag*, 2:775–83, here citing 783.4.

On one occasion Gtsang smyon strings some of these names together, calling himself *dur khrod myul ba'i rnal 'byor pa sangs rgyas rgyal mtshan gtsang pa he ru ka rus pa'i brgyan can sogs du ma'i ming can*; *Bde mchog mkha' 'gro snyan rgyud kyi nang longs spyod rdzogs pa sku'i gdams pa smin lam yid bzhin nor bu*, 1:367–457, here citing 456.7–457.1.

INTERMEZZO

1. Rgod tshang ras pa, 84.3–6. My translation of this passage is somewhat tentative in places. I have omitted a few words of which I could not make definitive sense.

2. *chos rje dbus pa yang de dus dbus smyon du ma grags par/ la las bla ma thel pa zer la las bla ma ri pa zer ba . . . mtshon gyis mi tshugs pa'i rnal 'byor pa smyon pa gcig*; Rgod tshang ras pa, 67.3–4; Larsson, *Crazy for Wisdom*, 165–7; Roberto Vitali, *The Kingdoms of Gu.ge Pu.hrang, According to mNga'.ris rgyal.rabs by Gu.ge mkhan.chen Ngag.dbang grags.pa* (Dharamsala: Tho.ling gtsug.lag.khang lo.gcig.stong 'khor. ba'i rjes.dran.mdzad sgo'i go.sgrig tshogs.chung, 1996), 532.

3. The entire story runs Rgod tshang ras pa, 67.4–71.3.

4. Smyug la paN chen and Lha mthong lo tsA ba, 440.2–443.4.

5. Rgod tshang ras pa, 98.2–6. The blessing would appear to read (including its many spelling errors): *OM tuk thum rag sha/ ya ma ra ja mje sbreng / ma mo'i glig pa thim rgyob/ khal pa'i gzhong la ma ra ya/ tu ru mu ru kub tshum bung brtsag khyu/ bung bu'i kyab nas thal tshub lang lang hUM hUM phaT swahA*.

    Kun dga' bzang po's attempt to exorcise this spirit is reminiscent of an episode from his biography in which, after a female patron had asked him for a blessing to ensure that sons and wealth would come to her household, he proceeded to urinate in all its pots and pans, which ultimately brought good fortune; Smyug la paN chen and Lha mthong lo tsA ba, 566.3–567.2.

6. Rgod tshang ras pa, 200.7–201.7.

7. Gtsang smyon is said to have shared his disciple Rtogs ldan blo gros bkra shis with Dbus smyon, as one of the *thun mong gi rtogs ldan brgyad*; Rgod tshang ras pa, 266.5.

CHAPTER 4

1. This autobiographical text, *Phyi dka' ba spyad tshul gyi lo rgyus*, is contained in the *Bka' brgyud gser 'phreng* of the 'Ba' ra Bka' brgyud, and discussed in Smith, "Golden Rosaries of the Bka' brgyud Schools," in *Among Tibetan Texts*, 39–51,

here citing 50–51 (essay first published in 1970). The translation here is Smith's, but I have replaced his Wylie transliterations of proper nouns with phonetic transcriptions. On Mon rtse pa kun dga' dpal ldan, who was associated with the 'Brug pa Bka' brgyud, see Roberts, *Biographies of Rechungpa*, 30, 96. Mon rtse pa kun dga' dpal ldan should not be confused with Chos rje mon rtse pa, a disciple of Gtsang smyon who appears in the epigraph to the intermezzo.

2. Byang chub rgyal mtshan's rise to power and the formation of the Phag mo gru regime is descrbed in Tsepon W. D. Shakabpa, *Tibet: A Political History* (New Haven, CT: Yale University Press, 1967), 73–82; Kapstein, *Tibetans*, 116–18; Leonard van der Kuijp, "On the Life and Political Career of Ta'i-si-tu Byang-chub Rgyal-mtshan (1302–?1364)," in *Tibetan History and Language: Studies Dedicated to Uray Géza on his Seventieth Birthday*, ed. Ernst Steinkellner, 277–327 (Vienna: Arbeitskreis für tibetische und buddhistische studien universität wien, 1991); Olaf Czaja, *Medieval Rule in Tibet: The Rlangs Clan and the Political and Religious History of the Ruling House of Phag mo gru pa* (Vienna: Austrian Academy of Sciences Press, 2014), 111–96.

3. The founder of what would become the Phag mo gru subsect of the Bka' brgyud was named Rdo rje rgyal po (1110–1170). He came to be referred to as Phag mo gru pa after taking up residence at a place called Phag mo gru, "Sow's Ferry Crossing."

4. Kapstein, *Tibetans*, 121. Kapstein refers to the rise of the Dge lugs as "the most important" development in Tibetan religious culture during the fifteenth century, 119. See also David Snellgrove and Hugh Richardson, *A Cultural History of Tibet* (Boston, MA: Shambhala, 1995), 180–83; Stein, *Tibetan Civilization*, 80–81; Mills, *Identity, Ritual and State*, 19–22; Tucci, *Tibetan Painted Scrolls*, 1:85–6; and Hor gtsang 'jigs med, *Mdo smad lo rgyus chen mo las lo rgyus spyi'i gzhung shing gi skor* (Dharamsala: Library of Tibetan Works and Archives, 2009), 1:507.21–509.11.

5. PaN chen bsod nams grags pa's *Deb ther dmar po gsar ma* records how a lord of the Gong dkar district arranged for the printing of the works of Tsong kha pa, following a directive from *gong ma* Grags pa rgyal mtshan; Giuseppe Tucci, *Deb ther dmar po gsar ma [The New Red Annals]: Tibetan Chronicles*, vol. 1 (Serie Orientale Roma 24. Rome: Istituto Italiano per il Medio ed Estremo Oriente, 1971), 237. Below we will see that ShAkya mchog ldan was forced to study the Dge lugs system for a time.

6. Tucci, *Deb ther dmar po gsar ma*, 216, 240–41; Phun tshogs tshe ring, *Deb ther kun gsal me long* (Bod ljongs mi dmangs dpe skrun khang, 1987), 227.7–229.8; Turrell Wylie, "Monastic Patronage in 15th-century Tibet," *Acta Orientalia Academiae Scientiarum Hungaricae* 34, no. 103 (1980): 319–20; Rachel McCleary and Leonard van der Kuijp, "The Market Approach to the Rise of the Geluk School, 1419–1642," *Journal of Asian Studies* 60, no. 1 (2010): 160; Kapstein, *Tibetans*, 120; Czaja, *Medieval Rule*, 210.

On the support offered by Lha sa-area Phag mo gru administrators, such as the Sne'u pa, Brag dkar ba/Brag khar ba, and so on, see Per K.Sørensen and

Guntram Hazod, *Rulers on the Celestial Plain: Ecclesiastic and Secular Hegemony in Medieval Tibet: A Study of Tshal Gung-thang* (Vienna: Österreichische Akademie der Wissenschaften and Tibetan Academy of Social Sciences of the Autonomous Region Tibet, 2007), 49–52; Sørensen, "Lhasa Diluvium: Sacred Environment at Stake: The Birth of Flood Control Politics, the Question of Natural Disaster Management and their Importance for the Hegemony over a National Monument in Tibet," *Lungta* 16 (Spring 2003): 112–13.

7. This last fact is according to Bshes gnyen tshul khrims, *Lha sa'i dgon tho rin chen spungs rgyan* (Lhasa: Bod ljongs mi dmangs dpe skrun khang, 2001), 40.4. On the founding of Dga' ldan, see *Dpyid kyi rgyal mo'i glu dbyangs* by the Fifth Dalai Lama, translated in Zahiruddin Ahmad, *A History of Tibet by Ṅag-dBaṅ Blo-bZaṅ rGya-mTSHo, the Fifth Dalai Lama of Tibet* (Bloomington: Research Institute for Inner Asian Studies, Indiana University, 1995), 173–4, and Tucci, *Tibetan Painted Scrolls*, 2:645; Phun tshogs tshe ring, *Deb ther kun gsal me long*, 229.9–230.2; Dung dkar blo bzang 'phrin las, *Bod kyi chos srid zung 'brel skor bshad pa* (Dharamsala: Library of Tibetan Works and Archives, 1982), 79.9–15; Wylie, "Monastic Patronage," 320–21; McCleary and van der Kuijp, "Market Approach," 160–61; Kapstein, *Tibetans*, 120; Czaja, *Medieval Rule*, 210.

8. Tucci, *Deb ther dmar po gsar ma*, 240–41; Dung dkar blo bzang 'phrin las, *Chos srid zung 'brel*, 79.20–80.2; Wylie, "Monastic Patronage," 321; McCleary and van der Kuijp, "Market Approach," 161; Bshes gnyen tshul khrims, *Lha sa'i dgon tho rin chen spungs rgyan*, 47.18–51.4.

9. Tucci, *Deb ther dmar po gsar ma*, 190, 217; *Dpyid kyi rgyal mo'i glu dbyangs*, translated in Ahmad, *History of Tibet by the Fifth Dalai Lama*, 178, and Tucci, *Tibetan Painted Scrolls*, 2:646. See also Shakabpa, *Tibet*, 83; Czaja, *Medieval Rule*, 212–13. For a description of Rab brtan kun bzang 'phags's life, see Bo dong paN chen phyogs las rnam rgyal, *Rab brtan kun bzang 'phags kyi rnam thar* (Bod ljongs mi dmangs dpe skrun khang, 1987); *Dpal ldan shar ka ba'i gdung rabs brgyan gyi 'phreng ba* ("The Chronicles of Gyantse") in Tucci, *Tibetan Painted Scrolls*, 2:665–8; and Franco Ricca and Erberto Lo Bue, *The Great Stupa of Gyantse: A Complete Tibetan Pantheon of the Fifteenth Century* (London: Serindia, 1993), 18–31.

10. Dung dkar blo 'phrin las, *Chos srid zung 'brel*, 80.3–8; Wylie, "Monastic Patronage," 321–2; McCleary and van der Kuijp, "Market Approach," 161; Bshes gnyen tshul khrims, *Lha sa'i dgon tho rin chen spungs rgyan*, 52.17–57.22; Czaja, *Medieval Rule*, 210.

11. Bshes gnyen tshul khrims, *Lha sa'i dgon tho rin chen spungs rgyan*, 58.1–60.5.

12. For a list of these monasteries, drawn from Bshes gnyen tshul khrims, *Lha sa'i dgon tho rin chen spungs rgyan*, see DiValerio, "Subversive Sainthood," 287–9.

13. On the founding of Bkra shis lhun po, see Wylie, "Monastic Patronage," 322–3. According to *Deb ther dmar po gsar ma*, at this time Ngor chen kun dga' bzang po, founder of Ngor monastery, approached Rin spungs pa Nor bu bzang po and requested that he prevent the building of the monastery and convert the

area's existing Dge lugs monasteries to the Sa skya tradition. Nor bu bzang po said that doing so would be inappropriate. See Tucci, *Deb ther dmar po gsar ma*, 239–40; José Ignacio Cabezón and Geshe Lobsang Dargyay, *Freedom from Extremes: Gorampa's "Distinguishing the Views" and the Polemics of Emptiness* (Boston, MA: Wisdom, 2007), 44. However, in *Dpyid kyi rgyal mo'i glu dbyangs*, the Fifth Dalai Lama states that this story is incorrect; translated in Ahmad, *History of Tibet by the Fifth Dalai Lama*, 162, and Tucci, *Tibetan Painted Scrolls*, 2:642; Nor brang o rgyan, *Dpyid kyi rgyal mo'i glu dbyangs kyi 'grel pa yid kyi dga' ston* (Beijing: Mi rigs dpe skrun khang, 1993), 405.9–20.

Czaja has arrived at a different understanding of these events, *Medieval Rule*, 223–5. He argues that the Rin spungs pas did not fully seize Gzhis ka rtse until 1446 (not around 1434, as many sources suggest), and that the reason they did not block the establishment of Bkra shis lhun po was that other noble families of Gtsang, with whom the Rin spungs pas were keen to strengthen relations, were patronizing the project.

Bsod nams rgya mtsho (1543–1588) received the title "Dalai Lama" in 1578 from the Mongol ruler Altan Khan. His two prior incarnations were then labeled the first and second Dalai Lamas retroactively.

14. Luciano Petech, *The Kingdom of Ladakh c. 950–1842* (Roma: Instituto Italiano per il Medio ed Estremo Oriente, 1977), 167–8; Mills, *Identity, Ritual and State*, 20. Roberto Vitali, *The Dge lugs pa in Gu ge and the Western Himalaya (Early 15th – Late 17th Century)* (Dharamsala: Amnye Machen Institute, 2012), contains a wealth of information related to this issue.

15. Hor gtsang 'jigs med, *Mdo smad lo rgyus chen mo*, 483.5–494.21. This last fact, regarding the *BaiDU rya ser po*, is mentioned on 493.15–19.

16. Hor gtsang 'jigs med, *Mdo smad lo rgyus chen mo*, 478.22–479.4.

17. Sørensen and Hazod talk of Lha sa as the "geo-political axis of orientation" for Tibetans; *Rulers on the Celestial Plain*, 20. See also Sørensen, "Lhasa Diluvium," 113–14; Czaja, *Medieval Rule*, 209–210. The relationship between Tsong kha pa's *smon lam chen mo*, earlier prayer festivals organized by other religious groups, and the New Year's festivities put on by the Phag mo gru government is a topic deserving of further research.

18. Hor gtsang 'jigs med, *Mdo smad lo rgyus chen mo*, 499.15–501.9; Thub bstan phun tshogs, *Bod kyi lo rgyus spyi don pad+ma rA ga'i lde mig* (Si khron mi rigs dpe skrun khang, 1996), 2:709–712; David P. Jackson, "The Earliest Printings of Tsong-kha-pa's Works: The Old Dga'-ldan Editions," in *Reflections on Tibetan Culture: Essays in Memory of Turrell V. Wylie*, ed. Lawrence Epstein and Richard F. Sherburne, 107–116 (Studies in Asian Thought and Religion, vol. 12. New York: Edwin Mellen, 1990). For a wider discussion of printing projects in central Tibet in the fifteenth century, see Marta Sernesi, "A Manual on Nāropa's Six Yogas by sPyan snga Nyer gnyis pa (1386–1434): Tucci Tibetan Collection 1359," *Indo-Iranian Journal* 53 (2010): 143–5.

19. On the Dge lugs monastic network, see Newland, "Debate Manuals in dGe lugs Monastic Colleges," in *Tibetan Literature: Studies in Genre*, ed. José Ignacio Cabezón and Roger Jackson (Ithaca, NY: Snow Lion, 1996), 205–6; Sørensen, "Lhasa Diluvium," 113; Hor gtsang 'jigs med, *Mdo smad lo rgyus chen mo*, 501.10–502.12; Dung dkar blo bzang 'phrin las, *Chos srid zung 'brel*, 79.15–19.

20. The six monasteries are mentioned in Bshes gnyen tshul khrims, *Lha sa'i dgon tho rin chen spungs rgyan*, 26.12–30.10, 113.1–116.13, 117.11–118.6, 154.1–12, 159.1–160.12, 161.12–21. On the effect the spread of Dge lugs had on the other sects, see Tucci, *Tibetan Painted Scrolls*, 1:40; Dung dkar blo bzang 'phrin las, *Chos srid zung 'brel*, 80.14–17. Following the decline of the Rin spungs pas, there would be serious fighting between the 'Bri gung pas and the Phag mo gru–Dge lugs regime in the 1520s and 30s, during which monasteries were seized and forcibly converted; Tucci, *Deb ther dmar po gsar ma*, 200–201; Hor gtsang 'jigs med, *Mdo smad lo rgyus chen mo*, 511.1–6; Dung dkar blo bzang 'phrin las, 84.13–85.5; Sørensen, "Lhasa Diluvium," 118.

21. 'Bri gung dkon mchog rgya mtsho (Ra se zla ba), *'Bri gung chos 'byung* (Beijing: Mi rigs dpe skrun khang, 2003), 407–8; quotation from 402. This theme is repeated, 411–14. The date for the composition of the text comes from 'Bri gung bstan 'dzin pad ma'i rgyal mtshan, *'Bri gung gdan rabs gser phreng* (Bod ljongs bod yig dpe rnying dpe skrun khang, 1989), 3.2. 'Bri gung dkon mchog rgya mtsho's *'Bri gung chos 'byung* is based on this much earlier text, with some comments added.

22. Hugh Richardson, "The Karma-pa Sect: A Historical Note," in *High Peaks, Pure Earth: Collected Writings on Tibetan History and Culture*, ed. Michael Aris, 338–59 (London: Serindia, 1998), here citing 345–9 (essay first published in 1958); Shakabpa, *Tibet*, 83–5.

23. *Dpyid kyi rgyal mo'i glu dbyangs*, translated in Ahmad, *History of Tibet by the Fifth Dalai Lama*, 161; and Tucci, *Tibetan Painted Scrolls*, 2:641–2. See also Nor brang o rgyan, *Dpyid kyi rgyal mo'i glu dbyangs kyi 'grel pa yid kyi dga' ston*, 402.13–404.14; Shakabpa, *Tibet*, 86; Phun tshogs tshe ring, *Deb ther kun gsal me long*, 240.3–241.3. Yar lung pa a 'bum has written a history of the Rin spungs pas, *Dpal ldan rin chen spungs pa sger gyi gdung rabs che long tsam zhig*, which draws largely from *Dpyid kyi rgyal mo'i glu dbyangs*, but adds more details and dates, some of which are derived from *Chos 'byung mkhas pa'i dga' ston*. See also Sa skya'i spyi 'thus ga zi tshe rings po, *Bstan pa'i sbyin bdag chen po sa skyong rin spungs pa'i skor*, in *Chos kyi blo gros* 2:39–41 (Mandi, India: Dzongsar Institute, Chos kyi blo gros rtsom sgrig khang, 2009).

24. *phag mo gru pa nang zhig gi lo; stag lo'i sde gzar chen mo*. Ehrhard, "Holy Madman of dBus," 219; Tucci, *Deb ther dmar po gsar ma*, 219; Tucci, *Tibetan Painted Scrolls*, 1:28–9; Dung dkar blo bzang 'phrin las, *Chos srid zung 'brel*, 80.18–81.13; Shakabpa, *Tibet*, 86; Hor gtsang 'jigs med, *Mdo smad lo rgyus chen mo*, 509.4–11; Kapstein, *Tibetans*, 122; Czaja, *Medieval Rule*, 220.

25. *phag gru bas gtsang phyogs rin spung ba la shor;* Sum pa mkhan po ye shes dpal 'byor, from the *Re'u mig,* published within *Dpag bsam ljon bzang,* vol. 3, ed. Lokesh Chandra (New Delhi: International Academy of Indian Culture, 1959), 47.2. As stated in note 13, although many of the histories claim that the Rin spungs pas took Gzhis ka rtse in 1434 or 1435, Czaja, has suggested that they did not achieve this until 1446.

26. Czaja, *Medieval Rule,* 19, 209, 227, 252; Tucci, *Deb ther dmar po gsar ma,* 220; Peter Schwieger, "Significance of Ming Titles Conferred upon the Phag mo gru Rulers: A Reevalution of Chinese–Tibetan Relations during the Ming Dynasty," in *The Earth Ox Papers: Proceedings of the International Seminar on Tibetan and Himalayan Studies, Held at the Library of Tibetan Works and Archives, September 2009 on the Occasion of the "Thank you India" Year,* ed. Roberto Vitali, 313–28, special issue, *Tibet Journal* (Autumn and Winter 2009, Spring and Summer 2010).

    On *gong ma* Grags pa 'byung gnas's not being able to go to Gtsang for the customary inspection tour, see Czaja, 221–2. The next *gong ma,* Kun dga' legs pa, did make such tour, in around 1458, but became displeased when the Rin spungs pas were insufficiently courteous to him, 227.

27. *gong ma sde srid kyi bka' khrims kyi shing rta chen po'i kha lo pa rnams;* Nor brang o rgyan, *Dpyid kyi rgyal mo'i glu dbyangs kyi 'grel pa yid kyi dga' ston,* 402.14–15; translation drawn from Tucci, *Tibetan Painted Scrolls,* 2:641. For an alternative translation, see Ahmad, *History of Tibet by the Fifth Dalai Lama,* 161.

    As Phun tshogs tshe ring summarizes in *Deb ther kun gsal me long,* the Rin spungs pas *zhi drag gnyis ka'i thabs la brten nas phag gru'i srid dbang rim bzhin 'phrog,* 241.19–20. See Hugh Richardson, "The Political Role of the Four Sects in Tibetan History," in *High Peaks, Pure Earth: Collected Writings on Tibetan History and Culture,* ed. Michael Aris, 420–30 (London: Serindia, 1998), here citing 424 (essay first published in 1976).

28. *dpon tshab thel gtong.* Ehrhard, "Holy Madman of dBus," 219–20; Tucci, *Deb ther dmar po gsar ma,* 226–8; Tucci, *Tibetan Painted Scrolls,* 1:30. Nor brang o rgyan, *Dpyid kyi rgyal mo'i glu dbyangs kyi 'grel pa yid kyi dga' ston,* 390.5–18, 406.8–407.10; translated in Ahmad, *History of Tibet by the Fifth Dalai Lama,* 154–5, 162–3, and Tucci, *Tibetan Painted Scrolls,* 2:640, 642. Dung dkar blo bzang 'phrin las, *Chos srid zung 'brel,* 83.6–17; Czaja, *Medieval Rule,* 20–21, 242, 246, 249. Mtsho skyes rdo rje's dates are as given by Czaja. Ehrhard suggests 1450–1510.

29. Czaja, *Medieval Rule,* 20, 225–7, 229, 233.

30. Czaja, *Medieval Rule,* 250; Tucci, *Deb ther dmar po gsar ma,* 228; *Dpyid kyi rgyal mo'i glu dbyangs,* translated in Ahmad, *History of Tibet by the Fifth Dalai Lama,* 157, and Tucci, *Tibetan Painted Scrolls,* 2:641; Nor brang o rgyan, *Dpyid kyi rgyal mo'i glu dbyangs kyi 'grel pa yid kyi dga' ston,* 394.21–395.4; Shakabpa, *Tibet,* 88–9; Rgod tshang ras pa, 258.6. Yar lung pa a 'bum, *Dpal ldan rin chen spungs pa sger gyi gdung rabs che long tsam zhig,* in *Bod kyi rgyal rabs phyogs bsdebs kyi nang*

gses (Dharamsala: Library of Tibetan Works and Archives, 1985) mentions two daughters had by Don yod rdo rje, 133.2–3.

31. A brief biography is offered in Ko zhul grags pa 'byung gnas and Rgyal ba blo bzang mkhas grub, *Gangs can mkhas grub rim byon ming mdzod* (Lanshou: Kan su'i mi rigs dpe skrun khang, 1992), 1613–14; and in Dung dkar blo bzang 'phrin las, *Dung dkar tshig mdzod chen mo* (Beijing: Krung go'i bod rigs dpe skrun khang, 2002), 1915. Other details are drawn from Czaja, *Medieval Rule*, 487–8, 565. Don yod rdo rje's dates are given as according to Czaja.

32. Tucci, *Deb ther dmar po gsar ma*, 224–5; Czaja, *Medieval Rule*, 20, 235–8. For information on how these events are described differently in other sources, including *Dpyid kyi rgyal mo'i glu dbyangs*, the *Re'u mig*, and later histories, like Dung dkar blo bzang 'phrin las, *Chos srid zung 'brel*, and Shakabpa, *Tibet*; see DiValerio, "Subversive Sainthood," 303–7.

33. The efforts of Smon lam dpal ba are mentioned in Nor brang o rgyan, *Dpyid kyi rgyal mo'i glu dbyangs kyi 'grel pa yid kyi dga' ston*, 407.23–408.9; translated in Ahmad, *History of Tibet by the Fifth Dalai Lama*, 163, and Tucci, *Tibetan Painted Scrolls*, 2:642; Sum pa mkhan po, *Dpag bsam ljon bzang* (Sarnath: Mongolian Lama Guru Deva, 1965), 24.9–10, 200.18–19, and in Tucci, 2:654.

34. Tucci, *Deb ther dmar po gsar ma*, 189, 226; Czaja, *Medieval Rule*, 240. Among the alternative presentations offered by other sources, some say that there were in fact two separate campaigns against Rgyal rtse: one in 1485, which was unsuccessful, and one in 1488, in which they achieved their aim. Shakabpa, *Tibet*, 88; Wylie, "Monastic Patronage," 325.

35. Tucci, *Deb ther dmar po gsar ma*, 227; Czaja, *Medieval Rule*, 243.

36. Sørensen, "Lhasa Diluvium," 115–16; Czaja, *Medieval Rule*, 245.

37. Tucci, *Deb ther dmar po gsar ma*, 228; Czaja, *Medieval Rule*, 246, 249.

38. Tucci, *Deb ther dmar po gsar ma*, 229–30; Ehrhard, "Holy Madman of dBus," 220; *Dpyid kyi rgyal mo'i glu dbyangs*, translated in Ahmad, *History of Tibet by the Fifth Dalai Lama*, 164, and Tucci, *Tibetan Painted Scrolls*, 2:640; Nor brang o rgyan, *Dpyid kyi rgyal mo'i glu dbyangs kyi 'grel pa yid kyi dga' ston*, 391.17–392.8; Czaja, *Medieval Rule*, 251–3.

39. These include *nang so, drung, sgar pa, sde pa, sde pa sgar pa, sde srid, sa skyong, chos rgyal, chos skyong ba'i rgyal po, sa skyong chos kyi rgyal po, stobs kyi rgyal po, mi'i dbang po, sa skyong mi'i dbang po,* and others.

40. *dbus gtsang ru bzhi'i bdag po sa skyong don yod rdo rje*; Dpa' bo gtsug lag phreng ba, *Chos 'byung mkhas pa'i dga' ston*, 2006, 556.10; repeated in Si tu paN chen and 'Be lo tshe dbang kun khyab, *Bsgrub brgyud karma kaM tshang*, 1:569.4. The second passage is in *Chos 'byung mkhas pa'i dga' ston*, 2006, 561.25–27.

41. Si tu paN chen and 'Be lo tshe dbang kun khyab, *Bsgrub brgyud karma kaM tshang*, 2:55.4; 1:668.6, 672.2; DiValerio, "Subversive Sainthood," 372–3.

42. Czaja, *Medieval Rule*, 488–9; Tucci, *Deb ther dmar po gsar ma*, 230, 232–3, 240; *Dpyid kyi rgyal mo'i glu dbyangs*, translated in Ahmad, *History of Tibet by the Fifth*

Dalai Lama, 164, and Tucci, *Tibetan Painted Scrolls*, 2:642; Nor brang o rgyan, *Dpyid kyi rgyal mo'i glu dbyangs kyi 'grel pa yid kyi dga' ston*, 408.22–410.3; Hor gtsang 'jigs med, *Mdo smad lo rgyus chen mo*, 509.22–510.12. Ngag dbang rnam rgyal's dates are given as according to Czaja, 565.

43. Czaja, *Medieval Rule*, 21, 249.

44. *Dpyid kyi rgyal mo'i glu dbyangs*, translated in Ahmad, *History of Tibet by the Fifth Dalai Lama*, 155–9, and Tucci, *Tibetan Painted Scrolls*, 2:640–41; Nor brang o rgyan, *Dpyid kyi rgyal mo'i glu dbyangs kyi 'grel pa yid kyi dga' ston*, 391.17–393.12; Tucci, *Deb ther dmar po gsar ma*, 230–33; Dung dkar blo bzang 'phrin las, *Chos srid zung 'brel*, 84.2–12; Czaja, *Medieval Rule*, 260–61. Exemplifying their fallen status, the Rin spungs pas tried to involve themselves with the recognition of the Fifth Zhwa dmar, but were blocked from doing so; Czaja, 257.

45. Sørensen, "Lhasa Diluvium," 113–14.

46. Hor gtsang 'jigs med, *Mdo smad lo rgyus chen mo*, 509.17–21. According to many historians, either during the period the Rin spungs pas controlled Lha sa, or during the 1520s and 1530s, when the Phag mo gru–Dge lugs regime was fighting with the 'Bri gung Bka' brgyud and a number of monasteries were forcibly converted, some Dge lugs monks in Dbus took to keeping two different hats, one red and one yellow, which they would wear when they were outside and inside (or they had a single hat that was red on the inside and yellow on the outside, which they would flip inside-out when they came and went), so as to appear to be conforming to a conversion forced upon them, or simply to avoid being antagonized by the Bka' brgyud pas or their allies; Dung dkar blo bzang 'phrin las, *Chos srid zung 'brel*, 84.19–85.5; Nor brang o rgyan, *Dpyid kyi rgyal mo'i glu dbyangs kyi 'grel pa yid kyi dga' ston*, 305.18–306.6; 'Bri gung dkon mchog rgya mtsho, *'Bri gung chos 'byung*, 427; Shakabpa, *Tibet*, 90.

   Similarly, Tucci, *Deb ther dmar po gsar ma*, 223, maintains that in the 1460s the monks of Rtse thang monastery were commanded (it is unclear by whom) to change their hats from yellow to red—signifying a conversion (back) from Dge lugs to Bka' brgyud—although many monks did not comply, continuing to wear a yellow hat with only a small patch of red on it, or wearing no hat at all; Czaja, *Medieval Rule*, 233; Nor brang o rgyan, 390.8–12, 406.23–407.4. Whether these stories are the product of oral traditions or more historically factual, they are a telling indicator of the sectarian tensions of the time.

47. Sum pa mkhan po ye shes dpal 'byor, *Dpag bsam ljon bzang*, 1965, 24.6–10; translated in Tucci, *Tibetan Painted Scrolls*, 2:654. Dung dkar blo bzang 'phrin las, *Chos srid zung 'brel*, 82.22–83.2. In his *Re'u mig*, Sum pa mkhan po says the Fourth Zhwa dmar "invited" or perhaps "led" (*drangs*) the army from Gtsang into Dbus; contained within *Dpag bsam ljon bzang*, 1959, 3:51.22–52.1. Elsewhere in his histories, Sum pa mkhan po uses *drangs* unambiguously in the sense of leading troops.

48. Dung dkar blo bzang 'phrin las, *Chos srid zung 'brel*, 83.11–17. Richardson also addresses these events, "Political Role of the Four Sects," in *High Peaks, Pure Earth*, 424–5.

49. *rgyal ba blo bzang grags pa dang bcas pa ma 'gran/ zhwa dmar nag la 'thab kha ma 'gran*; 'Brug pa kun legs, *'Brug pa kun legs kyi rnam thar*, 202.6–7. The first line is about Tsong kha pa, which I cannot resolve definitively. Stein takes the line as meaning that no one can compete with Tsong kha pa in terms of "règles (de conduite monastique)"; *Vie et chants*, 319. I suspect that this line is a play on Tsong kha pa's personal name, Blo bzang grags pa, saying that none is "more famous," *grags pa*, than he. Stein reads *'thab kha* as *thab kha*, referring to "réalisations spirituelles," but admits an uncertainty over this.

50. Dpa' bo gtsug lag phreng ba describes the Fourth Zhwa dmar as a refuge for all the inhabitants of central and western Tibet, protecting them from fear; *Chos 'byung mkhas pa'i dga' ston*, 2006, 587.7–9. According to this version of history, in around 1498 the Zhwa dmar worked to ensure that Se ra and Dga' ldan monasteries would not be destroyed by troops from Gtsang and Bya, who had arrived in the Lha sa area, and that local administrators would not be harmed; 581.26–30. The story is repeated in Si tu paN chen and 'Be lo tshe dbang kun khyab, *Bsgrub brgyud karma kaM tshang*, 1:615, with the Karma pa inserted into it. *Chos 'byung mkhas pa'i dga' ston* describes another occasion when the Zhwa dmar convinced the Rin spungs pas not to send troops to Lho stod; 2006, 585.6–14.

51. This is my translation, based on Tucci, *Deb ther dmar po gsar ma*, 195; the Tibetan is on 60a.

52. Dung dkar blo bzang 'phrin las, *Dung dkar tshig mdzod chen mo*, 36.

53. The twelfth abbot of Stag lung monastery, Ngag dbang grags pa dpal bzang, is said to have had a patron–preceptor relationship with the Rin spungs pas after meeting Nor bu bzang po, which carried over into his having a similar connection with Mtsho skyes rdo rje and Don yod rdo rje, both of whom he met on numerous occasions in the 1480s and 90s between the Sne gdong area and Chu shul lhun po rtse; Stag lung ngag dbang rnam rgyal, *Stag lung chos 'byung* (Bod ljongs bod yig dpe rnying dpe skrun khang, 1992), 428, 438–55; Sørensen, "Lhasa Diluvium," 116.

54. The story begins at Dpa' bo gtsug lag phreng ba, *Chos 'byung mkhas pa'i dga' ston*, 2006, 549.25; it is retold in Si tu paN chen and 'Be lo tshe dbang kun khyab, *Bsgrub brgyud karma kaM tshang*, starting at 1:558.7; and in Sørensen, "Lhasa Diluvium," 114–15.

55. Sørensen and Hazod, *Rulers on the Celestial Plain*, 51.

56. Dpa' bo gtsug lag phreng ba, *Chos 'byung mkhas pa'i dga' ston*, 2006, 582.28, 585.20–21; Si tu paN chen and 'Be lo tshe dbang kun khyab, *Bsgrub brgyud karma kaM tshang*, 1:617.1, 621.2; Sørensen, "Lhasa Diluvium," 116.

57. *las 'bras kyi shugs 'di gang gis kyang dgag par ma nus pas/ yun du ma gnas pa . . .* The Tibetan is from Nor brang o rgyan, *Dpyid kyi rgyal mo'i glu dbyangs kyi 'grel*

Notes   275

pa yid kyi dga' ston, 408.18–20; translated in Ahmad, *History of Tibet by the Fifth Dalai Lama*, 163, and Tucci, *Tibetan Painted Scrolls*, 2:642. In his commentary, Nor brang o rgyan states that this monastery was called Karma dgon gsar thub bstan chos 'khor, that it was built in 1503, and that it was destroyed by monks from Se ra and 'Bras spungs. Dpa' bo gtsug lag phreng ba's *Chos 'byung mkhas pa'i dga' ston* mentions the founding of a Thub chen chos 'khor on the east side of Lha sa, 2006, 563.30–564.2; repeated in Si tu paN chen and 'Be lo tshe dbang kun khyab, *Bsgrub brgyud karma kaM tshang*, 1:586.4. According to Dung dkar blo bzang 'phrin las, the monastery was called Karma dgon gsar or Dgon gsar thub bstan chos 'khor, and was built in 1503 on the east side of Lha sa; *Dung dkar tshig mdzod chen mo*, 26; Dung dkar blo bzang 'phrin las, *Chos srid zung 'brel*, 83.18–84.1. See also Wylie, "Monastic Patronage," 326. Shakabpa, *Tibet*, 87–8, presents the construction and destruction of this (?) monastery as having occurred much earlier, so that Don yod rdo rje's campaign into central Tibet in 1480 was in retaliation for this attack from representatives of the Dge lugs sect.

58. Tucci, *Tibetan Painted Scrolls*, 1:40, mentions two monasteries, built near Se ra and 'Bras spungs, one for the Zhwa dmar and the other for the Karma pa. According to Richardson, two Karma pa monasteries were built near 'Bras spungs and Se ra "in order to overawe" the Dge lugs pas during the twenty years the Rin spungs pas controlled Lha sa; the one near 'Bras spungs was called Yam mda' phur thub dbang legs bshad gling; Richardson, "Karma-pa Sect," in *High Peaks, Pure Earth*, 347.

59. This terminology is used in Sum pa mkhan po ye shes dpal 'byor, *Dpag bsam ljon bzang*, 1965, 24.10–11; and echoed by Dung dkar blo bzang 'phrin las, *Chos srid zung 'brel*, 83.23, and by many other historians in their discussions of this period.

60. *rang shugs kyis med par byas 'dod. . . . kar dge gnyis pha wang dang nyi 'od ltar gyur*; Sum pa mkhan po, *Dpag bsam ljon bzang*, 1965, 24.10–16.

61. Sources disagree about when this monastery was established, offering dates of 1480, 1490, and 1503. According to the account of the Fourth Zhwa dmar's biography given in Dpa' bo gtsug lag phreng ba, *Chos 'byung mkhas pa'i dga' ston*, he had visions regarding Yangs pa can monastery starting in 1501 (*lcags bya*), 2006, 583.8–11; laid the foundation (*rmang bting*) for the future monastery in 1503 (*chu phag*), 584.22–4; the construction is described thereafter, continuing through 1504 (*shing byi*). Repeated in Si tu paN chen and 'Be lo tshe dbang kun khyab, *Bsgrub brgyud karma kaM tshang*, 1:617.4–5, 619.6–7. For more on the history of Yangs pa can, see Bshes gnyen tshul khrims, *Lha sa'i dgon tho rin chen spungs rgyan*, 220.1–228.9.

Some of this confusion may stem from the fact that in 1490 (*lcags khyi*) a Sa skya pa named Mus rab 'byams pa thugs rje dpal founded a monastery called Thub bstan yangs pa can; Sum pa mkhan po, *Re'u mig*, in *Dpag bsam ljon bzang*, 1959, 3:52.21–22. Sørensen, "Lhasa Diluvium," 116, mentions a temple within

Dga' ldan monastery also called Yangs pa can, showing that this was a commonly used name.

62. Czaja, *Medieval Rule*, 250, 487.

63. My argument over the next few paragraphs draws extensively from Wylie,
"Monastic Patronage," 324–8. Wylie was working under the assumption that
Yangs pa can was built in 1490, and could thus prove useful in the Rin spungs
pas's successful military campaign against Lha sa in 1498. I believe Yangs pa can
to have been built after this campaign. Nevertheless, much of Wylie's thinking
about the strategic intent behind the monastery is still applicable.

64. The strategic location of this monastery is suggested by the fact that it also played
a role in the struggle between the Gtsang pa sde srid and the Fifth Dalai Lama's
regime in the seventeenth century; Dung dkar blo bzang 'phrin las, *Dung dkar
tshig mdzod chen mo*, 1846.

65. Dpa' bo gtsug lag phreng ba, *Chos 'byung mkhas pa'i dga' ston*, 2006, 595.16–17;
1986, 1166.11–12; Ehrhard, "Holy Madman of dBus," 243.

66. It was during this time that the Second Dalai Lama founded Chos 'khor rgyal
monastery, near Dwags po, in 1509; Wylie, "Monastic Patronage," 326–7; Tucci,
Tibetan Painted Scrolls, 1:41; Sørensen and Hazod, *Rulers on the Celestial Plain*, 52.

67. *chos lugs kyi grub mtha' so so'i bar gyi 'thab rtsod dag ni phyi tshul nas bltas na sangs
rgyas kyi bstan pa srung skyob ched du yin pa ltar snang yang / don dam du dpal
'byor gyi khe phan dang chab srid kyi dbang cha rtsod pa'i 'thab rtsod cig kyang red*;
Don grub rgyal, <<*Mi la ras pa'i rnam thar* >> *gyi rtsom pa po'i lo rgyus*, in *Dpal
don grub rgyal gyi gsung 'bum*, 3:38.12–16.

68. Komarovski, *Visions of Unity*, 19–20.

69. This last fact is according to Dpa' bo gtsug lag phreng ba, *Chos 'byung mkhas
pa'i dga' ston*, 2006, 587.20; Si tu paN chen and 'Be lo tshe dbang kun khyab,
Bsgrub brgyud karma kaM tshang, 1:642.4. The Rin spungs pas's patronage of
these various endeavors is described in Czaja, *Medieval Rule*, 212, 217–18, 221,
228–9, 483–5; *Dpyid kyi rgyal mo'i glu dbyangs*, translated in Ahmad, *History
of Tibet by the Fifth Dalai Lama*, 162, and Tucci, *Tibetan Painted Scrolls*, 2:642;
Nor brang o rgyan, *Dpyid kyi rgyal mo'i glu dbyangs kyi 'grel pa yid kyi dga' ston*,
404.17–406.7; Tucci, *Deb ther dmar po gsar ma*, 238–9; 'Gos lo tsA ba, *Deb ther
sngon po*, 1:414.1–7; Roerich, *Blue Annals*, 340; and three texts contained in vol. 17
(*tsa*) of the *Collected Works* of ShAkya mchog ldan: *Rje btsun byams pa mgon po'i
sku brnyan bzhengs pa'i dkar chag lo rgyus*, 243–76; *Gtsang rong byams chen chos
sde'i par gsar pa rnams kyi dkar chag tu gnang ba*, 229–38; and *Gzhis ka rin spung
kyi phyag mdzod du bsdu ba'i deb gter chen mo'i shis brjod*, 238–9.

70. On the relationship between the Rin spungs pas and Go ram pa, see Cabezón
and Dargyay, *Freedom from Extremes*, 39–40, 43–4.

71. Tucci saw this regional competition as an important factor in the struggle that
defined this time period, *Tibetan Painted Scrolls*, 1:27, 29–30.

72. On the former conflict, see Sørensen and Hazod, *Rulers on the Celestial Plain*, 55–6. On the latter, see Melvyn C. Goldstein, *A History of Modern Tibet, 1913–1951: The Demise of the Lamaist State* (Berkeley: University of California Press, 1989).

73. *dbus gtsang gi sde 'khrug langs pa*; Smyug la paN chen and Lha mthong lo tsA ba, 608.2.

74. Kun dga' grol mchog, *PaNDi ta chen po shAkya mchog ldan gyi rnam par thar pa*, 228.4; Czaja, *Medieval Rule*, 251. On ShAkya mchog ldan's relationship with the Rin spungs pas during his lifetime, see Komarovski, *Visions of Unity*, 19, 42, 44, 105–6. Don yod rdo rje is, like Dbus smyon, listed in ShAkya mchog ldan's biography as one of his disciples; Kun dga' grol mchog, 230.1; Komarovski, 43, 329.

75. Stag lung ngag dbang rnam rgyal, *Stag lung chos 'byung*, 449.

76. *Chos 'byung mkhas pa'i dga' ston*, 2006, 591.4–11; Si tu paN chen and 'Be lo tshe dbang kun khyab, *Bsgrub brgyud karma kaM tshang*, 1:646.4–8.

77. Kun dga' grol mchog, *PaNDi ta chen po shAkya mchog ldan gyi rnam par thar pa*, 5.6; Komarovski, *Visions of Unity*, 49–50.

78. Komarovski, *Visions of Unity*, 88–9, 91–4, 96, 100.

79. Komarovski, *Visions of Unity*, 28. See also 19–20, 29–30, 43–4, and many other places throughout.

80. Komarovski, *Visions of Unity*, 3.

81. Offering a glimpse of how such symbolic legitimation was established, Dpa' bo gtsug lag phreng ba states that the Seventh Karma pa once traveled to Rin spungs, which place "in the past was renowned in a prophecy of lord Mar pa." This suggests that the Rin spungs pas, their rule, and their association with the Bka' brgyud pas were asserted to have been preordained; *Chos 'byung mkhas pa'i dga' ston*, 2006, 562.24.

82. Dbus smyon encountered a *sa skyong chos kyi rgyal po* at Gzhis ka rtse; Smyug la paN chen and Lha mthong lo tsA ba, 503.2–6. Following Ehrhard, "Holy Madman of dBus," 231, I take this to be Rdo rje tshe brtan, older brother of Don yod rdo rje. Shortly after this, the yogin encounters *sa skyong chos kyi rgyal po rdo rje tshe brtan* at Rin spungs, 506.4–5. On what is known about Rdo rje tshe brtan, see Czaja, *Medieval Rule*, 239. It seems he was responsible for maintaining the family's holdings from their base at Rin spungs. The yogin meets *mi yi dbang po dpal ldan kun tu bzang po*, Don yod rdo rje's father, at Rin spungs, 506.6–507.6; he meets Mtsho skyes rdo rje near 'Phan yul, 540.2–4; letter described, 609.4–5.

83. There has been some uncertainty regarding this genealogy. Dpa' bo gtsug lag phreng ba, *Chos 'byung mkhas pa'i dga' ston*, asserts a woman known as *dpon sa gser khang ma* to be a daughter of the *sde pa sgar pa*, which title usually refers to Don yod rdo rje (2006, 656.22, 657.18–19; 1986, 1285.15–16, 1287.10–11); she was given in marriage to someone from the estate of Rin chen rtse at Snye mo. She was a devotee of the Eighth Karma pa and Mi nyag rab 'byams pa mgon po dpal

(who was also a disciple of Dbus smyon) (*Chos 'byung mkhas pa'i dga' ston*, 2006, 591.21–22; 1986, 1158.24–1159.1). Yar lung a 'bum follows this version of events, saying that Don yod rdo rje had a daughter named *dpon sa gser khang rgyal mo*, who was given in marriage to Snye mo rin chen rtse pa; *Dpal ldan rin chen spungs pa sger gyi gdung rabs che long tsam zhig*, 133.3. She would give birth to Smyug la paN chen ngag dbang grags pa (*Chos 'byung mkhas pa'i dga' ston*, 2006, 592.12; 1986, 1160.7–8). Czaja, *Medieval Rule*, 488, 565, has accepted *gser khang ma*'s father as being Don yod rdo rje. This cannot be correct, as this would make Smyug la paN chen (1463–1512) the grandson of Don yod rdo rje (1462/3–1512).

Ehrhard, "Holy Madman of dBus," 235, has offered an alternative geneology, which I accept. In his reading, the *sde pa sgar pa* referred to in *Chos 'byung mkhas pa'i dga' ston* as the father of *gser khang ma* (2006, 657.18; 1986, 1287.10) is not Don yod rdo rje, but his grandfather, Nor bu bzang po. That would make *gser khang ma* Don yod rdo rje's aunt, and Smyug la paN chen his cousin.

In the *Life of the Madman of Ü*, Smyug la paN chen and Lha mthong lo tsA ba, 654.1–2, it is said that the sponsorship for his reliquary was offered *cho 'brang gi do shal chen po bsod nams kyi srad bu la 'chang ba'i bdag mo gser khang nas . . .*; *gser khang* may be intended as part of the woman's title, or as referring to her place of residence. Clearly her ancestry is praised.

Smyug la paN chen's association with Gser khang is further confirmed when, in his *Miscellaneous Writings*, 'Brug pa kun legs meets Smyug la paN chen at that place; *'Brug pa kun legs kyi rnam thar*, 456.6.

It could also be the case that there was more than one woman in the family known as *gser khang ma*.

84. Smyug la paN chen and Lha mthong lo tsA ba, 498.1–5; 499.1–4. Ehrhard, "Holy Madman of dBus," 230–31, assumes the patron for this meditation center to be Don yod rdo rje; alternatively, it may have been the lord of Rgyal rtse.

85. The great gathering at Zam bu lung is described, Smyug la paN chen and Lha mthong lo tsA ba, 504.1–506.1; the fact that Don yod rdo rje and the yogin had met there is mentioned 510.1–2. The meeting at Ras mda' is 510.1–4. The phrase *yon mchod thugs mthun* is also used to describe the yogin's relationship with Mtsho skyes rdo rje, 540.2–4.

86. Smyug la paN chen and Lha mthong lo tsA ba, 510.5–6, 518.6–519.2, 547.3.

87. Their meetings are described, Smyug la paN chen and Lha mthong lo tsA ba, 479.5–480.3, 569.6–570.6, 582.1–3. On Bkra shis dar rgyas, see Roerich, *Blue Annals*, 1086–90; 'Gos lo tsA ba, *Deb ther sngon po*, 2:1265.10–1270.6; Toni Huber, *The Cult of Pure Crystal Mountain: Popular Pilgrimage and Visionary Landscape in Southeast Tibet* (New York: Oxford University Press, 1999), 245; Aris, *Hidden Treasures and Secret Lives*, 72, 74–5; Leonard W. K. van der Kuijp, "On the Composition and Printings of the *Deb gter sngon po* by 'Gos lo tsā ba gzhon nu dpal (1392–1481)," *Journal of the International Association of Tibetan Studies* 2 (2006): 1–46; *Dpyid kyi rgyal mo'i glu dbyangs*, translated in Ahmad, *History of Tibet by the Fifth Dalai Lama*, 183, and Tucci, *Tibetan Painted Scrolls*,

2:647–8; Nor brang o rgyan, *Dpyid kyi rgyal mo'i glu dbyangs kyi 'grel pa yid kyi dga' ston*, 440.18–441.18. In Czaja's estimation, *Medieval Rule*, 241, 474–5, the profile of the house of Bya was greatly raised as a result of Bkra shis dar rgyas's alliance with the Karma Bka' brgyud. Bkra shis dar rgyas and Mtsho skyes rdo rje are listed among those who made offerings after the death of Thang stong rgyal po, the famous saint sometimes counted among the "holy madmen"; Stearns, *King of the Empty Plain*, 431.

88. Smyug la paN chen and Lha mthong lo tsA ba, 1494 edition, 51a4; 1972, 659.6–660.1.

89. Gtsang smyon he ru ka, *Rje btsun gtsang smyon he ru ka'i mgur 'bum*, 4a7–9b3; Larsson, *Crazy for Wisdom*, 167–71.

90. The yogin's various contacts with the kings of Mnga' ris gung thang are mentioned in Rgod tshang ras pa, 93.7, 161.6, 172.3–5, 176.2–3, 221.3–4, 229.6, 244.7–245.2. At 198.5–6 Lha btsun rin chen rnam rgyal is said to be *gung thang rgyal po'i sras*, a son of the king. See also Roberts, *Biographies of Rechungpa*, 37–8, 64; Larsson, *Crazy for Wisdom*, 262, 266.

91. Rgod tshang ras pa, 67.5–7, 153.6, 155.3, 161.6, 177.7, 195.2, 198.2, 221.7–222.2. According to Petech, on visits around 1480, 1488, and 1500, the yogin met with three successive rulers of Glo bo smon thang; Luciano Petech, "The 'Bri-guṅ-pa sect in Western Tibet and Ladakh," in *Selected Papers on Asian History* (Roma: Istituto Italiano per il Medio ed Estremo Oriente, 1988), 362–3. His attempt to mediate in the fighting is described in Rgod tshang ras pa, 184.4–188.7; Larsson, *Crazy for Wisdom*, 176–7. See also Vitali, *Kingdoms of Gu.ge Pu.hrang*, 532–7; Petech, "'Bri-guṅ-pa sect in Western Tibet and Ladakh," 363.

92. His dealings with Gu ge are mentioned in Rgod tshang ras pa, 198.2, 221.5. His contacts with lords of Tsha 'da' or Tsha mda' are mentioned 52.2, 57.6.

93. Rgod tshang ras pa, 32.1–34.6, 39.1–4, 120.4–121.6. A *bya yul sde pa* is mentioned as one of the patrons for the Swayambhūnāth stūpa, likely referring to a relative of Bkra shis dar rgyas, who died a few years before this project was undertaken, 223.2.

94. Rgod tshang ras pa, 158.2–4, 161.7. In this text, Don yod rdo rje is variously referred to as *sa skyong chos kyi rgyal po*, 213.7; *stobs kyi rgyal po*, 222.7; *chos skyong ba'i rgyal po*, 247.6; *rgyal po don yod rdo rje*, 251.5; *sa skyong mi'i dbang po*, 281.2; and often simply as the *sde pa*. The establishment of the hermitage is discussed in chapter 5.

95. *rgyal pas* [sic] *dbus gtsang thams cad kyi longs spyod zos pas*; Rgod tshang ras pa, 251.4–7; Larsson, *Crazy for Wisdom*, 183.

96. Rgod tshang ras pa, 254.1–256.1, 281.1–2; Kurtis Schaeffer, "Dying Like Milarépa: Death Accounts in a Tibetan Hagiographic Tradition," in *The Buddhist Dead: Practices, Discourses, Representations*, ed. Bryan Cuevas and Jacqueline Stone (Honolulu: University of Hawai'i Press, 2007), 221.

97. The former is at Rgod tshang ras pa, 234.4–235.3. According to the biography, Don yod rdo rje stated that the military action was to be against the *lho pa dgo dgos rgyal* [sic], but it was commonly believed that his real target was to be Rgyal

rtse. The latter instance is at 254.1–256.1, taking *mnga' rigs* to be a misspelling of *mnga' ris*. Larsson, *Crazy for Wisdom*, 182, 184.

98. Dpa' bo gtsug lag phreng ba, *Chos 'byung mkhas pa'i dga' ston*, 2006, 585.6–11; 1986, 1146.15–1147.4; Czaja, *Medieval Rule*, 251.

99. At Rgod tshang ras pa, 288.4–5, it is mentioned that *theg chen sbyin bdag rin dpungs gnyer chen nyid/ chos skyong mgon po* made an offering; this may refer to Ngag dbang rnam rgyal, Don yod rdo rje's cousin. Among the sponsors of the restoration of the Swayambhūnāth stūpa is listed a *rin dpungs blon chen nam mkha' dbang rgyal*, 222.7–223.1.

100. *phebs pa'i rten 'brel ma 'grig*; Rgod tshang ras pa, 258.6–259.1; Larsson, *Crazy for Wisdom*, 29, 185. Gtsang smyon was also once very disrespectful toward a lord of Sne'u rdzong, who represented the Phag mo gru regime in Lha sa; Rgod tshang ras pa, 43.7–46.2.

101. Smyug la paN chen and Lha mthong lo tsA ba, 610.5–611.2, 624.3–5. This latter letter was receieved in 1522, at which time the *gong ma* would have been Ngag dbang bkra shis grags pa.

102. Smith, "Introduction to *The Life of Gtsang smyon Heruka*," in *Among Tibetan Texts*, 60, with phonetic transcriptions inserted in place of Smith's Wylie transliterations of Tibetan proper nouns. Quoted and expanded upon in Quintman, *Yogin and the Madman*, 122.

CHAPTER 5

1. Rgod tshang ras pa, 214.5–7; Larsson, *Crazy for Wisdom*, 179.

2. *rang re dpon slob sngar lugs bzhin phyogs med kyi ri la bzhugs pa legs zhus pa . . . sgrub rgyud kyi bstan pa la mig rkyen bzang po cig 'jog pa*; Smyug la paN chen and Lha mthong lo tsA ba, 586.1–2. I have found no reference to Rtsi dmar dpal outside of this biography, which suggests that it did not remain in operation for long after Kun dga' bzang po's death.

3. The 1973 edition of the first half of the yogin's *rnam thar* is mislabeled as his *mgur 'bum*. I have not found a single composition attributed to him, neither within his biography nor elsewhere.

4. Smyug la paN chen and Lha mthong lo tsA ba, 592.3–4. According to Smith, Smyug la paN chen wrote a biography of Lha btsun pa kun dga' chos kyi rgya mtsho (1432–1505), a guru of 'Brug pa kun legs and Grags pa mtha' yas, titled *Ngo mtshar ut+pa la'i do shal byin brlabs kyi zil mngar 'ba byed*; Jamyang Namgyal [E. Gene Smith], "*Vie et chants de 'Brug-pa Kun-legs le yogin*, a Review," *Kailash* 1, no. 1 (1973): 97. Lo chen 'gyur med bde chen's was the only biography of Thang stong rgyal po carved into woodblocks and published in Tibet, perhaps in the seventeenth century; Stearns, *King of the Empty Plain*, 8–9.

5. Quintman, *Yogin and the Madman*, 156. Scholars who have worked on this material include Everett Goss, Stefan Larsson, Andrew Quintman, Peter Alan

Roberts, Kurtis Schaeffer, Marta Sernesi, E. Gene Smith, Francis Tiso, and others. See the bibliography for works by these scholars.

6. Much of what is presented in the next few paragraphs is drawn from Kurtis Schaeffer, *The Culture of the Book in Tibet* (New York: Columbia University Press, 2009), 54–69; Schaeffer, "The Printing Projects of Gtsang Smyon Heruka and his Disciples," in *Mahāmudrā and the Bka'-brgyud Tradition: Proceedings of the Eleventh Seminar of the International Association for Tibetan Studies, Königswinter 2006*, ed. Roger R. Jackson and Matthew T. Kapstein, 453–79 (Andiast: International Institute for Tibetan and Buddhist Studies, 2011); and Smith, "Introduction to *The Life of Gtsang smyon Heruka*," in *Among Tibetan Texts*. On the *Sangs rgyas dar po chos 'byung*, see Roberts, *Biographies of Rechungpa*, 47–9; Dan Martin, *Tibetan Histories: A Bibliography of Tibetan-Language Historical Works* (London: Serindia, 1997), 88.

7. Gtsang smyon seems not to have prioritized the *Life of Marpa*, as it is said to have been carved into woodblocks and printed with resources he had leftover from some other project; Rgod tshang ras pa, 235.5; Larsson, *Crazy for Wisdom*, 242–3; Marta Sernesi, "A Continuous Stream of Merit: The Early Reprints of gTsang smyon Heruka's Hagiographical Works," *Zentral-Asiatische Studien* 40 (2011): 181, 187.

   Gtsang smyon also wrote some short texts about songs, which I have not had access to. See Larsson, *Crazy for Wisdom*, 42–4. Larsson discusses the full range of Gtsang smyon's writings, 229–53.

8. Dngos grub dpal 'bar, 23b7. There is a similar passage in Rgod tshang ras pa's version of the *Life*, 246.5–7; Larsson, *Crazy for Wisdom*, 183.

9. The text is referred to as a *bstod pa*. Rgod tshang ras pa, 72.6–73.2; Quintman, *Yogin and the Madman*, 125–6; Schaeffer, "Printing Projects," 455. A three-folio text written by Gtsang smyon he ru ka, titled *Rje btsun gzhad* [sic] *pa rdo rje la gsol ba 'debs pa byin rlabs kyi gter mdzod*, NGMPP L803/5, does not seem to be the text of his original *bstod pa*.

10. Lha btsun rin chen rnam rgyal, 96.3–97.6; translated in Quintman, *Yogin and the Madman*, 126–7; Schaeffer, *Culture of the Book*, 54–5; Schaeffer, "Printing Projects," 454–5. Schaeffer points out that, according to his own biography, Lha btsun rin chen rnam rgyal would have a similar vision of a woman who commanded him to compile and print a new anthology of Mi la ras pa's songs that had not been included in Gtsang smyon's version.

11. *Yogin and the Madman*, 128–9; Rgod tshang ras pa, 137.7–138.7. The first and final brackets are mine. For an alternate translation, see Schaeffer, *Culture of the Book*, 56–7, and "Printing Projects," 455–6. This passage in Rgod tshang ras pa's version of the *Life* is closely based on one in Dngos grub dpal 'bar's earlier version, 16a3–16b2. There is also a passage in Lha btsun rin chen rnam rgyal's version of the *Life*, 97.6–98.3, based on that in Dngos grub dpal 'bar's.

12. Schaeffer, *Culture of the Book*, 55.

13. These two passages are in Quintman's translation, Tsangnyön Heruka, *Life of Milarepa*, 225, 227; their being drawn from the earlier text is established based on Quintman, *Yogin and the Madman*, 99, 101, 103.

14. Quintman, *Yogin and the Madman*, 135–6.

15. Quintman, *Yogin and the Madman*, 46, 99, 137, 140–41. It is worth noting that when the first biography of Gtsang smyon was written shortly after his death, Dngos grub dpal 'bar and others involved in the project decided to separate the biography and the yogin's songs into two separate texts. But in the latter two biographies, by Rgod tshang ras pa and Lha btsun rin chen rnam rgyal, his songs were once again incorporated into the narrative of his life. It seems that Gtsang smyon's innovation of a *Life* and a supporting *Collected Songs* did not fully catch on. See DiValerio, "Reanimating the Great Yogin," 35.

16. Quintman, *Yogin and the Madman*, 55, 137–8.

17. Quintman, *Yogin and the Madman*, 49, 69; Tsangnyön Heruka, *Life of Milarepa*, 87.

18. Roberts, *Biographies of Rechungpa*, 199. As Roberts describes, Gtsang smyon would make significant changes to the ways the relationships between Mi la ras pa and his disciples Sgam po pa and Ras chung pa are portrayed. For example, in earlier accounts Mi la ras pa gave his famous bare-butt teaching to Ras chung pa; in Gtsang smyon's version, he gives it to Sgam po pa, 216–20. Some later Tibetan authors would disagree with aspects of Gtsang smyon's version of history; Decleer, "The Melodious Drumsound All-Pervading: Sacred Biography of Rwa Lotsāwa: About Early Lotsāwa *rnam thar* and *chos 'byung*," in *Proceedings of the 5th Seminar of the International Association for Tibetan Studies, Narita 1989*, vol. 1, ed. Ihara Shōren and Yamaguchi Zuihō (Narita: Naritasan Shinshoji, 1992), 21, 23–7.

19. Donald Lopez, introduction to Quintman's translation, Tsangnyön Heruka, *Life of Milarepa*, x; Quintman, translator's introduction, xxvii; Quintman, *Yogin and the Madman*, 137–8, 169–72.

20. Quintman, *Yogin and the Madman*, 112, 122–3, 142–3, 148–9, 181; Roberts, *Biographies of Rechungpa*, 78–80.

21. Translation from Tsangnyön Heruka, *Life of Milarepa*, 166–7; Gtsang smyon he ru ka, *Mi la ras pa'i rnam mgur*, 180.13–182.12.

22. Translation from Tsangnyön Heruka, *Life of Milarepa*, 128–9; Gtsang smyon he ru ka, *Mi la ras pa'i rnam mgur*, 140.9–142.8.

23. A biography of Ba ri lo tsA ba is given in the *Blue Annals*, Roerich, 1021–3; 'Gos lo tsA ba, *Deb ther sngon po*, 2:1189.4–1191.12.

24. Translation from Tsangnyön Heruka, *Life of Milarepa*, 156; Gtsang smyon he ru ka, *Mi la ras pa'i rnam mgur*, 171.2–4. *Life of Milarepa*, 157–9; *Mi la ras pa'i rnam mgur*, 171.15–173.13. In their inability to see the need for Mi la ras pa's extreme asceticism, Pe ta and Mdzes se represent what ordinary people might well think. The text expresses a bitterness over this state of affairs, as in a song Mi la ras pa

laments, "In the four regions of Ü and Tsang / Pedant's dharma is prized, the meditator's, ignored"; *Life of Milarepa*, 154; *Mi la ras pa'i rnam mgur*, 168.9.

25. Quintman, *Yogin and the Madman*, 75, 101; Frances Tiso, "The Death of Milarepa: Towards a Redaktionsgeschichte of the Mila rnam thar Traditions," in *Tibetan Studies: Proceedings of the 7th Seminar of the International Association for Tibetan Studies, Graz 1995*, ed. Helmut Krasser, Michael Torsten Much, Ernst Steinkellner, and Helmut Tauscher (Vienna: Oesterreichischen Akademie der Wissenschaften, 1997), 2:994–5.

26. Translation from Tsangnyön Heruka, *Life of Milarepa*, 179; Gtsang smyon he ru ka, *Mi la ras pa'i rnam mgur*, 790.7–16.

27. Translation from Tsangnyön Heruka, *Life of Milarepa*, 180; Gtsang smyon he ru ka, *Mi la ras pa'i rnam mgur*, 790.17–791.3.

28. Tsangnyön Heruka, *Life of Milarepa*, 191; Gtsang smyon he ru ka, *Mi la ras pa'i rnam mgur*, 804.19–805.2.

29. Translation from Tsangnyön Heruka, *Life of Milarepa*, 199; Gtsang smyon he ru ka, *Mi la ras pa'i rnam mgur*, 813.15–17. Rgod tshang ras pa, 25.6; Larsson, *Crazy for Wisdom*, 95.

30. Wylie, "Reincarnation: A Political Innovation in Tibetan Buddhism," in *Proceedings of the Csoma de Kőrös Memorial Symposium, held at Mátrafüred, Hungary, September 24–30, 1976*, ed. Louis Ligeti, 579–86 (Budapest: Akadémiai Kiadó, 1978); E. Gene Smith, "Padma dkar po and His History of Buddhism," in *Among Tibetan Texts*, 81.

31. Schaeffer, *Culture of the Book*, 59; Schaeffer, "Printing Projects," 457. On the broader printing culture of the time, see Franz-Karl Ehrhard, *Early Buddhist Block Prints from Mang-yul Gung-thang* (Lumbini: Lumbini International Research Institute, 2000).

32. Schaeffer, *Culture of the Book*, 62.

33. Rgod tshang ras pa, 139.6–7; Quintman, *Yogin and the Madman*, 130.

34. Rgod tshang ras pa, 148.1–5; Quintman, *Yogin and the Madman*, 130–31.

35. Rgod tshang ras pa, 147.6–7. Quintman, *Yogin and the Madman*, 132–3, 129.

36. Quintman, *Yogin and the Madman*, 131; Schaeffer, "Printing Projects," 464–6, 470; Sernesi, "Continuous Stream of Merit," 188. At least one additional set of blocks for the *Life of Marpa* would be carved.

37. Quintman, *Yogin and the Madman*, 27, 83, 87, 89, 119–20.

38. This story is of much earlier provenance, since a similar version of the tale was included in the version of the *Life* of Mi la ras pa penned by Bla ma zhang in the twelfth century; Quintman, *Yogin and the Madman*, 65–6.

39. This story was told to me on numerous occasions during my conversations with Tibetans about the holy madman phenomenon.

40. Rgod tshang ras pa, 244.6.

41. Andrew Quintman brought this to my attention in a personal communication, November 2006. For an example of a twentieth-century Tibetan quoting

this line in response to the chaos he observed during the Cultural Revolution, see Melvyn C. Goldstein, Dawei Sherap, and William R. Siebenschuh, *A Tibetan Revolutionary: The Political Life and Times of Bapa Phüntso Wangye* (Berkeley: University of California Press, 2004), 254.

42. Lha btsun rin chen rnam rgyal, 47.6–48.1; Larsson, *Crazy for Wisdom*, 157–8; Stearns, *King of the Empty Plain*, 74.

43. *smyon pa'i spyod pa 'dra ba.* The episode begins in Gtsang smyon he ru ka, *Mi la ras pa'i rnam mgur*, 729.11; the song begins at 734.4. In Garma C. C. Chang, *The Hundred Thousand Songs of Milarepa*, by Tsangnyön Heruka, 2 vols. (Boston, MA: Shambhala, 1977), this episode is titled "The Meeting with Dhampa Sangje," 606–614. On this song see Robert Everett Goss, "The Hermeneutics of Madness: A Literary and Hermeneutical Analysis of the 'Mi-la'i-rnam-thar' by Gtsang-smyon Heruka" (ThD diss., Harvard University, 1993), 67–9.

44. *yul mi rnams kyis 'jig rten thams cad dang mi mthun pa'i smyon pa zhig tu mthong;* Ngag dbang mkhas grub, *Rje btsun mi la bzhad pa'i rdo rje'i gsung mgur smyo ma'i 'grel pa myo ba sangs byed,* in *The Collected Works of Nag-dban-mkhas-grub, Kyai-rdor Mkhan-po of Urga* (Leh: Smanrtsis shesrig spendzod, 1972–1974), 2:79.4.

45. *mig 'phrul mkhan gyi sgyu 'am smyo spyod du mthong ba;* Ngag dbang mkhas grub, *Rje btsun mi la bzhad pa'i rdo rje'i gsung mgur smyo ma'i 'grel pa myo ba sangs byed,* 82.3–85.4. For an example of the role this song has played in shaping conceptions of "holy madness," see the opening of Larsson, *Crazy for Wisdom.*

46. *spyod lam bltas na smyon pa 'dra;* Gtsang smyon he ru ka, *Mi la ras pa'i rnam mgur,* 156.16; Tsangnyön Heruka, *Life of Milarepa,* 143. *ci yang mi shes pa'i smyon spyod dang tho co;* Mi la ras pa'i rnam mgur, 790.17–18; *Life of Milarepa,* 180.

47. Rgyal thang pa's text is described in Quintman, *Yogin and the Madman,* 72–5, and elsewhere. The passage in which the onlooker calls the yogin a madman is translated by Goss, "Hermeneutics of Madness," 69. Gtsang smyon he ru ka, *Mi la ras pa'i rnam mgur,* 162.16–163.6; Tsangnyön Heruka, *Life of Milarepa,* 149.

48. Gtsang smyon he ru ka, *Mi la ras pa'i rnam mgur,* 8.5–6; Tsangnyön Heruka, *Life of Milarepa,* 11; Quintman, *Yogin and the Madman,* 272. Mi la ras pa'i rnam mgur, 79.19–80.8; *Life of Milarepa,* 69.

49. Tsangnyön Heruka, *Life of Milarepa,* 108, 212–13, 11.

50. Rgod tshang ras pa, 4.5, 148.5–149.3; Quintman, *Yogin and the Madman,* 164.

51. *snyigs dus mi la ras pa dang dngos su 'jal;* Dngos grub dpal 'bar, 26b3; Larsson, *Crazy for Wisdom,* 187; Quintman, *Yogin and the Madman,* 166. Rgod tshang ras pa, 152.7–153.2; Larsson, 58–9; Quintman, 163–5.

52. Quintman, *Yogin and the Madman,* chap. 5: "The Yogin and the Madman: A Life Brought to Life."

53. See Larsson, *Crazy for Wisdom,* 76, 121; Quintman, *Yogin and the Madman,* 124, 161.

54. Tsangnyön Heruka, *Life of Milarepa*, 220; Gtsang smyon he ru ka, *Mi la ras pa'i rnam mgur*, 834.8–9.

55. Ehrhard, "Editing and Publishing," 154; Larsson, *Crazy for Wisdom*, 42; Quintman, *Yogin and the Madman*, 155.

56. Rgod tshang ras pa, 245.6. On the terminology of *snyan brgyud* and *snyan rgyud*, and this body of literature in general, see Larsson, *Crazy for Wisdom*, 83–9, 243–50; Quintman, *Yogin and the Madman*, 40–42, 235; Roberts, *Biographies of Rechungpa*, 1–2; Marta Sernesi, "Milarepa's Six Secret Songs: The Early Transmission of the *bDe mchog snyan brgyud*," *East and West* 54, nos. 1–4 (2004), 251–87; Sernesi, "The Aural Transmission of Saṃvara: An Introduction to Neglected Sources for the Study of the Early Bka' Brgyud," in *Mahāmudrā and the Bka'-brgyud Tradition: Proceedings of the Eleventh Seminar of the International Association for Tibetan Studies, Königswinter 2006*, ed. Roger R. Jackson and Matthew T. Kapstein, 179–209 (Andiast: International Institute for Tibetan and Buddhist Studies, 2011); Fabrizio Torricelli, "Padma dkar po's Arrangement of the *bDe mchog snyan brgyud*," *East and West* 50, nos. 1–4 (2000): 359–86.

57. *Bde mchog mkha' 'gro snyan rgyud kyi gzhung 'brel sa gcad dang shrags pa*, in Gtsang smyon he ru ka, *Bde mchog mkha' 'gro snyan rgyud*, 1:5–360, here citing 354.3–6. *snyan rgyud yi ger bkod pa*; Rgod tshang ras pa, 208.4.

58. Rgod tshang ras pa, 24.7–25.3.

59. Dngos grub dpal 'bar, 17a3–7; Larsson, *Crazy for Wisdom*, 246.

60. Beyond the two incomplete collections printed in 1971 as the *Bde mchog mkha' 'gro snyan rgyud*, a third is described by Sernesi, "Aural Transmission of Saṃvara," 197–8. A *dkar chag* for Gtsang smyon's *yig cha* is still extant. Many of the texts mentioned in the *dkar chag* are included in either of the two partial collections, and in separate manuscripts preserved by the NGMPP. Some scholars with knowledge of these materials have suspected that some Aural Transmission texts may have been printed around the time of Gtsang smyon, but no hard evidence of this has been found.

    Zhang lo tsA ba (died in 1237) (not to be confused with Bla ma zhang) had also compiled a collection of Aural Transmission teachings, as would the third and fourth hierarchs of the 'Brug pa Bka' brgyud, 'Jam dbyangs chos kyi grags pa (the son of Bkra shis dar rgyas of Bya), and Pad+ma dkar po; Roberts, *Biographies of Rechungpa*, 50, 53; Sernesi, "Aural Transmission of Saṃvara," 184–90; Sernesi, "Milarepa's Six Secret Songs," 252; Fabrizio Torricelli, "Zhang Lo tsā ba's Introduction to the Aural Transmission of Śaṃvara," in *Le Parole e i Marmi: Studi in Onore di Raniero Gnoli nel suo 70. Compleanno*, ed. Raffaele Torella, 2:875–96 (Rome: Istituto Italiano per l'Africa e l'Oriente, 2001).

61. On this text, see Fabrizio Torricelli, "The Tibetan text of the *Karṇatantravajrapada*," *East and West* 48, nos. 3–4 (1998): 385–6; and Glenn H. Mullin, *The Practice of the Six Yogas of Naropa* (Ithaca, NY: Snow Lion, 1997), 35–41. The commentary is known by various names, including the *Bde mchog mkha' 'gro snyan rgyud*

kyi gzhung 'brel sa gcad dang sbrags pa, as in Gtsang smyon he ru ka, *Bde mchog mkha' 'gro snyan rgyud*, 1:5–360. The text was completed in a *kun dga'* year, which likely refers to 1494. Discussed in Roberts, *Biographies of Rechungpa*, 36–7.

62. This last issue is discussed in *Bde mchog mkha' 'gro snyan rgyud kyi nang longs spyod rdzogs pa sku'i gdams pa smin lam yid bzhin nor bu*, in Gtsang smyon he ru ka, *Bde mchog mkha' 'gro snyan rgyud*, 1:367–457, here citing, 431.1–455.2.

63. *Snyan rgyud 'khrul 'khor gsal ba'i me long*, in Gtsang smyon he ru ka, *Bde mchog mkha' 'gro snyan rgyud*, 1:681–7, here citing 687.4–5.

64. *nor phyir gdams ngag tshong ba rnams la mi gter phyir. . . bka' rgya dam po yod*; Gtsang smyon he ru ka, *Rgya gar gsang spyod kyi don bsdus rtsa ba*, NGMPP L513/1, 10b4.

65. Mar pa chos kyi blo gros, trans., *Snyan rgyud rdo rje'i tshig rkang*, in Gtsang smyon he ru ka, *Bde mchog mkha' 'gro snyan rgyud*, 2:1–6, here citing 6.5–6; Mullin, *Practice of the Six Yogas of Naropa*, 41; Sernesi, "Milarepa's Six Secret Songs," 255. Gtsang smyon he ru ka, *Mi la ras pa'i rnam mgur*, 117.19–119.6; Tsangnyön Heruka, *Life of Milarepa*, 105–6.

66. See Tsangnyön Heruka, *Life of Milarepa*, 116, 230. This is also told in *Bde mchog mkha' 'gro snyan rgyud kyi gzhung 'brel sa gcad dang sbrags pa*, in Gtsang smyon he ru ka, *Bde mchog mkha' 'gro snyan rgyud*, 1:5–360, here citing 10.6–12.2, 355.5–356.3. See also Sernesi, "Milarepa's Six Secret Songs," 259.

67. For Gtsang smyon's presentation of the central lineage, passing through Rechungpa, see *Bde mchog mkha' 'gro snyan rgyud kyi gzhung 'brel sa gcad dang sbrags pa*, in Gtsang smyon he ru ka, *Bde mchog mkha' 'gro snyan rgyud*, 1:5–360, 10.6–12.2; and in longer form, 22.2–113.7. These presentations are discussed in detail by Larsson, *Crazy for Wisdom*, 85–9.

68. Gtsang smyon he ru ka, *Mi la ras pa'i rnam mgur*, 680.6–11; Chang, *Hundred Thousand Songs of Milarepa*, 2:549. Chang mistakenly takes *rdo rje rnal 'byor ma* as "Vajra Ḍākinī." Rgod tshang ras pa, 159.2–7. On Ngan dzong pa's work to systematize some of the Aural Transmission teachings, see Quintman, *Yogin and the Madman*, 40–42.

69. Rgod tshang ras pa, 7.2–8.1.

70. Rgod tshang ras pa, 115.6–116.4; Sernesi, "Aural Transmission of Saṃvara," 193–4. Gtsang smyon did eventually write some texts on the *Hevajra Tantra*; Rgod tshang ras pa, 51.3, 127.6, 135.4, 207.3; Larsson, *Crazy for Wisdom*, 250–51.

71. Rgod tshang ras pa, 38.2–4; Larsson, *Crazy for Wisdom*, 135–6. The deity told Gtsang smyon that people would soon arrive to offer texts explicating ritual practices in which he figures, which began the next day. This suggests that Gtsang smyon may have been actively collecting sources connected to the Aural Transmission even at this early phase of his life, as various texts pertaining to Mahākāla are included among Gtsang smyon's *yig cha* of the Aural Transmission. According to Rgod tshang ras pa, when Sangs rgyas rgyal mtshan was one year old, his mother had a dream in which she was visited by a black man with his

hair in a topknot, wearing ornaments made of bone, who imparted (to her?) instructions on the *Ḍākiṇī*-Saṃvara Aural Transmission and other unspecified Bka' brgyud teachings; 15.7–16.2; Larsson, 69.

72. Rgod tshang ras pa, 49.2–4, 173.7–174.2, 175.5–6; Larsson, *Crazy for Wisdom*, 155, 175. On this statue see Dowman, *A Buddhist Guide to the Power Places of the Kathmandu Valley* (Thamel: Himalayan Buddhist Meditation Centre, 2007), 42–4. Gtsang smyon's worshipping this statue is mentioned in a Newari-language source, as described in Alexander von Rospatt, "The Past Renovations of the Svayambhūcaitya," in *Light of the Valley: Renewing the Sacred Art and Traditions of Svayambhu*, ed. Tsering Palmo Gellek and Padma Dorje Maitland (Cazadero, CA: Dharma, 2011), 174.

The statue is referred to in Tibetan as *bod thang mgon po*, as it sits on the "Tibetan field," so called because it was where the ministers of the Tibetan king Srong btsan sgam po purportedly waited for the king of Nepal to hand over his daughter Bhṛkuti for marriage. To this day the impressive statue remains the subject of vibrant cultic activity.

73. *'Pho ba zab mo*, in *Bde mchog mkha' 'gro snyan rgyud*, 1:703–7, here citing 705.5–706.2, 707.4. In *Snyan rgyud gsal ba'i zhal gdams*, Gtsang smyon defends his setting this text to paper by saying that he did so only for the sake of his disciples, and at their request; in *Bde mchog mkha' 'gro snyan rgyud*, 1:697–701, here citing 698.2, 701.2. He also states that he confessed (*mtholo* [*sic*] *bshags*) to the lineage lamas and to the *ḍākiṇīs* for setting this text to paper, perhaps preemptively mitigating whatever punishment that would otherwise have come to him for doing so; 701.3. For similar comments, see *Dbang gsum pa'i nyams len mkha' 'gro'i gsang lam*, in *Bde mchog mkha' 'gro snyan rgyud*, 2:759–74, here citing 774.1–3. This last text was likely composed by Gtsang smyon, although it is not explicitly identified as such.

74. Rgod tshang ras pa, 245.1–246.7; Larsson, *Crazy for Wisdom*, 182–3; Sernesi, "Aural Transmission of Saṃvara," 196.

75. *mkha' 'gro'i gsang tshig yi ger med pa snyan rgyud gyi gdams ngag rnams gsal bar yi ger bkod pa las/ ma sring mkha' 'gro'i tshogs kyi bzod par mdzod*; Gtsang smyon he ru ka, *Chos drug gi 'khrid yig gsal ba'i sgron me*, NGMPP L560/6, 14b3.

76. Quintman, *Yogin and the Madman*, 34; Roerich, *Blue Annals*, 427–36; 'Gos lo tsA ba, *Deb ther sngon po*, 1:511.12–522.14.

77. *Bde mchog mkha' 'gro snyan rgyud kyi gzhung 'brel sa gcad dang sbrags pa*, in Gtsang smyon he ru ka, *Bde mchog mkha' 'gro snyan rgyud*, 1:5–360, here citing 31.1–39.3; *Phyag rgya chen po bsam gyis mi khyab pa*, in Gtsang smyon he ru ka, *Bde mchog mkha' 'gro snyan rgyud*, 2:51–68.

78. Dngos grub dpal 'bar, 17a7. Sernesi has arrived at similar conclusions, "Aural Transmission of Saṃvara," 181, 195, 201–3.

79. Rgod tshang ras pa, 210.1–214.2, 235.4; Quintman, *Yogin and the Madman*, 151, 268–9. On the struggle between Bka' brgyud groups for control of these sites,

and Gtsang smyon's activities in the area, see Huber, "A Guide to the La-Phyi Maṇḍala: History, Landscape and Ritual in South-Western Tibet," in *Maṇḍala and Landscape*, ed. A. W. Macdonald, 233–86. Emerging Perceptions in Buddhist Studies, no. 6. (Delhi: D. K. Printworld, 1997).

80. Rgod tshang ras pa, 178.7–180.4, 183.1–4; Vitali, *Kingdoms of Gu.ge Pu.hrang*, 399–400.

81. Von Rospatt, "Past Renovations," 170–71.

82. Von Rospatt, "Past Renovations," 161–2. Will Tuladhar-Douglas cites scholarship suggesting that Swayambhūnāth was a holy site from perhaps as early as 400 CE; *Remaking Buddhism for Medieval Nepal: The Fifteenth-Century Reformation of Newar Buddhism* (New York: Routledge, 2006), 139.

83. Alexander von Rospatt, "On the Conception of the Stūpa in Vajrayāna Buddhism: The Example of the Svayambhūcaitya of Kathmandu," *Journal of the Nepal Research Centre* 11 (1999): 130–32; Dowman, *Buddhist Guide to the Power Places of the Kathmandu Valley*, 17–21, 29; Hem Raj Shakya, *Śrī Svayambhū Mahācaitya*, trans. Min Bahadur Shakya (Kathmandu: Svayambhu Vikash Mandal, 2004).

84. Von Rospatt, "Past Renovations," 158. This number does not include the many occasions on which only more superficial repairs, like those under Gtsang smyon, were carried out.

85. Information on Śāriputra is derived from Arthur McKeown, "From Bodhgayā to Lhasa to Beijing: The Life and Times of Śāriputra (c. 1335–1426), Last Abbot of Bodhgayā" (PhD diss., Harvard University, 2010); von Rospatt, "Past Renovations," 169–71.

86. Rgod tshang ras pa, 49.4–50.3; 172.2, 176.3. On the yogin's second visit, see Todd Lewis and Lozang Jamspal, "Newars and Tibetans in the Kathmandu Valley: Three New Translations from Tibetan Sources," *Journal of Asian and African Studies* 36 (1988): 187–211. One night in 1680 an actual madman climbed atop the stūpa, fell, and died; Shakya, *Śrī Svayambhū Mahācaitya*, 203.

87. The section on the renovation of the stūpa runs 208.4–229.5 in Rgod tshang ras pa. See von Rospatt, "Past Renovations," 171–4; Stefan Larsson, "Tsangnyön Heruka's Sixteenth-Century Renovation of the Svayambhū Stūpa," in *Light of the Valley: Renewing the Sacred Art and Traditions of Svayambhu*, ed. Tsering Palmo Gellek and Padma Dorje Maitland, 208–230 (Cazadero, CA: Dharma, 2011); Larsson, *Crazy for Wisdom*, 178–80; Schaeffer, *Culture of the Book*, 65–7. Dngos grub dpal 'bar, Lha btsun rin chen rnam rgyal, and Rgod tshang ras pa's respective versions of the *Life* all have very similar passages describing the renovation. See DiValerio, "Reanimating the Great Yogin," 27, 45.

88. Tuladhar-Douglas, *Remaking Buddhism for Medieval Nepal*, 106–7, 153.

89. Rgod tshang ras pa, 216.5–7. Von Rospatt suspects that these numbers are exaggerated, "Past Renovations," 172–3. Schaeffer gives an alternative accounting, drawn from Lha btsun rin chen rnam rgyal's version of the *Life*; *Culture of the Book*, 66.

90. Schaeffer, *Culture of the Book*, 65; von Rospatt, "Past Renovations," 173.

91. Rgod tshang ras pa, 217.3–7.

92. Rgod tshang ras pa, 218.1–6; Schaeffer, *Culture of the Book*, 66. Viśvakarman was also associated with the carving of woodblocks; Schaeffer, 62, 65.

93. *grub thob min na su yin*; Dngos grub dpal 'bar, 23a1–2; Larsson, *Crazy for Wisdom*, 180.

94. Shakya, *Śrī Svayambhū Mahācaitya*, 538–42.

95. Rgod tshang ras pa, 226.4–7.

96. Rgod tshang ras pa, 220.6–226.3.

97. Rgod tshang ras pa, 235.4–5, 246.6.

98. Von Rospatt, "Past Renovations," 174–5; Larsson, *Crazy for Wisdom*, 268.

CHAPTER 6

1. 'Brug pa kun legs, *'Brug pa kun legs kyi rnam thar*, 49.16–50.1; Stein, *Vie et chants*, 101–2.

2. Although 'Brug pa kun legs spent time in areas that are today within the borders of Bhutan, he does not seem to have had a special association with the place during his lifetime. He was, however, closely connected with the 'Brug pa Bka' brgyud through his family. In fact, the Tibetan name for Bhutan, 'Brug yul, did not gain currency until the seventeenth century, after the 'Brug pa sect had become prominent there under Zhabs drung Ngag dbang rnam rgyal (1594–1651), bringing a mythology of 'Brug pa kun legs along with them. See Karma Phuntso, *The History of Bhutan* (Noida, Uttar Pradesh: Random House India, 2013), 147–50.

3. Stein, *Tibetan Civilization*, 154; Dowman, *Divine Madman*, 28.

4. Both of these stories were told to me by Tibetans born in Tibet but living in India in 2009. The first is in Dowman, *Divine Madman*, 87–9; Tshe dbang bstan 'dzin, *'Gro ba'i mgon po kun dga' legs pa'i rnam thar mon spa gro sogs kyi mdzad spyod rnams* (Dharamsala: Tibetan Cultural Printing Press, 1981), 7.7–13.12. The second is in Dowman, 134–6; Tshe dbang bstan 'dzin, 44.7–50.9. On the circulation of stories about 'Brug pa kun legs among Tibetans, see Kun mchog dge legs, Dpal ldan bkra shis, and Kevin Stuart, "Tibetan Tricksters," *Asian Folklore Studies* 58, no. 1 (1999): 5–30; and Michiyo Hoshi, ed., *Texts of Tibetan Folktales*, vol. 5, *Studia Tibetica*, 10 (Tokyo: Toyo Bunko, 1985): 149–204.

5. Editions of the text printed under the first and third titles are described in the bibliography, as the work of Tshe dbang bstan 'dzin. A handwritten manuscript with the title *Chos rje 'brug pa kun legs kyi rnam par thar pa rgyas pa'i lho'i bskor* was used by Andreas Kretschmar in his study, *'Brug pa kun legs: Das wundersame Leben eines verrückten Heiligen* (Sankt Augustin: VGH Wissenschaftsverlag, 1981).

6. Tshe dbang bstan 'dzin, *Mon spa gro sogs kyi mdzad spyod rnams*, 4.1–3. John Ardussi, "'Brug-pa Kun-legs, The Saintly Tibetan Madman" (MA thesis,

University of Washington, 1972), 204; Stein, *Vie et chants*, 17; Jamyang Namgyal, "*Vie et chants*, a Review," 94–5.

7. German, trans. Franz-Karl Ehrhard, *Der Heilige Narr* (Frankfurt am Main: Barth, 1983, 2005); Spanish, *La Divina Locura Drukpa Künléy* (Madrid: Miraguano, 1988, 2001); French, *Le Fou Divin* (Paris: Albin Michel, 1984, 2012); Romanian, trans. Octavian Creț, *Nebunul Divin* (Bucharest: Firul Ariadnei, 2006).

8. For details on how sections of the 1981 Dharamsala edition of Tshe dbang bstan 'dzin's *Mon spa gro sogs kyi mdzad spyod rnams* correspond to specific pages in Dowman's translation, see DiValerio, "Subversive Sainthood," 404.

9. Dowman, *Divine Madman*, 158–9, 94–5, 169–70, 157–8, 164, 134–6, 141–3.

10. See comments by Choegyal Gyamtso Tulku and Keith Dowman in *Divine Madman*, 21, 31. Michael Aris addresses this view in "'The Boneless Tongue': Alternative Voices from Bhutan in the Context of Lamaist Societies," *Past and Present* 115 (1987): 145.

11. Dowman, *Divine Madman*, 37–8, 173.

12. Dowman, *Divine Madman*, 69–70, 77–81. Neither tale is included in the *Southern Cycle*.

13. Dowman, *Divine Madman*, 89.

14. Dowman, *Divine Madman*, 83, 103–4, 154–6, 39–41, 120–21.

15. Dowman, *Divine Madman*, 107. On Ngag dbang chos rgyal, see Jamyang Namgyal, "*Vie et chants*, a Review," 95; Stein, *Vie et chants*, 14, 17.

16. Dowman, *Divine Madman*, 63–4, 64–70.

17. *a kha kha/ skyug bro ba la/ 'brug pa kun legs smyon pa rang du dug*; Tshe dbang bstan 'dzin, *Mon spa gro sogs kyi mdzad spyod rnams*, 17.7–9; Dowman, *Divine Madman*, 90–92, 135.

18. Full titles for the four volumes are given in the bibliography under the work of 'Brug pa kun legs. Smith has referred to the contents of the first volume as 'Brug pa kun legs's "autobiographical reminiscences"; Jamyang Namgyal, "*Vie et chants*, a Review," 91.

19. Stein has suggested that Mon ban smyon pa is an alias of one Sde pa grub thob rin po che; *Vie et chants*, 25–6.

20. Ardussi, "'Brug-pa Kun-legs," 76. This thesis includes a partial translation of the second volume of the collection. The colophon to the first volume runs 268.21–271.18 in 'Brug pa kun legs, *'Brug pa kun legs kyi rnam thar*; Stein, *Vie et chants*, 418–22. The colophon to the second volume runs 399.4–16.

21. 'Brug pa kun legs, *'Brug pa kun legs kyi rnam thar*, 49.7–50.3; Stein, *Vie et chants*, 101–2. See also 'Brug pa kun legs, 36.6–18; Stein, 83–4. Stein discusses these passages, 25.

22. The date mentioned in the *gsol 'debs* is often taken as referring to 1529, which many have taken as indicating that this was the year of 'Brug pa kun legs's death. On these issues, see Ardussi, "'Brug-pa Kun-legs," 72–5; Stein, *Vie et chants*,

24–7; Jamyang Namgyal, "*Vie et chants*, a Review," 95, 98; DiValerio, "Subversive Sainthood," 414–21.

23. 'Brug pa kun legs, *'Brug pa kun legs kyi rnam thar*, 157.12–158.16; Stein, *Vie et chants*, 255–6.

24. 'Brug pa kun legs, *'Brug pa kun legs kyi rnam thar*, 50.12–51.12; Stein, *Vie et chants*, 102–3. 'Brug pa kun legs, 161.18–162.12; Stein, 262–3. 'Brug pa kun legs, 251.13–253.20; Stein, 395–9. 'Brug pa kun legs, 415.10–416.21; 423.11–16; 440.7–441.6; and starting at 456.7. Karma 'phrin las pa was also involved in this conversation, as he composed a document with answers to a set of twenty-six philosophical questions Smyug la paN chen had posed to 'Brug pa kun legs, in *The Songs of Esoteric Practice (mgur) and Replies to Doctrinal Questions (dris lan) of karma-'phrin-las-pa*, 198.1–210.1. Ehrhard discusses this correspondence in "Holy Madman of dBus," 240–41.

25. References are provided later in the chapter, when expanding on the relationship between 'Brug pa kun legs and Dbus smyon.

26. For information on some of the passages Dge bshes brag phug drew from the *Miscellaneous Writings*, and on the relationship between the *Miscellaneous Writings* and the *Southern Cycle*, see DiValerio, "Subversive Sainthood," 429–30.

27. 'Brug pa kun legs, *'Brug pa kun legs kyi rnam thar*, beginning at 3.14; Stein, *Vie et chants*, 42. Summarized in Stein, 14, and Ehrhard, "Holy Madman of dBus," 233. The detail that 'Brug pa kun legs was thirteen when his father was killed is supplied from a retelling of these events later in the first volume; 'Brug pa kun legs, 199.19; Stein, 317.

28. 'Brug pa kun legs, *'Brug pa kun legs kyi rnam thar*, 130.4–131.4, Stein, *Vie et chants*, 218–19.

29. 'Brug pa kun legs, *'Brug pa kun legs kyi rnam thar*, 184.15–17; Stein, *Vie et chants*, 295.

30. 'Brug pa kun legs, *'Brug pa kun legs kyi rnam thar*, 266.12–21; Stein, *Vie et chants*, 416.

31. 'Brug pa kun legs, *'Brug pa kun legs kyi rnam thar*, 5.12–17; Stein, *Vie et chants*, 44.

32. Tse dbang 'dzoms is mentioned in 'Brug pa kun legs, *'Brug pa kun legs kyi rnam thar*, 121.10. On the life of Bstan 'dzin rab rgyas, see John Ardussi, "Gyalse Tenzin Rabgye (1638–1696), Artist Ruler of 17th-century Bhutan," in *The Dragon's Gift: The Sacred Arts of Bhutan*, ed. Terese Tse Bartholomew and John Johnston, 88–99 (Chicago: Serindia, 2008). On these issues see Jamyang Namgyal, "*Vie et chants*, a Review," 95; Stein, *Vie et chants*, 14–17; Ardussi, "'Brug-pa Kun-legs," 6–7; Karma Phuntso, *History of Bhutan*, 149.

In one composition, 'Brug pa kun legs refers to *phru gu 'di rnams* as distracting him from his religious practice, which may suggest that he did have more than one child; 'Brug pa kun legs, 144.8, Stein, 236.

33. 'Brug pa kun legs, *'Brug pa kun legs kyi rnam thar*, 75.21–77.21; Stein, *Vie et chants*, 139–41. 'Brug pa kun legs, 101.9–102.4; Stein, 175. 'Brug pa kun legs, 120.15–121.9; Stein, 205–6. 'Brug pa kun legs, 220.18–222.3; Stein, 349–50.

34. 'Brug pa kun legs, *'Brug pa kun legs kyi rnam thar*, 96.14–22; Stein, *Vie et chants*, 168–9. 'Brug pa kun legs, 81.12; Stein, 145.

35. 'Brug pa kun legs, *'Brug pa kun legs kyi rnam thar*, 62.22–64.10; Stein, *Vie et chants*, 120–22.

36. 'Brug pa kun legs, *'Brug pa kun legs kyi rnam thar*, 52.19–54.3; Stein, *Vie et chants*, 105–7. Ardussi, "'Brug-pa Kun-legs," 2.

37. 'Brug pa kun legs, *'Brug pa kun legs kyi rnam thar*, 201.3–8; Stein, *Vie et chants*, 318. While passing through the Rin spungs pas' home territory, 'Brug pa kun legs observes how they had raised a large army to fight against the Nang so snel pa, who was in control of Lha sa; 'Brug pa kun legs, 18.17–19; Stein, 61.

38. 'Brug pa kun legs, *'Brug pa kun legs kyi rnam thar*, 482.5–488.7.

39. 'Brug pa kun legs, *'Brug pa kun legs kyi rnam thar*, 31.7–8; Stein, *Vie et chants*, 77. 'Brug pa kun legs, 11.14–12.5; Stein, 51–2. Beginning at 'Brug pa kun legs, 364.12; and 494.2–14.

40. 'Brug pa kun legs, *'Brug pa kun legs kyi rnam thar*, 387.14–390.8; Dowman, *Divine Madman*, 59–60. 'Brug pa kun legs, 544.7–14. 'Brug pa kun legs, 37.17; Stein, *Vie et chants*, 85.

41. 'Brug pa kun legs, *'Brug pa kun legs kyi rnam thar*, 105.11–107.17; Stein, *Vie et chants*, 181–4.

42. 'Brug pa kun legs, *'Brug pa kun legs kyi rnam thar*, 19.17–21.4; Stein, *Vie et chants*, 62–4.

43. *da lta'i chos 'chad pa 'di kun/ chos nor phyir 'tshong / phan sems med pa'i lto gos kyi phyir chos shod pa la/ shAkya thub pas bka' chad tshe phyi ma la bka' drin skyong ba zhu lags*; 'Brug pa kun legs, *'Brug pa kun legs kyi rnam thar*, 13.22–14.2; Stein, *Vie et chants*, 54. *chos dang nor rdzas brje mkhan rnams la phyag 'tshal lo*; 'Brug pa kun legs, 360.18–20.

44. 'Brug pa kun legs, *'Brug pa kun legs kyi rnam thar*, 218.2–18; Stein, *Vie et chants*, 345–6.

45. 'Brug pa kun legs, *'Brug pa kun legs kyi rnam thar*, 39.7–19; Stein, *Vie et chants*, 88. See also 'Brug pa kun legs, 44.21–45.13; Stein, 95; and 'Brug pa kun legs, 118.2–119.20; Stein, 201–3.

46. 'Brug pa kun legs, *'Brug pa kun legs kyi rnam thar*, 22.1–12; Stein, *Vie et chants*, 66. 'Brug pa kun legs, 24.20–26.1; Stein, 69–70. 'Brug pa kun legs, 43.5–11; Stein, 92–3; Dowman, *Divine Madman*, 64.

47. 'Brug pa kun legs, *'Brug pa kun legs kyi rnam thar*, 73.19–74.17; Stein, *Vie et chants*, 136–7.

48. 'Brug pa kun legs, *'Brug pa kun legs kyi rnam thar*, 110.2–10; Stein, *Vie et chants*, 188.

49. Dowman, *Divine Madman*, 110. There is no episode like this in the *Southern Cycle* or the *Miscellaneous Writings*.

50. Rgod tshang ras pa, 191.3–192.5. 'Brug pa kun legs, *'Brug pa kun legs kyi rnam thar*, 79.17–83.15; Stein, *Vie et chants*, 143–8.

51. Smyug la paN chen and Lha mthong lo tsA ba, 601.2–4. 'Brug pa kun legs, *'Brug pa kun legs kyi rnam thar*, 412.2–414.13; 423.16–425.7; 409.3–412.2; 416.22–418.8; 476.13–477.8. See Ehrhard, "Holy Madman of dBus," 240–41. In another passage 'Brug pa kun legs discusses the mode of dress taken on by the followers of Dbus smyon and Gtsang smyon; 'Brug pa kun legs, 274.16–275.9.

52. Terese Tse Bartholomew and John Johnston, eds., *The Dragon's Gift: The Sacred Arts of Bhutan* (Chicago: Serindia, 2008), contains a few statues and paintings of 'Brug pa kun legs, dating from the seventeenth century and later. In each case he is depicted playing a Tibetan lute or *sgra snyan*, perhaps indicating a life of enjoyment and leisure.

53. Aris, "Boneless Tongue," 143–8; Michael Aris, *Bhutan: The Early History of a Himalayan Kingdom* (Warminster, England: Aris and Phillips, 1979), 196. Tales of 'Brugs pa kun legs are also told and acted out by bards in Ladakh, on the far opposite side of the Tibetan cultural world. See Patrick Sutherland and Tashi Tsering, *Disciples of a Crazy Saint: The Buchen of Spiti* (Oxford: Pitt Rivers Museum, 2011).

54. Aris, "Boneless Tongue," 148–53. Tshe dbang bstan 'dzin, *Mon spa gro sogs kyi mdzad spyod rnams*, 57.1–61.2; Dowman, *Divine Madman*, 138. Françoise Pommaret and Tashi Tobgay have also addressed the relationship between the legend of 'Brug pa kun legs and more popular forms of literature in "Bhutan's Pervasive Phallus: Is Drukpa Kunley Really Responsible?" (unpublished essay). Aris comments on how the historical 'Brug pa kun legs differs from that of popular memory; *Hidden Treasures*, 86, 88, 97.

CHAPTER 7

1. Lo chen 'gyur med bde chen, *Thang stong rgyal po'i rnam thar ngo mtshar kun gsal nor bu'i me long gsar pa* (Bir: Kandro, 1976), 184.1–2. My translation is based on Stearns, *King of the Empty Plain*, 271.

2. *Rwa lung dkar brgyud gser 'phreng: Brief Lives of the Successive Masters in the Transmission Lineage of the Bar 'brug-pa Dkar-brgyud-pa of Rwa-lung* (Palampur: Sungrab Nyamso Gyunphel Parkhang, Tibetan Craft Community, 1975–8), 3:99.1–106.4. Rwa smyon's verse biography was written in 1432 by Shes rab bzang po (1400–1438), his younger brother, who took the throne of Rwa lung after his death. Mentioned in Stein, *Vie et chants*, 9; Ardussi, "'Brug-pa Kun-legs," 204.

3. Dur khrod smyon pa is mentioned in Rgod tshang ras pa, 261.1–2, and in Lha btsun rin chen rnam rgyal, 109.2. Stag lung smyon pa is mentioned in Rgod

tshang ras pa, 108.7, 260.3. A Stag lung smyon pa, likely the same person, is mentioned in Ma pham rdo rje, *Rnal 'byor gyi dbang phyug grags pa mtha' yas dpal bzang po'i rnam thar mgur 'bum*, 101.5–102.1. Dbus sdings smyon pa is mentioned in Ma pham rdo rje, 235.3–6.

4. *Gangs can 'dir ston pa'i rgyal tshab dpal sgam po pa'i khri gdung 'dzin pa'i dam pa rnams kyi gtam bai DUrya'i phreng ba*, 56b6–65a5, in *Rare Texts from Tibet: Seven Sources for the Ecclesiastic History of Medieval Tibet*, ed. Per K. Sørensen and Sonam Dolma, 45–50, 191–247 (Text F) (Lumbini: Lumbini International Research Institute, 2007). Sgam smyon is also mentioned in a 1617 guide-book to the monastery and the surrounding retreat centers, by Sgam po pa mi pham chos kyi dbang phyug phrin las rnam rgyal dpal bzang po (1589–1633), *Gdan sa chen po dpal dwags lha sgam po'i ngo mtshar gyi bkod pa dad pa'i gter chen*, 28b6–29a2, in Sørensen and Dolma, *Rare Texts from Tibet*, 248–273 (Text G). Sgam smyon is mentioned in Stein, *Vie et chants*, 9. There seems to have been another "Madman of Gam," Sgam smyon phyag rdor nor bu; Roberts, *Biographies of Rechungpa*, 33.

5. On Lha sa'i smyon ma, see Roerich, *Blue Annals*, 258, 984; 'Gos lo tsA ba, *Deb ther sngon po*, 1:316.12–13, 2:1143.8–14; Martin, *Tibetan Histories*, 24; Per K. Sørensen and Guntram Hazod, *Thundering Falcon: An Inquiry into the History and Cult of Khra-'brug, Tibet's First Buddhist Temple* (Vienna: Österreichische Akademie der Wissenschaften, 2005), 250–51. On Smyon pa be re, see Roerich, 997–8; 'Gos lo tsA ba, 2:1160.9–1161.5. On Thod smyon bsam grub/Thod pa bsam grub, see Roerich, 481, 597, 986, 988; 'Gos lo tsA ba, 1:571.13, 2:703.17, 1145.3–18, 1147.15; Stag lung ngag dbang rnam rgyal, *Stag lung chos 'byung*, 716; Ardussi, "'Brug-pa Kun-legs," 27; Edou, *Machig Labdrön and the Foundations of Chöd*. On Smyon ma rgyal le lcam, see Roerich, 930; 'Gos lo tsA ba, 2:1084.8–1085.1. On Cog ro smyon pa, see Roerich, 688, 912; 'Gos lo tsA ba, 2:806.1–2, 1065.2; Stag lung ngag dbang rnam rgyal, 715. On Rgya smyon chung/Smyon pa don ldan, see Roerich, 876; 'Gos lo tsA ba, 2:1024.18–1025.5; Davidson, *Tibetan Renaissance*, 330.

6. On Khams smyon d+harma seng ge and this text, see Dan Martin, "Padampa Sangye: A History of Representation of a South Indian Siddha in Tibet," in *Holy Madness: Portraits of Tantric Siddhas*, ed. Rob Linrothe, 116.

7. I was told of La rtse smyon pa by Mkhan po tshul rnams rin po che, during an interview on September 23, 2009. La rtse refers to the man's clan. Another *bla ma smyon pa* specializing in *gcod*, who would have lived in the late nineteenth or early twentieth century, is mentioned in 'Bri gung dkon mchog rgya mtsho, *Grub pa'i dbang phyug chen po a mgon rdo rje 'chang gi rnam thar rags bsdus bka' brgyud bstan pa'i mdzes rgyan* (Bod ljongs mi dmangs dpe skrun khang, 2004), 47.20–48.13. This text will be discussed further below. Thang stong rgyal po is also associated *gcod*; Stearns, *King of the Empty Plain*, 18–20, 63.

8. Sgo smyon, Karma srid bral, is mentioned in Si tu paN chen and 'Be lo tshe dbang kun khyab, *Bsgrub brgyud karma kaM tshang*, 2:65.7.

9. Stearns, *King of the Empty Plain*, 62; Stein, *Tibetan Civilization*, 275–6.

10. On Dben sa smyon pa, Chos rdo rje, see E. Gene Smith, "Siddha Groups and the Mahāsiddhas in the Art and Literature of Tibet," in *Holy Madness: Portraits of Tantric Siddhas*, ed. Rob Linrothe, 69. On Smyon pa ldom chung see Roerich, *Blue Annals*, 1030; 'Gos lo tsA ba, *Deb ther sngon po*, 2:1200.1–10; Dan Martin, "Lay Religious Movements in 11th- and 12th-Century Tibet: A Survey of Sources," *Kailash* 18, nos. 3–4 (1996): 39.

11. Martin, "Star King and the Four Children of Pehar," 186.

12. Cyrus Stearns, *Hermit of Go Cliffs: Timeless Instructions from a Tibetan Mystic* (Boston, MA: Wisdom, 2000), 15. The song quoted is from 46–7. Ko brag pa uses the term "madman" in other senses as well, 38–9, 106–7. A biography of Ko brag pa is included in the *Blue Annals*, Roerich, 726–8; 'Gos lo tsA ba, *Deb ther sngon po*, 2:851.1–853.18.

13. Nyag re se bo, *Grub thob nyag re se bo'i skyes rabs rnam thar ma 'ongs lung bstan zhal chems nyams mgur*, compiled and edited by AtsArya dge bshes gle dgon thub bstan byang chub, Bkra shis tshe ring, and Brag g.yab grags pa tshe ring (Dharamsala: 'Gro phan gtsug lag dpe skrun khang and A myes rma chen bod kyi rig gzhung zhib 'jug khang, 2008), 39.18–20. See also 22.14, 23.15, 29.13–15, 30.7, 33.19, 49.15, 54.15.

14. Nyag re se bo, *Grub thob nyag re se bo'i skyes rabs rnam thar*, 19.1–8; *grub thob kyi tshul du brtul zhugs du ma bsten*, 54.18–19. See also 32.6, 49.10, 54.10–11. He is referred to as Myang re se bo in Sangs rgyas dar po, *Sangs rgyas dar po chos 'byung*, 110.7.

15. Bsod nams 'od zer, *Grub chen u rgyan pa'i rnam thar* (Bod ljongs bod yig dpe rnying dpe skrun khang, 1997), 105.18–106.3, 135.2–17, 176.20–177.3, 241.15–242.19. See also Smith, "Golden Rosaries of the Bka' brgyud Schools," in *Among Tibetan Texts*, 46; Roerich, *Blue Annals*, 696–703; 'Gos lo tsA ba, *Deb ther sngon po*, 2:816.3–822.14.

16. Suzanne Bessenger, "Echoes of Enlightenment: The Life and Legacy of Sonam Peldren (1328–1372)" (PhD diss., University of Virginia, 2009), 154–66.

17. Hanna Havnevik, *The Life of Jetsun Lochen Rinpoche (1865–1951) as Told in Her Autobiography* (Oslo: University of Oslo Press, 1999), 2:412–13.

18. *ngas smyo ba yin lugs kyi glu 'di smras so*. Blo bzang tshe ring, *Shug gseb rje btsun sku zhabs kyi rnam thar* (Lhasa: Mi rigs dpe skrun khang, 1997), 130.6, 131.12, 145.1–22. For songs in which Shug gseb rje btsun mentions *brtul zhugs*, see 110.14, 175.23, the former also including a rhetoric of madness.

19. Havnevik, *Life of Jetsun Lochen Rinpoche*, 2:410–11, 458–9, 492–3.

20. 'Bri gung dkon mchog rgya mtsho, *A mgon rdo rje 'chang gi rnam thar*, 43.17–20; 17.21–18.22.

21. 'Bri gung dkon mchog rgya mtsho, *A mgon rdo rje 'chang gi rnam thar,* 17.14–21; Dowman, *Divine Madman,* 63–4.

22. *'bri 'bangs smyon pa ra se dkon mchog rgya mtsho;* 'Bri gung dkon mchog rgya mtsho, *A mgon rdo rje 'chang gi rnam thar,* 101.13–14. For another version of his life, see 'Bri gung pa chos 'byor, *'Bri gung mtshams pa grub thob a mgon rin po che'i rnam thar,* Ngag rgyun lo rgyus deb phreng dang po, Oral Histories Series, no. 1 (Dharamsala: Library of Tibetan Works and Archives, 1996).

23. The *mkhan po* who told me this story himself noted that it was just like the one told about 'Brug pa kun legs. 'Brug pa kun legs, *'Brug pa kun legs kyi rnam thar,* 387.14–390.8; Dowman, *Divine Madman,* 59–61. See also Larsson, *Crazy for Wisdom,* 19.

24. The story was told to me during an interview with Mkhan po tshul rnams rin po che, August 22, 2009. *grub pa'i mdzad spyod ltar byed pas kun spyod gnam du gshegs pa . . . smyon pa'i lam mkhan lta bu'i bshes gnyen;* Rdza dpal sprul rin po che, *Kun bzang bla ma'i zhal lung* (Chengdu: Si khron mi rigs dpe skrun khang, 1991), 215.3–9; Patrul Rinpoché, *The Words of My Perfect Teacher,* trans. Padmakara Translation Group (Boston, MA: Shambhala, 1998), 140.

25. Gedün Chöpel and Jeffrey Hopkins, *Tibetan Arts of Love: Sex, Orgasm and Spiritual Healing* (Ithaca, NY: Snow Lion, 1992), 15–7; Donald S. Lopez Jr., *The Madman's Middle Way: Reflections on Reality of the Tibetan Monk Gendun Chopel* (Chicago: University of Chicago Press, 2006), 11, 230–36; Heather Stoddard, *Le Mendicant de l'Amdo* (Paris: Société d'ethnographie, 1985), 248–67; Larsson, *Crazy for Wisdom,* 6–7.

26. Melvyn C. Goldstein, *On the Cultural Revolution in Tibet: The Nyemo Incident of 1969* (Berkeley: University of California Press, 2009).

27. On Sding chen smyon pa, see Stein, *Tibetan Civilization,* 276. On the pen name in general, see Hor gtsang 'jigs med, *Khrag thigs las skyes pa'i ljang myug: deng rabs bod kyi rtsom rig dang de'i rgyab ljongs, 1980–2000* (Dharamsala: Youtse, 2000), 97–9; and comments by various authors in Lauran Hartley and Patricia Schiaffini-Vedani, eds., *Modern Tibetan Literature and Social Change* (Durham, NC: Duke University Press, 2008), 143, 153, 248–51, 272–3. See also Bkra shis don grub (A smyon), *Ston gyi rang sgra* (Xining: Mtsho sngon mi rigs dpe skrun khang, 1999); Bya dor phun tshogs dbang phyug (Gangs smyon), *Skyug bro ba'i 'jig rten* (Delhi: Archana, 2007); and Yar kaH 'jam dbyangs phrin las ('Brug smyon klu gdong), *Gtsang gsum 'phyo ba'i skya rengs* ('Dzam gling zhi bde par khang and Bod gzhung shes rig par khang, 2003).

28. See his autobiography, Ye shes rgya mtsho rin po che (Klu smyon he ru kaH), *Rgyal khab med pa'i mi (homeless person): mi lo sum bcu'i rags zin (1969–2002).* According to Pema Bhum, *klu* here is a tribal name, probably not carrying the meaning of a serpent spirit, "'Heartbeat of a New Generation' Revisited," translated by Lauran Hartley, in *Modern Tibetan Literature and Social Change,* ed.

Hartley and Schiaffini-Vedani, 143. Some more details on the use of the pen name "madman" are offered in DiValerio, "Subversive Sainthood," 667–8.

29. See, for example, 'Bri gung lam mkhyen rgyal po, *Smyo glu a ho ma*, in *'Char ka'i 'bod pa* 3 (2009): 15–17 (Dehradun: Bka' brgyud mtho slob rtsom sgrig khang); and the collection by Karma pa XV Mkha' khyab rdo rje, *Zhal gdams su btags pa'i smyon tshig nam mkha'i sprin sgra*, in his *Gsung 'bum*, vol. 9 (*ta*), 823–78 (Paro: Lama Ngodrup and Sherab Drimey, 1979–81).

30. The first exchange is in Ma pham rdo rje, *Grags pa mtha' yas dpal bzang po'i rnam thar mgur 'bum*, 38.4–6. Grags pa mtha' yas interacts with Dbus smyon, 63.3, 335.4–336.2; receives the *lung* for his biography, 255.2; interacts with Gtsang smyon, 105.2–3; meets 'Brug pa kun legs, 150.2–151.2. He mentions *brtul zhugs smyon spyod*, 167.6; *smyon pa'i brtul zhugs*, 289.3. He praises his master as *lha btsun smyon pa*, 358.1, 364.1. For more on Grags pa mtha' yas, see DiValerio, "Subversive Sainthood," 373–89.

31. See Manfred Gerner, *Chakzampa Thangtong Gyalpo: Architect, Philosopher and Iron Chain Bridge Builder*, translated from German by Gregor Verhufen (Thimphu: Centre for Bhutan Studies, 2007).

32. On the question of Thang stong rgyal po's dates, see Stearns, *King of the Empty Plain*, 11–14. His time at the stūpa is described, 70, 193. Gtsang smyon's stay there is told in Dngos grub dpal 'bar, 10a7–10b1; Rgod tshang ras pa, 44.6–7; Lha btsun rin chen rnam rgyal, 40.2–3.

33. Stearns, *King of the Empty Plain*, 68; Lha btsun rin chen rnam rgyal, 40.1–2.

34. The traditional use and meanings of the terms *'khrul zhig* and *zhig po*, which occasionally appear in discussions of topics pertaining to the history of "holy madmen," are deserving of further study.

35. Nam mkha' 'jigs med (Kong smyon), *Kong smyon 'khrul zhig nam mkha' 'jigs med rig pa brtul zhugs kyi spyod la gzhol pa'i tshul chos brgyad tshul chos kyi mnya' gnon rig pa gcer mthong ngo sprod kyi thol glu*, in *Rnal 'byor gyi dbang phyug chen po lha btsun nam mkha' 'jigs med kyi gsung 'bum* (New Delhi: Jurme Drakpa, 1974), 1:367.1–370.1, 422.3–4. On Nam mkha' 'jigs med, see Franz-Karl Ehrhard, " 'Turning the Wheel of the Dharma in Zhing sa Va lung': The dPal ri sPrul skus (17th to 20th Centuries)," *Bulletin of Tibetology* 44, nos. 1–2 (2008): 5–29.

36. Stearns, *King of the Empty Plain*, 65–6, 109, 117. The Practice of the Observance and the Secret Practice are mentioned at times throughout the biography.

37. Stearns, *King of the Empty Plain*, 149, 162, 160. Stearns has shown that some stories of Thang stong rgyal po's being called a madman are present in the earlier versions of his biography as well; 67–8.

38. Stearns, *King of the Empty Plain*, 139. Dngos grub dpal 'bar, 18b2–5; Rgod tshang ras pa, 174.2–4; Lha btsun rin chen rnam rgyal, 44.5–45.1.

39. Lo chen 'gyur med bde chen, *Thang stong rgyal po'i rnam thar ngo mtshar kun gsal nor bu'i me long gsar pa*, 184.2; Dngos grub dpal 'bar, 8a6–8b2; Rgod tshang

ras pa, 30.2–6; Lha btsun rin chen rnam rgyal, 17.4–7. Stearns, *King of the Empty Plain*, 543, points out the similarity between these passages. For other examples of Gtsang smyon's having encounters in which a similar set of questions are asked, see Lha btsun rin chen rnam rgyal, 47.4–6, 58.1–2; and numerous occasions in the other two versions of the *Life*. For another example of Thang stong rgyal po's being asked the same basic questions, see Stearns, 201. See also Larsson, *Crazy for Wisdom*, 111, 145–7, 157.

40. Dowman, *Divine Madman*, 45; Brag phug dge bshes dge 'dun rin chen, *'Gro ba'i mgon po chos rje kun dga' legs pa'i rnam thar rgya mtsho'i snying po mthong ba don ldan* (Kalimpong: Mani Printing Works, 1971), 15.6. Herbert Guenther, *Ecstatic Spontaneity: Saraha's Three Cycles of Dohā* (Berkeley, CA: Asian Humanities Press, 1993), 4.

41. *sprang smyon dge 'dun rgya mtsho*. Glenn H. Mullin, *Mystical Verses of a Mad Dalai Lama* (Wheaton, IL: Quest / Theosophical Publishing, 1994), xiv. This explanation is quoted by Larsson, *Crazy for Wisdom*, 8.

42. Stein, *Vie et chants*, 61; *'Brug pa kun legs, 'Brug pa kun legs kyi rnam thar*, 18.19–21.

43. Yamamoto, *Vision and Violence*, 246–54; Davidson, *Tibetan Renaissance*, 327–31; Larsson, *Crazy for Wisdom*, 13–14.

44. Linrothe, *Holy Madness*. In his article, "Siddha Groups and the Mahāsiddhas," E. Gene Smith casually refers to various *siddhas* as "holy madmen," seemingly influenced by the title of the exhibition; 63, 64.

45. Fabrice Midal, *Chögyam Trungpa: His Life and Vision*, trans. Ian Monk (Boston, MA: Shambhala, 2005), 311, 464, 466–7, 340, 342, 164. For other descriptions of Trungpa's life, corroborating many details of Midal's account, see Stephen Butterfield, *The Double Mirror: A Skeptical Journey into Buddhist Tantra* (Berkeley, CA: North Atlantic, 1994), and John Riley Perks, *The Mahāsiddha and His Idiot Servant* (Putney, VT: Crazy Heart, 2004).

46. Midal, *Chögyam Trungpa*, 434, 313.

47. Fabrice Midal, ed., *Recalling Chögyam Trungpa* (Boston, MA: Shambhala, 2005), 246. See also, Midal, *Chögyam Trungpa*, 161–2.

48. Midal, *Chögyam Trungpa*, xxv, 311, 153.

49. Tom Clark, *The Great Naropa Poetry Wars, with a Copious Collection of Germane Documents Assembled by the Author* (Santa Barbara, CA: Cadmus, 1980), 23–4, 59–60. For a brief description of Trungpa and the way those around him interpreted his actions, see Larsson, *Crazy for Wisdom*, 20–21.

50. Chögyam Trungpa, *Crazy Wisdom*, ed. Sherab Chödzin (Boston, MA: Shambhala, 2001), 12, 173, 118, 10; connection with Padmasambhava mentioned, 21, 29, 53, 63, 111, 112, 167; connection with *upāya*, 112, 169, 175.

51. Chögyam Trungpa, *Crazy Wisdom*, 59, 66–7, 58, 174, 79–80.

52. Chögyam Trungpa, *Crazy Wisdom*, 105, 179–80.

53. Midal, *Chögyam Trungpa*, 154. According to Janet Gyatso, Trungpa was using this term as early as 1974; personal communication, October 31, 2010.

54. Larsson, *Crazy for Wisdom*, 9.

55. Midal, "Introduction," in *Recalling Chögyam Trungpa*, 5; Françoise Bonardel, "Tantric Alchemy and the Transmission of Dharma: At the Heart of the Western Mandala," in *Recalling Chögyam Trungpa*, 35–56, here citing 52. See also Reginald A. Ray, "Chögyam Trungpa as a *Siddha*," in *Recalling Chögyam Trungpa*, 197–220.

56. An article by Ramesh Bjonnes titled "Fat, Naked, and Enlightened: The Crazy Yogis of Love," *Elephant Journal*, October 17, 2010 (http://www.elephantjournal.com/2010/10/fat-naked-and-enlightened-ramesh-bjonnes/), states: "The Buddhist tradition is of course well known for its *crazy wisdom* teachers. Marpa, Milarepa, and Drukpa [Künlé] are some of the more famous of the wild ones from the past, while Chögyam Trungpa was contemporary." Midal compares Trungpa to 'Brug pa kun legs; *Chögyam Trungpa*, 154.

57. Dowman, *Divine Madman*, 28–9. Cited, for example, in Marcy Braverman, "Possession, Immersion, and the Intoxicated Madness of Devotion in Hindu Traditions" (PhD diss., University of California, Santa Barbara, 2003), 253.

58. Georg Feuerstein, *Holy Madness: Spirituality, Crazy-Wise Teachers, and Enlightenment* (Prescott, AZ.: Hohm, 2006), xxix.

59. Feuerstein, *Holy Madness*, 94.

60. Feuerstein, *Holy Madness*, 344. Feuerstein singles out Tibetan Buddhism as "highly relevant to the discussion of crazy wisdom," xiii.

61. The broader influence Trungpa and Dowman have had on the ways people worldwide think about "holy madness" can also be observed in the psycho-analyst Sudhir Kakar's *Mad and Divine: Spirit and Psyche in the Modern World* (Chicago: University of Chicago Press, 2009), and in Surya Das, *Wisdom Tales From Tibet* (San Francisco, CA: Harper, 1992), 251–2.

Tibetan Spellings

Akhu Tönpa	*a khu ston pa*
Amdo	*a mdo*
Amgön Rinpoché	*a mgon rin po che*
Ani Lochen	*a ni lo chen*
Barawa Gyeltsen Pelzang	*'ba' ra ba rgyal mtshan dpal bzang*
Bari Gang	*ba ri sgang*
Bari Lotsāwa	*ba ri lo tsA ba*
Barkor	*bar skor*
Belo Tsewang Künkhyap	*'be lo tshe dbang kun khyab*
Bodong Rinchen Tsemo	*bo dong rin chen rtse mo*
Chödrak Gyatso	*chos grags rgya mtsho*
Chödrak Yeshé	*chos grags ye shes*
Chödzé Abhaya	*chos mdzad a b+ha ya*
Chögyam Trungpa	*chos rgyam drung pa*
Chögyel Lhünpo	*chos rgyal lhun po*
Chokro Penchen Rinchen Samtenpa	*cog ro paN chen rin chen bsam gtan pa*
Chökyi Drakpa	*chos kyi grags pa*
Chongyé	*'phyongs rgyas*
Chöpel Zangmo	*chos 'phel bzang mo*
Chöwang Lhündrup	*chos dbang lhun grub*
Chubar	*chu bar, chu dbar, chu 'bar*
Chungtsang	*chung tshang*
Chushül	*chu shur, chu shul*
Chuworipa Künga Namgyel	*chu bo ri pa kun dga' rnam rgyal*
Dakla Gampo	*dwags la sgam po, dwags lha sgam po*
Dakmema	*bdag med ma*
Dakpo	*dwags po*
Dakpo Penchen Tashi Namgyel	*dwags po paN chen bkra shis rnam rgyal*
Dakpo Rapjampa Chögyel Tenpa	*dwags po ram 'byams pa chos rgyal bstan pa*

Damzhung	*'dam gzhung*
Densa Til	*gdan sa mthil*
Desi Sangyé Gyatso	*sde srid sangs rgyas rgya mtsho*
Dharma Sengé	*d+harma seng ge*
Dingri Langkhor	*ding ri glang 'khor*
Do Khyentsé Yeshé Dorjé	*mdo mkhyen rtse ye shes rdo rje*
Döl	*dol*
Dölpopa	*dol po pa*
Döndrup Gyel	*don grub rgyal*
Döndrup Tseten Dorjé	*don grub tshe brtan rdo rje*
Dönyö Dorjé	*don yod rdo rje*
Doring Künpangpa	*rdo rings kun spangs pa*
Dorjé Tseten	*rdo rje tshe brtan*
Drak Yerpa	*brag yer pa*
Drakar Taso	*brag dkar rta so*
Drakarwa Rinchen Pel	*brag dkar ba rin chen dpal*
Drakchokpa Rinchen Zangpo	*brag lcog pa rin chen bzang po*
Drakpa Gyeltsen	*grags pa rgyal mtshan*
Drakpa Tayé	*grags pa mtha' yas*
Drakpuk Geshé Gendün Rinchen	*dge bshes brag phug dge 'dun rin chen*
Drepung	*'bras spungs*
Dreyül Dzongkar	*'bras yul rdzong dkar*
Dreyül Kyemö Tsel	*'bras yul skyed mos tshal*
Drigu Tso	*gri gu mtsho*
Drikung	*'bri khung, 'bri gung*
Drikung Til	*'bri gung mthil, 'bri gung thel*
Drin	*brin*
Driu Lhé	*dri'u lhas*
Dröpuk	*grod phug*
Drukchen	*'brug chen*
Drukpa	*'brug pa*
Drukpa Künlé	*'brug pa kun legs*
Drupwang Tseten Rinpoché	*grub dbang tshe brtan rin po che*
Dungkar Lozang Trinlé	*dung dkar blo bzang 'phrin las*
Dza Patrül Rinpoché	*rdza dpal sprul rin po che*
Dzesé	*mdzes se*
Dzongkar	*rdzong dkar, rdzong kha*
Five Long Life Sisters	*tshe ring mched lnga, tshe rings mched lnga*
Forest of Glorious Samantabhadra	*dpal kun tu bzang po'i nags khrod*
Fortress of the Expanse of Being	*chos dbyings nam mkha'i rdzong*
Four-Doored Kakṇi stūpa	*ka ka Ni sgo bzhi ma, ka ka ni sgo bzhi ma,*
	kag Ni sgo bzhi ma

Gampopa	*sgam po pa*
Ganden	*dga' ldan*
Geluk	*dge lugs*
Gendenpa	*dge ldan pa*
Gendün Chöpel	*dge 'dun chos 'phel*
Gendün Drup	*dge 'dun 'grub*
Gendün Gyatso	*dge 'dun rgya mtsho*
Ger	*sger*
Geshé Chapu	*dge bshes brag phug*
Gö Lotsāwa Zhönnu Pel	*'gos lo tsA ba gzhon nu dpal*
Gongkar	*gong dkar*
Gorampa Sönam Sengé	*go ram pa bsod nams seng ge*
Götsang Repa Natsok Rangdröl	*rgod tshang ras pa sna tshogs rang grol*
Götsangpa Gönpo Dorjé	*rgod tshang pa mgon po rdo rje*
Great Prayer Festival	*smon lam chen mo*
Gugé Purang	*gu ge pu hrang*
Gurpa	*gur pa*
Gya	*rgya*
Gyama	*rgya ma*
Gyantsé	*rgyal mkhar rtse, rgyal rtse*
Gyeltangpa Dechen Dorjé	*rgyal thang pa bde chen rdo rje*
Gyeltsen Pel	*rgyal mtshan dpal*
Gyelwang Drukpa	*rgyal dbang 'brug pa*
Gyümé	*rgyud smad*
Gyütö	*rgyud stod*
Hortsang Jikmé	*hor gtsang 'jigs med*
Ja	*bya*
Jamchen	*byams chen*
Jamchen Chöjé Śākya Yeshé	*byams chen chos rje shAkya ye shes*
Jamgön Kongtrul	*'jam mgon kong sprul*
Jamyang Chökyi Drakpa	*'jam dbyangs chos kyi grags pa*
Jangchup Gyeltsen	*byang chub rgyal mtshan*
Jetsün Zhepa Dorjé	*rje btsun bzhad pa rdo rje*
Jokhang	*jo khang*
Jonang	*jo nang*
Jowo	*jo bo*
Jozang Sthavira	*jo bzang gnas brtan*
Kadampa	*bka' gdams pa*
Kagyü	*bka' rgyud, bka' brgyud*

Kangtsuk cave	*rkang tshug phug*
Karma	*karma*
Karma Dröndül Nyönpa	*karma 'gro 'dul smyon pa*
Karma Sidrel	*karma srid bral*
Karma Trinlepa	*karma 'phrin las pa*
Kham	*khams*
Kharak	*kha rag, mkha' rag, mkha' reg*
Kharkha	*mkhar kha*
Khedrup Jé Gelek Pelzang	*mkhas grub rje dge legs dpal bzang*
Khön	*'khon*
Kodrakpa Sönam Gyeltsen	*ko brag pa bsod nams rgyal mtshan*
Könchok Gyeltsen	*dkon mchog rgyal mtshan*
Kongpo	*kong po*
Künga Lekpa	*kun dga' legs pa*
Künga Penjor	*kun dga' dpal 'byor*
Künga Zangpo	*kun dga' bzang po*
Künkhyen Sangyé Pel	*kun mkhyen sangs rgyas 'phel*
Küntu Zangmo	*kun tu bzang mo*
Küntu Zangpo	*kun tu bzang po*
Künzang Chökyi Nyima	*kun bzang chos kyi nyi ma*
Künzang Nyida Pembar	*kun bzang nyi zla dpal 'bar*
Kya-lhuk cave	*phug pa skya lhug*
Kyepo Dar	*skyes po dar*
Kyichu	*skyid chu*
Ladakh	*la dwags*
Lama Zhang	*bla ma zhang*
Lampar monastery	*lam 'phar dgon*
Lang	*rlangs*
Lapchi	*la phyi, lab phyi*
Latö Lho	*la stod lho*
Latsé Khyenrap	*la rtse mkhyen rab*
Latsé Madman	*la rtse smyon pa*
Latsé Powerful One	*la rtse stobs ldan*
Lé monastery	*gla dgon, gle dgon, bla dgon*
Lhasa	*lha sa*
Lhatong Lotsāwa Shényen Namgyel	*lha mthong lo tsA ba bshes gnyen rnam rgyal*
Lhatsün Künga Chökyi Gyatso	*lha btsun kun dga' chos kyi rgya mtsho*
Lhatsün Rinchen Namgyel	*lha btsun rin chen rnam rgyal*
Lhokha	*lho kha*
Lhünpo fortress	*lhun po rtse*
Liberation Park	*thar pa gling*

Lingrepa	*gling ras pa*
Little Madman of Gya	*rgya smyon chung*
Lochen Gyurmé Dechen	*lo chen 'gyur med bde chen*
Lodrö Tashi	*blo gros bkra shis*
Lower Nyang	*myang smad*
Lowo Möntang	*glo bo smon thang*
Machik Lapdrön	*ma gcig lab sgron*
Mad Beré	*smyon pa be re*
Mad Domchung	*smyon pa ldom chung*
Mad Dönden	*smyon pa don ldan*
Mad Lu, the Heruka	*klu smyon he ru kaH*
Mad Mantrika of Zahor	*za hor sngags smyon*
Mad Monk of Mön	*mon ban smyon pa*
Mad Tsöndrü	*brtson 'grus smyon pa*
Madman of the Charnel Ground	*dur khrod smyon pa*
Madman of Chokro	*cog ro smyon pa*
Madman of [Dakla] Gam[po]	*sgam smyon*
Madman of Dingchen	*sding chen smyon pa*
Madman of the Drukpa	*'brug smyon*
Madman of the Empty Valley	*lung stong smyon pa*
Madman of Go	*sgo smyon*
Madman of Kham	*khams smyon*
Madman of Kong[po]	*kong smyon*
Madman of Nyak	*nyag smyon*
Madman of Ra[lung]	*rwa smyon*
Madman of Taklung	*stag lung smyon pa*
Madman of Tsang, the Heruka	*gtsang smyon he ru ka*
Madman of Ü	*dbus smyon*
Madman of Üding	*dbus sdings smyon pa*
Madman of Ur	*dbur smyon*
Madwoman Gyel-lecham	*smyon ma rgyal le lcam*
Madwoman of Lhasa	*lha sa'i smyon ma*
Marpa Chökyi Lodrö	*mar pa chos kyi blo gros*
Marpori	*dmar po ri*
Martsang	*smar tshang*
Medro Gungkar	*mal gro gung dkar*
Menlungpa	*man lungs pa*
Mikyö Dorjé	*mi bskyod rdo rje*
Milarepa	*mi la ras pa, mid la ras pa*
Mipam Drakpa Gyeltsen	*mi pham grags pa rgyal mtshan*
Mönlam Pelwa	*smon lam dpal ba*
Möntsepa Künga Lekzang	*mon rtse pa kun dga' legs bzang*

Möntsepa Künga Pelden	*mon rtse pa kun dga' dpal ldan*
Mount Kailash	*gangs ti se, gangs rin po che, ti se*
Nakartsé	*sna dkar rtse*
Nam Tso	*gnam mtsho*
Namkha Gyeltsen	*nam mkha' rgyal mtshan*
Namkha Jikmé	*nam mkha' 'jigs med*
Namkha Pelzang	*nam mkha' dpal bzang*
Namkha Wangpo	*nam mkha' dbang po*
Namkha Zangpo	*nam mkha' bzang po*
Nangchen	*nang chen*
Nedong	*sne gdong*
Nenying	*gnas rnying*
Neudzong	*sne'u rdzong*
New Kadampa	*bka' gdams gsar ma*
Ngaki Wangpo	*ngag gi dbang po*
Ngari Gungtang	*mnga' ris gung thang*
Ngawang Chögyel	*ngag dbang chos rgyal*
Ngawang Drakpa	*ngag dbang grags pa*
Ngawang Jikdrak	*ngag dbang 'jigs grags*
Ngawang Khedrup	*ngag dbang mkhas grub*
Ngawang Lozang Gyatso	*ngag dbang blo bzang rgya mtsho*
Ngawang Namgyel	*ngag dbang rnam rgyal*
Ngawang Tashi Drakpa	*ngag dbang bkra shis grags pa*
Ngawang Tenzin	*ngag dbang bstan 'dzin*
Ngendzongpa	*ngan rdzong pa*
Ngödrup Pembar	*dngos grub dpal 'bar*
Ngok Lotsāwa	*rngog lo tsA ba*
Ngorpa	*ngor pa*
Norbu Dé	*nor bu sde*
Norbu Dzom	*nor bu 'dzom*
Nyakré Sewo	*nyag bre se bo, nyag re se bo*
Nyang	*myang*
Nyel	*gnyal*
Nyemo	*snye mo*
Nyendo	*snye mdo*
Nyingma	*rnying ma*
Nyingro Menchukha	*nying ro sman chu kha*
Nyiwa	*rnyi ba*
Nyukla	*gnyug la, snyug la, smyug la*
Nyukla Penchen	*smyug la paN chen*
Ölkha	*'ol kha*

Onjung	*'o 'byung*
Orgyen Lingpa	*o rgyan gling pa*
Padampa Sangyé	*pha dam pa sangs rgyas*
Pakmodrupa	*phag mo gru pa*
Pawo	*dpa' bo*
Pelgyé	*dpal rgyas*
Pelkhor Chödé	*dpal 'khor chos sde*
Pelnam	*dpal nam*
Pelzang Butri	*dpal bzang bu khrid*
Pema Chödrön	*pad+ma chos sgron*
Pema Karpo	*pad+ma dkar po*
Pema Lingpa	*pad+ma gling pa*
Penjor Gyelpo	*dpal 'byor rgyal po*
Penyül	*'phan yul*
Peta	*pe ta*
Puma Tso	*phu ma mtsho*
Ralung	*rwa lung*
Ramoché	*ra mo che*
Rangjung Dorjé	*rang byung rdo rje*
Rapten Künzang Pak	*rab brtan kun bzang 'phags*
Rasé Dawa Könchok Gyatso	*ra se zla ba dkon mchog rgya mtsho*
Rechen cave	*ras chen phug*
Rechung cave	*ras chung phug*
Rechungpa	*ras chung pa*
Renda	*ras mda'*
Rinchen Zangpo	*rin chen bzang po*
Rinpung	*rin chen dpungs, rin spung, rin spungs*
Rong	*rong*
Sakya	*sa skya*
Śākya Chokden	*shAkya mchog ldan*
Sakya Paṇḍita	*sa skya paNDi ta*
Samdé	*bsam sde*
Samdrup Dé	*bsam grub sde*
Samdrup, the Mad Skull Cup	*thod smyon bsam grub*
Samten Ling	*bsam gtan gling*
Sangyé Darpo	*sangs rgyas dar po*
Sangyé Gyeltsen	*sangs rgyas rgyal mtshan*
Sera	*se ra*
Serdokchen	*gser mdog can*
Serkyi Jakyib	*gser gyi bya skyibs*

Shang	*shangs*
Shangdrön Gang	*shangs 'gron khang, shangs 'gron po sgang*
Shangpa	*shangs pa*
Shara Rapjampa Sangyé Sengé	*sha ra rab 'byams pa sangs rgyas seng ge*
Shigatsé	*gzhis ka rtse, gzhis ka bsam 'grub rtse*
Shuksep Jetsün	*shug gseb rje btsun*
Shuksep Lochen Rinpoché	*shug gseb lo chen rin po che*
Situ Penchen	*si tu paN chen*
Six Fortresses	*rdzong drug*
Sönam Drakpa	*bsod nams grags pa*
Sönam Peldren	*bsod nams dpal 'dren*
Śrī Lopen Repa Jampel Chö-lha	*zrI lo paN ras pa 'jam dpal chos lha*
Sumpa Khenpo	*sum pa mkhan po*
Tago	*rta mgo*
Taklung	*stag lung*
Taktsé	*stag rtse*
Tamdrin Tseten	*rta mgrin tshe brtan*
Tangtong Gyelpo	*thang stong rgyal po*
Tashi Dargyé	*bkra shis dar rgyas*
Tashi Lhünpo	*bkra shis lhun po*
Tedung	*ste dung*
Tenzin Rapgyé	*bstan 'dzin rab rgyas*
Tölung	*stod lung*
Tongwa Dönden	*mthong ba don ldan*
Tri Namgyel Dé	*khri rnam rgyal sde*
Trinlé Chödrön	*'phrin las chos sgron*
Troru Khenpo Tsenam	*khro ru mkhan po tshe rnam*
Tsakpuwa	*rtsag phu ba*
Tsamda	*tsha mda', tsha 'da'*
Tsang	*gtsang*
Tsangpa Desi	*gtsang pa sde srid*
Tsangpa Gyaré	*gtsang pa rgya ras*
Tsangpo	*gtsang po*
Tsari	*tsa ri, tsA ri, rtsa ri*
Tselpa	*tshal pa*
Tsetang	*rtsed thang*
Tsewang Dzom	*tshe dbang 'dzoms*
Tsewang Tenzin	*tshe dbang bstan 'dzin*
Tsimar Pel	*rtsi dmar dpal*
Tsokyé Dorjé	*mtsho skyes rdo rje*
Tsongkhapa Lozang Drakpa	*tsong kha pa blo bzang grags pa*

Tsopema	*mtsho pad+ma*
Tsuklak Trengwa	*gtsug lag phreng ba*
Tsurpu	*tshur phu, mtshur phu*
Tupten Chökhor	*thub bstan chos 'khor*
Ü	*dbus*
Upper Nyang	*myang stod*
Urgyenpa Rinchen Pel	*u rgyan pa rin chen dpal*
Urgyenpa Sengé Pel	*u rgyan pa seng ge dpal*
Uyuk	*'u yug*
Wang Drukgyel	*wang 'brug rgyal*
Wangchuk Gyeltsen	*dbang phyug rgyal mtshan*
Wensa Madman Chö Dorjé	*dben sa smyon pa chos rdo rje*
Yamchilwa	*g.yam spyil ba*
Yamdrok Tso	*yar 'brog mtsho*
Yanggönpa	*yang dgon pa*
Yangpachen	*yangs pa can*
Yargyap	*yar rgyab*
Yarlung	*yar lung*
Yeshé Gyatso Rinpoché	*ye shes rgya mtsho rin po che*
Yöl Rinchen Ling	*yol rin chen gling*
Zambulung	*zab phu lung, zam bu lung*
Zelmo cave	*zal mo brag*
Zhalu	*zhwa lu*
Zhaluwa Gelong Khyenrap	*zhwa lu ba dge slong mkhyen rab*
Zhingkyong Drukdrak	*zhing skyong 'brug grags*
Zhung	*gzhung*
Zilnön Dorjé	*zil gnon rdo rje*

Works Cited

TIBETAN-LANGUAGE SOURCES

NGMPP: Nepal–German Manuscript Preservation Project
TBRC: Tibetan Buddhist Resource Center

Karma pa III Rang byung rdo rje (1284–1339). *Brtag gnyis rnam bshad dri med 'od* [*Stainless Light Explaining the Two-Parted*]. Seattle, WA: Nitartha International, 2006.

Karma pa XV Mkha' khyab rdo rje (1871–1922). *Gsung 'bum*. 10 vols. Paro: Lama Ngodrup and Sherab Drimey, 1979–81. (Reproduced from a print of the xylographs carved at Dpal spungs monastery.)

Karma 'phrin las pa (1456–1539). *Do ha skor gsum gyi Ti ka 'bring po sems kyi rnam thar ston pa'i me long: A commentary on the three cycles of dohā composed by the great Saraha*. Thimphu: Druk Sherig, 1984.

——. *The Songs of Esoteric Practice (mgur) and Replies to Doctrinal Questions (dris lan) of karma-'phrin-las-pa*. New Delhi: Ngawang Topgay, 1975. (Reproduced from prints of the 1539 woodblocks.)

Kun dga' grol mchog (1507–1565/66). *PaNDi ta chen po shAkya mchog ldan gyi rnam par thar pa zhib mo rnam 'byed pa* [the *Life* of Śākya Chokden]. In *Collected Works of Śākya mchog ldan*, vol. 16 (*ma*): 1–234.

Ko zhul grags pa 'byung gnas and Rgyal ba blo bzang mkhas grub. *Gangs can mkhas grub rim byon ming mdzod*. Lanshou: Kan su'i mi rigs dpe skrun khang, 1992.

Bkra shis don grub (A smyon). *Ston gyi rang sgra*. Xining: Mtsho sngon mi rigs dpe skrun khang, 1999.

Khro ru mkhan po tshe rnam. *Dpal mnyam med mar pa bka' brgyud kyi grub pa'i mtha' rnam par nges par byed pa mdor bsdus su brjod pa dwags brgyud grub pa'i me long*. Sarnath: WA Na bka' brgyud nyam skyong tshogs pa skabs so bzhi pas dpar skrun zhus, 2007.

Mkhas grub rje dge legs dpal bzang (1385–1438). *Rgyud sde spyi'i rnam par gzhag pa rgyas par brjod*. See Ferdinand Lessing and Alex Wayman, *Mkhas grub rje's Fundamentals of the Buddhist Tantras (Rgyud sde spyiḥi rnam par gźag pa rgyas par brjod)*. The Hague: Mouton, 1968.

Gangs can 'dir ston pa'i rgyal tshab dpal sgam po pa'i khri gdung 'dzin pa'i dam pa rnams kyi gtam bai D Urya'i phreng ba [Multiple authors]. In *Rare Texts from Tibet: Seven Sources for the Ecclesiastic History of Medieval Tibet*, edited by Per K. Sørensen and Sonam Dolma, 45–50, 191–247 (Text F). Lumbini: Lumbini International Research Institute, 2007.

'Gos lo tsA ba gzhon nu dpal (1392–1481). *Deb ther sngon po [Blue Annals]*. 2 vols. Chengdu: Si khron mi rigs dpe skrun khang, 1984.

Rgod tshang ras pa sna tshogs rang grol (1482–1559). *Rnal 'byor gyi dbang phyug rgod tshang ras chen pa'i rnam thar tshigs gcad ma dngos grub rgya mtsho* [the verse auto-biography of Götsang Repa]. Eight folios. NGMPP L978/7.

———. *Gtsang smyon he ru ka phyogs thams cad las rnam par rgyal ba'i rnam thar rdo rje theg pa'i gsal byed nyi ma'i snying po* [the *Life* of the Madman of Tsang]. Edited by Lokesh Chandra. New Delhi: Sharada Rani, 1969. (Unless specified, all citations of Rgod tshang ras pa refer to this text.)

———. Untitled verse praise of the Madman of Tsang. One folio. Written at Rtsa ri on the occasion of finishing his biography of the Madman of Tsang. NGMPP L803/5.

Sgam po pa mi pham chos kyi dbang phyug phrin las rnam rgyal dpal bzang po (1589–1633). *Gdan sa chen po dpal dwags lha sgam po'i ngo mtshar gyi bkod pa dad pa'i gter chen*. In *Rare Texts from Tibet: Seven Sources for the Ecclesiastic History of Medieval Tibet*, edited by Per K. Sørensen and Sonam Dolma, 248–273 (Text G). Lumbini: Lumbini International Research Institute, 2007.

Ngag dbang mkhas grub (1779–1838). *Rje btsun mi la bzhad pa'i rdo rje'i gsung mgur smyo ma'i 'grel pa myo ba sangs byed* [*Dispelling Insanity: A Commentary on the Crazy Song Sung by Lord Mila, Laughing Vajra*]. In *The Collected Works of Nag-dban-mkhas-grub, Kyai-rdor Mkhan-po of Urga*, vol. 2 (*kha*): 75–97. Leh: Smanrtsis shesrig spendzod, 1972–1974.

Dngos grub dpal 'bar (1456–1527). *Rje btsun gtsang pa he ru ka'i thun mong gi rnam thar yon tan gyi gangs ri la dad pa'i seng ge rnam par rtse ba* [the *Life* of the Madman of Tsang]. A copy from the original 1508 xylograph owned by E. Gene Smith is preserved by the TBRC.

Nyag re se bo (1141?–1201). *Grub thob nyag re se bo'i skyes rabs rnam thar ma 'ongs lung bstan zhal chems nyams mgur*. Compiled and edited by AtsArya dge bshes gle dgon thub bstan byang chub, Bkra shis tshe ring, and Brag g.yab grags pa tshe ring. Dharamsala: 'Gro phan gtsug lag dpe skrun khang and A myes rma chen bod kyi rig gzhung zhib 'jug khang, 2008.

Stag lung ngag dbang rnam rgyal (1571–1626). *Stag lung chos 'byung (Brgyud pa yid bzhin nor bu'i rtogs pa brjod pa ngo mtshar rgya mtsho)*. Bod ljongs bod yig dpe rnying dpe skrun khang, 1992.

Thub bstan phun tshogs. *Bod kyi lo rgyus spyi don pad+ma rA ga'i lde mig.* 2 vols. Si khron mi rigs dpe skrun khang, 1996.

Dung dkar blo bzang 'phrin las (1927–1997). *Dung dkar tshig mdzod chen mo (Mkhas dbang dung dkar blo bzang 'phrin las mchog gis mdzad pa'i bod rig pa'i tshig mdzod chen mo shes bya rab gsal).* Beijing: Krung go'i bod rigs dpe skrun khang, 2002.

———. *Bod kyi chos srid zung 'brel skor bshad pa.* Dharamsala: Library of Tibetan Works and Archives, 1982. (First published in Beijing: Mi rigs dpe skrun khang, 1981.)

Don grub rgyal (1953–1985). <<*Mi la ras pa'i rnam thar* >> *gyi rtsom pa po'i lo rgyus.* In *Dpal don grub rgyal gyi gsung 'bum,* 3:27–53. Beijing: Mi rigs dpe skrun khang, 1997.

Dwags po paN chen bkra shis rnam rgyal (1512/13–1587). *Dpal kye'i rdo rje zhes bya ba'i rgyud kyi rgyal po'i 'grel pa.* Si khron mi rigs dpe skrun khang, 2002.

Nam mkha' 'jigs med (Kong smyon, 1597–1650). *Kong smyon 'khrul zhig nam mkha' 'jigs med rig pa brtul zhugs kyi spyod la gzhol pa'i tshul chos brgyad tshul chos kyi mnya' gnon rig pa gcer mthong ngo sprod kyi thol glu.* In *Rnal 'byor gyi dbang phyug chen po lha btsun nam mkha' 'jigs med kyi gsung 'bum,* 1:369–474. New Delhi: Jurme Drakpa, 1974.

Nor brang o rgyan. *Dpyid kyi rgyal mo'i glu dbyangs kyi 'grel pa yid kyi dga' ston (Gangs can yul gyi sa la spyod pa'i mtho ris kyi rgyal blon gtso bor brjod pa'i deb ther rdzogs ldan gzhon nu'i dga' ston dpyid kyi rgyal mo'i glu dbyangs kyi 'grel pa yid kyi dga' ston).* Beijing: Mi rigs dpe skrun khang, 1993.

PaN chen bsod nams grags pa (1478–1554). *Deb ther dmar po gsar ma.* See Giuseppe Tucci, *Deb ther dmar po gsar ma [The New Red Annals]: Tibetan Chronicles,* vol. 1. Serie Orientale Roma 24. Rome: Istituto Italiano per il Medio ed Estremo Oriente, 1971.

Pad+ma dkar po, 'Brug chen IV (1527–1592). *Chos 'byung bstan pa'i pad+ma rgyas pa'i nyin byed ('Brug pa'i chos 'byung).* Published as *Tibetan Chronicle of Padma-dkar-po,* edited by Lokesh Chandra. New Delhi: International Academy of Indian Culture, 1968.

Dpa' bo gtsug lag phreng ba (1504–1564/66). *Chos 'byung mkhas pa'i dga' ston (Dam pa'i chos kyi 'khor lo bsgyur ba rnams kyi byung ba gsal bar byed pa mkhas pa'i dga' ston) [Scholar's Feast].* Beijing: Mi rigs dpe skrun khang, 1986, 2006.

Phun tshogs tshe ring. *Deb ther kun gsal me long.* Bod ljongs mi dmangs dpe skrun khang, 1987.

Bo dong paN chen phyogs las rnam rgyal (1375–1451). *Rab brtan kun bzang 'phags kyi rnam thar (Rgyal rtse chos rgyal gyi rnam par thar pa dad pa'i lo thog dngos grub kyi char 'bebs).* Bod ljongs mi dmangs dpe skrun khang, 1987.

Bya dor phun tshogs dbang phyug (Gangs smyon). *Skyug bro ba'i 'jig rten.* Delhi: Archana, 2007.

Brag phug dge bshes dge 'dun rin chen [Geshé Chapu] (1926–1997). *'Gro ba'i mgon po chos rje kun dga' legs pa'i rnam thar rgya mtsho'i snying po mthong ba don ldan* [the *Life* of Drukpa Künlé]. Kalimpong: Mani Printing Works, 1971.

Blo bzang tshe ring. *Shug gseb rje btsun sku zhabs kyi rnam thar* (*Gangs shug ma Ni lo chen rig 'dzin chos nyid bzang mo'i rnam par thar pa rnam mkhyen bde ster*). Lhasa: Mi rigs dpe skrun khang, 1997.

'Bri gung dkon mchog rgya mtsho (Ra se zla ba). *Grub pa'i dbang phyug chen po a mgon rdo rje 'chang gi rnam thar rags bsdus bka' brgyud bstan pa'i mdzes rgyan.* Bod ljongs mi dmangs dpe skrun khang, 2004.

———. *'Bri gung chos 'byung.* Beijing: Mi rigs dpe skrun khang, 2003.

'Bri gung bstan 'dzin pad ma'i rgyal mtshan. *'Bri gung gdan rabs gser phreng* (*Nges don bstan pa'i snying po mgon po 'bri gung pa chen po'i gdan rabs chos kyi byung tshul gser gyi phreng ba*). Bod ljongs bod yig dpe rnying dpe skrun khang, 1989.

'Bri gung pa chos 'byor. *'Bri gung mtshams pa grub thob a mgon rin po che'i rnam thar.* Ngag rgyun lo rgyus deb phreng dang po, Oral Histories Series, no. 1. Dharamsala: Library of Tibetan Works and Archives, 1996.

'Bri gung lam mkhyen rgyal po. *Smyo glu a ho ma.* In *'Char ka'i 'bod pa* 3:15–17. Dehradun, India: Bka' brgyud mtho slob rtsom sgrig khang, 2009.

'Brug pa kun legs (born 1455). *'Brug pa kun legs kyi rnam thar* [Miscellaneous Writings]. The four volumes are titled: (1) *Rnal 'byor pa'i ming can kun dga' legs pa'i rnam thar byung tshul lhug par smra pa zhib mo'i rtsing mo ha le ho le sna zin spu zin nas bkod pa;* (2) *Rnal 'byor gyi dbang phyug chen po kun dga' legs pa'i rnam thar gsung 'bum rgya mtsho las dad pa'i ku shas chu thigs tsam blangs pa ngo mtshar bdud rtsi'i zil mngar;* (3) *Rnal 'byor pa'i ming can kun dga' legs pa'i nyams la shar ba'i 'phral gyi chos spyod 'dra dang nyams 'char ci byung ma byung bris pa skyag gtad gang yang med pa 'ga' zhig;* (4) *Rnal 'byor gyi dbang phyug kun dga' legs pa'i gsung 'bum 'thor bu.* Beijing: Bod ljongs mi dmangs dpe skrun khang, 2005. (2012 edition has different pagination.)

Ma pham rdo rje. *Rnal 'byor gyi dbang phyug grags pa mtha' yas dpal bzang po'i rnam thar mgur 'bum ngo mtshar nor bu'i 'phreng ba.* Gangtok: Gonpo Tseten, 1977. (Reproduced from tracings from prints of the central Tibetan woodblocks.)

Mar pa chos kyi blo gros (1012–1097), trans. *Snyan rgyud rdo rje'i tshig rkang* [*Karṇatantravajrapada*]. In Gtsang smyon he ru ka, *Bde mchog mkha' 'gro snyan rgyud* (*Ras chung snyan rgyud*): *Two Manuscript Collections of Texts from the Yig cha of Gtsang-smyon He-ru-ka,* 2:1–6. Leh: Smanrtsis shesrig spendzod, 1971.

———. *'Bum chung nyi ma* (*Dpal mar pa lo tsA'i kye'i rdo rje'i rtsa rgyud brtag pa gnyis pa'i 'grel pa*) [*Sun of the Little Collection*]. Dehradun: Srong btsan dpe mdzod khang, 2005.

Smyug la paN chen ngag dbang grags pa (1458–1515) and Lha mthong lo tsA ba bshes gnyen rnam rgyal (born 1512). Part I, *Dpal ldan bla ma dam pa grub pa'i khyu mchog phyogs thams cad las rnam par rgyal ba'i spyod pa can rje btsun kun dga' bzang po'i rnam par thar pa ris med dad pa'i spu long g.yo byed.* Part II, *Rje btsun kun dga' bzang po'i rnam par thar pa ris med dad pa'i spu long g.yo byed ces bya ba las/ rim par phye ba gnyis pa phrin las rgyan gyi rnga sgra* [the *Life of the Madman of Ü*]. An edition from the 1494 woodblocks for the first part of the biography, in fifty-one folios, is preserved by the NGMPP, E1581/11. An *dbu can* manuscript of the first part of the biography, also in fifty-one folios, is preserved by the NGMPP, L117/1. An *dbu can* manuscript of the complete biography, in eighty-six folios, is preserved by the NGMPP, L855/29. The complete biography was printed in *Bka' brgyud pa Hagiographies: A Collection of Rnam Thar of the Eminent Masters of Tibetan Buddhism*, compiled and edited by Khams sprul don brgyud nyi ma, vol. 2: 383–660. Palampur, Himachal Pradesh: Sungrab Nyamso Gyunphel Parkhang, Tibetan Craft Community, 1972. In 1973 the first part of the biography was printed in Delhi, mislabeled as *Dbus smyon kun dga' bzang po'i mgur 'bum*. Unless stated otherwise, all references to Smyug la paN chen and Lha mthong lo tsA ba refer to the 1972 edition.

Gtsang smyon he ru ka (1452–1507). *Rgya gar gsang spyod kyi don bsdus rtsa ba. dbu med* manuscript. Ten folios. NGMPP L513/1.

———. *Chos drug gi 'khrid yig gsal ba'i sgron me. dbu can* manuscript. Fourteen folios. NGMPP L560/6. Composed at Rtsa ri in 1487 (*me mo lug*).

———. *Rje btsun gtsang pa he ru ka'i mgur 'bum rin po che dbang gi rgyal po thams cad mkhyen pa'i lam ston* [the *Collected Songs* of the Madman of Tsang]. Xylograph completed in 1508. Twenty-eight folios. A copy owned by E. Gene Smith is preserved by the Tibetan Buddhist Resource Center.

———. *Rje btsun gzhad* [sic] *pa rdo rje la gsol ba 'debs pa byin rlabs kyi gter mdzod*. Three folios. NGMPP L803/5. Printed by Rgod tshang ras pa at Ras chung phug.

———. *Bde mchog mkha' 'gro snyan rgyud (Ras chung snyan rgyud): Two Manuscript Collections of Texts from the Yig cha of Gtsang-smyon He-ru-ka*. 2 vols. Leh: Smanrtsis shesrig spendzod, 1971. Vol. 1 contains what is known as the Bya btang 'phrin las dpal 'bar manuscript; vol. 2 contains the Gra dkar rab 'jam pa manuscript.

———. *Rnal 'byor gyi dbang phyug chen po mi la ras pa'i rnam mgur* [the *Life* and *Collected Songs* of Milarepa]. Xining: Mtsho sngon mi rigs dpe skrun khang, 2005. (This edition inserts the contents of the *mgur 'bum* into the eleventh chapter of the *rnam thar*.)

Tshar chen chos rje blo gsal rgya mtsho (1502–1566). *Rje btsun rdo rje 'chang chen po kun spangs chos rje'i rnam thar ngo mtshar dad pa'i spu long g.yo ba*. Thimphu: National Library of Bhutan, 1985.

Tshe dbang bstan 'dzin (1574–1643/44). *'Gro ba'i mgon po kun dga' legs pa'i rnam thar mon spa gro sogs kyi mdzad spyod rnams* [*Southern Cycle*]. Dharamsala: Tibetan Cultural Printing Press, 1981.

———. *'Brug pa kun legs kyi rang rnam (Grub pa'i dbang phyug chen po rnal 'byor kun dga' legs pa'i dpal gyi rnam par thar pa)*. [Recent Chinese edition; no publication information. 83 pages.]

Rdza dpal sprul rin po che (1808–1887). *Kun bzang bla ma'i zhal lung (Snying thig sngon 'gro'i khrid yig)*. Chengdu: Si khron mi rigs dpe skrun khang, 1991.

Zhwa dmar [Red Hat] IV Chos grags ye shes (1453–1524). *Dam chos dgongs pa gcig pa'i gsal byed: A detailed explanation of the 'Bri-guṅ Bka'-brgyud Dgoṅs gcig teaching.* Bir: D. Tsondu Senghe, the Bir Tibetan Society, 1992.

Yar kaH 'jam dbyangs phrin las ('Brug smyon klu gdong). *Gtsang gsum 'phyo ba'i skya rengs.* Published jointly by 'Dzam gling zhi bde par khang and Bod gzhung shes rig par khang, 2003.

Yar lung pa a 'bum. *Dpal ldan rin chen spungs pa sger gyi gdung rabs che long tsam zhig.* In *Bod kyi rgyal rabs phyogs bsdebs kyi nang gses*, 125–34. Dharamsala: Library of Tibetan Works and Archives, 1985. (The title for the collection given on the coverboard reads *Mi rje 'ba' nyag a thing mchog nas phyogs bsdus gces gsog gnang ba'i bod dpe'i khongs rim pa bdun pa'o: sngon gyi gtam me tog gi phreng ba.* Another copy of *Rin chen spungs pa sger gyi gdung rabs* is preserved by the TBRC. Both editions abruptly end in mid-sentence, followed by a note stating that the original source manuscript was cut off.)

Ye shes rgya mtsho rin po che (Klu smyon he ru kaH). *Rgyal khab med pa'i mi (homeless person): mi lo sum bcu'i rags zin (1969–2002).* [No publication information. 219 pages.]

Rwa lung dkar brgyud gser 'phreng: Brief Lives of the Successive Masters in the Transmission Lineage of the Bar 'brug-pa Dkar-brgyud-pa of Rwa-lung. 4 vols. Palampur: Sungrab Nyamso Gyunphel Parkhang, Tibetan Craft Community, 1975–8. (Reproduced from the 1771–2 woodblocks.)

Lo chen 'gyur med bde chen (1540–1615). *Thang stong rgyal po'i rnam thar ngo mtshar kun gsal nor bu'i me long gsar pa* [the *Life* of Tangtong Gyelpo]. Bir: Kandro, 1976. (Reproduced from the eighteenth-century woodblocks.)

ShAkya mchog ldan (1428–1507). *Collected Works of Śākya mchog ldan.* 24 vols. Thimphu: Kunzang Tobgyey, 1995. (Originally published in 1975.)

Bshes gnyen tshul khrims. *Lha sa'i dgon tho rin chen spungs rgyan.* Lhasa: Bod ljongs mi dmangs dpe skrun khang, 2001.

Sa skya'i spyi 'thus ga zi tshe rings po. *Bstan pa'i sbyin bdag chen po sa skyong rin spungs pa'i skor.* In *Chos kyi blo gros* 2:39–41. Mandi, India: Dzongsar Institute, Chos kyi blo gros rtsom sgrig khang, 2009.

Sa ra ha [Saraha]. *Mi zad pa'i gter mdzod man ngag gi glu.* In *Dege Tengyur*, vol. shi: 28b–33b. Tohoku no. 2264.

Sangs rgyas dar po. *Sangs rgyas dar po chos 'byung (Bka' brgyud chos 'byung rin po che spungs pa'i 'od stong 'khyil* or *Bde gshegs bstan pa'i gsal byed bka' rgyud chos kyi 'byung gnas rin po che spungs pa'i 'od stong 'khyil ba)* [*History of the Kagyü: The Combined Luster of a Heap of Jewels*]. Undated block print. NGMPP L392/14. A copy lent by Tashi Tsering (Dharamsala) was used during research.

Si tu paN chen chos kyi 'byung gnas (1699/1700–1774) and 'Be lo tshe dbang kun khyab. *Bsgrub brgyud karma kaM tshang brgyud pa rin po che'i rnam par thar pa rab 'byams nor bu zla ba chu shel gyi phreng ba.* New Delhi: D. Gyaltshan and Kesang Legshay, 1972.

Sum pa mkhan po ye shes dpal 'byor (1704–1788). *Dpag bsam ljon bzang* [*Excellent Wish-Fulfilling Tree*]. Two editions are referenced: Sarnath: Mongolian Lama Guru Deva, 1965; and New Delhi: International Academy of Indian Culture, 1959. Vol. 3 of the latter, edited by Lokesh Chandra, contains the text of the *Re'u mig* [*Chronological Tables*].

Bsod nams 'od zer. *Grub chen u rgyan pa'i rnam thar*. Bod ljongs bod yig dpe rnying dpe skrun khang, 1997.

Hor gtsang 'jigs med. *Khrag thigs las skyes pa'i ljang myug: deng rabs bod kyi rtsom rig dang de'i rgyab ljongs, 1980–2000*. Dharamsala: Youtse, 2000.

———. *Mdo smad lo rgyus chen mo las lo rgyus spyi'i gzhung shing gi skor*. Dharamsala: Library of Tibetan Works and Archives, 2009. (This is the first in a six-volume series.)

Lha btsun rin chen rnam rgyal (1473–1557). *Grub thob gtsang pa smyon pa'i rnam thar dad pa'i spu slong g.yo ba* [the *Life* of the Madman of Tsang]. In Gtsang smyon he ru ka, *Bde mchog mkha' 'gro snyan rgyud*, 1:1–129. (Unless specified, all citations of Lha btsun rin chen rnam rgyal refer to this text.) An *dbu can* manuscript, in 165 folios, is preserved by the NGMPP, E2601/7.

———. Untitled verse praise of the Madman of Tsang. Written in 1522. Two editions, from different sets of woodblocks, are preserved by the NGMPP: contained within L803/5, in three folios, and in L581/6, also in three folios.

EUROPEAN-LANGUAGE SOURCES

Ahmad, Zahiruddin. *A History of Tibet by Ṅag-dBaṅ Blo-bZaṅ rGya-mTSHo, the Fifth Dalai Lama of Tibet*. Bloomington: Research Institute for Inner Asian Studies, Indiana University, 1995.

Ardussi, John. "'Brug-pa Kun-legs, The Saintly Tibetan Madman." MA thesis, University of Washington, 1972.

———. "Gyalse Tenzin Rabgye (1638–1696), Artist Ruler of 17th-Century Bhutan." In *The Dragon's Gift: The Sacred Arts of Bhutan*, edited by Terese Tse Bartholomew and John Johnston, 88–99. Chicago: Serindia, 2008.

Ardussi, John, and Lawrence Epstein. "The Saintly Madmen in Tibet." In *Himalayan Anthropology: The Indo-Tibetan Interface*, edited by James Fisher, 327–37. The Hague: Mouton, 1978.

Aris, Michael. *Bhutan: The Early History of a Himalayan Kingdom*. Warminster, England: Aris and Phillips, 1979.

———. "'The Boneless Tongue': Alternative Voices from Bhutan in the Context of Lamaist Societies." *Past and Present* 115 (1987): 131–64.

———. *Hidden Treasures and Secret Lives: A Study of Pemalingpa (1450–1521) and the Sixth Dalai Lama (1683–1706)*. London and New York: Kegan Paul International, 1989.

Bartholomew, Terese Tse, and John Johnston, eds. *The Dragon's Gift: The Sacred Arts of Bhutan*. Chicago: Serindia, 2008.

Bessenger, Suzanne. "Echoes of Enlightenment: The Life and Legacy of Sonam Peldren (1328–1372)." PhD diss., University of Virginia, 2009.

Bjonnes, Ramesh. "Fat, Naked, and Enlightened: The Crazy Yogis of Love." *Elephant Journal*, October 17, 2010. http://www.elephantjournal.com/2010/10/fat-naked-and-enlightened-ramesh-bjonnes/.

Bogin, Benjamin. "The Dreadlocks Treatise: On Tantric Hairstyles in Tibetan Buddhism." *History of Religions* 48, no. 2 (2008): 85–109.

Bonardel, Françoise. "Tantric Alchemy and the Transmission of Dharma: At the Heart of the Western Mandala." In *Recalling Chögyam Trungpa*, edited by Fabrice Midal, 35–56. Boston, MA: Shambhala, 2005.

Braverman, Marcy. "Possession, Immersion, and the Intoxicated Madness of Devotion in Hindu Traditions." PhD diss., University of California, Santa Barbara, 2003.

Brick, David. "The Origin of the *Khaṭvāṅga* Staff." *Journal of the American Oriental Society* 132, no. 1 (2012): 31–9.

Butterfield, Stephen. *The Double Mirror: A Skeptical Journey into Buddhist Tantra*. Berkeley, CA: North Atlantic, 1994.

Cabezón, José Ignacio, and Geshe Lobsang Dargyay. *Freedom from Extremes: Gorampa's "Distinguishing the Views" and the Polemics of Emptiness*. Boston, MA: Wisdom, 2007.

Campany, Robert Ford. *Making Transcendents: Ascetics and Social Memory in Early Medieval China*. Honolulu: University of Hawai'i Press, 2009.

Caplan, Lionel, ed. *Studies in Religious Fundamentalism*. Albany: State University of New York Press, 1987.

Chang, Garma C. C. *The Hundred Thousand Songs of Milarepa*, by Tsangnyön Heruka. 2 vols. Boston, MA: Shambhala, 1977. (First published in 1962.)

Chaoul, Alejandro. *Chöd Practice in the Bön Tradition*. Ithaca: Snow Lion, 2009.

Chögyam Trungpa. *Crazy Wisdom*. Edited by Sherab Chödzin. Boston, MA: Shambhala, 2001.

———. *Cutting Through Spiritual Materialism*. Boston, MA: Shambhala, 2002.

Clark, Tom. *The Great Naropa Poetry Wars, with a Copious Collection of Germane Documents Assembled by the Author*. Santa Barbara, CA: Cadmus, 1980.

Collins, Steven. *Nirvana and Other Buddhist Felicities: Utopias of the Pali Imaginaire*. Cambridge: Cambridge University Press, 1998.

Cüppers, Cristoph, and Per K. Sørensen. *A Collection of Tibetan Proverbs and Sayings: Gems of Tibetan Wisdom and Wit*. Stuttgart: Franz Steiner Verlag, 1998.

Czaja, Olaf. *Medieval Rule in Tibet: The Rlangs Clan and the Political and Religious History of the Ruling House of Phag mo gru pa*. Vienna: Austrian Academy of Sciences Press, 2014.

Dalton, Jacob P. *The Taming of the Demons: Violence and Liberation in Tibetan Buddhism*. New Haven, CT: Yale University Press, 2011.

Das, Surya. *Wisdom Tales from Tibet*. San Francisco, CA: Harper, 1992.

Davidson, Ronald. *Indian Esoteric Buddhism: A Social History of the Tantric Movement*. New York: Columbia University Press, 2002.

———. *Tibetan Renaissance: Tantric Buddhism in the Rebirth of Tibetan Culture*. New York: Columbia University Press, 2005.

Decleer, Hubert. "The Melodious Drumsound All-Pervading: Sacred Biography of Rwa Lotsāwa: About Early Lotsāwa *rnam thar* and *chos 'byung*." In *Proceedings of the 5th Seminar of the International Association for Tibetan Studies, Narita 1989*, vol. 1, edited by Ihara Shōren and Yamaguchi Zuihō, 13–28. Narita: Naritasan Shinshoji, 1992.

DiValerio, David. *The Life of the Madman of Ü*. Oxford University Press. Forthcoming, 2016.

———. "Reanimating the Great Yogin: On the Composition of the Biographies of the Madman of Tsang." *Revue d'Etudes Tibétaines* 31 (2015): 25–49.

———. "Subversive Sainthood and Tantric Fundamentalism: An Historical Study of Tibet's 'Holy Madmen.'" PhD diss., University of Virginia, 2011.

Dowman, Keith. *A Buddhist Guide to the Power Places of the Kathmandu Valley*. Thamel: Himalayan Buddhist Meditation Centre, 2007.

———. *The Divine Madman: The Sublime Life and Songs of Drukpa Kunley*. Varanasi and Kathmandu: Pilgrims, 2000. Translated into German by Franz-Karl Ehrhard as *Der Heilige Narr: Das liederliche Leben und die lästerlichen Gesänge des tantrischen Meisters Drukpa Künleg*; Frankfurt am Main: Barth, 1983, 2005. Translated into Spanish as *La Divina Locura Drukpa Künléy: Andanzas de un Yogui Tántrico Tibetano del Siglo XVI*; Madrid: Miraguano, 1988, 2001. Translated into French as *Le Fou Divin: Drukpa Kunley, Yogi Tantrique Tibétain*; Paris: Albin Michel, 1984, 2012. Translated into Romanian by Octavian Creţ as *Nebunul Divin: viaţa sublimă a marelui maestru tantric Drukpa Kunley*; Bucharest: Firul Ariadnei, 2006.

Dreyfus, Georges. "Tibetan Scholastic Education and the Role of Soteriology." *Journal of the International Association of Buddhist Studies* 20, no. 1 (1997): 31–62.

Edou, Jerome. *Machig Labdrön and the Foundations of Chöd*. Ithaca, NY: Snow Lion, 1996.

Ehrhard, Franz-Karl. *Early Buddhist Block Prints from Mang-yul Gung-thang*. Lumbini: Lumbini International Research Institute, 2000.

———. "Editing and Publishing the Master's Writings: The Early Years of rGod tshang ras chen (1482–1559)." In *Edition, éditions: L'écrit au Tibet, évolution et devenir*, edited by Anne Chayet et al., 129–61. Munich: Indus Verlag, 2010.

———. "The Holy Madman of dBus and His Relationships with Tibetan Rulers of the 15th and 16th Centuries." In *Geschichten und Geschichte: Historiographie und Hagiographie in der asiatischen Religionsgeschichte*, edited by Peter Schalk, 219–46. Uppsala: Uppsala University Library, 2010.

———. "'Turning the Wheel of the Dharma in Zhing sa Va lung': The dPal ri sPrul skus (17th to 20th Centuries)." *Bulletin of Tibetology* 44, nos. 1–2 (2008): 5–29.

Farrow, G. W., and I. Menon. *The Concealed Essence of the Hevajra Tantra, with the Commentary "Yogaratnamālā."* Delhi: Motilal Banarsidass, 1992.

Feuerstein, Georg. *Holy Madness: Spirituality, Crazy-Wise Teachers, and Enlightenment.* Prescott, AZ: Hohm, 2006.

———. *Holy Madness: The Shock Tactics and Radical Teachings of Crazy-Wise Adepts, Holy Fools, and Rascal Gurus.* Harmondsworth: Penguin, 1991.

Foucault, Michel. *History of Madness.* Translated by Jonathan Murphy and Jean Khalfa. New York: Routledge, 2006. [This edition includes Foucault's famous works on madness first published in 1961 and 1967.]

———. *Madness and Civilization: A History of Insanity in the Age of Reason.* Translated by Richard Howard. New York: Vintage, 1988.

———. *Power/Knowledge: Selected Interviews and Other Writings, 1972–1977.* Edited by Colin Gordon. New York: Pantheon, 1980.

Gedün Chöpel and Jeffrey Hopkins. *Tibetan Arts of Love: Sex, Orgasm and Spiritual Healing.* Ithaca, NY: Snow Lion, 1992.

Gerner, Manfred. *Chakzampa Thangtong Gyalpo: Architect, Philosopher and Iron Chain Bridge Builder.* Translated from German by Gregor Verhufen. Thimphu: Centre for Bhutan Studies, 2007.

Goldstein, Melvyn C. *A History of Modern Tibet, 1913–1951: The Demise of the Lamaist State.* Berkeley: University of California Press, 1989.

———. *On the Cultural Revolution in Tibet: The Nyemo Incident of 1969.* Berkeley: University of California Press, 2009.

Goldstein, Melvyn C., Dawei Sherap, and William R. Siebenschuh. *A Tibetan Revolutionary: The Political Life and Times of Bapa Phüntso Wangye.* Berkeley: University of California Press, 2004.

Goss, Robert Everett. "The Hermeneutics of Madness: A Literary and Hermeneutical Analysis of the 'Mi-la'i-rnam-thar' by Gtsang-smyon Heruka." ThD diss., Harvard University, 1993.

Gray, David B. *The Cakrasamvara Tantra (The Discourse of Śrī Heruka) (Śrīherukābhidhāna): A Study and Annotated Translation.* New York: American Institute of Buddhist Studies, Columbia University Press, 2007.

Guenther, Herbert. *Ecstatic Spontaneity: Saraha's Three Cycles of Dohā.* Berkeley, CA: Asian Humanities Press, 1993.

Gutschow, Kim. "The Practice of Tibetan Medicine in Zangskar: A Case of Wind Disorder." In *Healing at the Periphery: Ethnographies of Tibetan Medicine in India,* edited by Laurent Pordié. Durham, NC: Duke University Press, forthcoming.

Gyatso, Janet. "The Literary Transmission of the Traditions of Thang-stong rGyal-po: A Study of Visionary Buddhism in Tibet." PhD diss., University of California at Berkeley, 1981.

Harding, Sarah. *Machik's Complete Explanation: Clarifying the Meaning of Chöd.* Ithaca, NY: Snow Lion, 2013.

Hartley, Lauran, and Patricia Schiaffini-Vedani, eds. *Modern Tibetan Literature and Social Change.* Durham, NC: Duke University Press, 2008.

Havnevik, Hanna. *The Life of Jetsun Lochen Rinpoche (1865–1951) as Told in Her Autobiography.* 2 vols. Oslo: University of Oslo Press, 1999.

Herriot, Peter. *Religious Fundamentalism and Social Identity.* New York: Routledge, 2007.

Huber, Toni. *The Cult of Pure Crystal Mountain: Popular Pilgrimage and Visionary Landscape in Southeast Tibet.* New York: Oxford University Press, 1999.

———. "A Guide to the La-Phyi *Maṇḍala*: History, Landscape and Ritual in South-Western Tibet." In *Maṇḍala and Landscape*, edited by A. W. Macdonald, 233–86. Emerging Perceptions in Buddhist Studies, no. 6. Delhi: D. K. Printworld, 1997.

Jackson, David P. "The Earliest Printings of Tsong-kha-pa's Works: The Old Dga'-ldan Editions." In *Reflections on Tibetan Culture: Essays in Memory of Turrell V. Wylie*, edited by Lawrence Epstein and Richard F. Sherburne, 107–116. Studies in Asian Thought and Religion, vol. 12. New York: Edwin Mellen, 1990.

Jamgön Kongtrul ['Jam mgon kong sprul]. *Buddhist Ethics.* Translated by the International Translation Committee. Ithaca: Snow Lion, 1998.

Jamyang Namgyal [E. Gene Smith]. "*Vie et chants de 'Brug-pa Kun-legs le yogin*, a Review." *Kailash* 1, no. 1 (1973): 91–9.

Kakar, Sudhir. *Mad and Divine: Spirit and Psyche in the Modern World.* Chicago: University of Chicago Press, 2009.

Kapstein, Matthew. *The Tibetans.* Malden, MA, and Oxford: Blackwell, 2006.

Karma Phuntso. *The History of Bhutan.* Noida, Uttar Pradesh: Random House India, 2013.

Kerouac, Jack. *The Dharma Bums.* New York: Penguin, 1986.

Kinsley, David. "'Through the Looking Glass': Divine Madness in the Hindu Religious Tradition." *History of Religions* 13, no. 4 (1974): 270–305.

Kleinberg, Aviad. *Prophets in Their Own Country: Living Saints and the Making of Sainthood in the Later Middle Ages.* Chicago: University of Chicago Press, 1992.

Komarovski, Yaroslav. *Visions of Unity: The Golden Paṇḍita Shakya Chokden's New Interpretation of Yogācāra and Madhyamaka.* Albany: State University of New York Press, 2012.

Kretschmar, Andreas. *'Brug pa kun legs: Das wundersame Leben eines verrückten Heiligen.* Sankt Augustin: VGH Wissenschattsverlag, 1981.

Kun mchog dge legs, Dpal ldan bkra shis, and Kevin Stuart. "Tibetan Tricksters." *Asian Folklore Studies* 58, no. 1 (1999): 5–30.

LaCapra, Dominick. "Rethinking Intellectual History and Reading Texts." *History and Theory* 19, no. 3 (1980): 245–76.

Larsson, Stefan. "The Birth of a Heruka: How Sangs rgyas rgyal mtshan became gTsang smyon Heruka: A Study of a Mad Yogin." PhD diss., University of Stockholm, Institutionen för etnologi, religionshistoria och genusstudier, 2009.

———. *Crazy for Wisdom: The Making of a Mad Yogin in Fifteenth-Century Tibet.* Leiden: Brill, 2012.

———. "Tsangnyön Heruka's Sixteenth-Century Renovation of the Svayambhū Stūpa." In *Light of the Valley: Renewing the Sacred Art and Traditions of Svayambhu,* edited by Tsering Palmo Gellek and Padma Dorje Maitland, 208–30. Cazadero, CA: Dharma, 2011.

———. "What Do the Childhood and Early Life of Gtsang smyon Heruka Tell Us about His Bka' brgyud Affiliation?" In *Mahāmudrā and the Bka'-brgyud Tradition: Proceedings of the Eleventh Seminar of the International Association for Tibetan Studies, Königswinter 2006,* edited by Roger R. Jackson and Matthew T. Kapstein, 425–52. Andiast: International Institute for Tibetan and Buddhist Studies, 2011.

Lessing, Ferdinand, and Alex Wayman. *Mkhas grub rje's Fundamentals of the Buddhist Tantras (Rgyud sde spyiḥi rnam par gźag pa rgyas par brjod).* The Hague: Mouton, 1968.

Lewis, Todd, and Lozang Jamspal. "Newars and Tibetans in the Kathmandu Valley: Three New Translations from Tibetan Sources." *Journal of Asian and African Studies* 36 (1988): 187–211.

Linrothe, Rob, ed. *Holy Madness: Portraits of Tantric Siddhas.* New York: Rubin Museum of Art, 2006.

Lopez, Donald S., Jr. *The Madman's Middle Way: Reflections on Reality of the Tibetan Monk Gendun Chopel.* Chicago: University of Chicago Press, 2006.

Martin, Dan. "Lay Religious Movements in 11th- and 12th-Century Tibet: A Survey of Sources." *Kailash* 18, nos. 3–4 (1996): 23–55.

———. "Padampa Sangye: A History of Representation of a South Indian Siddha in Tibet." In *Holy Madness: Portraits of Tantric Siddhas,* edited by Rob Linrothe, 109–123. New York: Rubin Museum of Art, 2006.

———. "The Star King and the Four Children of Pehar: Popular Religious Movements of 11th- to 12th-Century Tibet." *Acta Orientalia Academiae Scientiarum Hungaricae* 49, nos. 1–2 (1996): 171–95.

———. *Tibetan Histories: A Bibliography of Tibetan-Language Historical Works.* London: Serindia, 1997.

Marty, Martin E., and R. Scott Appleby, eds. *Fundamentalisms Observed.* Chicago: University of Chicago Press, 1991.

McCleary, Rachel M., and Leonard W. J. van der Kuijp. "The Market Approach to the Rise of the Geluk School, 1419–1642." *Journal of Asian Studies* 60, no. 1 (2010): 149–80.

McDaniel, June. *The Madness of the Saints: Ecstatic Religion in Bengal.* Chicago: University of Chicago Press, 1989.

McKeown, Arthur. "From Bodhgayā to Lhasa to Beijing: The Life and Times of Śāriputra (c. 1335–1426), Last Abbot of Bodhgayā." PhD diss., Harvard University, 2010.

Michiyo Hoshi, ed. *Texts of Tibetan Folktales*. Vol. 5, *Studia Tibetica*, 10. Tokyo: Toyo Bunko, 1985.

Midal, Fabrice. *Chögyam Trungpa: His Life and Vision*. Translated by Ian Monk. Boston, MA: Shambhala, 2005.

———, ed. *Recalling Chögyam Trungpa*. Boston, MA: Shambhala, 2005.

Mills, Martin A. *Identity, Ritual and State in Tibetan Buddhism: The Foundations of Authority in Gelukpa Monasticism*. New York: RoutledgeCurzon, 2003.

Mullin, Glenn H. *Mystical Verses of a Mad Dalai Lama*. Wheaton, IL: Quest / Theosophical Publishing, 1994.

———. *The Practice of the Six Yogas of Naropa*. Ithaca, NY: Snow Lion, 1997.

Munson, Henry. "Fundamantalism." In *The Routledge Companion to the Study of Religion*, edited by John R. Hinnells, 337–54. New York: Routledge, 2005.

Napper, Elizabeth. "Ethics as the Basis of a Tantric Tradition: Tsong kha pa and the Founding of the dGe lugs order in Tibet." In *Changing Minds: Contributions to the Study of Buddhism and Tibet in Honor of Jeffrey Hopkins*, edited by Guy Newland, 107–31. Ithaca, NY: Snow Lion, 2001.

Newland, Guy. "Debate Manuals in dGe lugs Monastic Colleges." In *Tibetan Literature: Studies in Genre*, edited by José Ignacio Cabezón and Roger Jackson, 202–16. Ithaca, NY: Snow Lion, 1996.

Norman, Alexander. *Secret Lives of the Dalai Lama: The Untold Story of the Holy Men Who Shaped Tibet, From Pre-History to the Present Day*. New York: Doubleday, 2008.

Orofino, Giacomella. "The Great Wisdom Mother and the Gcod Tradition." In *Tantra in Practice*, edited by David Gordon White, 396–416. Princeton, NJ: Princeton University Press, 2000.

Patrul Rinpoché. *The Words of My Perfect Teacher*. Translated by the Padmakara Translation Group. Boston, MA: Shambhala, 1998.

Pema Bhum, "'Heartbeat of a New Generation' Revisited." Translated by Lauran Hartley. In *Modern Tibetan Literature and Social Change*, edited by Lauran Hartley and Patricia Schiaffini-Vedani, 135–47. Durham, NC: Duke University Press, 2008.

Perks, John Riley. *The Mahāsiddha and His Idiot Servant*. Putney, VT: Crazy Heart, 2004.

Petech, Luciano. "The 'Bri-guṅ-pa sect in Western Tibet and Ladakh." In *Selected Papers on Asian History*, 355–68. Roma: Istituto Italiano per il Medio ed Estremo Oriente, 1988.

———. *The Kingdom of Ladakh c. 950–1842*. Roma: Istituto Italiano per il Medio ed Estremo Oriente, 1977.

Pommaret, Françoise, and Tashi Tobgay. "Bhutan's Pervasive Phallus: Is Drukpa Kunley Really Responsible?" Unpublished essay.

Quintman, Andrew. *The Yogin and the Madman: Reading the Biographical Corpus of Tibet's Great Saint Milarepa.* New York: Columbia University Press, 2014.

Ray, Reginald A. "Chögyam Trungpa as a *Siddha.*" In *Recalling Chögyam Trungpa,* edited by Fabrice Midal, 197–220. Boston, MA: Shambhala, 2005.

Rhoton, Jared Douglas. *A Clear Differentiation of the Three Codes: Essential Distinctions among the Individual Liberation, Great Vehicle, and Tantric Systems.* New York: State University of New York Press, 2002.

Ricca, Franco, and Erberto Lo Bue. *The Great Stupa of Gyantse: A Complete Tibetan Pantheon of the Fifteenth Century.* London: Serindia, 1993.

Richardson, Hugh. *High Peaks, Pure Earth: Collected Writings on Tibetan History and Culture.* Edited by Michael Aris. London: Serindia, 1998.

Roberts, Peter Alan. *The Biographies of Rechungpa: The Evolution of a Tibetan Hagiography.* Abingdon and New York: Routledge, 2007.

Roerich, George N. *The Blue Annals.* Delhi: Motilal Banarsidass, 1996. (First published in 1949.)

Rozenberg, Guillaume. *Renunciation and Power: The Quest for Sainthood in Contemporary Burma.* Translated by Jessica Hackett et al. New Haven, CT: Yale University Southeast Asian Studies, 2010.

Ruthven, Malise. *Fundamentalism: The Search for Meaning.* New York: Oxford University Press, 2004.

Samuel, Geoffrey. *Civilized Shamans: Buddhism in Tibetan Society.* Washington, DC: Smithsonian Institution Press, 1994.

Schaeffer, Kurtis. *The Culture of the Book in Tibet.* New York: Columbia University Press, 2009.

———. "Dying Like Milarépa: Death Accounts in a Tibetan Hagiographic Tradition." In *The Buddhist Dead: Practices, Discourses, Representations,* edited by Bryan Cuevas and Jacqueline Stone, 208–33. Honolulu: University of Hawai'i Press, 2007.

———. "The Printing Projects of Gtsang Smyon Heruka and his Disciples." In *Mahāmudrā and the Bka'-brgyud Tradition: Proceedings of the Eleventh Seminar of the International Association for Tibetan Studies, Königswinter 2006,* edited by Roger R. Jackson and Matthew T. Kapstein, 453–79. Andiast: International Institute for Tibetan and Buddhist Studies, 2011.

Schwieger, Peter. "Significance of Ming Titles Conferred upon the Phag mo gru Rulers: A Reevalution of Chinese–Tibetan Relations during the Ming Dynasty." In *The Earth Ox Papers: Proceedings of the International Seminar on Tibetan and Himalayan Studies, Held at the Library of Tibetan Works and Archives, September 2009 on the Occasion of the "Thank you India" Year,* edited by Roberto Vitali, 313–28. Special issue, *Tibet Journal* (Autumn and Winter 2009, Spring and Summer 2010).

Sernesi, Marta. "The Aural Transmission of Saṃvara: An Introduction to Neglected Sources for the Study of the Early Bka' Brgyud." In *Mahāmudrā and the Bka'-brgyud Tradition: Proceedings of the Eleventh Seminar of the International Association for Tibetan Studies, Königswinter 2006*, edited by Roger R. Jackson and Matthew T. Kapstein, 179–209. Andiast: International Institute for Tibetan and Buddhist Studies, 2011.

———. "A Continuous Stream of Merit: The Early Reprints of gTsang smyon Heruka's Hagiographical Works." *Zentral-Asiatiche Studien* 40 (2011): 179–237.

———. "A Manual on Nāropa's Six Yogas by sPyan snga Nyer gnyis pa (1386–1434): Tucci Tibetan Collection 1359." *Indo-Iranian Journal* 53 (2010): 121–63.

———. "Milarepa's Six Secret Songs: The Early Transmission of the *bDe mchog snyan brgyud*." *East and West* 54, nos. 1–4 (2004): 251–87.

Shakabpa, Tsepon W. D. *Tibet: A Political History*. New Haven, CT: Yale University Press, 1967.

Shakya, Hem Raj. *Śrī Svayambhū Mahācaitya*. Translated by Min Bahadur Shakya. Kathmandu: Svayambhu Vikash Mandal, 2004.

Smith, E. Gene. *Among Tibetan Texts: History and Literature of the Himalayan Plateau*. Edited by Kurtis Schaeffer. Boston, MA: Wisdom, 2001.

———. "Siddha Groups and the Mahāsiddhas in the Art and Literature of Tibet." In *Holy Madness: Portraits of Tantric Siddhas*, edited by Rob Linrothe, 62–75. New York: Rubin Museum of Art, 2006.

Snellgrove, David. *The Hevajra Tantra: A Critical Study*. 2 vols. Oxford: Oxford University Press, 1959.

———. *Indo-Tibetan Buddhism*. Boston, MA: Shambhala, 2002. (First published in 1987.)

Snellgrove, David, and Hugh Richardson. *A Cultural History of Tibet*. Boston, MA: Shambhala, 1995. (First published in 1968.)

Sørensen, Per K. "Lhasa Diluvium: Sacred Environment at Stake: The Birth of Flood Control Politics, the Question of Natural Disaster Management and their Importance for the Hegemony over a National Monument in Tibet." *Lungta* 16 (Spring 2003): 85–134 [special edition titled *Cosmogony and the Origins*].

Sørensen, Per K., and Guntram Hazod, with Tsering Gyalbo. *Rulers on the Celestial Plain: Ecclesiastic and Secular Hegemony in Medieval Tibet: A Study of Tshal Gung-thang*. Vienna: Österreichische Akademie der Wissenschaften and Tibetan Academy of Social Sciences of the Autonomous Region Tibet, 2007.

———. *Thundering Falcon: An Inquiry into the History and Cult of Khra-'brug, Tibet's First Buddhist Temple*. Vienna: Österreichische Akademie der Wissenschaften, 2005.

Stearns, Cyrus. *Hermit of Go Cliffs: Timeless Instructions from a Tibetan Mystic*. Boston, MA: Wisdom, 2000.

———. *King of the Empty Plain: The Tibetan Iron-Bridge Builder Tangtong Gyalpo*. Ithaca, NY: Snow Lion, 2007.

———. *Luminous Lives: The Story of the Early Masters of the Lam 'Bras Tradition in Tibet*. Boston, MA: Wisdom, 1996.

Stein, R. A. *Tibetan Civilization*. Translated by J. E. Stapleton Driver. Stanford, CA: Stanford University Press, 1972.

———. *Vie et chants de 'Brug-pa Kun-legs le yogin*. Paris: G.-P. Maisonneuve et Larose, 1972.

Stoddard, Heather. *Le Mendicant de l'Amdo*. Paris: Société d'ethnographie, 1985.

Sutherland, Patrick, and Tashi Tsering. *Disciples of a Crazy Saint: The Buchen of Spiti*. Oxford: Pitt Rivers Museum, 2011.

Tambiah, Stanley Jeyaraja. *The Buddhist Saints of the Forest and the Cult of Amulets*. Cambridge: Cambridge University Press, 1984.

Tatz, Mark. *Asanga's Chapter on Ethics with the Commentary of Tsong-kha-pa*. Studies in Asian Thought and Religion, vol. 4. Lewiston, NY: Edwin Mellen, 1986. [Translation of Tsong kha pa's *Byang chub gzhung lam*.]

———. "Whom is Tsong-kha-pa Refuting in His *Basic Path to Awakening?*" In *Reflections on Tibetan Culture: Essays in Memory of Turrell V. Wylie*, ed. Lawrence Epstein and Richard F. Sherburne, 149–63. Studies in Asian Thought and Religion, vol. 12. New York: Edwin Mellen, 1990.

"The Three Divine Madmen." In *The Dragon Yogis: A Collection of Selected Biographies and Teachings of the Drukpa Lineage Masters*, 41–9. Gurgaon: Drukpa Publications, 2009.

Tiso, Frances. "The Death of Milarepa: Towards a Redaktionsgeschichte of the Mila rnam thar Traditions." In *Tibetan Studies: Proceedings of the 7th Seminar of the International Association for Tibetan Studies, Graz 1995*, edited by Helmut Krasser, Michael Torsten Much, Ernst Steinkellner, and Helmut Tauscher, 2:987–95. Vienna: Oesterreichischen Akademie der Wissenschaften, 1997.

———. *Liberation in One Lifetime: Biographies and Teachings of Milarepa*. Isernia, Italy: Proforma, 2010.

———. "A Study of the Buddhist Saint in Relation to the Biographical Tradition of Milarepa." PhD diss., Columbia University, 1989.

Torricelli, Fabrizio. "Padma dkar po's Arrangement of the *bDe mchog snyan brgyud*." *East and West* 50, nos. 1–4 (2000): 359–86.

———. "The Tibetan text of the *Karṇatantravajrapada*." *East and West* 48, nos. 3–4 (1998): 385–423.

———. "Zhang Lo tsā ba's Introduction to the Aural Transmission of Śaṃvara." In *Le Parole e i Marmi: Studi in Onore di Raniero Gnoli nel suo 70. Compleanno*, edited by Raffaele Torella, 2 vols. 2:875–96. Rome: Istituto Italiano per l'Africa e l'Oriente, 2001.

Tsangnyön Heruka [Gtsang smyon he ru ka]. *The Life of Milarepa*. Translated by Andrew Quintman. New York: Penguin, 2010.

Tucci, Giuseppe. *Deb ther dmar po gsar ma* [*The New Red Annals*]: *Tibetan Chronicles*, vol. 1. Serie Orientale Roma 24. Rome: Istituto Italiano per il Medio ed Estremo Oriente, 1971.

————. *Tibetan Painted Scrolls*. 3 vols. Rome: La Libreria della Stato, 1949.

Tuladhar-Douglas, Will. *Remaking Buddhism for Medieval Nepal: The Fifteenth-Century Reformation of Newar Buddhism*. New York: Routledge, 2006.

van der Kuijp, Leonard W. K. "On the Composition and Printings of the *Deb gter sngon po* by 'Gos lo tsā ba gzhon nu dpal (1392–1481)." *Journal of the International Association of Tibetan Studies* 2 (2006): 1–46.

————. "On the Life and Political Career of Ta'i-si-tu Byang-chub Rgyal-mtshan (1302–?1364)." In *Tibetan History and Language: Studies Dedicated to Uray Géza on his Seventieth Birthday*, edited by Ernst Steinkellner, 277–327. Vienna: Arbeitskreis für tibetische und buddhistische studien universität wien, 1991.

van Manen, Johan. "A Contribution to the Bibliography of Tibet." *Journal and Proceedings of the Asiatic Society of Bengal* 18, new series (1922): 445–525.

Vitali, Roberto. *The Dge lugs pa in Gu ge and the Western Himalaya (Early 15th–Late 17th Century)*. Dharamsala: Amnye Machen Institute, 2012.

————. *The Kingdoms of Gu.ge Pu.hrang, According to mNga'.ris rgyal.rabs by Gu.ge mkhan.chen Ngag.dbang grags.pa*. Dharamsala: Tho.ling gtsug.lag.khang lo.gcig. stong 'khor.ba'i rjes.dran.mdzad sgo'i go.sgrig tshogs.chung, 1996.

von Rospatt, Alexander. "A Historical Overview of the Renovations of the Svayambhūcaitya at Kathmandu." *Journal of the Nepal Research Centre* 12 (2001): 195–241.

————. "On the Conception of the Stūpa in Vajrayāna Buddhism: The Example of the Svayambhūcaitya of Kathmandu." *Journal of the Nepal Research Centre* 11 (1999): 121–47.

————. "The Past Renovations of the Svayambhūcaitya." In *Light of the Valley: Renewing the Sacred Art and Traditions of Svayambhu*, edited by Tsering Palmo Gellek and Padma Dorje Maitland, 157–206. Cazadero, CA: Dharma, 2011.

Wedemeyer, Christian K. *Āryadeva's Lamp that Integrates the Practices (Caryāmelāpakapradīpa): The Gradual Path of Vajrayāna Buddhism According to the Esoteric Community Noble Tradition*. New York: American Institute of Buddhist Studies, Columbia University Press, 2007.

————. *Making Sense of Tantric Buddhism: History, Semiology, and Transgression in the Indian Traditions*. New York: Columbia University Press, 2013.

Williams, Paul, with Anthony Tribe. *Buddhist Thought: A Complete Introduction to the Indian Tradition*. New York: Routledge, 2000.

Wylie, Turrell V. "Monastic Patronage in 15th-Century Tibet." *Acta Orientalia Academiae Scientiarum Hungaricae* 34, no. 103 (1980): 319–28.

————. "Reincarnation: A Political Innovation in Tibetan Buddhism." In *Proceedings of the Csoma de Kőrös Memorial Symposium, held at Mátrafüred, Hungary, September 24–30, 1976*, edited by Louis Ligeti, 579–86. Budapest: Akadémiai Kiadó, 1978.

Yamamoto, Carl S. *Vision and Violence: Lama Zhang and the Politics of Charisma in Twelfth-Century Tibet*. Leiden: Brill, 2012.

INTERVIEWS

Karma pa XVII O rgyan 'phrin las rdo rje, interview at Rgyud stod monastery, Himachal Pradesh (HP), India, August 4, 2009.

Mkhan po dkon mchog rnam dag, interview at Phyang monastery, Ladakh, July 22, 2009.

Mkhan po nyi ma rgyal mtshan, interview at Kagyu College, Dehradun, October 4, 2009.

Mkhan po 'phrin las thar chen, interview at Drikung Kagyu Monastery, Rewalsar, HP, September 29, 2009.

Mkhan po blo gsal tshe rgyal, interview at Smin grol gling monastery, Clement Town, Uttaranchal, India, October 10, 2009.

Mkhan po blo gsal rin po che, interview at Kamgar Druk College, Tashijong, HP, August 13, 2009.

Mkhan po tshul rnams rin po che, interview at Shes rab gling monastery, Bir, HP, numerous interviews between August 16 and September 28, 2009.

Mkhan po bsod nams bkra shis, interview at 'Dzi sgar bkra shis thub bstan chos 'khor dge 'phel gling monastery, Rewalsar, HP, September 29, 2009.

Mkhan po o rgyan tshe ring, interview at Rnying dgon dpal yul chos 'khor gling, Bir, HP, September 22, 2009.

Chos rgyal rin po che, interview at Byang chub ljong, HP, India, August 15, 2009.

Bla ma tshul khrims stobs ldan rin po che, interview at Karma Dupgyud Choeling Monastery, Choklamsar (near Leh), Ladakh, July 19, 2009.

Dbang 'dul rin po che, interview at the retreat center above Rewalsar lake, HP September 28, 2009.

Dbon sprul rin po che, interview at Drikung Kagyu Monastery, Rewalsar, HP, September 30, 2009.

Sman pa tshe dbang rta mgrin, former principal of the Sman brtsis khang. Interview at Sman rtsis khang, Mcleod Ganj, HP, September 7, 2009.

Tshangs gsar kun dga' rin po che, interview in Kathmandu, Nepal, July 13, 2013.

Index

Printed in Great Britain
by Amazon